DECLARATIONS OF INDEPENDENCE

The Revolutionary Age

FRANCIS D. COGLIANO, CHRISTA BREAULT DIERKSHEIDE,
ELIGA H. GOULD, AND PATRICK GRIFFIN, EDITORS

*Winner of the Walker Cowen Memorial Prize
for an outstanding work of scholarship
in eighteenth-century studies*

Declarations of Independence

INDIGENOUS RESILIENCE, COLONIAL RIVALRIES,
AND THE COST OF REVOLUTION

Christopher R. Pearl

UNIVERSITY OF VIRGINIA PRESS
Charlottesville and London

The University of Virginia Press is situated on the traditional lands of the Monacan Nation, and the Commonwealth of Virginia was and is home to many other Indigenous people. We pay our respect to all of them, past and present. We also honor the enslaved African and African American people who built the University of Virginia, and we recognize their descendants. We commit to fostering voices from these communities through our publications and to deepening our collective understanding of their histories and contributions.

University of Virginia Press
© 2024 by the Rector and Visitors of the University of Virginia
All rights reserved
Printed in the United States of America on acid-free paper

First published 2024

1 3 5 7 9 8 6 4 2

Library of Congress Cataloging-in-Publication Data

Names: Pearl, Christopher R., author.
Title: Declarations of independence : indigenous resilience, colonial rivalries, and the cost of revolution / Christopher R. Pearl.
Description: Charlottesville : University of Virginia Press, 2024. | Series: The revolutionary age | Includes bibliographical references and index.
Identifiers: LCCN 2024002738 (print) | LCCN 2024002739 (ebook) | ISBN 9780813951980 (hardcover) | ISBN 9780813951997 (paperback) | ISBN 9780813952000 (ebook)
Subjects: LCSH: Susquehanna Claim, 1753–1808. | Susquehanna Indians—Government relations. | Susquehanna River Valley—History—18th century. | United States—History—Revolution, 1775–1783. | United States—Politics and government—1775–1783. | BISAC: HISTORY / United States / Revolutionary Period (1775–1800) | HISTORY / Indigenous Peoples in the Americas
Classification: LCC F157.W9 P29 2024 (print) | LCC F157.W9 (ebook) | DDC 974.8004/97—dc23/eng/20240612
LC record available at https://lccn.loc.gov/2024002738
LC ebook record available at https://lccn.loc.gov/2024002739

Cover art: "The Indians giving a talk to Colonel Bouquet in a conference at a council fire, near his camp on the banks of Muskingum in North America in Oct. 1764." (Library of Congress Prints and Photographs Division, LC-DIG-pga-10838)
Cover design: TG Design

Dedicated to Owen S. Ireland, a historian, mentor, and friend whose unwavering passion for history and encouragement made this book possible

CONTENTS

ACKNOWLEDGMENTS   ix

Introduction   1

1. "The Foundation of Our Uneasiness": Mischief Makers and Native Americans in the Susquehanna River Valley, 1749   19

2. "Very Uneasy and Displeas'd": Displacement and Alienation on the Haudenosaunee Frontier, 1750–1754   43

3. "Bird on a Bow": The Rise of the Susquehanna Nations and a War for Independence in the Northern Susquehanna River Valley, 1754–1758   61

4. Hearts and Mouths: An Uneasy Peace, 1758–1763   84

5. A "Diversity of Interests": Attempts to Separate People and Divide Land, 1763–1767   115

6. "A Great Run for the Lands on Susquehanna": The Treaty of Fort Stanwix, 1768   141

7. An Empire Divided: The Consequences of Fort Stanwix, 1768–1773   169

8. "A Spirit of Liberty and Patriotism Pervaded the People": The Creation of a Squatter Republic in the Northern Susquehanna River Valley and the Beginning of the American Revolution, 1773–1776   192

9. "The Title of Savages": The Revolutionary War in the Northern Susquehanna River Valley, 1776–1783   217

Aftermath: Establishing the Revolution's "Value" in a "Rising Empire" of Liberty 249

NOTES 279

BIBLIOGRAPHY 311

INDEX 325

ACKNOWLEDGMENTS

There are many people to thank when publishing a book; it is rarely a solitary endeavor. Foremost among them is Nadine Zimmerli at the University of Virginia Press. Her guidance and belief in this project were instrumental. Crafting a second book was challenging: there were so many false starts, but Nadine's steadfast support has been invaluable. There are plenty of other people that need to be thanked. Linda Ries, Timothy Shannon, Patrick Spero, Paul Douglas Newman, and the other scholars involved in *Pennsylvania History*'s special issue on "Rethinking Pennsylvania's Eighteenth Century Borderlands" deserve special thanks. Not only was my contribution to that volume the beginning of this book project but their comments, criticisms, and encouragement forced me to think more broadly and dig deeper. The same could be said about Robert Parkinson. Every conversation I have with Rob not only generates new ideas but also reminds me why I love researching and teaching the American Revolution. His energy is infectious. I would also like to extend my gratitude to the Pennsylvania Historical Association. The individuals within this organization foster inspiring and immensely helpful discussions at the annual meetings and during casual gatherings over dinner and drinks. Special thanks to John and Lurene Frantz, Joe Heffley, Benjamin Scharff, Michael McCoy, and Jay Donis. Owen S. Ireland, who could be included on the previous list, is very much responsible for this book. He sparked my interest in Pennsylvania's Revolution nearly twenty years ago, and I have not tired of it since. I would also like to continue to thank my PhD advisors, Douglas Bradburn, Diane Sommerville, and J. David Hacker. I not only benefited from their training and mentoring but I continue to try to channel their critical evaluations and questions when I tackle any project. I am forever grateful.

I would be remiss if I didn't acknowledge Lycoming College, my home institution, which is situated on the Indigenous land this book is about. Throughout the process of writing this book, both the administration and the faculty provided unwavering support. A huge thank you to Marisa Sanchez in the Department of Art History for helping to find art for the cover. This book could also not have been done without the financial support I received from the History Department, the Faculty Personnel Committee, and the Humanities Research Center. They not only made it possible to get access to crucial collections but also allowed me to hire undergraduate researchers. Those students—Landon Corbin, Noah Lovecchio, Areesha Mian, and Mackenzie Holmes—have my deep appreciation. They've both contributed to the research for this book and taken the lead on their own publications and a podcast. Those projects aim to educate our local community about Williamsport's Native American roots, encouraging a critical examination of our shared past, present, and future. Lycoming College's Humanities Research Center, established in 2022 under Andrew Leiter's guidance, plays a significant role in that important work. Andrew's dedication secured a National Endowment for the Humanities grant that now helps facilitate such student initiatives and faculty research. This support enables us to address challenging questions for a broader audience. While this book represents a part of that collaborative effort, there's still much more work ahead.

Last, but certainly not least, I would like to thank my family. My wife, Kelley, is an endless reservoir of support and love. My kids, Ella and Jackson, have also been an intimate part of this project. I couldn't help but think of them as I researched and wrote this book. After all, the four of us often traveled to the many locations I write about in the book, even precariously standing along a busy road while I took pictures—that I never actually used but that clearly influenced my understanding of the historical landscape. In all, I am grateful to so many people, many of whom I will never have the time or space to name or explain.

DECLARATIONS OF INDEPENDENCE

Introduction

AS ALL AMERICANS AT some point learn or at least come to understand, July 4, 1776, was a day of immense importance. It was the day the Continental Congress adopted the Declaration of Independence, which Americans since that moment fête with food, family, friends, and, of course, fireworks. That ongoing annual celebration is exactly how some revolutionaries wanted it. Independence Day "will be the most memorable Epocha, in the History of America," John Adams mused, and he was "apt to believe that it will be celebrated, by succeeding Generations, as the great anniversary Festival" with "Pomp and Parade, with Shews, Games, Sports, Guns, Bells, Bonfires and Illuminations from one End of this Continent to the other from this Time forward forever more."[1]

That celebration Adams so vividly imagined continues to conjure staid but steady images of the day, and through it the meaning and legacy of the American Revolution itself. It was a moment when "the founders," such as John Hancock with his large, swooping signature, irritated with an overbearing British government and flush with ideas about liberty and freedom, affixed their names to a document declaring the United States an independent country where "all men are created equal," and they did so in one of the largest cities in the British colonies at the time, Philadelphia. Through that particular vision of the past, the city of Philadelphia, liberty, and independence have become nearly synonymous in the American and international imagination. On any given day in any given year, thousands of tourists eager to understand the American Revolution flock to Philadelphia. They line up to take a peek at the cracked Liberty Bell, which supposedly heralded the Revolution with its now silent chime, and to walk the halls and rooms of "Independence Hall," the "Birthplace of a Nation."[2]

Contrary to popular belief, the summer of 1776 wasn't defined by a singular meeting or a sole city. Declarations of independence were proclaimed across early America, in both urban centers and rural landscapes. Diverse revolutionaries, beyond just white male colonists, gathered in taverns, private homes, open fields, and communal spaces to assert their independence. Their stories and motivations, though, often diverge from the popular narrative of a momentous day securing sweeping rights, liberties, and freedoms for untold generations. In reality, this vision didn't even uniformly extend to all those participating in these gatherings.

The more accurate story of multiple birthplaces with multiple meanings is familiar to some modern residents of the small Pennsylvania town of Jersey Shore, located on the West Branch of the Susquehanna River about two hundred miles northwest from Independence Hall. American citizens there do not just celebrate the memory of elite, bewigged white men cramped in a small room in Philadelphia signing a piece of parchment. Instead, they gather to celebrate and remember a group of relatively poor white squatters on Indigenous land who met under the shade of a large elm tree on July 4, 1776, and also declared their independence from Great Britain. Those squatters even, locals say, wrote and signed their own declaration of independence, and they did so without knowing that Congress had done the same thing on the same day . . . or so goes popular lore.

Those celebrations in Jersey Shore are illuminating. For over thirty years, from at least 1960 to the mid-1990s, local citizens annually lined a small street to watch a group of men carrying rifles, wearing buckskin pants and hunting frocks made by members of the local Baptist church, and flying the "Don't Tread on Me" Gadsden Flag march through the town and reenact the signing of their own local declaration of independence. The gathered community also heard speeches from a small group of Native Americans who had ancestral ties to the land. Recently, the "pomp and parade" has receded. Now residents gather to hear a reading from the town crier trying to capture the essence of the frontier settlers' declaration of independence.[3]

Despite this shift, the perspective and recollection of the Revolution in Jersey Shore departs from the official narrative centered around

Independence Hall. While popular memory has blended the rights and liberties of the national and local declarations over time, creating a sense of identity tied to the "birth" of the United States, the celebration in Jersey Shore encapsulates distinct causes, peoples, emotions, outcomes, and consequences. In this small town, beyond the layers of lore and legend, we may find a more nuanced representation of the American Revolution itself. The Native Americans who called that land home and the squatters who convened on their land on that summer day in 1776 certainly believed so, albeit for vastly different reasons.

Grappling with popular lore and legend poses challenges. It is, for instance, debatable, if not unbelievable, that a group of frontier squatters met and drafted their own declaration of independence simultaneously with Congress, all while purportedly oblivious to the latter's actions. Contrary to prevailing notions about the frontier, the colonists on the West Branch of the Susquehanna River were not so isolated. They were acutely aware of goings on in the East and had long been integrated into the undertakings of the Continental Congress by 1776. Furthermore, the alleged declaration has never been found. Yet, modern residents staunchly embrace the myth, firmly believing that the elusive document to prove it lies buried somewhere deep under the muddied earth along the banks of the river, secreted away by settlers fearful of their proclaimed treason.

The idea of a lost declaration of independence is so grand that in 1948 U.S. Army engineers from Fort Belvoir, Maryland, believing the settlers had buried their declaration in a metal strong box, searched for it with a mine detector. Modern-day treasure hunters still poke around.[4] The Thomas T. Taber Museum in Williamsport, Pennsylvania, has a section dedicated to the local declaration, the local newspapers publish annual stories about it, and there are social media groups dedicated to that moment of local lore. The place where squatters supposedly met under the elm tree, later nicknamed by a folklorist the Tiadaghton Elm (it succumbed to Dutch elm disease in 1972) is now a state landmark with two different historical markers; the town of Jersey Shore still holds its annual "Tiadaghton Elm Ceremony" on July 4, and the local Sons of the American Revolution have their own "Tiadaghton" chapter.

The appeal of popular lore often lies in its connection to a kernel of truth or, at the very least, a kernel of evidence. While there might be no

FIGURE 1. Pennsylvania Historical Marker 1947HM00104, PA 220 northbound, northeast of Avis, dedicated April 30, 1947 (photo by author)

indication that settlers created a physical document while unaware of Congress's actions, numerous contemporary accounts attest to squatters on the West Branch gathering to assert their independence. According to those present at the "meeting on the banks of Pine Creek on the Fourth of July 1776," a "spirit of liberty and patriotism pervaded the people," with "Indipendence" being "all the talk." However, even such corroboration is, in the end, unsatisfying. The fact that they met together tells us little about their motivations or objectives. What, indeed, did "Indipendence" or "liberty and patriotism" signify for those squatters on Indigenous land? Equally crucial, what did it mean for the Native peoples who also considered that land their home? Both, after all, experienced and participated in the American Revolution.[5]

The answer to those questions are not lost, located on a settler declaration of independence buried amid the debris of future generations somewhere on the banks of the West Branch. There were and are plenty of other documents available to reconstruct what happened there and why, but

FIGURE 2. Pennsylvania Historical Marker 1947HM00103, SR 1016/old US 220, southeast of Avis, dedicated May 6, 1947 (photo by author)

digging into that part of the story, which confirms the kernel of one myth, also shatters larger ones. These documents reveal causes and consequences of the American Revolution that are wildly out of synch with a popular memory that lionizes the grand visions of equality, individualism, and a patriotic antigovernment propensity of revolutionaries that Americans celebrate each year. Such a memory sits uneasily aside the reality of the revolution as lived, experienced, and proclaimed by the actual people who met on the banks of Pine Creek on that hot July day and by the still more peoples, especially Indigenous ones, who fought to secure those very banks for themselves and their posterity.

From the vantage point of that small corner of the Susquehanna River Valley, it becomes abundantly clear that the American Revolution was much messier and more contradictory than Americans today understand. Just as the historical record makes clear that squatters on the West Branch met, it also makes clear that the equality their independence promised was narrowly defined. It certainly did not include Native peoples. Moreover, that same historical record reveals that those squatters on the West Branch believed individual liberty was relative to the needs of the "patriotic" community—a definition of belonging that excluded a host of individuals, including other British colonists. Moreover, those same settlers exclaimed that government was necessary, even desirable—just not the colonial and imperial governments claiming sovereignty at the time. The settlers came to those conclusions and held those beliefs because what underlined them all was concern about land—who had access to it, who had authority over it, and who could reap its rewards.

That revolution for land and limited liberty, as foreign as it seems today, was exactly what those squatters meeting on the "banks of Pine Creek" wanted. It promised to be transformative, a radical departure from their past experiences, reflecting their desires for the future. In the eight years preceding their July 4 meeting, these settlers had been illegally squatting on Native American land, defying Indigenous rights and sovereignty, the wishes of land speculators, the goals of Pennsylvania's colonial government, and the larger interests of the British Empire. All were "our enemies," they argued at the time. But their defiance involved much more than squatting on land others owned and resisting what they saw as the evils of the colonial and imperial governments. Dismissive of Native American rights and irritated with how land, resources, and power were allocated in Pennsylvania and the British Empire at large, these squatters made their way to the northern portion of the Susquehanna River Valley, illegally occupying roughly twenty-five miles of land along the West Branch, and erected their own independent republican government that they tellingly called "Fair Play." And they did all of this years before the heady summer of 1776.[6]

That Fair Play republic, those settlers well knew, existed on shaky ground. First and foremost, Native Americans rightfully detested that rudimentary republic for encroaching on their land. They complained to colonial officials and threatened war, proclaiming their own independence and sovereign authority over that land in the process. Land speculators as well as colonial and imperial officials too disliked this squatter republic. The speculators actively sought to acquire the land, while the officials aimed to either relocate the settlers to prevent conflict with Native Americans or advance the interests of politically connected speculators. Most times, however, officials and speculators were one and the same.

American independence, the Fair Play squatters thought, offered a glimmer of hope that new governments birthed in that independence would support the basic premises of their squatter republic as well as their rights to their "considerable improvements" (as they called their illegal claims to the land) against Native Americans, avaricious land speculators, and seemingly corrupt politicians.[7] These were reasonable assumptions. After all, patriots everywhere proclaimed American independence would undermine the power of both elite white men *and* Indigenous people. Not only did Pennsylvania's new state constitution, established in 1776 to replace Pennsylvania's colonial government, rail against elite white privilege while proclaiming the dawn of a limited (if still radical for its time) white male democracy, but even the Declaration of Independence itself, the founding document of the young, disjointed American republic, touted equal liberty while also pointing out its narrow applicability. The Declaration may have importantly stated that "all men are created equal," but it also made clear that this equality did not extend to everyone, especially "the merciless Indian Savages."[8]

Such revolutionary and exclusive rhetoric expressed patriotic assumptions everywhere but especially in the squatter republic on the West Branch where equal liberty quite literally meant, as those squatters said in their own words, that "the Poor distress'd People" would finally triumph over a "Cruel and Savage Enemy" as well as a "Set of men" with connections and "hard money."[9] Triumphing over those enemies to gain legal title to Native American land was inseparable from their vision of the revolution and its promise.

That exclusionary, antielite, and anti-Indigenous view of the American Revolution encapsulates the motivations for and consequences of a rural revolution erupting up and down Britain's mainland colonies. From the remote outposts of rural Georgia to the newly organized "frontier" counties of New Hampshire, many colonial inhabitants prioritized securing safe and independent landholdings for themselves and their descendants. This emphasis took center stage as they considered their support for American independence and the ensuing war to achieve it, significantly influencing the future of numerous Native nations and peoples in the process.[10]

Most colonial Americans, over 90 percent, after all, lived in rural areas well outside of urban centers. Of the nearly 450,000 colonial Pennsylvanians in 1776, only 40,000 lived in Philadelphia. During the eighteenth century, that rural population grew exponentially, shuffling colonists north, west, and south in search of land and opportunity, land occupied by Indigenous nations those settlers desired to replace, and sought after by prominent white men with the capital and political connections to purchase it all.[11] The early history of rural colonial settlers was in no small part defined by an ability, or inability, to secure land for the future. If we are to understand the Revolution and its consequences beyond the confines of Independence Hall and the various other cities dotting the eastern seaboard, we need to take seriously the quest for land and economic security that shaped the motivations and experiences of rural settlers such as those in the Fair Play republic on the West Branch as well as the land speculators and Native peoples they believed stood in their way.

Both the desire of speculators and the resilience of Native peoples defending their rights actively shaped the Fair Play settlers' understanding of the purpose of the American Revolution. When these settlers declared "themselves and the country free and independent of Great Britain," they believed that this separation would elevate their status, allowing them to thwart prominent speculators and appropriate Native American land through forcible dispossession or even eradication of the Native nations that lived there.[12] As those Fair Play settlers consistently declared, they *deserved*, because of their dedication to American independence, state recognition of their land rights and state support "to extirpate" Native peoples "from the face of the earth." That was, they thought, the purpose of the Revolutionary War, or as they later called it, "the late unhappy Indian War."[13] More significant still, that vision of the Revolution's purpose coupled with the Fair Play settlers' experiences during the war received both statewide and even national attention, even commendation, by war's end.[14]

The ferocity and violence of that language and vision of the American Revolution's purpose also underscores a simple but often overlooked fact—the American Revolution wasn't solely a struggle between Britain and its colonies; it also encompassed, and in many cases revolved around, the future of Native peoples and their lands in an independent America. Threats to Native American land and sovereignty proliferated across North America during the Revolution, intensifying as the war progressed. By the war's end, Americans, regardless of their residence in rural or urban areas, perceived forcibly dispossessing Native Americans as the Revolution's true "Value." In the process, "conquest" and "empire" became the watchwords of the day.[15] What happened on that small corner of the West Branch of the Susquehanna River helps illuminate how and why that critical transition occurred and its costs for everyone involved.[16]

Significantly, Native nations and peoples were acutely aware of the Revolution's objectives and potential repercussions. As a prominent member of the Seneca Nation asserted, "the Desire" to "extirpate us from the Earth" and "possess our Lands" was "the Cause of the present War." In response, Native Americans too convened in various locations, rallying clan, kin, and nation to declare they were "free and independent," expressing a willingness to fight and sacrifice for their land and sovereignty. This sentiment was not a newfound response but had been articulated and acted on for years. Over a decade earlier, Britain's superintendent of Indian affairs, William Johnson, had explained that Native nations regarded themselves as "a free people who had independent Lands, which were their ancient possessions."[17]

By 1776, squatters and settlers like those in the Fair Play republic seriously threatened that independence. More important still, the states and Congress only encouraged that threat, harnessing settler wishes and desires to win the war and secure their own fledgling and beleaguered sovereign authority.[18] Therefore, the American Revolution intensified long held feelings in Native communities of the need to defend their land and sovereignty. As many Native Americans proclaimed during the Revolutionary War, "Subjection & slavery" was their future if American colonists achieved their own independence for "liberty." It was and is a striking irony.[19]

Many peoples throughout America thus fought for liberty, sovereignty, and independence during the American Revolution, but what those terms meant and what they would mean for the futures of the various peoples who used them were often at odds. On the West Branch of the Susquehanna River, the territory the Fair Play republic claimed and its citizens desired and fought for comprised the last bastion of Indigenous land in the Susquehanna River Valley that had been contested for nearly half a century. It should be no surprise that the Indigenous nations there continued to proclaim their own liberty, independence, and sovereignty. The struggle of both Native peoples and American colonists to achieve these venerable revolutionary ideals in that region, though, as Pennsylvania's chief justice put it in 1791, "was an offence that tended to involve this country in blood."[20] And it did.

Yet, the Revolutionary War was a complex conflict extending beyond a simple narrative of white Americans versus Native Americans or American colonies against the British Empire. Early Americans, be they Indigenous or colonial, also engaged in internal conflicts over land and independence. The multifaceted layers of power, conflicting interests, and deep-seated animosities that characterized eighteenth-century America erupted during the Revolution. In the thirteen colonies, longstanding clashes among colonists came to a head. Different colonies grappled for power and territory, and within each colony a myriad of regional, ethnic, religious, class, and social distinctions often fueled discord. Native peoples were equally diverse, with distinct cultures, languages, and governing structures. They had independent nations, alliances, and enemies, and held unique visions of their pasts and futures. Even within individual nations, internal disagreements among clan and kin groups were common. Power, land, sovereignty, cultural differences, and past histories underscored those differences, and they were lasting.

The Revolutionary War, which rapidly transitioned into a contest for land and sovereignty, heightened existing disparities within and between Native Americans and colonists. This transformation turned the Revolution into a complex and tumultuous civil war for everyone, a common occurrence when seeking independence in a diverse landscape like North America. Independence within this framework became a subjective concept, shaped by the conflicting interests and perceived power dynamics prevalent in early America. Attaining one group's notion of independence frequently entailed, paradoxically, dependence or even destruction for another. Essentially, as is often observed, those experiencing oppression can simultaneously act as oppressors.

In the tumultuous theater of Revolutionary America, the Northern Susquehanna River Valley stood out as a battleground where conflicting visions of independence played out in gruesome detail. This landscape witnessed a brutal saga of raids, counterraids, scorched-earth campaigns, and senseless massacres. Here, colonists turned on one another, Native Americans clashed over the war and their futures, and all the while both groups fought each other. Entire towns, whether inhabited by Indigenous or American communities, were razed to the ground. The toll was staggering—countless lives were lost, combatants and noncombatants alike, all sacrificed in the pursuit of independence. It was a macabre dance, performed under the banner of liberty, an ironic quest for freedom that often meant the opposite for those caught in its deadly embrace.

The violent repercussions stemming from various declarations of independence were not sudden; they were deeply rooted in a prolonged and intricate history. Rather than emerging from a period of peace, the Revolutionary War in the Susquehanna River Valley was just one significant episode in an enduring struggle over land, sovereignty, and independence involving Native Americans and European colonists that had been raging for well over thirty years. This protracted conflict was intricately interwoven into the American Revolution and its aftermath. Divergent memories, histories, and animosities, shaped by experiences spanning generations, converged, comingled, and clashed during this revolutionary struggle.

It is not difficult to imagine why. The Fair Play republic, a focal point of intense Revolutionary War violence, existed within a larger contested territorial zone. This zone was a perpetual battleground in the eighteenth century, witnessing relentless conflicts within, between, and among Native nations, speculators, financiers, government officials, military officers, common white soldiers, and ordinary white farmers vying for control. This expansive region spanned most of present-day northcentral Pennsylvania, also known as the Northern Susquehanna River Valley. This valley commences just south of the confluence of the East and West Branches of the Susquehanna River, extending northeast and northwest through fertile flatlands, enclosed by what both Native peoples and white colonists termed "endless mountains." It stood as a continuous theater where declarations of independence were proclaimed, won, and lost.

This area's history also transcends mere geographic boundaries. Positioned in the center of a rich and tangled history, the Northern Susquehanna River Valley shaped and was shaped by the struggle for land, sovereignty, and independence to the north, the home of the Mohawk, Oneida, Onondaga, Cayuga, Seneca, and Tuscarora, who comprised the Six Nations or Haudenosaunee, "the people of the Longhouse." Similar connections extended southeast to the Lehigh Valley and southwest beyond the Alleghany Mountains into the Ohio River Valley. Even places as distant as Illinois left an imprint on and were influenced by the Northern Susquehanna River Valley. By the mid-eighteenth century, this valley had captured the attention of people on both sides of the Atlantic Ocean, residing in diverse colonies, empires, and nations. From London to Paris, Montreal to Albany, Hartford to Wyoming, Philadelphia to Shamokin, Onondaga to Williamsburg, Pine Creek to Logstown, individuals were keenly interested in and actively sought to control the valley, with force if necessary.

Throughout the eighteenth century, the Northern Susquehanna River Valley was closely linked to these seemingly distant lands and peoples due to the diverse multiethnic population residing in or vying for control of the region. Indigenous refugees, displaced from their ancestral homes to the east, north, and south, found a home in this valley, particularly after the disastrous "Walking Purchase" of 1737. The Lenni Lenape, or Delaware, encompassing the Unalachtigo, Unami, and sometimes the Munsee (who often identified as a separate people), displaced from their lands east and west of the Delaware River, established roots in the river valley. Seeking refuge from racial violence, multiethnic Indigenous Christians also sought solace there after fleeing Moravian missions in the Lehigh Valley. Additionally, the Northern Susquehanna River Valley became a haven for other refugee peoples, including Algonquian-speaking Nanticoke and Conoy from present-day Maryland, Shawnee from the south and west, and Mohican and Esopus from the northeast. Siouan-speaking Saponi and Tutelo from the Piedmont, along with a small group of Muskogean-speaking peoples from further south likewise called the Northern Susquehanna River Valley home during the eighteenth century.

By the middle of the eighteenth century, these diverse groups either coexisted in multiethnic towns or lived as close but separate neighbors.

Multiethnic towns like Nescopeck, Lackawacka, Wyoming, and Wyalusing thrived along the North and East Branches; Shamokin marked the forks; and Ostonwackin, Wenschpochkechung, Great Island, Bald Eagle, and many other towns dotted the tributary creeks branching out from the West Branch. In the 1720s and again in the 1750s, several multiethnic communities in the valley confederated, establishing their own councils complete with diplomats, speakers, and interpreters, and asserted their claim over the Northern Susquehanna River Valley. While modern historians and contemporaries often refer to them as "the Susquehanna Indians," I prefer to call them the Susquehanna Nations, a term that captures their intimately connected lives while still preserving their distinct identities. The Northern Susquehanna River Valley had a dynamic social landscape as different peoples continually formed new associations, confederacies, alliances, and even shared spaces, envisioning and pursuing collective futures. Despite their shared dreams, these communities retained their individual identities, lineages, histories, and at times lingering animosities toward one another.[21]

Like all dreams, these aspirations were not easily realized. The Haudenosaunee also asserted their claim to the Northern Susquehanna River Valley through the right of conquest from the Iroquoian-speaking Susquehannock after the Beaver Wars in the seventeenth century. By the mid-eighteenth century, the Six Nations had a well-established presence in the region, residing in the diverse multiethnic towns scattered across the fertile valleys, densely covered mountains, rolling hills, and navigable creeks that made the Northern Susquehanna River Valley desirable for farming, hunting, and fishing.

The valley wasn't just valuable for its rich resources. It held a strategic importance due to the Wyalusing, Shamokin, and Sheshequin paths. These routes facilitated the movement of warriors, traders, diplomats, and missionaries along the Susquehanna River and its tributaries, connecting the region to Onondaga, the heart of the Haudenosaunee and home to the most revered symbol of the Six Nations' unity and history, the Grand Council Fire, the Fire That Never Dies. The Seneca, Cayuga, and Oneida, as guardians of the corridors leading to Onondaga, especially those opening onto the Susquehanna River, carried the responsibility of safeguarding the land for the well-being and safety of their people.

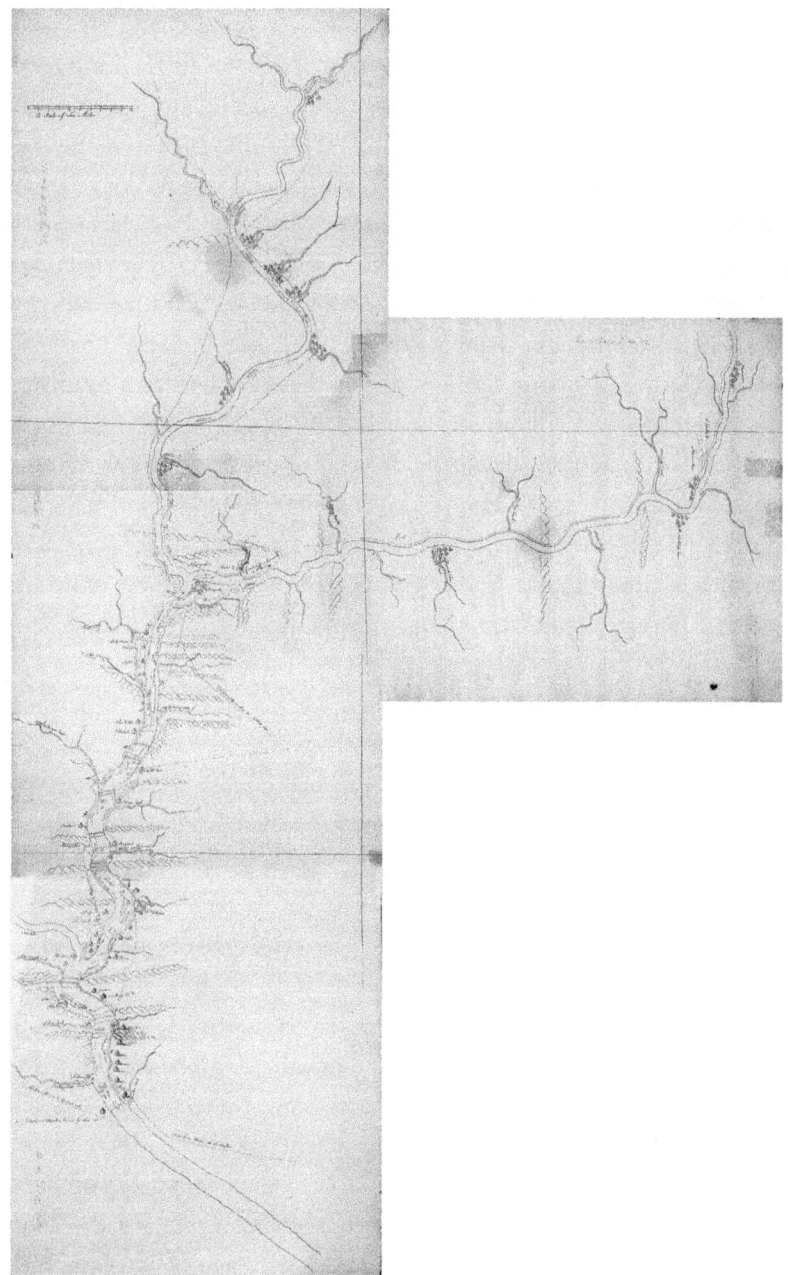

FIGURE 3. Map of General William Clapham's march along the Susquehanna River, ca. 1756, pen on paper (DP f.037.10–13, Moravian Archives, Bethlehem, Pennsylvania)

The Six Nations not only laid claim to the land but also asserted their dominance over the Susquehanna Nations. Whether Delaware, Shawnee, Nanticoke, or Conoy, Saponi or Tutelo, Mohican or Esopus, all were considered by the Six Nations as tributaries, props of the Longhouse, envisioned as conquered children, women, nephews, and cousins. Many of these supposed tributaries had been displaced to the Northern Susquehanna River Valley due to that perceived status, and as a result they consistently contested their position, striving for their own independence. Their resilience and continual pursuit of autonomy and sovereignty significantly influenced the history of the Northern Susquehanna River Valley.

The Haudenosaunee and the Susquehanna Nations were not the only Indigenous people who laid claim to the valley or had an interest there. Many of the Native nations living beyond the Alleghany Mountains in the Ohio River Valley shared clan and kinship connections with the Susquehanna Nations. They also shared many of the same grievances. Like the Susquehanna Nations, the Ohio Nations were a multiethnic people composed of various displaced Native polities claimed by the Haudenosaunee as tributaries. Many had also lived for a time in the Northern Susquehanna River Valley, and even after they moved west continued to take up seasonal residence on the North and West Branches of its defining river. In essence, any clear ethnic, geographic, or national boundaries demarcating space in the Northern Susquehanna River Valley is nearly impossible to establish because, as one Haudenosaunee explained, there was an "abundance of Indians . . . moving up and down" the river.[22] European American missionaries as well as land-hungry speculators and settlers who traversed the valley also couldn't help but comment on the mosaic of multiethnic "Indian Villages" and individual farms that peppered the countryside. "Its rare to hear two Indians talking in one Language," one missionary staying in the large Indigenous town of Shamokin wrote in his diary.[23]

While there was a struggle within and between different Native American communities for control of and sovereignty over the Northern Susquehanna River Valley, European Americans were also involved, and just like Native Americans, they fought between and among themselves. Separated by class, ethnicity, religion, and nationality, European Americans living up and down North America jockeyed for the fertile lands of the valley. Since at least 1749, the Northern Susquehanna River Valley captured their attention, becoming part of a fantasy where they dreamed of economic independence and future riches. Whether confined to a cramped space on a ship, experiencing a long and arduous journey across the Atlantic Ocean from the German provinces or Irish plantations, trying to eke out some kind of subsistence in a small cabin, sitting comfortably in a merchant's counting house, listening to a sermon in their local church, or even drinking at a tavern or debating in a council chamber or a legislative session, they all shared in the dream, and they were willing to fight each other and the Native peoples who lived there to obtain it.

The tumultuous journey of these diverse communities as they pursued their dreams and futures in the Northern Susquehanna River Valley laid the groundwork for a revolutionary upheaval that would profoundly shape the very foundations of the United States. This book delves into this history, unraveling the protracted struggle for independence in the Northern Susquehanna River Valley as it unfolded. Commencing in 1749 with a treaty between the Six Nations and Pennsylvania, which granted 2 million acres of Delaware land to the proprietors of Pennsylvania, the narrative unfolds through a series of movements and wars for independence that that treaty helped inspire. It culminates with another treaty with the Haudenosaunee in 1784 after yet another war for independence, ultimately shaping the modern boundaries of the state of Pennsylvania and revealing the true costs of that revolutionary struggle.

That 1784 treaty marked the official conclusion of both the Fair Play republic on the West Branch as well as the hard-fought quest for independence by the Susquehanna Nations. Armed with the land "ceded" by the Haudenosaunee in that treaty, and acknowledging the Fair Play settlers' "Service and their Suffering" during the Revolutionary War, the commonwealth of Pennsylvania granted these squatters the rights to their once-illegal claims. In doing so, the state effectively assimilated the Fair Play republic into the revolutionary framework, concurrently displacing the numerous Indigenous nations who had similarly served, suffered, and fought for their independence on that land—many of whom were never even consulted about their future. As the Fair Play settlers envisioned when they gathered on Indigenous land on July 4, 1776, American "Independence" realized their dreams, wishes, and hopes for the future, but it also entailed the destruction of the dreams, wishes, and hopes of others.[24] When citizens gather to celebrate American Independence today, whether in Philadelphia or the other small towns throughout the United States, this history is an important part of its enduring legacy, silently echoing, like the Liberty Bell, through time.

1

"The Foundation of Our Uneasiness"

MISCHIEF MAKERS AND NATIVE AMERICANS IN THE SUSQUEHANNA RIVER VALLEY, 1749

On Thursday, June 26, 1749, a small group of Haudenosaunee delegates and representatives of some of their proclaimed tributaries living just west of the Susquehanna River at the headwaters of the Juniata—the Tutelo, Nanticoke, and Conoy—unceremoniously entered the city of Philadelphia. The trip, while not spur of the moment, was also not widely advertised. Nevertheless, these travelers didn't raise any suspicions in the city. The newspapers did not report on the delegation, nor did the city's leaders initially comment about it or gossip to others. It was normal for Native peoples to make their way to Philadelphia. Well over a decade earlier, the Haudenosaunee and the Pennsylvania government had made a grand alliance, carving a figurative road from Onondaga—the heart of the Six Nations—to Philadelphia, establishing an official "council fire" for both "to sitt down by & take Council together." Since then, Haudenosaunee delegates routinely came to the city for trade, to make and restore peace, or to prevent war. Those last two goals were the reason for their arrival in the city in the summer of 1749.[1]

That summer, Haudenosaunee land, sovereignty, and power were under threat. Over the previous few months, Pennsylvania squatters had been settling west of the Susquehanna River, particularly at the base of the Juniata River as well as south of that river near Great Cove and about forty-two miles north at Penn's Creek, disrupting the towns and hunting grounds claimed by the Haudenosaunee and occupied by the tributaries they promised to protect. This was not the first time the Haudenosaunee and their tributaries had complained about squatters there.² Just a few years earlier, a group of squatters and colonial traders had clashed with Native peoples at the headwaters of the Juniata and nearly shattered the alliance between the proprietary colony and the Six Nations. While the squatters fled that time and the governor issued a proclamation barring settlement west of the Susquehanna River, more settlers had come in that clash's wake.³

The anger the Haudenosaunee felt about the scenario around the Juniata River was compounded by similar problems experienced across their lands. Everywhere they looked in the 1740s it seemed as if "ye English or White people intended to destroy" them.⁴ Feeling surrounded and downright exasperated by 1749, Haudenosaunee delegates and their tributaries traveled along the paths, roads, and rivers that led to the council fire in Philadelphia to air their grievances. Meeting with the governor a few days after their arrival that June, three Seneca and two Onondaga, speaking for the "tributary Nations" who traveled with them (rarely did tributaries speak for themselves at council), argued that the land the squatters occupied was the home and "hunting Ground" of the Nanticoke, Conoy, Mohican, Tutelo, and Delaware, as well as "other Indian" refugees who had been displaced from their ancestral homes and were now under the protection and authority of the Six Nations. Since "our Boundaries are so well known," the Haudenosaunee speakers demanded the squatters "be made to remove instantly with all their effects."⁵

This was not a demand the Pennsylvania government, nor any of the British colonies, could take lightly. Just a year earlier marked the end of King George's War, which had enmeshed Natives, British, and French in a violent conflict over the bounds of empires as well as Native American sovereignty. During that struggle, the British colonies had pinned their survival on their growing relationship with the Haudenosaunee and the perceived power the Haudenosaunee had over their proclaimed tributaries such as those Tutelo, Nanticoke, and Conoy who traveled to Philadelphia in the summer of 1749.

The Haudenosaunee were one of the most powerful, feared, and revered people in North America, and their friendship seemed the only thing holding back a host of Native nations from supporting Britain's enemy, France. According to one important Pennsylvania official, the Haudenosaunee and their tributaries could muster over nine thousand warriors and therefore were "our only Security against the ffrench."⁶ James Logan, who shaped much of Pennsylvania's Indian diplomacy, said simply, "If we lose the Iroquois, we are gone."⁷ The Haudenosaunee also knew of their significance to the British. As an important Onondaga speaker put it, the Six Nations controlled a vast "frontier Country between your Enemy and You, so that we have been your Guard."⁸

Importantly, King George's War had not ended France's imperial designs in North America. In fact, around the same time the Haudenosaunee and their tributaries met with Pennsylvania officials that June, a large force of French soldiers and their Native American allies traveled from Montreal to the Ohio River Valley, stopping along the way to place metal plates emblazoned with the French royal arms and an inscription declaring France's possession "of the said river Ohio and of all those which empty into it, and of all the lands on both sides as far as the sources of the said rivers."⁹

That declared expansion was, to say the least, inauspicious, especially since King George's War had seriously strained Britain's relationship with the Haudenosaunee and nearly split the Six Nations apart. The Seneca, the most western and populous of the Six Nations, veered toward the French while the easternmost nation, the Mohawk, swung toward the British.¹⁰ Those nations in the middle—the Onondaga, Cayuga, Oneida, and Tuscarora—cared less about European alliances and more about holding together the "great peace" that had united the Haudenosaunee since the beginning of their league when Hiawatha and Deganawidah planted the "Great Tree of Peace" centuries earlier. To make matters worse, King George's War had also weakened the Haudenosaunee's authority in the eyes of some of their tributaries, many of whom the French and their Native allies continued to court. If Pennsylvania's government did not act against the squatters, recognizing the legitimacy of Haudenosaunee claims and protection over the land and peoples in the region, it could further cripple Haudenosaunee supremacy, giving France a serious advantage in a new war that was likely to occur sooner than anyone expected. There was a certain "darkness visible" in the late 1740s.¹¹

Despite that visible darkness, Pennsylvania's governor, James Hamilton, as well as the Haudenosaunee and their tributaries had other conflicting problems and interests to contend with when they came to the city's council fire in the summer of 1749. France may have represented a significant external threat, but there were also internal issues to deal with that made any mutually agreeable solution extremely difficult to achieve. The land west of the Susquehanna River represented the hopes, wishes, and desires of not just the Haudenosaunee and their tributaries but the proprietors of Pennsylvania, the Penns, as well as elite speculators, and a growing number of cash-strapped colonists and incoming European immigrants. All of those hopes and dreams clashed, making the fight to obtain them more than a just a struggle between Europeans and Native Americans over the extent of their sovereign authority, but rather for the survival and futures of the various peoples involved. Often, sovereignty and survival were one and the same.

Governor Hamilton faced a serious predicament when he came to the council fire to hear Haudenosaunee complaints that June. Hamilton's superior and the main proprietor of Pennsylvania at that time, Thomas Penn, a smart yet petulant man reared as an elite with a certain self-importance, was cash-strapped, debt-ridden, and facing mounting political opposition in his colony looking to diminish his power. Because of Penn's poor economic circumstances and political factionalism, he was actively angling to extend his colony's jurisdiction west of the Susquehanna River, especially north of the Blue Mountains, where squatters were now settling. Obtaining that land would bring money to his depleted coffers from land sales and his ever-increasing quitrents (a feudal remnant that required landholders to pay a perpetual annual fee to the proprietor above and beyond basic taxes). Acquiring that land could also assure the political allegiance of some important officials in his colony.[12]

As Penn well knew, many of his supporters had struck it rich by speculating in land. In Pennsylvania, one observer noted, "It is almost a proverb" that "every great fortune made here within these 50 years has been by land." And because this "immense country" was ripe for "land jobbing," those with connections constantly looked to the proprietor to fulfill their desires; he was their cash cow, their benefactor.[13] After all, political allegiance was often acquired by a proprietary ability to sate people's appetite for land and the wealth and status it conveyed. That was how it had always been done in the colony. As early as 1685, just three years after Thomas Penn's father, William Penn, had received a royal grant from King Charles II making him and his growing family "Lords of the Soil" over a large swath of land cascading west of the Delaware River, the founding proprietor made it clear that for those people who were "of aid to me and Diligent, I will be kind to them in land and other things."[14]

Like father like sons. After William Penn died in 1718, his heirs continued the practice of dispensing lands at discount prices to men who supported them. His sons, especially those from his second marriage—John, Thomas, and Richard—embraced their supporters' speculations in return for political allegiance, often measuring their "inclination" to bestow land and offices in "proportion to the service" performed for them. If men proved loyal and useful, the sons returned the favor.[15] When James Burd, a young colonist on the make, sought to "settle in some way suitable to the interest of my family," he cultivated a relationship with Thomas Penn. Burd knew he had "small stock" but was willing to show the proprietor that he was and would remain a "servant . . . of the Proprietary Family."[16] Burd's appeals paid off. He received an appointment as a justice of the peace, became the commander of a new fort poised to extend Pennsylvania's jurisdiction north and west of the Susquehanna River into Native American country, and was able to purchase from Penn good land with a rentable mill.[17] Edward Shippen, a political juggernaut in Lancaster County who controlled a vast patronage machine through his connections to the proprietors and other prominent families in the province, advised his own son that if he wanted an office and good land he needed to make sure that Thomas Penn "should think it worth his while to Secure your Friendship for the Time to come."[18] For someone like Shippen, a prominent politician who already garnered Penn family respect, Penn's continued patronage offered power, place, and security for his children. For young people like Burd such a connection offered a chance to make it into the higher social circles of an early modern world.

The interconnectedness of proprietary patronage, political power, and land speculation becomes unmistakably clear in the success of William

Allen. He stood as a staunch ally of the proprietors and set his sights on the Susquehanna River Valley. Born and raised in Pennsylvania, the son of a wealthy Philadelphia merchant, he skillfully cultivated a relationship with the Penns. During the early 1700s, while still in his teens, Allen journeyed to England, obtaining a law degree from the esteemed Middle Temple in London. There, he forged connections with influential figures close to the Penn family, granting him access to serve as a legal advisor to the proprietors. Upon his return to the colonies in the late 1720s, Allen passionately advocated for proprietary rights. Notably, he even provided financial support to William Penn's sons, assisting them in settling the remaining mortgage on the province, alleviating their inherited debts. Additionally, Allen solidified his ties to the proprietary family by orchestrating the marriage between his daughter Anne and John Penn, the son of Richard Penn.[19]

The proprietors rewarded Allen for his loyalty. After about 1728, Allen held or had occupied at one time, often concurrently, the offices of legislator, common councilman, recorder, and mayor of Philadelphia; justice of the peace; boundary commissioner; and eventually chief justice of the colony's supreme court. Not only had Allen attained numerous positions and powerful placements but he also benefited through the acquisition of land. Proprietary land office records show many grants of large tracts of land to Allen starting in 1733.[20] What those records don't show is that Allen's acquisitions began much earlier and depended on his relationship with the proprietary family. In 1725, for instance, Allen bought 10,000 acres of rich alluvial land directly from the estate of the recently deceased William Penn Jr. for £741, well below the established price for most everybody else. Not only did Allen get a deal but the land purchased was above the forks of the Delaware River and owned by Native Americans, particularly the Lenni Lenape, or Delaware. In addition, Allen purchased 15,000 acres near the Delaware and Lehigh rivers for £1,000 from Thomas Penn and an additional 5,000 acres in what would be part of Nazareth Township in Northampton County from Laetitia Penn Aubrey for £500, all of which, again, was owned by Native Americans. Allen sold this last purchase just a few years later to George Whitefield, the famous evangelical preacher, for a hefty profit of £1,700.[21] By the mid-eighteenth century, about the same time Native delegates made their way to the city, Allen had acquired no less than 75,000 acres, 64,000 of which he purchased directly from members of the proprietary family.[22] Yet, he still wanted more, especially west of the Susquehanna River.

The intersecting desires of the Penn family and their close associates were not the only interests Governor Hamilton had to weigh when he met with Haudenosaunee delegates and their tributaries in the early summer of 1749. The squatters west of the Susquehanna River also posed a serious problem that threatened to upend his colony. Squatters inundated the lands his political allies and kin owned and wanted. Hamilton was, for example, related by marriage to William Allen. Those squatters also added fuel to the factional politics that often embroiled the colony in turmoil, and, just as important, threatened to disrupt the perceived harmony and goodwill with Native peoples that the proprietors publicly cultivated as the definitive image of their father and his "peaceable kingdom." The image and memory of William Penn as a fair and somewhat avuncular figure often brought Native peoples to the table to negotiate and sell more land in the first place.[23]

William Penn's reputation, as recounted in even mid-eighteenth-century legend, depicted him as a leader who was content with acquiring only the land necessary for his colony. He was known to respect the ongoing land use of Native Americans, often paying for purchased lands multiple times over. These actions were a routine part of his business dealings. This approach earned him the title "Brother Onas," "Onas" being a clever play on the Iroquoian word for "pen" or "quill," signifying a trusted ally or, at the very least, a more favorable figure compared to other Europeans laying claim to Indigenous lands. Throughout the eighteenth century, the memory of Penn as "Brother Onas" persisted, shaping the perceptions of both Native peoples and Pennsylvania officials. Remarkably, even Thomas Penn, who inherited his father's title but not his stance on recognizing Native American rights, commissioned Benjamin West's famous painting *Penn's Treaty with the Indians,* now exhibited in Harrisburg, Pennsylvania's state capital. Ironically, the land that city sits on served as a refuge for the displaced Delaware depicted in the painting.[24]

Although William Penn was never as virtuous as often remembered, his memory was at least rooted in a semblance of truth. By 1749, that semblance no longer reflected the colony. John, Thomas, and Richard were not

FIGURE 4. Benjamin West, *Penn's Treaty with the Indians*, 1771–1772. (Pennsylvania Academy of the Fine Arts)

their father when it came to working with Native peoples. Moreover, William Penn did not have to navigate the same financial, political, and demographic pressures as they did. To be sure, William Penn never had it easy, financially or otherwise, but his province had fundamentally changed by the time his sons came to power. Many of the squatters the Haudenosaunee and their "tributaries" complained about in the summer of 1749 were evidence of that fact.

Many of them were recent immigrants hailing from the German provinces and the Scots plantations in Ireland (often called the Ulster Scots or Scots-Irish). Those immigrants were part and parcel of a demographic and economic transformation that was forever changing Pennsylvania's political, social, cultural, and diplomatic future. Moreover, by the mid-eighteenth century, economic stratification and the attendant poverty it heralded grew parallel to this significant rise in the colonial population (which nearly doubled every twenty years). Such changes, coupled with a land policy started by William Penn and fully embraced by his sons that benefited a small cadre of wealthy and connected land speculators, put serious strains on access to land, created a great deal of factional turmoil, and threatened to upend the very ideas undergirding William Penn's "peaceable kingdom."[25]

According to Richard Peters, a haughty proprietary ally, avid land speculator, and secretary of the land office who traveled to the squatter settlements around the Juniata, the "families" he encountered "were not large, nor Improvements considerable." In most cases, squatters claimed few acres and their dwellings consisted of "only a few Logs piled, and fastened to one another." Many of the settlers were so destitute that Peters, who was also an Anglican minister, felt compelled to give "them money" and offer short-term and "rent-free" leases on "several of my own Plantations" that were still "vacant." While Peters could not make the same offer to everyone as far too "many settlements were found," he fervently believed that these "poor" people, who he thought "were only prompted by a Desire to make Mischief," should be grateful for his "good Usage" and the opportunity to learn the value of labor as tenants on his landed estates. He could not bring himself to come to any other conclusion. The lands they settled were "no better, nay not so good as many vacant Lands within the purchased Parts of the Province." Why, he must have asked himself, were they there, disrupting the peace and image of the province, if they could legitimately purchase or rent better land elsewhere?[26]

The way Peters brushed off the squatters by labeling them morally corrupt troublemakers should make modern readers pause. Describing them as merely causing "mischief" hardly encapsulated the true situation. By 1749, squatting had become a common reality for many residents of colonial Pennsylvania. Much like the speculators tied to the proprietary family, the desire to own land was a driving force behind immigration to the colony and the internal migration of people north, south, and west. The allure of prospects in the colonies was so strong that aspiring landowners were willing to undertake perilous transatlantic journeys from German provinces or Irish plantations. They even indentured themselves and their children as servants to fund their passage. After 1717, over eighty thousand German-speaking people fled Europe due to overpopulation, poverty, and limited land, driven by the widespread belief in the availability of land and opportunities in America. In many ways, these migrants were also speculators, banking on their future. However, although they shared aspirations with influential figures like William Allen, their ability to realize these dreams vastly differed from his. It did not take long for Pennsylvania's newcomers to experience that difference.[27]

Gottlieb Mittelberger, a Lutheran pastor from the Duchy of Württemberg who left his native country for Pennsylvania around the same time Native delegates entered the city of Philadelphia in the summer of 1749, was shocked by just how much reality contrasted with expectations. Through his now famous travel narrative *Journey to Pennsylvania,* Mittelberger tried to dissuade potential migrants from making the arduous voyage to Pennsylvania. Not only did he describe the horrors of transatlantic travel and the exploitation of indentured servitude but he made it clear that any suffering the migrants endured would not be repaid with land and opportunity. "Our German people who emigrate," he stated, "do not get land." The reason, he argued, was quite simple. The price of land in the colony was "already quite high" and is "increasing from year to year, especially because the English see that so many people, anxious to own farms or plantations, are coming to the country every year." Cultivated land, especially land with a house, barn, and stable, was completely out of reach, and "rich Englishmen have already bought up from the Indians all the remote land far and near, where all is as yet wild and wooded, in order to sell it again to the Europeans who are coming to the country."[28]

Mittelberger's depiction, though biased by its purpose, was not far from the mark. Of the migrants who willingly or unwillingly indentured themselves in the prospect of better opportunities, only one in ten realized a semblance of their dreams.[29] By the time Mittelberger arrived in the colony, landlessness was on the rise and so were land prices. Tenants and other landless wage laborers were quickly outnumbering the rest of the rural community. In some towns, the landless accounted for over half of the population, and those colonists rarely achieved a lifestyle beyond mere solvency.[30]

Although well-off colonists often argued otherwise, poverty was a fact of life for many Pennsylvanians, creating a great deal of resentment against the proprietors and their allies. The often talked about labor scarcity in the province, which some elites thought mitigated pervasive poverty with high wages, did not actually mean steady work with life sustaining wages for everyone, or even a majority of able-bodied laborers. Living poor was both typical and, for many with dreams of economic independence, unacceptable. But it was also a reality that too many with the power to change the situation ignored. At the same time that "governors, colonels, and the Lord knows who" else sat around extravagant dinner tables gossiping about "lands, Madeira wine, fishing parties, or politics," officials of the Pennsylvania Hospital for the Sick Poor tried to point out "the common Distresses of Poverty" which existed all around them as men, women, and children died in the streets from starvation, exposure, and disease. For the growing number of poor people, life seemed close to a Hobbesian hellscape; it was "nasty and brutish."[31] Suffice it to say, with the ability to acquire land difficult and poverty on the rise, the specter of impoverishment motivated many would-be landowners to achieve their dreams illegally as squatters.[32] As early as 1725, the "poorer sort" had few options but to stay put and live "very hard" or squat on land "beyond the limits of settlement and speculative holdings" in the hopes that their small improvements might someday become their freeholds and a chance to make it for their posterity.[33]

To achieve financial security many ordinary Pennsylvanians moved about, frequently to find land they could call their own. As in the larger Atlantic world, mobility was a part of life in Pennsylvania. Throughout the rural countryside, which was home to over 90 percent of the population, between 50 and 60 percent of inhabitants moved in and out of towns every five years. Tenants, wage laborers, servants released from their indentures, and small farmers consistently moved about the colony and into other colonies in search of land and opportunity.[34]

While necessity and most likely defiance motivated the growing number of poor colonists who elites called "freebooters" and "pirates" to "roam about like a Roving Tartar," looking to claim a plot of land, why they chose the land they squatted on is equally as important and had consequences for everyone who met at the council fire in the summer of 1749.[35] One contemporary quote about squatters is instructive. James Logan, writing about a group of squatters in 1731, found that they viewed it "against the Laws of God and Nature that so much Land should lie idle, while so many Christians wanted it to Labour on and raise their Bread." Such a sentiment, referencing the "laws of God and Nature," "idle" land, and Christian "Labour," highlights that squatters had a vision of land ownership at odds with both Native Americans and a host of characters who controlled access to land in Pennsylvania. After all, ordinary colonists didn't to any measurable degree squat on the land of middling white farmers. Instead, they squatted on the lands of the proprietors, speculators, and Native Americans who, they argued, did not have a legitimate claim to the land.[36]

Squatters' sentiments are understandable considering the circumstances. Speculators owned much of the available land for sale, and the definition of ownership was disputed during the colonial era. By 1749, Pennsylvania's factionalized politics revolved significantly around which land could be taxed, sparking widespread debate about the basis of land ownership in the proprietary colony. In colonial Pennsylvania, similar to other parts of British North America, there were essentially two categories of land: "located" and "unlocated." The defining factor between them hinged on a European concept of "use," often equated with "cultivation." Located land was identified by surveys and clear demarcations, showcasing permanent fixtures like cultivated fields, structures, pastures, and fences. In contrast, unlocated lands lacked evidence of intended "use" through permanent structures. Throughout much of the colonial period, only "settled," "improved," and "located" land was subject to taxation, further motivating land speculators to hoard as much "unlocated" land as possible.[37]

Such legal distinctions obviously did not reflect reality. As Pennsylvania's legislature noted, there existed "large tracts of valuable lands" legally defined as "located" but still tax-exempt because they were "held ... without intention of improvement ... in expectation of receiving hereafter higher prices for private advantage, by means whereof those lands remain uncultivated." At the same time, there were "many persons residing" on unlocated lands without "having property therein nor paying rent for the same." Yet, the legislators argued, these squatters "do actually hold and occupy" the land because of their cultivation, and therefore the land should be taxed. Using such terms as "hold," "occupy," and "improve" as the basis of taxation, the legislature came dangerously close to publicly recognizing squatters' legal claims to the lands they settled.[38]

The murkiness in the tax law among owning, holding, and occupying land reflected a deeper schism over the origins of property ownership. While the assembly questioned what constituted legitimate occupation and squatters proliferated the countryside, the proprietors and their land-speculating allies doubled down on a conception of ownership rooted in royal authority. The crown, claiming original jurisdiction from "sea to sea" in North America, granted William Penn and his heirs title to some of that land and royal authority by letters patent (a legal instrument that buttressed colonial possessions and governance). Therefore, the crown divested some of its right to the land to the proprietors, who then could sell or rent that same land to everyone else.[39]

Even in this context, significant conceptual and practical issues arose, not least of which was the fact that Native Americans existed. This fact led to the perplexing description of the land granted by the crown to the Penn family as "within the boundaries of this province not purchased of the Indians." This logic itself muddled any coherent notion of ownership as expressed by the proprietors and white colonial settlers alike. Initially, neither the crown nor the proprietors acquired the land from Native Americans claimed in the royal patent; such acquisitions occurred later. Adding to the confusion was the lack of a coherent imperial or colonial policy concerning the status of Native Americans or their lands within the British Empire. While the crown and other imperial administrators in England might issue directives, these often became obsolete with changes in leadership. Political turnovers were frequent in eighteenth-century England, impeding the establishment and execution of consistent imperial policies. On the ground, the situation was even more bewildering, as proprietors, Indian agents, governors, legislators, speculators, settlers, and Native peoples pursued their own interests. Eighteenth-century English jurists, trying to make sense of it all, simply declared that the crown owned the land by right of conquest.[40]

The conflicting view of Indigenous lands as conquered yet still "within" the province but "not purchased," combined with a Eurocentric understanding of legitimate "use," invited other interpretations of the origins of property that challenged the proprietors' claims and exacerbated the factional politics Governor Hamilton had to navigate in the summer of 1749. Just a few years before his meeting with Haudenosaunee delegates and their tributaries, one writer in the *American Magazine,* a monthly subscription published in Philadelphia by proprietary critic Andrew Bradford, stirred the pot when he declared that "no Man is naturally intitled to a greater Portion of the Earth than Another." Instead, the land "was made for the equal Use of all" by "the Almighty" through "the Laws of Nature, and ought therefore to be inviolably observed." Such a theory of ownership actuated itself "by the Improvement of any Part of it lying vacant, which is thereupon distinguished from the great Common of Nature, and made the Property of that Man, who bestowed his Labour on it." In sum, cultivating land constituted ownership.[41]

Such a theory could sit easily, though by no means comfortably, aside both the idea that Native American lands were "within" the colony but "not purchased," as well as the original authority of the crown, but had no place for proprietors or speculators monopolizing access to that land. As the same writer argued, "The Kings of England always held the Lands in America, ceded to them by Treaties," but unlike the assumptions of the proprietors and speculators, the kings held those lands "in Trust for their Subjects; which Lands, having lain uncultivated from the Beginning of the World, were therefore as free and as common for all to settle upon."[42]

More importantly for Hamilton, who had to deal with the ramifications of this article and those like it, this author explained that these "Rules of natural Justice" had been perverted by the "Mischief" not of squatters but of the proprietors and their cronies who "granted to a few Particulars" the "best Parts and most commodiously situated" lands "in such exorbitant Quantities, that the rest of the Subjects" are either left to buy the same land for "an extravagant Price" or go without. It only made sense that ordinary colonists should resist the proprietary government and seek other remedies to reap the rewards assured by nature, justified by God, and legitimized by the crown. Such a critique, calling on the Christian God and using such terms as "labor" and "natural law," seriously challenged the deferential view of land distribution as articulated by the proprietors and their supporters.[43]

That theoretical dispute not only challenged the proprietors and their allies but also fundamentally undermined Native American rights. Although the author in Bradford's *American Magazine* mentioned the importance of "Treaties," which provided a tacit recognition of Native American ownership, he never directly referenced Native Americans anywhere in his essay. It was a convenient omission, allowing him, like the squatters he supported, to declare Native American lands as "uncultivated from the Beginning of the World." Such a view of an immense "uncultivated" landscape ripe for the taking was not new or novel. It had informed colonial settlers' justification to occupy Indigenous lands as the will of "God and Nature" for decades. What "cultivation," "use," or "improvement" meant was consistently predicated on Eurocentric definitions that consciously discredited the practices and views of Native Americans. As early as 1630, English colonists had proclaimed over and again that "the *Indians* are not able to make use of the one fourth part of the Land, neither have they any settled places, as Townes to dwell in, nor any ground as they challenge for their owne possession."[44] It was exactly that view of "use" that Europeans wielded as a weapon to delegitimize the culture of racial others across "the Habitable Globe."[45]

For Native Americans who came to the city in the summer of 1749, however, their land was far from "Idle," "uncultivated," and unsettled; it was actively and extensively in use. For Native peoples, all parts of the landscape served essential purposes for farming, hunting, fishing, and living. Their land was broken up into seasonal hunting grounds, fowling locations, fishing camps, and farms. There were also cultivated woodlands that supplied fuel and construction materials, as well as the potash to make lye to process maize (corn) as a storable carbohydrate to sustain communities through the long winter months. Not only did Native peoples go through immense amounts of timber but the Haudenosaunee, for example, regularly cleared land each spring to make way for new farms, practicing swidden, a slash-and-burn horticulture, or shifting cultivation done to maintain soil productivity. Settled villages and hamlets too required extensive land because they moved every ten to twenty years, allowing nature to reclaim the land for future use. Where colonists saw uncultivated, abandoned, or wasted land, Native Americans saw purpose.[46]

If colonists needed visible evidence that jibed with a semblance of their idea of use, they could have looked no farther than the thousands of acres of farmland where Native Americans up and down North America used an efficient and effective agricultural method of companion planting where corn, beans, and squash (what the Haudenosaunee and many other Native peoples called the "three sisters") grew together, providing natural fertilization, weed control, and shade. This method extended not only the life of the soil but also the growing season. Even hunting required conscious cultivation. Selective burnings and planned reclamations produced the natural food supply that attracted the small and big game animals Native Americans depended on for subsistence and trade.[47]

None of that mattered to encroaching colonial settlers buoyed by their own ethnocentric ideologies. That reality fundamentally threatened Native American subsistence, which increasingly challenged their independence and power. The land and its bounty mattered, especially since by the eighteenth century many Native peoples depended on their lands for European trade and connections.

Europeans' consistent and early demand for furs and land in North America opened up a vast trade network among Native Americans, colonists, and consumers across the Atlantic Ocean, which brought new European manufactured goods into Indigenous lives, altering the alliances, power structures, and modes of life that had defined Native communities for generations. By the time the Haudenosaunee and their tributaries made their way to the city in 1749 to complain about squatters west of the Susquehanna River, almost all aspects of their material life depended on economic ties with Europe. They used European tools for farming and building, European weapons for hunting and war, while also cooking and eating with European kettles, pots, and spoons, and making clothing with European textiles using imported needles, thread, and scissors. As one British official stated simply, "A modern Indian cannot subsist without Europeans." Similarly, a Cherokee chief complained in 1750 that "every necessary Thing in Life we must have from the White People."[48]

Control of that important trade also brought authority to those Native nations who could monopolize it. In Britain's North American empire, Philadelphia became a central entrepôt in that matrix, and since the early 1730s the Haudenosaunee controlled the road to that city, and through it the power it conveyed. Dependency on the Atlantic economy, however, was a double-edged sword. It may have given power to those Native nations who could control it, but it also produced fierce competition for resources that all too often had deleterious effects on Native Americans' quality of life and their relationships with each other.

The commodification of animal pelts through the fur trade coupled with the ever-rising cost of and reliance on European goods often led to overhunting, requiring the accumulation of more hunting land and the defense of land that already existed. Such goals competed with the simple fact that the sale of land on generous terms to Europeans also, and more generally, granted the Native peoples who sold it access to critical trade relations. As a result, large Native polities like the Haudenosaunee sought to extend their sovereign authority over territories and peoples in ways that would protect their lands, gain new hunting grounds, and provide ample amounts of land they could sell to Europeans. Such a reality generated wars within and between Native nations over the land Europeans wanted but that also supplied the game that made trade with Europeans possible.[49] The quest for power and sovereignty among new and old rivals and enemies colored the surface of those contests, but the precarious nature of survival undergirded them all. Really, the two were interconnected.

That symbiotic relationship is evident in the Haudenosaunee's active expansion of sovereign authority across northeastern North America. Initially occupying what is now upstate New York, the Haudenosaunee faced significant demographic and political setbacks due to European contact, which brought diseases and conflicts. Nevertheless, they asserted control over vast areas and peoples, stretching from Canada south to the Cherokee River (now the Tennessee River). Their power did not solely stem from warfare but also from negotiation and the strategic inclusion of various Native nations. They integrated these nations as adopted captives or allied tributaries, establishing satellite towns governed by Haudenosaunee viceroys or headmen, expanding what they termed the "Covenant Chain." While some, like the Tuscarora, an Iroquoian-speaking people initially from the Carolinas, became full league members, the Haudenosaunee extended this status sparingly. Primarily, they coerced or enticed peoples from different regions to join as tributaries, relocating them to new satellite towns where they became integral components of "the Longhouse." This term symbolized the Haudenosaunee's expanding sovereign authority through the Covenant Chain. In exchange for protection and the preservation of their tribal structures, cultures, and languages, these tributaries relinquished their autonomy.[50]

Take, for example, the Haudenosaunee incorporation of the Yesay, a Siouan-speaking people from the Virginia Piedmont, Blue Ridge Mountains, and so-called Valley provinces near present-day Lynchburg, who would later be known as the Tutelo and Saponi. The Haudenosaunee had been waging war against them since the 1670s. The Yesay were, Haudenosaunee leaders said, their inveterate "enemies" who the Haudenosaunee would either "exterminate" or force "into the Covenant Chain as direct Tributaries." By 1722, the Haudenosaunee succeeded in conquering the Yesay, securing them as "props" and relocating them to the Juniata River and further north to Shamokin at the forks of the Susquehanna River, where they joined or would be joined by peoples with similar experiences such as the Nanticoke, Conoy, Delaware, Munsee, Mohican, and Shawnee, all under the authority of an Oneida headman, Shikellamy, charged by Onondaga to protect and project Haudenosaunee power over conquered lands and peoples in the Susquehanna River Valley.[51]

There were plenty of other Haudenosaunee satellite towns, and the creation of each one represented the incorporation of more and more lands and peoples into the Haudenosaunee's orbit "in order to," an observant British official noted, "make them [the Six Nations] more formidable." The incorporation of the Yesay not only brought more peoples within the "Covenant Chain," at least three hundred warriors, but gave the Haudenosaunee leverage to create new diplomatic and trade relations with colonial Virginians and authority over the land the Yesay had occupied and Virginians wanted. Once strengthened, the Haudenosaunee could also demand "larger presents from the English."[52]

By the 1740s, that expansive authority had been stretched to its limit. Haudenosaunee tributaries, treated no better than "slaves" according to Conrad Weiser (who grew up with and was adopted by the Mohawk), became more numerous than the Six Nations proper and rightfully questioned their status and the ability of the Haudenosaunee to make good on their promises of protection. As early as the 1720s, some of the tributaries in the Susquehanna River Valley confederated, forming their own separate and independent "Four Nations," but this group was ultimately overwhelmed by the Haudenosaunee and their British allies. Thoughts of independence, though, remained, and the constant undeterred encroachment of white squatters, like those west of the Susquehanna River, threatened to renew those calls for independence and upend Haudenosaunee power, exacerbating accumulating problems and making the struggle for sovereignty and survival all too real and perhaps more visceral. Early America from this vantage point was a world in motion, constant contention, and fluctuating power, not just for Europeans.[53]

In the summer of 1749, not only were Native nations regularly moving, contending with each other and land-hungry colonial officials they needed to placate for trade, but also battling against never-ending waves of rogue colonial settlers who actively coveted and changed the land Native Americans required for survival and fought wars to control. Frustratingly, colonial squatters did not abide by the boundaries of Native sovereignty nor the strictures of treaties, negotiations, or official proclamations because they disagreed with the basic assumptions that Native Americans and colonial leaders used to justify them in the first place. Squatters were, one official said, "troublesome settlers to the government and hard neighbors to the Indians."[54]

The threat posed to the Haudenosaunee and their tributaries in 1749 was far greater than poor colonists hacking out small homesteads at the base of a river and arguing with everyone about the definition of ownership; it was what those squatters guaranteed for the future. As one aging Delaware chief saw it, the squatters in and of themselves were not the problem. They could be "very good people and as Hospitable as we Indians." But once they came, "we lost our hunting Ground: for where one of those People settled, like pigeons, a thousand more would Settle."[55] It is no wonder that four Shawnee chiefs "said plainly" that squatters made it seem as if "the English would soon be too great a people in this Country."[56] And that greatness "Distroyed a Great quantity of game."[57] Squatters not only made "a vast and shameless havock of the Timber erecting only poor Cabbins" but they brought cattle and pigs to Indigenous land that roamed freely, trampling existing undergrowth, eating the foodstuffs that sustained wild herbivores, and destroying Native farmlands and food storages.[58] Colonial livestock, whose existence and management colonists viewed as central to "civilization" and "use," also compacted the soil by their sheer number and girth in ways that extended the time it took to melt accumulating snow during the winter months, which then resulted in devastating floods as the hot days of spring and summer took hold. There was a sort of compounding interest accruing from squatters that gobbled up and intimately changed the thoughtfully constructed Indigenous landscape.[59]

Tutelo, Saponi, Nanticoke, Conoy, Shawnee, and Delaware hunters, who had been displaced from their ancestral homes over the previous few decades and were now living in the Susquehanna River Valley, detested the cascading problems squatters brought, arguing that these invaders "drove away the Game and Spoiled the Indians Hunting" territory. Over forty members "of ye Six Nations," speaking on their tributaries' behalf, similarly complained that "your Settling heer In ye hart of our Cuntry has made our Game scurse" and farmlands less productive. Such circumstances were detrimental. If anything "prevented us from hunting" they would not be able to ensure the "Suport of our femelys much less providing any Skins to purchess any Cloathing fer our Wifes & Children." Many of their people, "now very pour," resorted to "beging for Some Reliufe," requesting clothes "to Cover thire Nackedness" and "powder & Lead" for hunting and "to prosecute ye Warr against our Enemys" for the very land and sovereign authority that established their power and guaranteed access to European markets.[60]

Since sovereignty and survival intermixed, encroaching squatters made "all ye Indian Nations Round you very Jelous that you have Some bad Designs against them."[61] Native Americans also understood the complicated origins of that "bad design." According to one prominent Delaware, Teedyuscung, who had dealt with squatters before and had been displaced from three homes in less than thirty years, it wasn't just the squatters' fault; rather, it was "the proprietors, who have purchased their Lands from us cheap," turned around and "sold them too dear to poor People, and the *Indians* have suffered for it." Without access to affordable land, colonists regularly encroached on what remained of Native American lands, altering the landscape in ways that hindered "us from Hunting, the only Means left us of getting our Livelihood." He, like many others, knew it was all connected, and that connection, he argued, was "the Foundation of our Uneasiness."[62]

During the summer of 1749, when the Haudenosaunee, their tributaries, and Pennsylvania government officials convened in Philadelphia, they grappled with this systemic and intricate issue. The squatters west of the Susquehanna River were merely a symptom. For the Haudenosaunee, aware of their precarious position, the remedy seemed evident: Governor

James Hamilton should forcibly remove the squatters and acknowledge Haudenosaunee sovereignty over the land and people to the river's west. Additionally, the governor ought to ensure measures preventing the squatters' return, perhaps by making land east of the river more accessible or easier to purchase for colonists. These actions would safeguard Haudenosaunee land temporarily and, if necessary, provide land they could sell in the future. However, for the Haudenosaunee's tributaries, any solution posed significant challenges. Displaced from their ancestral homes due to encroaching colonists and wars fought over land and sovereignty, their future, not just the immediate one, rested on the decisions of their Haudenosaunee protectors and the Pennsylvania government, whose interests rarely aligned with their own. Those conflicting interests challenged the negotiations that summer for Hamilton, the Haudenosaunee, and their proclaimed tributaries.[63]

Hamilton tried to use those interests to his advantage. Instead of directly addressing the Haudenosaunee requests and the concerns of their tributaries, he attempted to leverage the squatter settlements to purchase the disputed land to the west of the Susquehanna River. Simultaneously, he pledged to issue a proclamation demanding that squatters leave the area. This tactic could potentially benefit the province by obtaining desired land for the proprietors and their land-speculating partners, who would profit from the already developed land. Hamilton also hoped that the proclamation, without immediate enforcement, would temporarily ease tensions among the Native peoples and squatters living there. Some squatters might even choose to purchase the improved land. Moreover, Hamilton's plan artfully recognized the Haudenosaunee's control west of the Susquehanna River, assuming their authority over their tributaries, maintaining the alliance formed years ago—a relationship that Hamilton needed to preserve.[64]

For the Haudenosaunee delegates, such a purchase was out of the question and the proclamation was not enough. They faced the same reality as Governor Hamilton. Their hold over their tributaries, like Hamilton's tenuous grip over frontier squatters and speculators, was strained by war, special interests, politics, and trade, and because of that the Haudenosaunee's position as the predominant powerbroker in North America was under question. If the Haudenosaunee accepted Hamilton's solution and sold that land it would instantly threaten their claim over tributaries there, paving the way for the French and their Native allies to dominate the region. The French and their Indigenous allies, after all, also offered the Haudenosaunee's proclaimed tributaries protection, which, if successful, could eclipse the power wielded by the Six Nations. In short, Hamilton's solution was fraught with difficulties.

Nevertheless, the Haudenosaunee also wanted to maintain their relationship with the Pennsylvanians. The Six Nations could not simply deny Hamilton's request, turn a blind eye to violence when his proclamation failed, and abandon a fruitful alliance. Too much depended on a peaceful relationship with the colony. It was a diplomatic tightrope that those few Haudenosaunee delegates who came to the city in late June did not want to walk. On July 4, 1749, after nearly a week of negotiation, they left Philadelphia loaded with the gifts the proprietary government handed out but without clearly resolving anything. Hamilton and the council, however, thought they had carried the negotiation in the province's favor, imagining that gifts along with time and circumspection would bring the Haudenosaunee around to accepting their solution. The land west of the Susquehanna River seemed within their grasp.[65]

Time, however, was not on the colony's side. The Haudenosaunee delegation that entered the city in late June only accounted for a small portion of the representatives Onondaga sent to Philadelphia that summer. In fact, as the delegation left the city, a much larger one was slowly making its way to the city. This larger group was supposed to have traveled with the other that spring, but delays and miscommunication (and a little factionalism) created some confusion. Nevertheless, in mid-July at Shamokin, both delegations crossed paths and had the ability to prepare a thoughtful yet forceful response to Governor Hamilton. By the time the second delegation reached Philadelphia that August they were in no mood to hear about weak proclamations and proprietary desires to purchase "the good Lands on the West side of Sasquehanna."[66]

Unlike the previous delegation, news of this one did create a stir in the city. At first, both the governor and many of his advisors did not want to welcome them, and they prepared to send messengers asking the delegation to turn back. That rebuff might spell disaster, or so Hamilton was told by those more knowledgeable about Haudenosaunee diplomacy. It was all a flurry and confusion in the city. Letters crisscrossed the colony and the Atlantic Ocean, runners pervaded the city's streets identifying larger accommodations and acquiring another round of gifts. Soon newspapers and magazines picked up the story, and they all described over "260 persons" representing "eleven different nations," specifically the "Senecas, Mohawks, Cayugas, Oneidas, Tuscaroras, Shawonese, Nanticokes, Delawares, Mohigans, and Tutelos" traveling to the city.[67]

This new delegation, Richard Peters whined, was far different than the one that just preceded it. Not only was it larger but it included some of the more prominent Haudenosaunee chiefs and speakers, such as Canassatego, who colonists described as "tall, well-made," "masculine," and exceedingly "strong" and "very active."[68] Peters was especially irritated because this larger and more prominent delegation behaved "very rudely," entering the city and instantly demanding to "speak only to the Governor & Council" to remind them that "by Treaties all white People were to have been hinder'd from settling the Lands not purchased of Us." Therefore, this new delegation asserted that if settlers continued to encroach on Haudenosaunee land west of the Susquehanna River, it either meant the colonists were no longer "obedient to you," which rendered Pennsylvania's government useless, or that colonists were doing so by "Instructions from the King or Proprietors," which threw into question the Haudenosaunee's alliance with the entire British Empire.[69]

Even the governor's proclamation to remove squatters was suspect since he must know that it would have "no better Effects . . . than former Ones of the same nature." To demonstrate a "better Regard" for the "Chain of Friendship," Canassatego demanded that Hamilton "use more vigorous measures & forcibly remove" the squatters so that that "Country may be entirely Left vacant." If he did not, Canassatego warned, the Six Nations could not "prevent the sad Consequences which will otherwise ensue," which the governor knew meant "much Bloodshed." Such a request required colonial authorities to recognize Haudenosaunee sovereignty and purposefully work, as "Brethren," to maintain the geographic boundaries demarcating sovereign powers.[70]

Despite this hardline approach, Canassatego was prepared to demonstrate the Haudenosaunee's continued friendship with the proprietary colony. Thoughtful diplomacy coupled with threats often had the desired effect. In return for recognizing Haudenosaunee authority west of the Susquehanna River, he proffered Hamilton a land deal east of the river. The governor's political and practical predicament was no secret to Canassatego, and he offered to sell the proprietors nearly 2 million acres of land from the east side of the Susquehanna River all the way to the Delaware River for a meager £500, or less than a shilling per acre. Canassatego knew that his land deal was more than accommodating. "The Proprietors," he argued, "receive immense Sums for the Lands we have sold to them."[71]

The governor, as Canassatego suspected, agreed to the land sale. Hamilton also dropped but did not entirely abandon his effort to purchase the land west of the Susquehanna River. Importantly, this sale reaffirmed Haudenosaunee sovereignty over much of the Susquehanna River Valley. The governor, happy with the sale, even agreed to send officials west of the Susquehanna River to physically evict squatters.[72]

However, Canassatego's land sale and the governor's commitments came with inherent issues. What of the Native peoples who still lived on the land Canassatego had just sold? Although the Haudenosaunee deemed them mere tributaries, they still had homes there, many of them ancient ones. What would they do and where would they go? What about ordinary colonists now squatting west of the Susquehanna River? How would they respond to physical removal? Would they fight back? More importantly, would either colonial squatters or proclaimed Indigenous tributaries join the growing chorus of voices questioning Haudenosaunee and proprietary leadership? Could they, either of them, smarting from the agreements made, start a new war? Such potential problems were exacerbated by the fact that the Haudenosaunee were fighting similar battles from New York to Virginia. It was, as Canassatego argued, an "extensive frontier," and the way everyone tried to solve the problems there did not fix but rather exacerbated what Teedyuscung called the "Foundation of our Uneasiness," shaping the future of the many peoples who lived and fought for independence, sovereignty, and survival along that frontier. In hindsight, 1749 was a critical year.

2

"Very Uneasy and Displeas'd"

DISPLACEMENT AND ALIENATION ON THE HAUDENOSAUNEE FRONTIER, 1750–1754

THE AUGUST 1749 MEETING between the governor and over 260 Haudenosaunee and their diverse tributaries ended amicably enough. To demonstrate "a substantial proof of your being welcome to the People of this Province," the proprietary government offered much needed gifts including 140 shirts; 10 barrels each of gunpowder, lead, and shot; over a dozen new guns; 36 hatchets; and a host of other goods such as lace, scissors, beads, cloth, and ribbon. The Six Nations' delegation also offered Pennsylvania a gift by selling 2 million acres of land for far less than they knew it was worth. Through those reciprocal gifts, the Haudenosaunee and Pennsylvania officials left the council fire that summer thinking they had established a better foundation for a lasting friendship and peace.[1]

Foundations, while necessary, are not always strong. The one created in the summer of 1749 was certainly not. As far as foundations go, this one was hastily constructed atop an old one riddled with cracks that continued to widen with stress, threatening to topple everything built on it. As a result, the meetings in the city that summer solved little. Squatters kept coming, the proprietary government still clamored for more land, and many of the Haudenosaunee's tributaries were displaced moving both north and west. Within five short years, the foundation was in shambles. New Native confederations with new leaders rose to significance in both the Northern Susquehanna River Valley and the Ohio River Valley alienated by Haudenosaunee authority and British power, and looking to pursue their own paths to security through independence.

The problems began almost immediately after the meetings in the summer of 1749. Governor James Hamilton and his advisors waffled about removing squatters west of the Susquehanna River. Although they had promised Canassatego, they feared using force could spark internecine conflict or at the very least give political ammunition to the proprietors' opponents. Meanwhile, squatters proliferated, and the Grand Council of Chiefs at Onondaga grew tired of Hamilton's inaction. Finally, after months of prodding by the Onondaga Council and messages from Shamokin, the governor and his council pieced together a removal effort.[2]

Naturally, the Haudenosaunee and their tributaries were still wary that whatever the governor and his advisors planned would "prove like many former Attempts; the People will be put off now, and next Year come again." To ensure the Pennsylvanians made good on their promises, the Onondaga Council sent its own representatives to oversee the removal. These were a relatively young yet significant group, including the sons of the Oneida headman Shikellamy from Shamokin, as well as Saiuchtowano, a "man of note" among the Six Nations, and Sattelihu, more commonly known as Andrew Montour, a rising negotiator and go-between who spoke Mohawk, Oneida, Wyandot, Delaware, Miami, and Shawnee, as well as French and English. He was also the son of an Oneida war captain charged with managing the Six Nations' relationship with the Shawnee, and more importantly, he was raised by his mother, Isabelle or Elizabeth Couc, more popularly known as "Madam Montour," who was of mixed Indigenous (Algonquian) and French ancestry. Adopted by the Haudenosaunee at a young age, Madam Montour rose to significance as a multilingual go-between, interpreter, and leader, favored by colonial governors, European missionaries, and diplomats. After a successful stint as the "intrepretress" for New York's governor Robert Hunter, she migrated to the Northern Susquehanna River Valley in the late 1720s, and by the 1740s controlled a large, multiethnic town on the West Branch of the Susquehanna River called Otstonwakin. Not only did she garner significant respect from both European and Indigenous nations, but her daughters, nieces, and granddaughters became important leaders all across the Northern Susquehanna River Valley. The Montour name and legacy still endure from Pennsylvania to Canada through her descendants as well as the appropriated placenames of towns, rivers, businesses, and schools along the West and North branches of the Susquehanna River.[3]

When these young yet important delegates made their way to the headwaters of the Juniata, meeting Pennsylvania's reticent government officials on the road, they had demands. Not only did they want the squatters removed but they "insisted on our burning the Cabbin[s]," leaving a visible warning to future squatters. Richard Peters, heading the removal effort, noted that the Six Nations' representatives "repeatedly" complained "that their Hunting-ground was every Day more and more taken from them and that there must infallibly arise Quarrels between their Warriors and these Settlers, which would in the End break the Chain of Friendship." Shikellamy's sons were the most direct, making it clear "that if all the Cabbins were left standing" they "would conceive such a contemptible Opinion of the Government" and "come themselves in the Winter, murder the people and set the Houses on Fire."[4]

As the council chiefs, Haudenosaunee delegates, governor, and his advisors all suspected, the removal effort was a disaster. At Juniata some colonial settlers threatened to kill Peters and were only subdued when they saw the Shikellamy brothers watching from a short distance away. Once removed, those squatters added to a growing chorus of irritated colonial voices disillusioned with a government that, they argued, kowtowed to Native Americans and only worked to benefit elite speculators and those involved in the lucrative Indian trade. That was a grievance that would continue to bedevil colonial politicians, the greater interests of the British Empire, and any peaceful relationship with Native peoples for years to come. One of the colonists removed from the area, the then eight-year-old Simon Girty, perhaps remembering this moment, became part of American folklore as a vengeful bogeyman terrorizing the backcountry.[5]

More significant was that the removal effort failed. It had barely begun before Richard Peters tired of the business. The season was wet, rainy, and cold, and then he got sick. It seems that whenever Peters left the city he needed to find a doctor to be bled or to give him strong purgatives called "Vomits" and other herbal remedies. In short, it was slow going, Peters was irritable, he detested frontier accommodations, and he did not want to be there in the first place. After he removed settlers and burned cabins on the

Juniata he was ready to give up. When again confronted by angry colonists as he trekked south of that river, some of whom the proprietary government had actually encouraged to settle there because of a land dispute with Maryland, he was done. Peters told those settlers that he would "decline their removal & consult the Governors further pleasure," and then made his way home to the comforts of Philadelphia.⁶

Unsurprisingly, squatters returned to the Juniata in just a few months and more arrived thereafter. In October, Peters complained that "the People over the Hills are combin'd against the Government, are putting in new Cropps & bid us Defiance." Although irritated, government officials like Peters did little but grumble, and the multiethnic Native peoples who lived there suffered. Soon deeply disenchanted, they left the Juniata for other quarters.⁷

Native American discontent is understandable, given their repeated displacement. For instance, the Conoy, who had long lived near the Potomac River, became Haudenosaunee tributaries in the early eighteenth century, relocating to the lower Susquehanna River Valley on land supposedly reserved for them by the proprietors. However, "the settling of the white People all round them had made Deer scarce, and that therefore they chose to remove to Juniata for the benefit of hunting." Yet again, they were "ill used by the white People," forcing another relocation. This history of uncertainty made their future seem bleak. Unfortunately, individuals like Peters, mirroring many colonial officials, showed little concern. It appeared that after reaffirming friendship with the Six Nations, Native peoples such as the Conoy were disregarded. Peters viewed those Indigenous people west of the Susquehanna as the "Scum of the Earth," describing them as a "mixed dirty sort of People."⁸

While squatters continued to pour across the Susquehanna River, Canassatego's sale of land east of it also created havoc. When he sold to the proprietors 2 million acres for a meager recompense he was gambling on the future. He thought parting with that land could maintain Haudenosaunee authority over the many and various Native tributaries living in what Canassatego saw as the Haudenosaunee's "frontier Country," especially north and west of the Susquehanna River. Therefore, he stipulated to the governor that he sold land to the east so "the People" who squatted west of the Susquehanna River would "go and settle" in this new purchase. Settlers would be removed, have a motivation not to return, and Haudenosaunee sovereignty would remain intact. Or so Canassatego hoped.[9]

Such a hope required not only a more successful removal effort than what actually occurred but also changing entrenched proprietary land policies benefiting speculators so squatters could "go and settle" in the new purchase. That would never happen. Once Canassatego sold that land, the proprietors and their officials thought they could do with it what they pleased. From the governor and his council's perspective, the end of the lengthy negotiations with Canassatego resulted in a legal transfer of land that did not really require getting caught up in the rigmarole of how everyone got there.[10]

Plus, the governor never exactly agreed to much during the proceedings. He may have assented to forcibly evicting squatters and even sat, listened, and went through the motions of the proceedings, but he had no intention of incorporating any of what Canassatego said into the legal instrument that would define the sale of land. That reality, coupled with the tenuousness of Haudenosaunee sovereignty on either side of the Susquehanna River, made Canassatego's diplomatic maneuvers deeply problematic. Everyone involved should have seen the problems for the future. Most likely they did and chose to ignore them. Easy fictions are more digestible than hard truths.[11]

The Ohio Nations, a diverse group of Native peoples displaced due to treaties, warfare, and diseases, were one of those hard truths, and they were desperately looking for an opportunity to strengthen themselves and their diplomatic position away from Onondaga. Like other Native nations along the early American frontier, the Ohio Nations grappled with threats to their land and survival. France vied for control of the Ohio Valley, while in the summer of 1749, as the Haudenosaunee reaffirmed their ties with land-hungry Pennsylvanians in Philadelphia, Virginia speculators began surveying the frontier, including the Ohio Valley. These speculators claimed that the Haudenosaunee had relinquished the valley to them on behalf of their tributaries in 1744 and they now sought to validate that claim.[12]

Needless to say, the Ohio Nations had to do something to protect their future because the Haudenosaunee showed little interest or ability to do

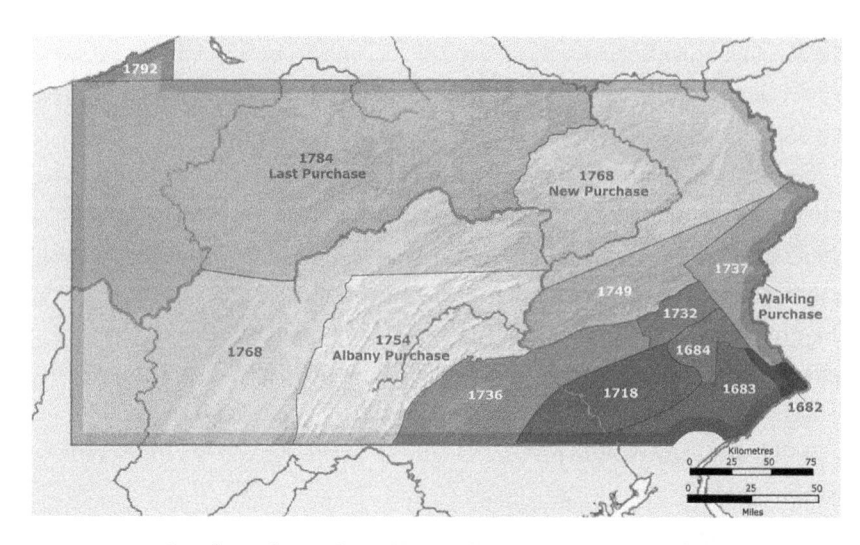

FIGURE 5. Land purchases from Native Americans in Pennsylvania

so. Less than a month after Peters's botched removal of squatters, the Ohio Nations seized the moment and sent envoys to the Juniata Valley offering the Native peoples who lived there land and protection if they joined the Ohio Nations, thus increasing their strength. Many of the Ohio Nations, especially the Delaware and Shawnee, envisioned the Ohio Nations' territory as encompassing much of the Susquehanna River Valley including the West Branch of the Susquehanna River, which they used for trade, travel, and hunting. Moreover, the Ohio Nations claimed they would actually protect Native American interests and maintain control over a large and growing country. That argument was more than mere bluster. As a Cayuga chief meeting with the governor of New France warned in May 1750, the Ohio Valley was the home of "a Republic composed of all sorts of Nations."[13] Unsurprisingly, some but certainly not all of the Haudenosaunee's tributaries living in the Juniata Valley found the Ohio Nations' entreaties to join them enticing and moved west. The others either stayed or trekked north to the West and East Branches of the Susquehanna River, many of whom would see the Ohio Nations as allies soon enough.[14]

The Ohio Nations used their growing numbers as leverage to assert their authority and even independence from Onondaga. As the Ohio Nations explained in a message to Governor Hamilton, since they "have got many to join us, and are become a great Body," they should "be taken notice of as such." Frustrated with Haudenosaunee land sales, they demanded Pennsylvania officials include them in any negotiations in the future. They especially wanted, they said, "Part of the Value" and a say over "any lands [that] shall be sold." The Pennsylvanians seriously considered it. Realizing the strength of the Ohio Nations and fearful of the Virginians as much as the French, some Pennsylvania officials thought recognizing the Ohio Nations as an independent people and thus gaining them as allies could create a sort of counterweight west of the Appalachian Mountains to rival other colonies and empires looking to take hold of the land.[15]

This was not the first time Pennsylvania officials dealt with the Ohio Nations, but they often skirted around the edges of any public recognition of that peoples' independence from the Six Nations, which was relatively easy to do early on. A number of Seneca and Cayuga had moved to the Ohio Valley years earlier. Some of them the Onondaga Council recognized as viceroys or "Half-Kings," but over time those viceroys began to associate more with the displaced people in the Ohio Valley and less with the Six Nations at Onondaga. Yet, the existence of these Haudenosaunee viceroys allowed Pennsylvania officials to refer to the Ohio peoples as "Brethren of the Six Nations," artfully blurring the distinction between Haudenosaunee leaders who lived and spoke for the people in Ohio with those who spoke on behalf of Onondaga.[16]

By midcentury, that distinction was much harder to keep up and posing diplomatic problems that the savviest of colonial officials had difficulty navigating. The Ohio Nations had become "a people of Note, & are grown very numerous," one official explained, which, he thought, required recognizing their difference from the Six Nations.[17] Regardless of how necessary such a change seemed, it was a difficult position to take as it would surely irritate the Six Nations, who "did not like" it when any colony made "treaties with these Indians, whom they called Hunters, and young and giddy Men and Children." The Six Nations "were their Fathers, and if the English wanted anything from these childish People they must first speak to their Fathers."[18] Whatever the Pennsylvanians chose to do diplomatically with the Ohio Nations, then, could alienate one or the other peoples.

The Ohio Nations were only part of the problem for the Onondaga Council and the colony of Pennsylvania. Canassatego's 1749 land sale also alienated the Native nations east of the Susquehanna River. That was especially risky since there were a host of people who called that land home. Delaware, Munsee, Shawnee, Nanticoke, Tutelo, Mohican, and a number of other Native peoples had moved, been displaced to, or had ancient claims there. When Canassatego sold that land, the people who lived there, like the Native peoples living along the Juniata, had few options but to fight or remove north and west, potentially adding to a growing and resentful populations. That problem became evident when the colonial government tried to physically establish its claim to the land it purchased from Canassatego, letting loose deep-seated animosities in the process.

Unlike Hamilton's dillydallying over the removal of squatters, it took him less than a month to commission a deputy to survey the new purchase "for the Proprietaries Use." That surveyor, Edward Scull, accompanied by a justice of the peace and three others, barely made it "within the late Purchase" before they were "overtook" by, Scull guessed, two Munsee, Mohican, or Esopus Indians "sent by their King Tattenhick." Scull should have known this would happen. Surveyors with their chains, logbooks, and compasses were long a source of contention in Indian country. Many Native peoples called a surveyor's compass a "Land Stealer."[19] Yet, Scull was still somehow stunned that he had been challenged, demanding a meeting with the king, who, he was informed, "could speak English."[20]

The next day, gaining an audience with Tattenhick, Scull, far from respectful, instantly berated the king for stopping him from "surveying the Land." Scull also "informed him" that the Haudenosaunee had sold this land to the proprietors, waving the "Draught of the Purchase" and the "Deed" in front of the leader's face. Mustering all the specters of authority he could, Scull imperiously asked "Tattenhick to give him a positive answer whether he was determined to oppose him in the Execution of the Governor's Orders" based on a "Deed" from the Six Nations.[21]

Scull may have believed in the governor's power and Haudenosaunee sovereignty, but Tattenhick did not. According to the king, this land "belonged to him and his People." If the Six Nations "had disposed of it they had done what they had no Right to do." Two days later, Tattenhick and "six Indians with their Guns" surrounded the surveyor and his party, "insisting on our leaving the Parts, which we did the same day." While Scull could not positively communicate who he encountered, modern scholars have identified King Tattenhick as a Delaware leader who would soon be known as Teedyuscung and rise to significance in the Northern Susquehanna River Valley, seriously challenging both the Six Nations and the proprietary colony.[22]

His resistance reflected nearly fifty years of experience that not only shaped his response to Scull but also defined the rest of his life. Born around 1700 near modern-day Trenton, New Jersey, this Delaware leader, who early on was known to colonists as "Honest John," spent his formative years with his father, a Captain Harris, fighting against colonial encroachment in West Jersey and trying to eke out a living selling homemade brooms and baskets. By 1730, Captain Harris and his family, including Honest John, irritated by colonial settlers and unable to achieve a dependable subsistence, resettled his family west of the Delaware River in the Lehigh Valley.[23]

Although the Delaware River served and still serves as a boundary between Pennsylvania and New Jersey, it did not hold the same jurisdictional significance for the Delaware. Moreover, their move elevated the status of Honest John's family. His father became the chief or sachem of a growing multiethnic village at Pocopoco near modern-day Jim Thorpe, Pennsylvania. Honest John's older half-brother, called Captain John, also became a leading figure in the neighboring town of Welagameka.[24]

Such positions mattered. Although the Pennsylvania government and Onondaga Council often tried to interfere with Delaware governance by elevating one "king" to negotiate on the Delaware's behalf, local sachems and village elders continued to hold most of the power. To be sure, some of those village sachems and elders rose to significance beyond their local communities, receiving the respect of multiple villages, but that status was acquired organically rather than by the fiat of a colonial governor or representatives from Onondaga. Even then, the power chiefs wielded was never absolute but had to reflect the needs, wants, and interests of the larger community. "A chief," one Moravian missionary noted, "may not presume to rule over the people as in that case he would immediately be forsaken by the whole tribe."[25]

The towns led by Honest John's family at Pocopoco and Welagameka quickly became the center of a large and prosperous community of Delaware, Munsee, and refugee Shawnee, Tutelo, and Mohican people. It was here that Honest John created a new life, forging alliances and communal ties with other Native peoples. It was also there that he created connections with other prominent Delaware leaders such as his uncle, Nutimus, who had migrated from West Jersey many years earlier. Not only was Nutimus the sachem of a large village in the Lehigh River Valley, but because of his outspoken dedication to the Delaware people, rather than what either the Pennsylvanians or Onondaga wanted, he garnered significant influence with many of the Delaware and other refugee communities living in the valley. Honest John respected Nutimus, and he, and eventually his sons, looked to Nutimus for guidance throughout their lives. It was around this time that Nutimus also began grooming Honest John to become a significant leader in his own right.[26]

Despite the prosperity of those first few years in the Lehigh Valley, it did not take long before Honest John and his family experienced the same problems they faced in West Jersey. By 1734, just four years after their arrival, colonial settlers began to invade the Lehigh Valley. One year later surveyors clandestinely made their way to that valley, and then Pennsylvania's land agent, James Logan, started selling off the surveyed land to speculators. Some speculators like William Allen, who claimed thousands of acres in the area, had begun their acquisitions nearly a decade earlier.[27]

Logan also had interests there. He had purchased a dubious deed to a potentially lucrative iron deposit on Nutimus's land from a local Delaware who had no right to sell that land in the first place. That was often how colonists like Logan operated, treating individual Native people from a particular nation as if they had the authority to sell all or most of their people's lands. When those purchases didn't work out, which they rarely did, colonial officials used those sales to take whole nations to task for failing to uphold "original" agreements. Often colonial officials did all of this in the hopes of initiating a new and larger land sale to confirm the legitimacy of the "original" dubious purchase. It was a vicious cycle that most aggressive speculators knew was a long con that could alienate Native peoples, but they did it anyway.[28]

Regardless of Logan's chicanery, he had excited the proprietors, who began making plans to establish thousands of acres in the Lehigh Valley as their own manors populated by rent-paying tenants. It was a land baron's dream. Soon the indebted sons of William Penn began imagining windfall profits. Nudged by Logan, the prospects became so alluring that the proprietors claimed legal title to all of the Lehigh Valley by using a questionable "deed" that had no signatures, signs, or seals supposedly negotiated with the Delaware by William Penn in 1686, which culminated in the now infamous "Walking Purchase" of 1737.[29]

News of this purported deed rocked the Native American communities in the Lehigh Valley, though everyone knew it was a sham. That "deed," or at least what we now know was the basis of it, had been clarified during a well-documented meeting among William Penn, James Logan, and Delaware leaders way back in 1700. Since that year, numerous private transactions had confirmed its settled status. Yet the Penns, through Logan, brandished the same "deed" again in the 1730s to extend Pennsylvania's jurisdiction over the Lehigh Valley. Honest John's new home was in danger.[30]

The pressure to resist Pennsylvania's designs was immense. In conference after conference, Delaware leaders such as Nutimus and Captain Harris questioned the legitimacy of the deed and tried to reason with proprietary officials. Finally, after much back and forth and a lot of tension, they came to an agreement. The Delaware acquiesced to ceding the Penn brothers some land but not all of what the proprietors wanted or claimed. Instead of a boundary north of the Kittatinny Mountains (the northern boundary of the Lehigh Valley), the Delaware agreed to a more southerly one around Tohiccon Creek, which was basically the same boundary agreed to in 1700. The exact line, however, according to the new agreement, would still need to be charted by a day and a half's walk.[31]

For their part, the Delaware thought the walk a mere formality. Not only were "walks" standard units of measurement in early land sales, but Pennsylvania's walkers, Delaware leaders believed, would "follow the Course of the [Delaware] River till they came to Tohiccon Creek & then" would "follow the Course of said Creek till they finish'd their Journey." At the conference establishing the necessity of the walk, Logan even produced a map that made it seem as if the walkers would follow Tohiccon Creek. That map, however, did not include clear geographical markers. What Delaware leaders thought was Tohiccon Creek was actually a northern section of the Lehigh River. With that map and the agreement made, the Penns and their land agents commissioned some of the fastest runners in the province, some of whom were known to be men of "ill fame," to "walk" the new boundary along paths speculators hired people to clear and chart. By the end of that day-and-a-half "walk," Pennsylvania laid claim to over 1 million acres encompassing most of the Lehigh Valley.[32]

Honest John, with his father, brothers, and probably two sons, participated in several meetings between the Delaware and Pennsylvania officials opposing the "Walking Purchase." Despite the Delaware's claims that they hadn't sold the land and that the "walk" was unfair, Pennsylvania remained obstinate. Throughout these meetings, Honest John witnessed Pennsylvania officials disparaging Nutimus, Captain Harris, and the Delaware community in general. In one such instance, James Logan openly criticized Nutimus, branding him "weak" and "knavish," belittling the significance of the Delaware people. In another meeting, Logan depicted Nutimus as no bigger than his pinkie finger while asserting himself as "a great, big man" by stretching his arms wide. Logan also implied that failure to agree to the land sale could lead to Delawares' isolation from trade or worse. This manipulative tactic was Logan's well-honed strategy. A decade earlier, he had used similar deceitful and forceful tactics to dispossess Delaware, Shawnee, and some Conoy along the Schuylkill River and Brandywine Creek. Although those nations had initially resisted, speculators and squatters inundated the land, and the Native peoples left their homes for both the Ohio and Northern Susquehanna River Valleys.[33]

Refusing to share a similar fate, Nutimus and other Delaware leaders appealed to the Six Nations for help. Not only did the Delaware regularly invite other Native nations to witness treaties and land sales, even granting them a share of the proceeds, but the Delaware often referred to the Six Nations as their "Uncles," a kinship term that represented the Haudenosaunee's power but also signified a connection and alliance. Native peoples used kinship terms to describe a host of positions and relationships in and among Native communities and with Europeans. Native peoples often called the British "brother" or the French "father." The Shawnee, Nanticoke, and Conoy referred to the Delaware as "grandfathers." But the status conveyed by these various kinship terms did not mean the subjugation of those who used them. Instead, those terms were meant to represent mutual respect and responsibilities expected of kin. Despite the Delaware's relationship with the Haudenosaunee, they were sadly disappointed in how their uncles responded.[34]

Just a year before the "Walking Purchase," the Six Nations had engaged in a conference with the Pennsylvanians convened by Logan to strengthen their ties with the proprietary government. This timing was deliberate. Frustrated by resistance from local Native Americans like Nutimus, James Logan courted the Six Nations, who were more open to the Penns' land aspirations. Leveraging his rapport with Shikellamy, a Haudenosaunee viceroy overseeing the Susquehanna River Valley, Logan, along with proprietors Thomas Penn, then visiting the colonies, and his older brother John (who made a surprise trip to avoid his creditors), organized "a great Treaty," a "League and Chain of Friendship and Brotherhood." This agreement not only created a grand alliance but also asserted the Haudenosaunee's sovereignty over the "Delawares, Canayes, & the other Indians living on Sasquehanna." According to the Onondaga Council, the proprietors, and officials, this treaty solidified the Six Nations' control over land "within" Pennsylvania but "not purchased of the Indians." During the same meeting, Logan persuaded the Six Nations to relinquish their claim to the Lehigh Valley, setting the stage for the "Walking Purchase."[35]

Ecstatic with what Logan had accomplished, Thomas Penn decided he would do everything in his power "to strengthen the hands of the Six Nations, and enable them to be the better answerable for their Tributaries."[36] For good reason, that relationship and the land deals it instigated turned the Penns' total profits from land sales from a meager £12,610 between 1701 and 1736 to a staggering £214,709 thereafter, equivalent in today's American dollars to $27,095,766, which at that time would have required a skilled tradesman to work more than 2 million days to earn. The funding to buttress the Penns' aristocratic pretensions had been achieved through and by the "Great Treaty" with the Six Nations in 1736.[37]

When the Delaware went to the Haudenosaunee for help with the Walking Purchase after that treaty, then, Logan and the proprietors held most of the cards. The Haudenosaunee could not disclaim their earlier agreement to cede the Lehigh Valley. If they did, they would undermine their diplomatic position by throwing into question the extent of their sovereign authority on either side of the Susquehanna River. As a result, during a meeting at Philadelphia in 1742 between the Six Nations, the Delaware, and the Pennsylvanians to settle the legitimacy of the Walking Purchase, Onondaga's representatives, Shikellamy and Canassatego, but particularly the latter, formally backed that purchase, confirming the dispossession of Nutimus, Honest John, his family, and the many other refugee peoples living in the Lehigh Valley.[38]

Perhaps all the more galling for Honest John and the many others affected by this meeting was that the Haudenosaunee speakers not only supported Pennsylvania but upbraided the Delaware leaders who resisted. Canassatego, speaking on behalf of the Six Nations, addressed "our Cousins the Delawares" as "a very unruly People." He wanted to take them all "by the Hair of the Head" and shake them "severely till you recover your Senses and become Sober." The Delaware's land, Canassatego argued, "is gone"; it went through their "guts" when they signed it away on Logan's deed. Therefore he "charge[d] them to remove instantly" to the Northern Susquehanna River Valley at "Wyomin or Shamokin" where "we shall have you more under our Eye." His demand, he argued, was final: "We don't give you the liberty to think about it." Nor, Canassatego claimed, could they or "any who shall descend from you" ever "meddle in Land Affairs" again. They were a "conquer'd" people, "made Women" and "Children" of the Haudenosaunee.[39]

That conquest never actually occurred. It was a fiction rooted in the "Great Treaty" with Pennsylvania. Moreover, Canassatego's use of terms like "Women" and "Children" to describe the Delaware was ambiguous considering the matrilineal culture and the importance of kinship for both the Delaware and Haudenosaunee. Yet, the terms Canassatego used were also situational, based on audience. In this scenario, in front of patriarchal Pennsylvanians, Canassatego clearly meant the Delaware were a subjugated people. As one important colonial interpreter thought, such kinship terms signify "a Subject or one that is under Command."[40] Thus began Honest

John's long experience with the combined power of the Pennsylvania government and Onondaga.

After the "Walking Purchase," Honest John and many but not all of the Native peoples living in the Lehigh Valley dispersed. While his older half-brother, Captain John, refused to move, hoping to purchase his land outright from the Pennsylvanians, some, like his uncle Nutimus, followed Canassatego's directive and moved to the Northern Susquehanna River Valley. Others, like his brother Captain Peter (also known as Young Captain Harris), moved to the Ohio Valley, and still others, including Honest John himself, moved northeast, remaining on what was left of Delaware land just beyond the new boundary. This new home is where Honest John was when Canassatego sold that land in the summer of 1749. Given Honest John's longer history, it is no surprise that he fought back, questioned the legitimacy of Haudenosaunee claims, and forced Pennsylvania's surveyor to abandon the area.[41]

Although initially successful in driving off Scull and his retinue, Honest John's resistance was short-lived. Like many others who encountered colonial land hunger and Haudenosaunee land sales, he was quickly overwhelmed by squatters and surveyors. Later that same year, or in early spring 1750, he left the home he had defended, making his way to a Christian Moravian mission town in the Lehigh Valley erected on land stolen from his people and purchased from speculators, in this case William Allen, where he was baptized, adopting the Christian name Gideon, a name with a militant origin in the Christian Bible's Book of Judges, and surely no coincidence.[42]

The multiple names used by Honest John thus far might seem confusing, but an individual with several names was relatively normal for Native peoples. Names rarely signified an internal personal identity granted at birth and kept forever but rather changed to reflect the particular social role and even power of that individual for the larger community and in the outside world. Even personal pronouns like "I" or "me" meant more in Native languages than the individual using it. "I am" in Lenape, for example, meant "I am the body of a man" or "my body is a Lenape." Delaware men also had at least two names in their lifetimes. The first, accorded by their parents around the age of six or seven, designated kinship connections as well as their possibilities for the future. The second was conferred by the larger community at a ceremony when they reached adulthood. Native peoples could also obtain new names as their social positions changed. Names were both fluid and powerful.[43]

Native peoples also used and accepted names given them by Europeans, such as Honest John. But therein lies a significant problem for any modern researcher trying to unearth the history and stories of individual Native peoples from sources written, curated, and edited by Europeans who often favored Christianized Native American names over Indigenous ones. Perhaps Honest John was known in Native communities as Tattenhick/Tatteneskund (as some spelled it) since his coming of age.[44] He could have also been known as something entirely lost to history, but we will never know for sure.

Honest John/Tattenhick turned Gideon, hoping his new name signifying his Christian conversion would provide security for the future, settled at Gnadenhutten, forging more connections with colonists as well as multiethnic Algonquin- and Siouan-speaking peoples. Like everything else in his life to that point, that too proved temporary. According to the Moravian minister who baptized him, Gideon did not conform to the strictures of the Christian mission. He was "a great sinner."[45] Just four years later, 1754, he left the mission town dissatisfied and moved northwest to Wyoming where he was identified by the name or at least the spelling of it most known to history, Teedyuscung, a name that some colonists translated as "one who makes the earth tremble," a significant transition for someone who once sold brooms called Honest John.[46]

Just because Teedyuscung eventually moved to Wyoming as Canassatego demanded years earlier does not mean he acquiesced to the authority of Onondaga. After all, the Six Nations were one of reasons he had to keep moving. As he explained much later, the Haudenosaunee, or "Minquas" as he called them, meaning "treacherous" in Delaware, "took us by the Hair of the Head, and removed Us off the Land: upon which, many of our People went to Allegheny, and others high up Susquehanna, very uneasy and displeas'd." Once "high up Susquehanna" in Wyoming, Teedyuscung consistently fought with Haudenosaunee overseers about the land he now lived on as well as the past deals that had dispossessed him and his family.⁴⁷

Tensions were so great that most Haudenosaunee representatives refused to even speak to him. When Teedyuscung did get a chance to meet with Six Nations' leaders they rebuked him for his recalcitrance. Just a year after his arrival at Wyoming, Teedyuscung obviously stirred the pot. Canyase, a Mohawk chief and "principal councilor" of the Six Nations, irritated with Teedyuscung, upbraided him. "We, the Mohocks, are Men; we are made so from above," he scolded Teedyuscung, "but the Delawares are Women and under our Protection, and of too low a kind to be Men." Therefore, Canyase wanted Teedyuscung to remember his people's place and "sit down and enjoy peaceably the Lands" the Six Nations "permitted them." Teedyuscung would not "sit down."⁴⁸ The tables were turning on the Six Nations. By the time Teedyuscung moved to the Northern Susquehanna River Valley, it seemed as if displaced and displeased Native Americans were "daily flocking there from all parts." Teedyuscung would use those growing numbers to his and his people's advantage.⁴⁹

Despite all the benefits and sweeping claims of the proceedings between the Pennsylvanians and the Haudenosaunee that dispossessed Teedyuscung and many others, old animosities remained and threatened to upend the power of Onondaga over their tributaries and the future of the proprietary colony. This was especially true as more and more tributaries were systematically displaced. While some of the peoples who relocated to the Northern Susquehanna River Valley or to the Ohio Valley recognized Onondaga's authority when it was mutually beneficial, they also resisted when Onondaga did not make good on its promises of protection. That protection, though, waned as the Haudenosaunee came to rely on their European allies for trade, authority, and survival, which ultimately required the use of land sales, and each new deed dispossessed and displaced more and more people.⁵⁰

Haudenosaunee land sales proved tricky for everyone involved. Not only did they dispossess numerous Indigenous people but they exacerbated the pressures white settlers placed on the land the Haudenosaunee and their tributaries still claimed. Despite their alliance with Pennsylvania, the

Grand Council of Chiefs at Onondaga could not change proprietary land policies that benefited speculators, which only resulted in more squatters inundating Native American land on the periphery of each new purchase, causing massive disturbances across the extensive Haudenosaunee frontier.[51] Squatters were like rippling waves erupting in the aftermath of a stone thrown in a pond. By the time Teedyuscung ventured to Wyoming not only was the Juniata occupied by squatters regardless of the Pennsylvania government's promises but the Ohio Valley was crawling with Virginia surveyors, Pennsylvania traders, and French officers, and Shamokin and the rest of the Northern Susquehanna River Valley at the edge of the 1749 purchase was under threat.[52]

Feeling besieged and disillusioned, some unknown members of the Six Nations, perhaps pro-French sympathizers irritated by Canassatego's acquiescence to British land hunger, assassinated the prominent Onondaga speaker.[53] Just as significant, Pennsylvania's old ally, Shikellamy, had also passed away from natural causes. Both deaths resulted in the elevation of new leaders, such as Canassatego's successor, Tohaswuchdioony, an Onondaga chief also known as The Belt, who had converted to Catholicism and had close ties with the French. Even Shikellamy's successor, his own son, John Shikellamy, looked uneasily at Pennsylvania.[54]

The younger Shikellamy increasingly indicated that the Northern Susquehanna River Valley was off limits. That land was not only "some of their best hunting Ground" but the home of the displaced people the Haudenosaunee claimed as tributaries. "No White Men," he told Pennsylvania officials, "should come and settle there."[55] Really, he had to resist further white encroachment. John Shikellamy was not the only person of authority in the valley. Teedyuscung, "uneasy and displeas'd," was also rising to significance. Within two short years of his arrival in Wyoming, Teedyuscung would again be a "king," but this time representing a much larger coalition of alienated Native nations, rivaling Shikellamy's authority and with it the suzerainty of Onondaga over the Northern Susquehanna River Valley.

3

"Bird on a Bow"

THE RISE OF THE SUSQUEHANNA NATIONS AND A WAR FOR INDEPENDENCE IN THE NORTHERN SUSQUEHANNA RIVER VALLEY, 1754–1758

DESPITE THE RISE OF Teedyuscung as well as the changing outlook from Onondaga and its regional satellite town, Shamokin, Pennsylvania's proprietors and their land-speculating allies refused to abandon their aspirations to acquire the Northern Susquehanna River Valley. In fact, their desires only grew when they found the land sold by Canassatego east of the Susquehanna River too rocky and insufficient and then learned of squatters trekking north toward more desirable land. Some of those squatter claims supposedly included rich iron and silver deposits, one of which Teedyuscung lived near at Wyoming. Moreover, there were constant murmurs that land companies from Virginia and Connecticut sought to extend their claims north and west of the Susquehanna River. There were even rumors that the French wanted to build a fort at Shamokin. If any of these projects were to succeed, the vast land granted to the Penns by King Charles II would be limited to the east side of the Susquehanna River and south of that river's East Branch. The proprietors' boom years could be coming to an end.[1]

Thomas Penn tried to safeguard his and his colony's future with another large land purchase from the Six Nations at a congress held at Albany, New York, in the summer of 1754. The Albany Congress, although popularly known to history as an intercolonial meeting at which the famous Benjamin Franklin proposed a grand colonial union, exhorting colonists, faced with a new war with France, to either "Join or Die," was also, and more importantly at the time, a meeting between colonial officials and the Haudenosaunee. As had been the case during King George's War, colonial officials sought Haudenosaunee help to counterbalance the imperial ambitions of France. They also wanted if possible to purchase more land. For Pennsylvania's proprietors the latter more than the former was the purpose of it all.[2]

Penn, who was obviously worried about the French, was just if not more concerned about the ambitions of his British colonial neighbors, especially Virginia and Connecticut. The Albany Congress, he thought, provided a kind of theatrical stage where he could publicly shore up his claims to a vast and profitable colony before an intercolonial audience. In his instructions to his agents attending the Albany Congress, especially his nephew John Penn and his secretary, Richard Peters, he urged them "to try, by all the means in their power to make a Purchase, and the Larger the better." Maybe they could even broker a deal with the Six Nations to buy "either the whole Province, or so much as to take in the Western Branch of the Susquehannah, called in their Language Senaxse." Most important of all, he wanted whatever purchase his agents accomplished to be included in the public record of the entire congress, thus deterring the aspirations of Virginia and Connecticut in one fell swoop.[3]

To Thomas Penn's and his agents' dismay, the Mohawk dominated the proceedings at Albany on behalf of the Six Nations. This was not a scenario the proprietors expected. In the previous few months, the proprietors' agents had cajoled Shikellamy's sons to attend the meeting and help negotiate the land deal the proprietors wanted. It seemed a sure thing. Yet, now the Mohawk rather than the Haudenosaunee leaders aligned with Pennsylvania controlled the meeting. In the short history of the relationship between the Haudenosaunee and Pennsylvania, the Mohawk had often derided the duplicity of the "Pens," preferring to deal with their neighbors in New York. When the Haudenosaunee and Pennsylvanians created Philadelphia's council fire in the 1730s, for example, the Mohawk were noticeably absent, and even after that rarely made their way to the city to negotiate, trade, or even speak to the Pennsylvanians.[4] Although proprietary representatives tried to work around the Mohawk at Albany by negotiating, or bribing, some of their old Haudenosaunee acquaintances and allies, it had little effect. Some Haudenosaunee representatives may have been disposed to the sale Penn wanted, but the Oneida absolutely refused to make a "final Determination" on any land sale "till the Arrival of the Mohocks." In sum, if Penn and his agents wanted to broker a deal, they had to go through the Mohawk.⁵

Fortunately for the Pennsylvanians, strained relations with New York pushed the Mohawk to pursue new alliances, especially the trade and benefits such connections offered. This made them more than willing to sell land situated in what Thomas Penn regarded as the northern and western regions of Pennsylvania. However, Hendrick, a significant leader among the Canajoharie Mohawk and a key Haudenosaunee spokesperson at the Albany Congress, initially resisted the Pennsylvanians' land requests. During discussions, Hendrick advised against selling "as much as they [the Penns] intended" and insisted on retaining the West Branch of the Susquehanna. That land was where "our Bones are scattered" and where they could "settle such of our Nations" who "shall come to us from the Ohio, or any others who shall deserve to be in our Alliance." Nevertheless, through prolonged negotiations and outright bribery, Hendrick eventually agreed. He sold the Penns much of "Senaxse" and a stretch of land west of the Susquehanna to the Ohio for four hundred pounds, plus five hundred pounds in gifts. They also made an agreement for additional compensation on colonists' settlement in the region north and west of the Alleghany Mountains. Overall, the original Albany agreement covered about 23,500 square miles, comprising over 50 percent of present-day Pennsylvania.⁶

As had happened in the past, neither the proprietary agents nor the Haudenosaunee delegates took into consideration the various peoples who actually inhabited that land. Complicating matters further, less than a week after the new land sale to the Pennsylvanians, Hendrick and other Six Nations headmen sold to John Lydius, an experienced land-jobber acting on behalf of Connecticut speculators, land in the Northern Susquehanna River Valley that overlapped with Pennsylvania's purchase and claims—the same land, moreover, that the Six Nations provided for the Delaware, Shawnee, Mohican, Nanticoke, and Conoy most recently displaced from the Schuylkill River, Brandywine Creek, and Lehigh Valley. Although the Grand Council at Onondaga would later disclaim both sales, and Pennsylvania's proprietors would have to give much of this purchase back a few years later, especially Senaxse and the land west of the Alleghany Mountains, the damage had been done. Wars for independence in both the Ohio and Northern Susquehanna River Valleys loomed on the horizon.[7]

Within a few months of the Albany Congress, Pennsylvania speculators gobbled up what land they could in the new purchase. The prospects were so alluring that some speculators did not even wait for the sale to become official before they started maneuvering. William Allen, for instance, bragged to a friend about how he knew beforehand that the proprietors would obtain "a new Indian Purchase" at Albany and how he was able to use that knowledge to dupe an unsuspecting family in England into selling him "all the good Land" in the upcoming purchase for next to nothing. Apparently, that family owned a claim to about eight thousand acres of land west of the Susquehanna River procured years earlier from the proprietary family in need of quick cash. Such claims to Native American lands were ubiquitous in Pennsylvania. Yet, in all such circumstances, such holdings were basically useless until the land was actually purchased from Native Americans.[8]

Allen offered the unsuspecting family eight hundred pounds for their eight thousand acres, which he told them was an excellent deal because "they never will make more it."[9] He, after all, would assume the potential risk, and besides, they had been holding onto it for so long without any recompense. They agreed, and with that early deal completed, Allen practically salivated over the profits to be made. It was not long before Allen went to the proprietary land office to make his purchase official and acquire more, but once he got there he must have quickly realized that he was not alone. Richard Peters was also maneuvering at the land office to make some profitable investments. Working with the sons of Pennsylvania's Indian agent, Conrad Weiser, Peters laid claim to thousands of acres of land west of the Susquehanna River, some of the same land he had traversed a few years earlier evicting squatters and burning cabins.[10]

Speculators like Allen and Peters were not the only colonists looking to benefit from the Albany Congress purchase. Squatters had been moving to that land for years, but as news and gossip about the prospects of a new purchase gripped the colony, squatters swarmed. For example, Jacob Beyerly and about forty other German families working with him tried to assert their right to "all Shamokin," going so far as to carve their names on the clapboards of a house to "forwarn everybody from this place." Irritated by ubiquitous "freebooters," William Allen complained that squatters had taken most of the "good lands" available, calculating that he owned roughly "thirty thousand acres . . . which is mostly occupied by these villains." Like Allen, Peters was also complaining about squatters on the lands he wanted or owned. When the Weiser brothers made their way to the Susquehanna River Valley on Peters's behalf, they found squatter families everywhere. Even the "trees" were "marked with 3 or 4 peoples names," the usual process by which squatters indicated the boundaries of their illegal claims. While speculators like Allen or Peters found squatters frustrating, it must have been infuriating for Native peoples as they watched white colonists build cabins and hack their initials into trees while surveyors with chains, compasses, and logbooks poured over *Native* land sold away to the Pennsylvanians by *their* supposed Haudenosaunee uncles.[11]

What happened next should come as no surprise. In October 1755, just over a year after the Albany Congress, many of the displaced Native peoples now living in the Ohio Valley (a large swath of which Penn also purchased at Albany from the Haudenosaunee) ignored Onondaga's calls for peace, asserted their independence, and went to war. The Ohio Nations were angry, one British official frantically reported, and would "act for themselves att this time without Consulting ye Onondago Council."[12]

The Ohio Nations' first military foray was no coincidence. Coordinated by Shingas, the prominent war chief of the Ohio Delaware, who colonists called "Shingas the Terrible," warriors from the Ohio Nations descended on the colonial settlements immediately west of the Susquehanna River near the Juniata River and Penn's Creek. As the Shikellamy brothers had warned Richard Peters years earlier, they "killed, scalped, and carried away all the men, women, and children" and "burned up" the homes where the inhabitants sought refuge. One Pennsylvanian was found "on his back barbarously burnt and two Tomhawks sticking in his forehead" next to the smoldering ashes of his home. Like those squatters who claimed their land rights by marking trees, "one of the Tomhawks" wedged in the man's head was "marked newly W. D." Thus began, in earnest, the Seven Years' War in Pennsylvania.[13]

The Seven Years' War, or the French and Indian War as Americans typically call it, started as a dispute among Virginia, the Ohio Nations, and the French over control of the forks of the Ohio River (modern-day Pittsburgh), but it rapidly became a global war between France and Britain over the extent of their empires. For Native peoples who got caught up in the whirlwind, it was a struggle for their land, sovereignty, and survival. As one Delaware elder asked British officials badgering him about why the Ohio Nations went to war, "Does not the Law of Nations permit, or rather command us all, to stand upon our Guard in order to Preserve our Lives, the Lives of our Wives and Children, our Property and Liberty?" "Let me tell you," he continued, answering his own question, "that was our case."[14]

The Ohio Nations, many of them at least, had no love for the French or their imperial ambitions, but neither did they love the British. "Your Nation," that same Delaware elder explained to a British official, "always shewed an Eagerness to settle our Lands, cunning as they were, they always encouraged a number of Poor People to settle upon our Lands: We protested against it several Times, but without any redress, or help." Other Delaware leaders were just as emphatic when the war broke out. "Why do you come to fight on our land?" they asked both French and British officials. "This makes everybody believe you want only to take & settle the Land." During this war, like the ones that preceded it and came after, Native peoples fought for their own causes, their own sovereignty, and their own security, not European ones, and they chose the alliances they made accordingly.[15]

From the Ohio Nations' perspective, then, the escalating war between avaricious empires would impact their future, not just at the forks but everywhere else. In this scenario, the Northern Susquehanna Valley was just as important as the lands to the west of it. For the Ohio Nations, particularly the Delaware and Shawnee, some of whom took up seasonal residence in the Northern Susquehanna River Valley, constantly traveled along the paths skirting the West Branch, and had kinship connections with the people who lived there, that valley, like the Ohio Valley, was a space worth defending.[16]

Who they should defend it from during the escalating conflict, though, was uncertain. In the early years of the war, many of the Native nations in the Ohio and Susquehanna River Valleys had struck a neutral stance, demanding their land and sovereignty be respected as they established relationships with both European empires. That started to change as war enveloped their country and the French, seeking Native allies, made their imperial ambitions seem less intrusive than British ones. The French even promised to protect Indigenous rights against avaricious British colonists. For their part, the British were not as diplomatically savvy as the French. Really, they never were. To be sure, the British tried, often using the same claims in their negotiations as the French, but those claims increasingly rang hollow in Native American ears.[17]

The challenge for Native Americans dealing with the British came from the conflicting messages they heard. Different British representatives had opposing views, creating confusion. While some pledged to honor Indigenous rights, others, like Edward Braddock, the commander-in-chief of the thirteen colonies, stated that once the French were dealt with, the British would claim the land because "no Savage should." And then there was discord among the British colonies themselves. Pennsylvania clashed with Virginia, Maryland, and Connecticut over borders and competed for relationships with the Six Nations, even speaking ill of Massachusetts and other New England colonies to Native groups. Despite attempts like the Albany Congress to resolve such intercolonial rivalries, disagreements persisted. For Native peoples navigating British diplomacy, these inconsistencies were more than frustrating.[18]

There were also practical issues at play for Native peoples. British colonists were far more numerous than French ones in North America. The British seemed akin to "Musketoes and Nitts in the Woods," who "if they get once a fast hold, it will not be" in anyone's "power to drive them away again." Obviously, Britain and its colonists were the enemy, or, at least for many Native peoples wary of both European empires, the greater of two evils. It did not help matters that Britain and its colonies, despite the fact that the French were "much inferior to them in Strength and Numbers," seemed militarily inept during the first few years of the war. Not only were the different colonies fighting between and among themselves but some colonies, like Pennsylvania, could barely pass laws to muster troops or even fund a war. The British, some Native peoples argued, "appeared to them like fools" who "could neither guard against surprise, run or fight."[19] Obviously, it would do no good to back a losing horse when so much was at stake.

French promises and the October 1755 raids by Ohio warriors in the Juniata Valley and at Penn's Creek, though, did not instantly motivate the multiethnic people living in the Northern Susquehanna River Valley to "take up the Hatchet" against the British. The Susquehanna nations may have shared similar grievances and had clan and kinship connections with many of the Ohio Nations who went to war, but they were in a difficult situation. Like the colonists, they too were often divided, a product of the constant migration of new peoples to the area and the way the Haudenosaunee settled and governed their tributaries as distinct yet subordinate nations. Some of them like the Mohican and the Delaware had even been enemies in the past. Moreover, with the Six Nations to their north, Pennsylvania to their south, and the Ohio Nations and their French allies to their west, the Native peoples in the Northern Susquehanna River Valley needed to act cautiously.[20]

Constantly viewed as client peoples, children, or women by the Haudenosaunee and British officials who elevated the status of the Six Nations, the various peoples in the Northern Susquehanna River Valley experienced a grueling dependence. As they were often told by British officials, "you, who are only Cousins and Dependents on the Six united Nations," had no power to question Haudenosaunee-backed British policy.[21] Moreover, the British controlled the easiest trade routes that those nations desperately needed. Two hard spring frosts had devastated the year's crop yield, which a summer drought only accentuated. While accustomed to seasons of want and plenty, the Native peoples in the Northern Susquehanna River Valley were also dangerously low on powder and shot, which threatened the hunting season. Combined with a poor harvest, that could mean starvation. Access to trade was utterly necessary.[22]

For at least eight months, from April to November 1755, the Native peoples living in the Northern Susquehanna River Valley pleaded with Pennsylvania officials for arms, ammunition, and access to trade. Some of them were even willing to go to war against the French if they could get needed supplies. In a meeting in Philadelphia that August, Scarouady, an Oneida leader from Logstown and "a man of Authority among the Six Nations, and of great Experience and Eloquence" allied with the British and trying to maintain Haudenosaunee control over both the Ohio and Northern Susquehanna River Valleys, argued that "one word of Yours will bring the Delawares to join You." The same could be said of the Nanticoke and other Northern Susquehanna Nations.[23] In meeting after meeting, the Susquehanna peoples, or rather the representatives of the Six Nations speaking on their behalf, beseeched "Brother Onas & the People of Pennsylvania not to leave us in the lurch, but to supply us with necessaries." Even Teedyuscung proclaimed his continued friendship with Pennsylvania if he and his people could get supplies they required. In all, they eagerly waited for "Brother Onas" to meet "the earnest request of us the Warriors, the Councellors, and our Wives and Children."[24]

Pennsylvania's new governor, Robert Hunter Morris, found himself under "particular Difficulties about making a proper Answer" to these requests. Disputes between the governor and the assembly had reached a peak over support for the war and how to pay for it. The assembly proposed funding it by taxing "proprietary and other unlocated lands" and demanded control over the dispensation of any public expenditures. The governor couldn't acquiesce to either demand. As a representative of the proprietors and the crown, he had to abide by both proprietary and royal wishes. The proprietors would not allow a law that taxed "their estates," and royal officials would resist a colonial law that challenged the king's authority, as exercised by the colonial governor, over public funds. Morris lamented that "he was not able to afford the Delawares assistance." All he could do was express "our hearty thanks to the Delawares and Nanticokes" and tell them to "wait." He hoped that would buy him enough time to broker a deal with the assembly.[25]

Time was something he did not have. In early November 1755, Charles Brodhead, a young frontier trader from the Lehigh Valley and the beneficiary of a six-hundred-acre estate granted to his father by the proprietors and legitimized by the "Walking Purchase," met with "the Indians settled at Wyomink," including Teedyuscung. Brodhead found that town in shambles and the people their near starvation. He sent a message to Governor

Morris that the "Delawares, Shawonee, & Minisinks [Munsee]" and a growing number of Chickasaw from the southeast at Wyoming desperately needed "proper encouragements from us" with "proper Provisions" to carry them through the winter. They seemed "very true to the English Interest at this time," but, he cautioned, "how long they may so continue without receiving" help "from us is hard to determine." If that was not bad enough, the various Native peoples living there interpreted the constant requests to "wait" as meaning that they were "sunk so low among the White People as to be forgot by them."[26]

As the two branches of the government fought between themselves, representatives of the French and their Native American allies in the Ohio Valley offered the peoples living in the Northern Susquehanna River Valley access to presents, trade goods, and "assurances of re-instating them in the Possession of the Lands they have sold to the English."[27] Shingas started sending envoys in October. All along the West Branch from Great Island (just east of present-day Lock Haven, Pennsylvania) to the town Wenschpochkechung (present-day Williamsport, Pennsylvania) and up the North Branch at Nescopeck (Nutimus's new home in present-day Luzerne County) and Wyoming (where Teedyuscung lived), Delaware and Shawnee warriors carrying British scalps encouraged the several different Susquehanna Nations to take up "the Hatchet from the French to destroy the English" for as long as "there remain'd one alive."[28] While the Susquehanna peoples initially demurred, hoping for supplies from "Brother Onas," such overtures became increasingly hard to rebuff.[29] According to Silver Heels, also known as Aroas, a Seneca representative, it was not long before a "great many" of the Susquehanna peoples, in need of supplies, "greedily" took up the "hatchet."[30]

The need for trade and the vacillation of the Pennsylvania government were not the only reasons an alliance with the French and their Native allies appealed to the refugee peoples in the Northern Susquehanna River Valley. Britain's superintendent of Indian affairs in the north, William Johnson, understood there were longer-term grievances involved. When "those Delaware & Shawanese Indians who live nearest to the Ohio being seduced by the French, went amongst their Brethren who dwelt on the Susquehanna," they had little difficulty propagating "those prejudices against the good Intentions of the English." Indeed, he explained to British officials in London, "the Great Patents of Land which had been purchased & taken up in those parts & our extended scattered Settlements beginning to crowd upon the Indians, had been a long Eye sore to them, infected them with Jealousy & disgust towards the English & they prepared them to be more easily influenced."[31]

That jealousy and disgust was exacerbated by the war itself and "the ill success" of British "arms." In July 1755, General Edward Braddock, heading one of the largest and longest overland campaigns in history to that point, was soundly defeated and then killed on the banks of the Monongahela River by an outnumbered French force and their Native American allies. It was, Governor Morris thought, "the most shameful blow that ever English Troops received." For many Native peoples on the fence, it seemed as if the French would soon be the "masters of all that part of the country."[32]

That "shameful blow," followed by what happened in the Juniata River Valley, also sharpened racial tension and divisions in the British colonies often erupting in violence. When the Native people living in the Northern Susquehanna River Valley learned of Braddock's "Defeat & Death" and then the raids by Ohio warriors, they feared that British colonists would vent their rage on them. That fear was confirmed by Charles Brodhead. When he visited Wyoming in early November, he outright claimed he knew "it was certainly you that did the mischief," going so far as to threaten that "the English will set out from all points against you" and "take severe Revenge."[33]

Considering the history of duplicity by Pennsylvania officials and escalating racial violence, it did not take much for Native peoples in the Northern Susquehanna River Valley to believe the boasting of colonists like Brodhead. As Delaware leaders told Haudenosaunee representatives during a meeting at Shamokin, "the white People will certainly kill us" they "will kill all the Indians." The British, they explained, have always "behaved very ill to us," and "we don't doubt if we would let things go on as they have done but they would subdue us and make Slaves of us."[34]

Even representatives of the Six Nations allied to the British feared traveling in Pennsylvania. They complained to the governor that "your People . . . think every Indian is against them; they blame us all without Distinction."[35]

The threat was so great that traveling Haudenosaunee from Shamokin, Ohio, and Onondaga had to wear clearly identifiable symbols of their loyalty and carry British flags and passes for their own safety. They even asked Governor Morris for an armed guard when they passed through the colony, new forts for their protection, and a place of refuge for their wives and children. Morris, receiving regular reports of the murder and violence committed by colonists on Native peoples, grumbled that the "unthinking people amongst us" did not make "a proper Distinction between our Friends and Enemy Indians." That reality would push the few Native allies his colony still had away and toward the French, but in the end he did not do anything about it. In fact, he soon made matters worse.[36]

By late November, many of the peoples living in the Northern Susquehanna River Valley harboring long-held grievances and facing the prospect of racially charged attacks without clear assertions for their safety from the colonial government, or even the necessary provisions to defend themselves, went to war against the British. Such an action was long in the making and involved much more than just fighting the British; it also required defying the council chiefs at Onondaga who still demanded that their "children" in the Northern Susquehanna River Valley support their British "Brethren." Despite Onondaga's stance, the different Susquehanna nations started meeting together, forming their own council to proclaim their independence for their safety. "We will," they declared, "do what we please."[37]

According to Pennsylvania colonist Charles Thomson, who often served as a clerk for Teedyuscung, "the Indians on Susquehannah" began to realize that there "divided State," where "every Tribe" formed a "distinct and independent government," could "one by one be easily crushed." To alter that future, they "resolved to new-model their Government, and out of the several Tribes to form one Nation." Even those "who had been Sachems before, now willingly, for the Sake of the public Good, resigned their Dignity, contenting themselves with a Place in the Council." While they didn't exactly become "one Nation"—the several nations kept their governing structures, languages, and cultures—they did confederate, becoming the Susquehanna Nations, a "very considerable Body" of peoples who "chose rather to attack than be attacked."[38]

The train of events explained above may have triggered the Susquehanna Nations' choice to go to war, but, as William Johnson explained to imperial officials, longtime grievances made those triggers possible. When asked why they went to war, representatives of the new Susquehanna Council rightly pointed out that "the English, from their first settling Pennsylvania, had murdered above one hundred of their people," had "cheated them out of a great deal of Land, and cheated them in Commerce continually." Such a "Memory" of "Maltreatment" only "armed them with double Fury."[39]

Teedyuscung was even more emphatic. During a meeting with Pennsylvanians at Easton, only a short distance away from his old home in the Lehigh Valley, the fifty-six year old Teedyuscung, described by contemporaries as an imposingly tall and heavy man, stomped on the floor, stating forcefully that "this very ground that is under me was my Land and Inheritance, and is taken from me by fraud," a reference to the "Walking Purchase" and a clear rebuke of the Pennsylvania proprietors and the power claimed by Onondaga. Infuriated, Richard Peters, the clerk of the meeting, dramatically threw down his pen and declared he would not take any more notes, hoping to remove Teedyuscung's complaint from the official record. Much to Peters's mortification, the past, as it often does, reverberated through time.[40]

That reverberation shaped the intensity of the war. "The Indians on Susquehannah," joining together, "ravaged and destroyed" their old homes on the "Frontiers of Pennsylvania, New-York, and New-Jerseys." They "lay waste every thing before them," Morris complained to Thomas Penn. "Even without" the French, "the [Susquehanna] Indians themselves may do more Mischief this Winter than twenty years will repair." One of the first settlements they hit was the home of that "imprudent" trader Charles Brodhead. Teedyuscung was among the leaders of the Susquehanna Nations who attacked Brodhead's home and other settlements around Pocopoco where his father had once been sachem, including the Moravian mission at Gnadenhutten where Teedyuscung lived after his baptism, earning him yet another nickname, "the War Trumpet."[41]

In this moment, Teedyuscung vehemently denied his tributary status, vocally and symbolically shedding the "petticoat" or underskirt the Haudenosaunee made for him as a woman for the "Breech Clout" typically worn by Native American men. Claiming to be a significant leader in his own right, he began referring to himself as a "king" in the messages he sent to neighboring leaders requesting they join him in the war.[42]

Although Thomas Penn and other proprietary officials would later try to denigrate his claim to power, it is clear that "Teedyuscung was the Person chosen King" by the Susquehanna Nations' new council.[43] Therefore, by going to war and throwing away the "petticoat," Teedyuscung proclaimed not only his independence but the independence of the Susquehanna Nations as well. That reality was not lost on William Johnson. Meeting with some representatives of the Six Nations, Johnson explained that the creation of the Susquehanna Council and the elevation of Teedyuscung threatened the Six Nations' "superiority over the Indians." If "you the Six Nations" will not "exert yourselves," Johnson warned, "you will not only lose that authority, but will have them your enemies."[44]

While the Haudenosaunee responded by sending deputies to the Susquehanna Nations reiterating old claims that "you are our women" and therefore should "do as we bid," it did not have the desired effect.[45] Circumstances had changed because of the war, and the Susquehanna Nations wanted to hear "no more" said "to us on that Head." They were now "men, and are determined not to be ruled any longer by you as Women." They would "cut off all the English" regardless of what Onondaga wanted. If the Haudenosaunee were not careful, the Susquehanna Nations would "make Women of you as you have done of us."[46] Even when Scarouady, who had the respect of many of the nations in the Northern Susquehanna River Valley, offered the Susquehanna Nations a belt of wampum to dissuade them from war, they refused to accept it or even touch it. They used a stick to push it away in a "contemptuous manner," throwing their peace pipes in a pile with the discarded wampum, all the while barraging Scarouady with "ill language." Similarly, when Paxinosa, a Shawnee leader in the Northern Susquehanna River Valley still loyal to the Haudenosaunee, requested the Susquehanna Nations, particularly the Delaware, hear out Onondaga's requests, they threatened to "knock" him "on the head."[47]

The Haudenosaunee faced limited options in responding to such threats and mistreatment. The Susquehanna Nations could mobilize a significant number of warriors, and retaliating against such challenges would only strengthen their ties with the Ohio Nations, particularly the Mingo (discontented members of the Six Nations in the Ohio and Susquehanna River Valleys). This posed a particular problem for Onondaga because the Mingo enjoyed the support of most northern Seneca, who outnumbered all other Six Nations combined.

The Susquehanna Nations also still referred to the northern Seneca as their "Uncles" while resisting Onondaga's suzerainty. During conflicts with the British, many Susquehanna Nations temporarily sought refuge in Seneca towns north of Tioga to protect their women and children. Despite no longer acknowledging "the Six nations in general as their Uncles, they would listen to what the Senecas said." This division created a dilemma for the other Six Nations. Their strength relied on perceived unity as the "Six united Nations," and alienating the Seneca risked lasting divisions among themselves.[48]

Needless to say, Onondaga may have wanted peace but the war continued, and before long it seemed as if the entire countryside was ablaze. The "country [was] so full of Smoke that we can scarce breathe," one settler wrote before fleeing his home in the Lehigh Valley. Even William Allen, safely ensconced in Philadelphia, expressed increasing fear: "We are now in the most deplorable situation imaginable in this province, every Day bringing fresh accounts of the murders committed by the Indians, and the panick is so great that it affects the people within twenty miles of this town."[49] He, like the people who bought, leased, or squatted on the land he owned, feared for the future. By the end of 1756, over seven hundred colonial inhabitants had been killed and many more were in captivity. Despite colonial reports and gossip mongering about "murders" committed by "our Savage neighbours," Native peoples were far more likely to capture and adopt than to commit outright slaughter. The Shawnee took three times as many captives as they killed. But their tactics did have the desired psychological effect. The "Pennsylvanians," one colonial Virginian thought, "are more scared than hurt."[50]

Any lingering doubts some Susquehanna Nations may have had about going to war were dispelled after Governor Morris declared war on the Delaware that spring. He issued a bounty offering $130 "for the Scalp of every male Indian of above Twelve Years old," $50 for women, and $120 for the capture of any child under the age of twelve. Without a clear way to distinguish friends from enemies, all Native Americans, even the recently interred, seemed fair game to roving groups of scalp hunters, many making more money from one scalp than several months of wages could provide. If the governor truly wanted to address the indiscriminate killing of "our Friends and Enemy Indians" by "unthinking people," this was not the solution. To worsen matters, the British enlisted the help of the Cherokee, old enemies of many people in the Susquehanna and Ohio River Valleys, especially the Shawnee. The number of Native peoples willing to go to war against the British grew, and for those few Susquehanna Nations still refusing, like "our Old Friend, Packsinosa, and his Family and Friends," they had no choice but to abandon their homes. They moved north seeking the protection of the Six Nations. Within a few years, Paxinosa, with eyes "running with Tears because of the Melancholy Sight; seeing our Country covered with Blood," relocated to the Ohio Valley.[51]

The partnership between the Susquehanna Nations and the French, alongside the Ohio Nations, didn't fare any better than their previous alliance with the British and the Haudenosaunee. The French and Ohio Nations often couldn't fulfill their promises of supplies and protection. The war had spread across North America and beyond, straining the Ohio Nations' resources while sparking conflicts worldwide involving Britain, France, Spain, Russia, Austria, and the Mughal Empire. By 1756, the French, preoccupied with the global conflict, essentially abandoned their North American officers at Fort Niagara. Moreover, hindered by the British Royal Navy's disruption of French trade routes, these officers could offer little beyond goodwill and meager supplies to their Native allies, including the Susquehanna Nations. Teedyuscung personally witnessed France's struggles. In June 1756, he led a Susquehanna Nations delegation to Fort Niagara seeking supplies and encouragement but discovered the French could barely sustain themselves. Similar to the British years earlier, French officers advised Teedyuscung and his people to wait. Despite this, they did honor Teedyuscung by offering him a new French officer's coat and hat.[52]

Within a month of that trip, the Susquehanna Nations, running out of ammunition and near starvation, were ready to negotiate with the British for peace. They may have been successful in their war effort thus far, but without any real help from the French, not to mention a respite to plant and hunt, it was hard to sustain. To feel out the British, the Susquehanna Nations again looked to Teedyuscung, who, donning his French coat and hat, claimed "that he was made King by Ten Nations," specifically "the United Six nations; Mohocks, Onondagoes, Oneidas, Senecas, Cayugas, and Tuscaroras, and Four others, Delawares, Shawnees, Mohickons and Munsies, who would all ratify what he should do."[53]

He might have cut an imposing figure, but he had no authority from the Six Nations, or at least the council chiefs at Onondaga, though he certainly had connections with the Seneca. Moreover, Teedyuscung was no more than a prominent leader of the Susquehanna Nations' council, easily disregarded if he did not express the will of the multiethnic people over whom he claimed to be king. The creation of the Susquehanna Council did not eradicate the desires of the nations who came together. They had instead confederated to form a diplomatic voice detached from Onondaga. In this sense, Teedyuscung was less a king and more an ambassador for a multinational people sharing some of the same enemies but not necessarily all of the same goals.[54]

Despite a bad turn in the war for his French allies and the pinch of hunger, Teedyuscung still sought the Susquehanna Nations' independence. Yet, he also had far too many interests to express and uphold to achieve it. Over the course of four conferences with the British held at Easton between 1756 and 1758, Teedyscung found his position more than difficult. For some of the Susquehanna Nations, he was there to achieve a lasting peace, a secure home, and access to trade and much needed gifts. For others, peace hinged on addressing long-held grievances, especially the Walking Purchase, the security of their land for the future, and forcefully securing their independence from both the British and the Haudenosaunee.[55]

And then there were the Six Nations, many of whom held Teedyuscung in contempt and deemed him a mere child who needed to recognize the continued authority of their council chiefs. The Six Nations caused Teedyuscung the most grief, especially by the last two Easton conferences at which many of the Six Nations were in attendance, particularly the Seneca. Disillusioned with the French war effort, the Seneca started to come back to the British fold, or were at least willing to stand neutral. Seneca neutrality in and of itself was a godsend for the British war effort. When the British captured Fort Niagara in 1759, for example, it was accomplished in large part because the Seneca gave no resistance. Fort Niagara had been built on Seneca land with Seneca permission.[56]

Teedyuscung's messages at those conferences mirrored tensions among the groups he represented and the Seneca's changing alliances. In July 1756, he sought peace, criticized the proprietary government for land and trade abuses, and aimed for independence from Onondaga. However, with limited Haudenosaunee representation, progress was minimal. In a later meeting, he moderated his stance, maintaining past grievances and emphasizing the need for a secure home and new trade with Pennsylvanians. Yet, challenges arose as Six Nations delegates disputed his quest for independence, while Pennsylvania officials eagerly aligned with any shifts in Six Nations diplomacy. With his people weary from war, lacking supplies, and no French aid, Teedyuscung had little choice but to accept Haudenosaunee authority for peace, access to British trade, and protection for his people in the Northern Susquehanna River Valley. Teedyuscung's varied interests also revealed that whatever peace was established could not endure indefinitely.[57]

The tenuousness of it all was readily apparent at the last Easton conference. Although Teedyuscung eventually agreed to peace, he also got "very drunk" and was overheard ranting "that he was King of all the nations and of all the world, and the Six Nations were fools." The only way to deal with the British was "to make war upon them and cut their throats."[58] Teedyuscung was prone to such outbursts when drunk, which was often enough in those days, but this display was less drunken bombast and more reflective of his frustration with the proceedings. Not only did the Haudenosaunee reprimand him during the conferences but despite his compromises, colonial officials undermined the legitimacy of his position, his claims, and his motives. Even some of the Susquehanna Nations started questioning his leadership.[59]

It was a slap in the face, especially since during the earlier proceeding at Easton the Pennsylvanians had easily referred to him as "King" with "subjects" of his own, even providing him with a "very large White Belt [of wampum], with the figures of Three Men in it," representing King George, the Six Nations, and "Teedyuscung the Delaware King," which importantly signified Teedyuscung's coequal and independent status.[60] By the last two Easton conferences that respect had given way to open and embarrassing ridicule and revile. With many Haudenosaunee in attendance, the Pennsylvanians dismissed Teedyuscung, calling him the creature of the proprietors' adversaries, particularly the assembly and the Quaker's Friendly Association (created to find their own lasting diplomatic path to peace). The Pennsylvanians also castigated him as a self-interested drunk using the situation to satisfy his own wants and desires for power. Pennsylvania officials even mocked him as a pretended revolutionary colluding with the proprietors' and the Six Nations' enemies to conjure up "imaginary" or "pretended" causes" about land fraud for the war.[61]

Teedyuscung was none of those things. To be sure, he often met with leading members of the Friendly Association, claimed powers far beyond his position, and all too often self-medicated with alcohol, but he also forcefully expressed the underlying feelings of many of the Susquehanna Nations over whom he claimed to be king. During the Easton conferences, he could and would vacillate about the power of Onondaga and the grievances against proprietary land fraud, but in the end he consistently upheld that the best way to restore peace was to give the Susquehanna Nations land they could call their own forever. An independent and secure future is what he wanted, regardless of how he got there.[62]

If we step back and look at all of Teedyuscung's requests at the conferences, that goal is readily visible. For instance, during the conferences he tried to work through his own interpreters and clerks to establish a written record from the Susquehanna Nations' point of view. In addition, during the negotiations he requested tutors not only to teach his people English but how to write it. What he wanted was to harness the authority of pen-and-ink diplomacy that his British "brethren" all too often wielded as a weapon of dispossession—a weapon he experienced firsthand. It should be no surprise that both imperial and proprietary officials branded his efforts as somehow "insolent."[63]

Some proprietary officials even claimed Teedyuscung made these requests so that their political adversaries could manipulate their own minutes of the proceedings and, worse yet, Teedyuscung's speeches, which they often thought were too good for him to come up with on his own. During the many meetings with Teedyuscung at Easton and even after, both imperial and proprietary officials did everything in their power to dissuade him from using his own clerks and walking away with his own written account of what went on. Irritatingly for those officials, "Teedyuscung persisted some time to have a Clerk, on Account of his Grandchildren, who ought to have something to shew in writing as well as the English." Such a written record, if it existed in 1686 or 1737, Teedyuscung thought, might have made a difference. As he explained about the Walking Purchase, "Somebody must have wrote wrong, and that makes the Land all bloody."[64]

His requests at Easton, then, were not exactly revolutionary or self-interested. He was willing to vocally recognize the Haudenosaunee as "Uncles" and the British as "brethren"; he was even willing to drop the dispute over the Walking Purchase as long as it meant clear and untrammeled security for his people in the future. Drawing on his history of displacement, Teedyuscung equated his and his people's current situation to that of a "Bird on a Bow," or "Bough," which, looking "about," did "not know where to go." He wanted to descend from the bough and "come down upon the Ground, and make that my own by a good Deed, and I shall then have a Home for Ever."[65]

In all, whether drunk and angry or sober and in a self-pitying mood (he often vacillated), he consistently requested permanency for his people. He wanted a clear written record, and what was worse to some Pennsylvania and Haudenosaunee officials, "a certain Tract of Land fixed" for "our own Use, and the Use of our Children" that would "not be lawful for us or our Children ever to sell." The written deed he wanted was for about 2 million acres encompassing not only his settlement at Wyoming but the forks of the Susquehanna River and nearly half of the West Branch, securing the future of the Susquehanna Nations. Such a deed, he argued, was necessary. As he explained to the Six Nations, "If you, my Uncles, or I die, our Brethren, the English, will say they have bought it from you, & so wrong my Posterity out of it." For all of the Susquehanna Nations' disagreements, they agreed on that underlying point: they wanted "certain" security for the future.[66]

Two prominent Delaware who often interpreted for Teedyscung, Joseph Tittamy and John Pumpshire, tried to explain this reality to Conrad Weiser. During a journey home from one of the earlier Easton conferences,

Tittamy and Pumpshire told Weiser that what "drawed the Delaware Indians' Heart from the English and their Indian Allies" had its roots not just in the fraudulent Walking Purchase but what came after. At Philadelphia in 1742, they complained, "Canassatego" both confirmed the legitimacy of that purchase and treated "the Delaware and Minisink Indians [Munsee]" as if they "were their Dogs" and "ordered them away from their own Land." However, "the Delaware and Minisink Indians, made no Reply" because Canassatego promised "he would give them Lands on Sasquehannah River, and instantly ordered them to Settle there, which the Delaware and Some of the Minisink Indians did."[67]

Although Canassatego was dead by the time of Seven Years' War, both Tittammy and Pumpshire complained that the spirit of his agreements lived on. At Albany, they pointed out, Hendrick had sold away the Susquehanna Nations' land to "the New England People" as well as "the Proprietaries of Pennsylvania," and those colonists treated them like "dogs" making them "terrible angry," thus they joined the French to "maintain their Lands." Therefore, if Pennsylvania truly wanted peace, its leaders needed "to lay out a large Tract of Land on Sasquehannah, and secure it so to their Posterity that none of them could sell and nobody buy it." These sentiments were not just those of Tittamy, Pumpshire, and Teedyuscung, or even just the Delaware, but, they explained, those of an "Indian Counsel" of the Susquehanna Nations.[68]

Weiser supported the plan but it posed significant challenges. Granting the Susquehanna Nations perpetual land ownership clashed with the proprietors' intentions and could challenge the sovereignty of the Six Nations on either side of the Susquehanna River. This could complicate past and future land deals, potentially favoring Virginia's and Connecticut's claims and necessitating compensation for the residing Native nations. To sidestep this issue, Pennsylvania upheld the terms of the "Great Treaty" of 1736 and subsequent agreements, recognizing the Six Nations, not their declared tributaries, as sovereign. This adherence meant Pennsylvania couldn't grant away Haudenosaunee land. Moreover, this approach aligned with the interests of various imperial officials reliant on "our Indians," the Six Nations.[69]

Initially, Thomas Penn was willing to "reserve" some lands for the Susquehanna Nations because he thought an established Native American presence might deter Connecticut settlers who had been looking to capitalize on John Lydius's purchase at Albany and create settlements on the land Penn desired along the North and West Branches of the Susquehanna River. But Penn also wanted the Susquehanna Nations "confined to the Forks" near Shamokin and outright refused land in perpetuity. He was especially reticent to give up those "Rich Lands of Wyomen."[70]

By the last Easton conference, Pennsylvania officials even abandoned that idea. When Teedyuscung again pressed for a deed to much of the Northern Susquehanna River Valley, the Haudenosaunee delegates refused and "went away angry." The Pennsylvania delegates, trying not to further enrage the Haudenosaunee, outright disclaimed any ability to help reserve land in the Northern Susquehanna River Valley for the Susquehanna Nations, even near Shamokin. Backed by the Pennsylvanians, the Six Nations made it clear that they would not go any farther than allowing the Susquehanna Nations the ability "to make *use* of those Lands in Conjunction with our People, and all the rest of our Relations," a far cry from the deed the Susquehanna Nations wanted.[71] In the end, with few choices left and his status diminished, Teedyuscung agreed, but he was not pleased and had not abandoned his plans. British and proprietary officials, however, were jubilant, believing that the arrangements made established a peace that buried "all Disputes about Land under Ground, so deep, that neither We, nor our Children, shall ever hear of them again."[72]

They didn't bury them deep enough. Wary of both the British and the Haudenosaunee, what happened at Easton proved to be an extremely tenuous peace for Teedyuscung and the Susquehanna Nations he represented, reflective of the tensions and animosities still brewing in the area. To be sure, the Susquehanna Nations walked away from those treaties with assurances that the Six Nations and the Pennsylvania government would *allow* them to live in the Northern Susquehanna River Valley. The Pennsylvania government even agreed to build homes for Teedyuscung and his people at Wyoming with a fair and easily accessible trade. The Haudenosaunee and Pennsylvanians also promised protection and assistance for the future, but those promises meant nothing without a deed. Both had offered the refugee peoples who lived in the Northern Susquehanna River Valley similar assurances in the past, and those assurances ultimately resulted in dispossession and displacement. For the Susquehanna Nations, peace at Easton solved little and they were again, at least according to Haudenosaunee and British officials, a subjugated people. It was, in the end, independence lost but not exactly forgotten.

4

Hearts and Mouths

AN UNEASY PEACE, 1758–1763

ALTHOUGH TEEDYUSCUNG HAD SOME very real reservations about the sincerity of the British and the Haudenosaunee at Easton, he took seriously the meetings and the agreements made there. Working hard to demonstrate his dedication to his renewed friendship with the British, Teedyuscung helped spread the message of peace west to the Ohio Valley. Using his sons Captain Bull and Captain Amos as representatives, he "gave the Halloo and published" what "passed between us to all the Indian Nations in this Part of the World, even the most distant have heard me." It worked. By early spring 1758, representatives of the Ohio Nations sent Teedyuscung a peace belt and an ancient calumet (a ceremonial pipe) to help him initiate talks with the British to broker a lasting peace.[1]

Using that authority to his advantage, Teedyuscung, whose name some started translating as "The Healer," traveled to Philadelphia to demonstrate his significance *and* further his quest for the security and independence of his people. Once in the city and in front of the governor, Teedyuscung proclaimed his "Great Work" accomplished. He brought "Eighteen Nations," representing people from "Sun Rising and the Sun Sett," together "as One," ready to end the war. He also went to Philadelphia to "put" the governor "in mind of what passed at Easton." From Teedyuscung's perspective, he had helped break French alliances in the Ohio Valley, and now the governor needed to "press on with all" his "might" to continue "what you have begun." For Teedyuscung, Easton was only a setback.[2]

Pennsylvania's governor, William Denny, who replaced Robert Morris after the first Easton conference, had little choice but to acknowledge

Teedyuscung's significance in this moment. The standard policy of mediating diplomatic matters through the Haudenosaunee had been shattered by the war. Despite what happened at the last Easton conference, both the Susquehanna and Ohio Nations still had vocal leaders who were "determined not to be ruled any longer by" the Six Nations "as Women." When Teedyuscung offered peace on behalf of "Eighteen Nations," then, Denny, facing public pressure to end the war, had few choices but to declare that this "news" gave him "the greatest Pleasure," proving that Teedyuscung was a "faithful Agent and Friend of Pennsylvania." The governor would not, he assured, forget that friendship. If "you continue to do your part," he told Teedyuscung, "nothing shall be wanting on mine."[3]

Despite the goodwill demonstrated and proclaimed, it did not take long for Teedyuscung and the Susquehanna Nations he represented to question the honesty as well as the memory of colonial officials. Just three years after his meeting with Governor Denny, Teedyuscung complained that although he had "been constantly employed in promoting the good work of Peace," it did not seem that everyone acted in kind. "Somethings," he warned, "look darkish." Ultimately, that darkness ended his life.[4] By the spring of 1763, Teedyuscung was dead, assassinated by land-hungry colonists looking to settle Wyoming, ushering in a new war for independence that shaped the Northern Susquehanna River Valley and much of early America for years to come.

That momentous "darkish" cloud Teedyuscung envisioned materialized almost instantly after the last Easton meetings. At nearly the same time Teedyuscung, his sons, and other British messengers and negotiators were spreading the news of peace, guaranteeing to anyone who would listen that "all Nations of Indians shou'd enjoy a Free Trade with their Brethren the English, and be protected in the Peaceable Possession of their Hunting Country," General Jefferey Amherst, the British commander-in-chief in North America, acted contrary to what was offered.[5] Unwilling to fathom Native sovereignty and worried about a dwindling treasury because of a long global war, he doled out parcels of Indigenous land to loyal officers and cut expenses by circumscribing gift giving and access to trade goods, particularly arms, ammunition, and gunpowder.[6]

Deeply steeped in the prejudices of the time, Amherst saw Native peoples as nothing more than "lazy rum drinking scoundrels" who should have access to "a little" powder and shot, but "the less" they can get "the better, for so long as they are deprived of it, they will do no mischief, for they cannot now get ammunition elsewhere." He wanted Native Americans dependent, which, he thought, would make them acquiescent. Amherst also contemplated lacing what little gifts the British gave to Native Americans with smallpox "to extirpate this execrable race," which a few British officers actually tried.[7]

Unsurprisingly, especially for Amherst's subordinates and colonial officials long versed in Indigenous diplomacy and trade, Native Americans complained that "traders are not suffered to go amongst them, Powder and Lead is prohibited being sold to them, and the General is giving away their Country to be Settled." Such "steps they say appears to them as if the English had a mind to Cut them off the face of the Earth."[8] The situation and experiences of Native peoples in the Northern Susquehanna River Valley made such fears palpable and the need for independence ever more desirable, if not necessary.

One of the most visible manifestations of Native American fears between 1758 and 1763 was Pennsylvania's Fort Augusta, erected at the Forks of the Susquehanna River near the important multiethnic town of Shamokin. Within just a few years of its construction, Native Americans, whether in the Ohio Valley; along the West, East, and North Branches of the Susquehanna River; or even in Onondaga increasingly pointed to "Fort Augusta as the greatest Eye sore to all the Indians."[9]

It had not always been that way. In fact, Haudenosaunee representatives from Ohio heartily approved the construction of the fort during the early years of the Seven Years' War. Kaghswaghtaniunt, also known as Belt of Wampum or Old Belt, a Mingo chief living on the upper Ohio River, advised Pennsylvania officials in early 1756 "to build a Fort at Shamokin" as a place for "such Indians as continue true to you . . . to come to, and to live in Security against your and their Enemies." He asserted such a fort would "strengthen your Interest very much." "Indeed, you lose Ground every day till this be done. Pray hasten the work." Similarly, Scarouady, the Oneida leader, called the intended fort "not a thing of little Consequence," as "it is

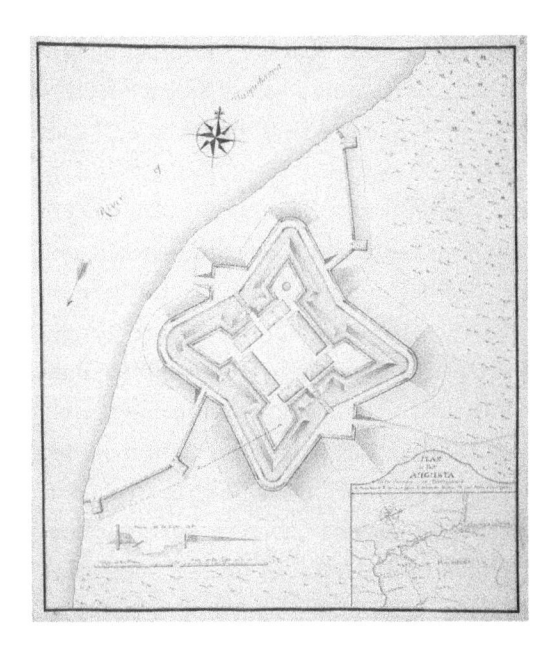

FIGURE 6. "Plan of Fort Augusta in the Province of Pansilvania," ca. 1760. (British Library Maps K.Top. 122.10)

of the greatest Importance to us as well as you."[10] Kaghswaghtaniunt and Scarouady also saw the fort as a potential place for trade and economic security for the various people who lived and hunted in the Northern Susquehanna River Valley. Heeding that advice, Pennsylvania's governor pushed the construction of the fort as a measure that would be a "means of securing the Sasquahana Indians to our Interest."[11]

Constructing a fort at Shamokin was not only about achieving harmony. It was, after all, a military installation at an important juncture. Situated at the forks of the Susquehanna River, the fort would command most traffic north and south. The central and well-trodden paths up and down the river would flow through and by the fort. As such, "the Susquehanna Indians" would be "obliged first to come" there "when they arrive on Our Frontiers," giving the settlements downriver protection. In effect, Fort Augusta could function as a gateway to police the activities of the Susquehanna Nations.[12]

Such a gateway with a police force was not what Kaghswaghtaniunt or Scarouady wanted or imagined. Nor was it what the Susquehanna Nations wanted as they had not been consulted. According to Governor Morris, who oversaw the initial planning of the fort, as soon as his men began constructing the fort he received "intelligence" that "ye Susquehannah Indians are much alarm'd at our Scheme of building a Fort at Shamokin & are jealous yt we intend to secure ye possession of *their* unpurchased Lands there."[13]

The Susquehanna Nations had good reason to be suspicious. For most of the eighteenth century they had been consistently belittled, ignored, and displaced, and now Pennsylvania had begun construction of a fortification on their land that by 1758 would become the largest provincial fort in Pennsylvania, even larger than Fort Duquesne (later the site of Fort Pitt). Built of upright logs facing the river with a surrounding moat and an outer stockade, Fort Augusta boasted four triangular bastions and sixteen mounted cannon that could produce a crossfire to cover any angle of entry. Inside, there was a forge, well, magazine, and quarters to house at least four hundred men. There was also a covered access to the river for easy supply and reinforcement.[14]

It was, to say the least, a formidable military structure made to overawe anyone who crossed its path, and to many Native Americans who lived near it, a constant annoyance that was ever expanding. As with most forts, colonial settlements materialized around it. While the war continued to keep squatters at bay, the fort itself invited their migration to the area it commanded. It was not long before the fort occupied nearly four thousand acres, much of it protected farmland producing wheat, corn, and a number of vegetables cultivated in a large garden (turnips alone took up ten acres) to provide for the troops and the growing "inhabitants" in the fort's orbit.[15]

Despite Indigenous misgivings, the fort quickly became a hub for trade, drawing numerous Native peoples seeking essential goods. Joseph Shippen, a prominent figure in Lancaster County and a newly promoted captain, meticulously recorded Native peoples' comings and goings at the fort. In January 1758, Shippen noted nearly one hundred arrivals, with fifty more in the following week. Some stayed, setting up temporary camps nearby. By February 13, faced with an overwhelming number of people, Shippen dispatched "a Party of 40 or 50" of his own men downstream to Fort Hunter. This action aimed to reduce "the number of Mouths here," as their existing food supply of "9,428 pds Flour" was barely "sufficient for the Garrison

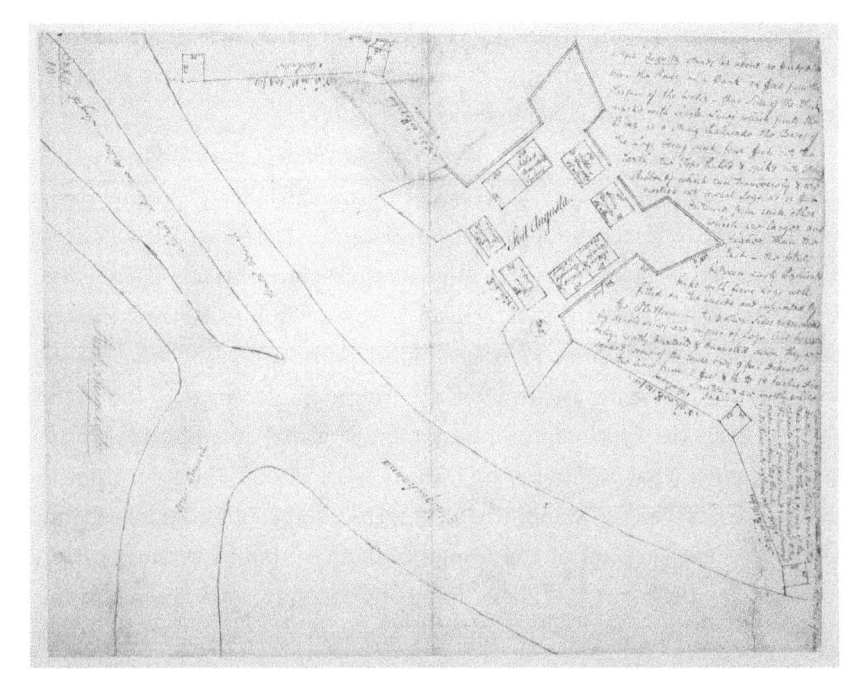

FIGURE 7. "A Drawn Plan of Fort Augusta in the Susquehanna Riv.," ca. 1756. (British Library Maps K.Top. 122.10)

and Indians (of whom we have now 52 prest)," estimating it would last only twenty-seven days.[16]

To his dismay, within the next few days nearly a dozen Delaware from the North Branch of the Susquehanna River came to the fort "to speak with me," and half a dozen more from the West Branch came to trade, which only added to the supply problem. "We have now 62 Indians" staying "here including Women & Children," Shippen wrote in his journal on February 15. At the same time, he dispatched an urgent letter to his commander and in-law, James Burd, that he now had "but 6,916 [pounds of] Flour." The limited provisions displeased Shippen so much that he requisitioned some battues sent for Native American trade goods to bring his soldiers' provisions instead. He would not "suffer any thing belonging to the Storekeepers or Suttlers to be brought up" until he had his supplies, which was sure to alienate

Native hunters making their way to the fort for the trade guaranteed at Easton. Needless to say, after Easton, Fort Augusta and the area it served teemed with "Business of Importance."[17]

It is not hard to imagine why. Within a few years of Fort Augusta's construction, according to several colonial officers in the fort, it seemed as if more and more Native peoples were making the Northern Susquehanna River Valley their home and Fort Augusta their place of trade. On July 20, 1761, one officer noted the arrival of "a small Tribe of strange Indians called Sappony's." That same officer reported the arrival of more Nanticoke, Conoy, Tuscarora, and other southern groups joining their kin in the valley.[18] Even the Philadelphia newspapers churned out reports informing the public "that a Number of Indians were at that Place, in order to trade with our People." Soon, it was reported, Indigenous "families from Allegheny" and "several of the Mingo Indians" would be settling within the vicinity of the fort.[19] William Johnson, trying to get a handle on the extent of settlements and the military strength of Native Americans in the Northern Susquehanna River Valley and elsewhere, compiled a rudimentary census documenting at least two hundred Nanticoke, Conoy, Tutelo, and Saponi warriors; the same number of Delaware; and over three hundred Cayuga, Oneida, and Tuscarora warriors in the Northern Susquehanna River Valley.[20]

Beyond their "Fighting Number," Johnson gave little account of the actual population of Native peoples living in the river valley, and that undercounting could be significant. Scholars have estimated that every one hundred warriors meant a population of roughly one thousand people, meaning, according to Johnson's rudimentary accounting, at least seven thousand people could have called the area their home or at least a temporary refuge. Even that number does not quite get at the population there because Johnson did not account for the seasonal "huntg Cabins" along and between the river's eastern, northern, and western branches. Those hunting settlements could add a significant number of people to the valley. Hunting was a community effort requiring large and small seasonal settlements that housed clan and kinship groups together—men, women, and children—from October to May, half of any given year.[21]

Needless to say, Native peoples in the Northern Susquehanna River Valley were numerous enough that both imperial and colonial authorities worried about them. Officers at Fort Augusta constantly fretted over "Indian tracks" found outside the fort and "whether the Indians [coming to the fort] were Friends or Enemies." For the young Captain Shippen, a lot went into such a determination. In his journal, he often justified his opinion of individual Native Americans by documenting a host of attributes, especially their ability to speak English and their willingness to share with him the strength and loyalty of local Native peoples. Obviously, Shippen reserved such a "good Opinion" to a select few. But that was the point of the fort. It was made to police people, gather intelligence, and protect the colony, not just facilitate trade and harmony.[22]

Shippen, fearful of his situation among so many Native Americans he did not trust, regardless of the peace established at Easton, tried to demonstrate to his Native visitors the true purpose of the fort. When Native Americans visiting the fort grew too numerous for his liking, he "ordered a false alarm to be created" and was heartened that his men turned out and took their posts "with the greatest alacrity and good Order." That was a general pattern. Shippen's commanding officer also ordered such displays in the hope they would prove to the growing Susquehanna Nations that "I am Prepar'd for War, I and my people are Warriors we live by fighting."[23] Meanwhile, the fortification's officers kept a watchful eye on the Native peoples and their habits. If any Indigenous person traded peltry for powder and shot, these officers could not help but document it and think it "a little suspicious."[24]

Despite all of the traffic, Native Americans also eyed the fort and the colonists around it with misgiving. Native peoples were eager to trade, but they questioned the purpose of the fort's existence after the peace at Easton. In February 1760, for example, Commander Burd sent a note to "all the Chiefs of the [Susquehanna] Indians that I had a message to deliver them," and "desired" they would meet at "my house" inside the fort. The next day, Burd "received a message from the Indians that they would not come into the Fort to my House least I should cut them all off." Burd had to resort to meeting the delegation outside the fort's walls at an "Indian store" operated by a Quaker attached to the Friendly Association.[25] Regardless of where Burd and the representatives of the Susquehanna Nations met, it was clear that the fort itself was a source of fear for the various peoples who lived, hunted, and traded in the valley.

Native American suspicion was compounded by an inadequate trade at the fort and the attitude of the colonial traders and military officers toward the Native peoples who ventured to the fort. Official trade was limited, and illegal traders operating outside the fort's walls ran rampant. The various illegal traders could raise prices and lower the value of skins at will. They also preferred to deal in liquor, a constant source of contention that created far more animosity than otherwise. Moreover, General Amherst's directives to limit access to powder and shot with official traders only served to drive up prices in the illegal trade. It wasn't just the price of ammunition that skyrocketed. The combination of demand, official trade restrictions, provincial fears of another war, and the attendant limitations on supply drove up the prices of all goods while at the same time lowering the value of skins and furs.[26]

The provincial commissioners, Friendly Association, and military officers in charge of overseeing trade at Fort Augusta tried to counteract these ill effects, but they could do little more than complain of their inability to do "any thing Effectually towards suppressing the illegal Traders at or near this place." Officials attempted to regulate the sale of liquor and rates of exchange, for example, but all to no avail. As James Irvine, the official store clerk, complained, he could not do anything as "Indian Evidence will not Convict them." The racial bias inherent in the legal system barred effectual action.[27] What was supposed to be a place for trade that could provide a semblance of independence and protection for the multiethnic people living in the Northern Susquehanna River Valley was quickly becoming a monument to their dependence.

In response, some Native peoples trying to trade either went away angry or threatened the traders with violence. It seemed, Native peoples protested, as if the traders were "depriving them of the Means of Subsisting."[28] Even Native Americans who wanted to "hold fast the same Friendship" established at Easton, which, they thought, put them on an equal footing with their British neighbors, took "it hard they should be denied Powder at this Place, that without it they are Poor and cannot support themselves."[29] One man was so upset that he became "very abusive, offering several times to strike" a trader "for not buying a wet Skin, Boasting at the same time of what he had done during the War & Could yet do." The Easton treaty may have brokered a peace, but its solution in the Northern Susquehanna River Valley, Fort Augusta, did not live up to expectations, and boasting became a prevalent feature of interaction on the northern frontier, with both Native peoples and British colonists mustering threats to intimidate each other.[30]

Official reaction to Native American boasting further alienated the Indigenous peoples making their way to the fort. After the young Indigenous man threatened to assault a trader for not buying his skins, a fort officer, fearing "mischief," overreacted and sent out a body of troops who "tied him & carried him into the Fort," which only brought the prisoner's family into the fray. "Much enraged," the enchained man's mother asked "what right the White People had to tie her Son."[31] She and her son, after all, were an independent people. Besides, she argued, one of the illegal traders got her son drunk to steal his peltry. To make matters worse, officers in the fort soon took the extreme position of outlawing "any Dealings with Indians on any pretense whatever," and even demanded Native Americans "not to Hunt nigh this Place," further disaffecting the numerous Native peoples living in the area.[32]

In sum, high prices, limited supplies, and colonial attitudes created severe tensions within and outside the fort's walls. In this scenario, even the trader associated with the Friendly Association, Nathaniel Holland, became suspect in the eyes of many Native peoples. James Burd noted in his diary that "an Indian attempted to kill" Holland, complaining of high prices.[33] Seneca, Cayuga, and Delaware chiefs and warriors similarly complained that Holland "provoked" them so "often" with his "ill usage and bad language" that they wanted "to do him Violence."[34]

By 1762, even the Six Nations detested Fort Augusta, especially because it threatened an uneasy peace in the valley. The Seven Years' War had exacerbated the tenuousness of Haudenosaunee authority over the Susquehanna Nations, and although the Easton treaty had reasserted Haudenosaunee power, the Susquehanna Nations' quest for independence had no prospect of ending if Onondaga did not at least use its proclaimed authority to represent those nations' interests. Removing the "eye sore" that was Fort Augusta and establishing a fair and equal trade were two items they had to address. Fort Augusta also represented very real threats to Haudenosaunee land far closer to home, which had rapidly been shrinking and more and more coming under threat. They too were now "penned up like Hoggs. There are Forts all around us, and therefore we are apprehensive that Death is coming upon us."[35]

In all, there was a general softening of the relationship between the Haudenosaunee and the Susquehanna Nations. Onondaga's representatives even began treating Teedyuscung with some respect. Perhaps they saw in him their future. As one important Haudenosaunee leader put it, it seemed as if the British would "serve me as you have done our cousins, the Delawares; you have got all their Land from them; all the Land hereabouts belonged to them once, and you have got it all." It was a terrifying reality given the present circumstances.[36]

At a treaty in August 1762 at Lancaster the Haudenosaunee sought to derail that future by demanding the evacuation of Fort Augusta. Thomas King, an Oneida chief from Oquaga on the North Branch of the Susquehanna River and an important Haudenosaunee overseer in both the Northern Susquehanna River Valley and the Ohio region, flatly told the governor, the now aged but experienced James Hamilton, the same James Hamilton who oversaw negotiations way back in the summer of 1749, "We the Six Nations have all consulted, and concluded" that "you will call your Soldiers away from Shamokin, for we have concluded a Peace." "For you to keep Soldiers there," he warned, "is not the way to live peaceable" because "your Soldiers are very often unruly." With the peace negotiated at Easton established, "there is no occasion for Soldiers to live there any longer."[37]

It was not just the soldiers that irritated King and the people he tried to represent. Fort Augusta and the settlements around it, he argued, undermined the initial agreement Hamilton's predecessors had made with the Haudenosaunee for the fort's construction. When "you [meaning the previous governors representing Pennsylvania] asked me [meaning all the Haudenosaunee] whether I was willing you should build a Fort at Shamokin," King stated, "you told me that you did not desire any greater quantity of my Land than what the Fort took up," and that when the war was concluded "you would go away." But since that time "you have planted Corn there." Not only had squatter settlements sprung up around the fort, but in 1760 some of the fort's officers, many of whom were members of leading families who got rich by speculating in land, surveyed "a Tract of Land . . . on the West Branch of Susquehanna above Shamokin," which caused "uneasiness to the Indians." It seemed as if the colonial government was trying "to take this Land by Force."[38]

If that was not reason enough to disparage the mere existence of the fort, King also argued that it did not meet their expectations for trade: "Our Hunters who have been down there, complain that when Indians come there and want provisions and Goods, they find the Store sometimes shut up, and they cannot be supplied with what they want." Even when the store was open, the supplies were limited and prices too high. Maybe, as colonial officials constantly argued, "the War has occasioned a rise in the price of Goods," but if that were the case, representatives of the Seneca and Cayuga argued, they should "be paid a higher price for their Skins and Furs in proportion"—a fair request.[39]

King did not want the fort completely abandoned; rather, he wanted the soldiers removed and the fort repurposed as a trading post. When "you take away your Soldiers, we desire you would keep your Trading House there" as well as a blacksmith and gunsmith to mend their "Guns & Hatchets, or do anything they may want." The current storekeepers and traders, though, had to go, and "honest Men placed in their Room." They particularly wanted Holland gone and "a more quiet man [put] in his place." Once established, this fort cum trading post would be the only one the Haudenosaunee would countenance in the region. "We desire you may have no trading Houses higher up the Susquehanna than Shamokin," King concluded.[40]

King and all the other Haudenosaunee speakers at Lancaster made it perfectly clear that they did not want any kind of colonial settlement, even trade posts, anywhere near the Northern Susquehanna River Valley besides Shamokin, especially along the West Branch. That branch was quickly becoming the last free bastion in the long history of the valley to that point, and it was seriously under threat. Nevertheless, despite the clear statements and fears articulated by King, other Haudenosaunee delegates, and members of the Susquehanna Nations, Hamilton ignored them and repeatedly asked to "let us go with our Canoes up the West Branch of Susquehannah as far as we can, & build a few Store Houses on the Banks of that river" to lower carrying costs and therefore prices. Hamilton had been trying to purchase that land for the proprietors since 1749 and knew all too well that these trading posts would give him a foothold in the region and could lead to a future sale.[41]

Thomas King answered the governor's repeated request with a resounding no. Wary, King spied in Hamilton's repeated proposal a pretext to take away their country. "You are always longing after my Land," King reprimanded Hamilton. He wanted it to stop. "You keep pressing me," and soon "you will push me out; for I shall have no place to live on nor hunt in, neither for me nor my Grandchildren; so I desire you will press no further." He did not want to experience the same reality "as our cousins, the Delawares." Hamilton, again ignoring him, kept asking, so much so that Kinderuntie, the "Head Warrior of the Seneca Nation, suddenly rose up" and chastised Hamilton. When "You" built Fort Augusta, "you told me you wanted none of our Lands," and "you promised to go away as soon as you drove the French away, yet you stay there & build Houses, and make it stronger and stronger every day, for this reason we entirely deny your request." King and Kinderuntie had good reason to be angry. Fort Augusta and Hamilton's repeated requests to build trading posts along the West Branch were only part of the problem they faced. As Pennsylvanians moved their way up the Susquehanna River, occupying settlements around the fort, Connecticut settlers were pushing west, threatening Wyoming and the land all along the West Branch.[42]

Connecticut land companies, tacitly backed by Connecticut's governor and legislature, asserted their right to most of modern-day northern Pennsylvania based on Connecticut's 1662 charter from Charles II granting that colony land all the way to the "Southern Sea." Seventeenth-century royal charters were often lax about geography, especially since many of the imperial officials who edited and approved those charters had only a rudimentary understanding of where one colony's land ended and another began. Even the maps they had available were unreliable. Pennsylvania's charter, granted twenty years after Connecticut's, is a case in point. Not only did those two charters clash, but the land the crown designated as

Pennsylvania also overlapped with what the crown had previously granted to New York, Maryland, and Virginia.[43]

Royal charters were only part of the equation when it came to the potential jurisdiction of any given colony. More often than not, charters precipitated a mad scramble to purchase the Indigenous lands those charters royally conveyed. Connecticut's land companies, notably the Susquehannah Company, leveraged Connecticut's charter to facilitate John Lydius's controversial land acquisition in the Northern Susquehanna River Valley from the Haudenosaunee in 1754. This move aimed to undermine Pennsylvania's land purchase at Albany, which similarly relied on charter rights.[44] Obtaining the land, therefore, would be decided on the ground, initiating another race between the two colonies to settle and secure their claims. Such an overarching description of this jurisdictional dispute does not capture the human component of it all that upended the lives of the Native peoples who actually lived there and the colonial settlers who took part in the game.

The effects, however, were not immediate after Lydius's purchase. The Seven Years' War stalled both Pennsylvania's and Connecticut's efforts to physically claim that land, but after peace had been established with the Susquehanna Nations at Easton, Connecticut land companies and their settlers began to stir. In September 1760, about forty Connecticut colonists settled at Cushietunk just west of the Delaware River near the Minisink with one hundred more settlers expected that spring. Less than two years later, in 1762, Connecticut settlers with 119 armed men as their guard began constructing a wagon road from Cushietunk over the mountains to Wyoming, which they completed in the middle of September while many of the local Susquehanna Nations, including Teedyuscung, were attending the conference at Lancaster. Just a month later over 150 settlers erected a settlement and sawmill about a mile north of Teedyuscung's village, and then some of those same settlers stole his horse. The Susquehanna Nations were again, as they complained earlier, treated like "dogs."[45]

Teedyuscung and the Susquehanna Nations detested this encroachment. For Teedyuscung, it must have felt like 1742 and 1749 all over again. Irritated, he amassed 150 warriors, threatening both the Connecticut settlers and Pennsylvania's governor that if something were not done, he and his people would "do themselves Justice," which might provoke another war.

Trying to stave off violence and another war that could reinvigorate the Susquehanna Nations' efforts to achieve independence, the Haudenosaunee also got involved. Haudenosaunee viceroy Thomas King, along with Robert White, a Nanticoke chief living on the West Branch, made their way to the Connecticut settlements "to warn them off."[46]

It had little effect. Despite the constant warnings that Connecticut's encroachment would "certainly bring on another Indian war," the Susquehannah Company ordered the "speedy beginning a Settlement of our Susquehannah purchase," and the settlers were determined to follow that directive. As the leaders of the Connecticut settlers told King and White, the settlers had rights to "the Wyomink Land, and if the Indians who lived there should hinder their Settlement they would fight it out with them, and the strongest should hold the Land." To make matters worse, rumors swirled through Indigenous communities that at least four thousand Connecticut settlers would descend on Wyoming and the West Branch within the year.[47]

In the face of Connecticut settlers pouring into the Northern Susquehanna River Valley, some of the Native inhabitants fled, and Teedyuscung, failing to receive a deed for the Susquehanna Nations and believing the Haudenosaunee had sold "those Lands" out from under him yet again, seriously contemplated moving to the Ohio region. In fact, the Ohio Nations had invited him to do so. Tamaqua, more popularly known as King Beaver, sent Teedyuscung a belt of wampum signifying their friendship and "desired that I and the Delawares, the Wapings [Wappinger] & Mohickons settled at Wyomink, would remove thence, and come and live at Allegheny." Alarmed, both the Six Nations and the Pennsylvania government scrambled, pleading with Teedyuscung to stay. They would, Governor Hamilton whined, be "very sorry if you remove from Wyoming." Teedyuscung and his people were the frontline of defense protecting the Northern Susquehanna River Valley from Connecticut settlers' westward march, and both the Six Nations and the Pennsylvania government knew it.[48]

To keep Teedyuscung in Wyoming, Thomas King, speaking on behalf of the Haudenosaunee, made a council "Fire for Teedyuscung at Wyoming." He wanted Teedyuscung "to sit there by the Fire side, and watch that Fire" because "our English Brethren cast an Eye upon that Land." If "any White people come there," he asked Teedyuscung to "tell them to go away for that Land belongs to your Uncles, the Six Nations." Official council fires were important spaces for the Haudenosaunee. They were powerful extensions of the council fire at Onondaga, and so very few existed. While creating a new council fire was a far cry from recognizing the independence of Teedyuscung and the Susquehanna Nations, it nonetheless represented that they were a people of some significance within the diplomatic hierarchy of the Six Nations. Hamilton too furthered the Susquehanna Nations' legitimacy as a significant people, making promises to Teedyuscung, assuring him that Pennsylvania would help protect Wyoming from Connecticut. Suddenly, Teedyuscung was again what the Haudenosaunee and the Pennsylvania government never really wanted him to be in the past, "a great man."[49] But, in the end, they needed him.

Teedyuscung agreed to stay. He had well-built homes in Wyoming, access to trade, and a steady supply of alcohol, something Pennsylvania traders continued to provide. Apparently, Teedyuscung could drink gallons of rum a day and remain sober, or so he boasted and others observed. But that was not all. He and his people were finally treated with respect. Without him and them, both the Six Nations and the Pennsylvanians could lose the Wyoming Valley to interlopers from Connecticut. He was the person who held the Susquehanna Nations together, and to keep him happy he was fêted as a king, provided with a near constant stream of presents, alcohol, and companions, so much so that his wife, a Christian Mohawk named Elizabeth, sought separation, which she had requested since at least 1756 for his "debauched way of living." She was especially upset that he had "took all the children but one from her" and tried to mold them in his image.[50]

Nothing, however, seemed to deter Connecticut's Susquehannah Company or its settlers. Not only did Teedyuscung and the Susquehanna Nations forewarn violence, but Hamilton issued proclamations threatening prosecution; General Jeffery Amherst wrote to Connecticut's governor, Thomas Fitch, to put a stop to settler encroachment; and even the crown's ministers got involved. In late March 1763, Britain's superintendent of Indian affairs, William Johnson, and some visiting Mohawk at Johnson Hall in upstate New York also entered into the fray, attempting to reason with Susquehannah Company officials.[51]

In March 1763, Colonel Eliphalet Dyer and Reverend Timothy Woodbridge, representatives of the Connecticut land company, traveled to Johnson's home seeking his and the Six Nations' support for their claims. With several Mohawk leaders in attendance, Johnson forthrightly explained the sheer scale of official resistance to the Susquehannah Company's designs and that its actions would start another general war. The visiting Mohawk were not so diplomatic. Visibly angry, they declared that the Haudenosaunee would "not part with the Lands in Question (thro' which is their great War path & where they have very good hunting)." If the Connecticut settlers persisted, they warned, it "would certainly occasion the whole 6 Nations & their Confederates to commence hostilities."[52]

None of that mattered. Unfazed, Dyer and Woodbridge "replyed that as the Company had the House of Representatives permission & right given them by virtue of the Claim of Connecticut to the Westward," as well as Lydius's "Deed [from the Haudenosaunee at Albany] & Expended much money thereon," they would "persist in their undertaking & shortly settle there [Wyoming] to a Considerable number, sufficient to maintain themselves in the possession thereof." Dyer and Woodbridge left the meeting in a huff, but they also made good on their militant promise.[53]

Less than a month after Dyer and Woodbridge's meeting with Johnson and the Mohawk, Teedyuscung, the now sixty-three-year old "great man" made "King by Ten Nations," was dead. On April 19, 1763, unknown assailants, most likely Connecticut settlers (though they later denied it), set fire to the outside of Teedyuscung's house built for him by Pennsylvanians as he lay asleep next to the council fire granted by the Haudenosaunee. Similar fires erupted across the village and by morning there were few buildings left. The loss of Teedyuscung was a heavy blow to the Susquehanna Nations. In many ways, he held that loose confederation of peoples and nations together, elevated their status in the eyes of both Onondaga and Pennsylvania, and was close to obtaining the independence he and his people so ardently sought.[54]

Despite his significance, there is no existing record of a condolence ceremony, not even a bead of wampum being exchanged on his behalf. It is unclear if or where he was even buried. British and colonial officials certainly did not comment. The historical record is quite literally silent when it comes to Teedyuscung's death. Some of those officials probably even welcomed it. He had been, for most of his later adult life, a thorn in their sides. William Johnson, the governor of Pennsylvania, nor even the members of the Quakers' Friendly Association documented anything about his death other than it occurred, and then only in passing as "the late Teedyuscung."[55]

But that silence did not reflect the indifference of his people; rather, it reflected that they did not have the time to mourn. Their home had been destroyed and Connecticut settlers were on the march. Within two weeks of Teedyuscung's death, nearly a dozen Connecticut families had settled Wyoming. By the end of April, 150 settlers arrived with cattle and the materials to construct cabins, mills, and blockhouses near the smoldering ashes of a once vibrant Susquehanna Nation town situated to stop the invasion of the Northern Susquehanna River Valley. As a result, the Susquehanna Nations living in Wyoming fled, many of them to towns in and around Great Island on the West Branch of the Susquehanna River, nearly one hundred miles west.[56]

While Teedyuscung may have been dead, the impact of his long history of dispossession, displacement, and struggle for independence lived on, especially through his sons. Still, as they would soon find, that was a hard row to hoe without their father's leadership. For all of his faults, and there were many, Teedyuscung knew how and when to strategically use threats, violence, and diplomacy for the security of his people, and now he was gone.[57]

After the assassination of Teedyuscung and the destruction of Wyoming, Native communities in the Northern Susquehanna River Valley divided over next steps. It seems the final Easton Treaty, coupled with Teedyuscung's death and the migration of new peoples to the valley, seriously tested much of what was left of the Susquehanna Council, though the Susquehanna Nations tried to maintain it. Some, such as Teedyuscung's son Captain Bull and Teedyuscung's son-in-law Mekawawlechon, who fled Wyoming for Great Island, demanded revenge against the Connecticut settlers. Others, such as Teedyuscung's old councilor Tepascowan and his uncle Nutimus, the aging Delaware chief and now nominal head of the Susquehanna Nations who also fled to Great Island, sought peaceful remedies. Considering Nutimus's experiences with violence and dispossession, he was a study in patience. He still thought the Easton agreements mattered and that he and his people had an ally in Pennsylvania and its proprietors. Therefore, Nutimus urged peace, hoping Pennsylvania's colonial government would act against these daring disturbers from New England.[58]

Nutimus's peaceful position won out. On June 2, Governor Hamilton, responding to "fresh Complaints from the Indians at Wyoming," particularly those of Captain Bull, issued another proclamation "requiring those Intruders" from Connecticut "forthwith to remove from the said Lands." He also commissioned James Burd and Thomas McKee, a seasoned frontier agent and trader, as justices of the peace and ordered them to go to Wyoming, read the proclamation, and persuade the Connecticut settlers to leave using "Expostulations & Arguments" but not violence.[59]

Initially, Hamilton's actions calmed tensions in the Northern Susquehanna River Valley. A few weeks after the proclamation, Job Chillaway, a Delaware interpreter from Wyalusing, a town just north of Wyoming, and Telenimut, a representative of the Six Nations "living a little way up the West Branch," went to Fort Augusta and expressed their approval of the proclamation and the governor's orders to Burd and McKee. They also let Burd know that Nutimus and the Susquehanna Nations along the West Branch felt "the same." Chillaway and Telenimut even promised Burd that they would let him know if these peaceful sentiments changed. "If anything happens" they told Burd, "we will let you know as two Brothers ought to do."[60]

To prove the goodwill of the Susquehanna Nations, representatives of the Susquehanna Council now living along the West Branch traveled to Fort Augusta a few days later. It was a veritable who's who of leaders. Representing the Delaware, Nutimus, Tepascowan, Teedyuscung's son Captain Bull, and his son-in-law Mekawawlechon attended along with Coshaughaways, representing the Munsee; Neguttewesta, the Shawnee; John Orby, the Nanticoke; and "Sam," the Conoy, with about "20 more Indians" most likely speaking for nations or factions that Pennsylvania officials found too insignificant or hostile to fully write down. As Chillaway and Telenimut related, these leaders came to Fort Augusta to express their continued friendship with Pennsylvania.[61]

Despite the professed mission of their meeting, Commander Burd still worried about the Susquehanna Nations' "sentiments." He even went so far as to order "all the Garrison under arms at their Posts, during" the meeting. For those leaders of the Susquehanna Nations on the fence, like Captain Bull and Mekawawlechon, it must have been difficult to listen to Burd and Nutimus's professions of peace under the watchful eye of armed colonial soldiers positioned on the walls and bastions of a controversial fort.[62]

For his part, Burd did have some reason to be fearful. Earlier that same month, "Indian Runners" from "the Westward" made their way to the Great Island carrying "English Scalps" and news of another war "with the English" erupting in the Illinois Country and Ohio River Valley. Ottawa war chief Pontiac was laying siege to Fort Detroit (some rumors suggested Pontiac had taken the fort), while Forts Miami, Michilimackinac, Venango, Le Boeuf, and Presque Isle fell to a combination of Delaware, Shawnee, Miami, Ojibwa, Wyandot, and Seneca warriors who challenged the peaceful stance of Onondaga. Native Americans in the Ohio Valley were also threatening Fort Pitt, and Shamokin Daniel, a former Moravian convert who moved back and forth between the Ohio and Northern Susquehanna River Valleys, was preparing to raid the Juniata Valley.[63] A new war for independence was in the offing.

This new war erupted because of the Seven Years' War, especially the fallout in Native communities after they learned about the terms the French had agreed to for peace in 1763. The formal peace agreement between the British and the French that ended the war in North America, the Treaty of Paris, seriously undermined the peace established with both the Susquehanna and Ohio Nations at Easton and Lancaster. Neither the French nor the British took into consideration their Native American allies when hammering out terms. Instead, through that agreement, the British gained French possessions in Canada as well as most of France's territory east of the Mississippi River, including the much sought-after Ohio region.[64]

Native peoples everywhere were obviously "under great Concern at ye Advantage ye English has Gain'd by the peace." They wanted to know how and "by what right" the "French had given up their Country." They were, after all, sovereign nations, which the treaties at Easton and Lancaster basically recognized. British-employed interpreters, middlemen, go-betweens, and officials up and down North America could not readily answer their questions in any satisfactory way. George Croghan, who had risen through the ranks to deputy superintendent of Indian affairs under William Johnson and was an avid land speculator himself, haphazardly told representatives of the Ohio Nations that the British would settle "only such parts of America as had been in Possession of the French & conquered by us during the War." That statement discounted the lands of Britain's Native allies within the territory the French claimed, and was so general in relation to Indigenous land that his statement only "seem'd to increase their Jealousy."[65] Jealousy was a bit of an understatement. Angst, anger, and even rage are far better nouns to represent Native American feelings. More important still, the Treaty of Paris, rather than instantly disrupting a peaceful coexistence, only confirmed for many Native peoples that previous treaties with the British were a sham.

Back in the Northern Susquehanna River Valley, Commander Burd and the officers at Fort Augusta were "much Alarm'd for the safety of the Garrison" when the Susquehanna Nations visited in June. This feeling was buttressed by the fact that colonists were daily "flying to the Interior parts of the province with the utmost precipitation." It was, some thought, "more easy to imagine than describe the distress of the back Inhabitants." Really, the fears that permeated Fort Augusta were unfounded. The Susquehanna Nations had "not yet Committed any Hostilities," and moreover had come to the fort to proclaim their peaceful intentions. Despite these facts, many colonists as well as some officials could not shake their belief that all Native Americans, including the Susquehanna Nations, were somehow involved. That imagination, if allowed to shape men and measures unchecked by facts, could and would result in what white colonists feared most, "a general war with the Indians."[66]

Facts, sadly, meant little. Although the Susquehanna Nations professed peace during their meeting at Fort Augusta in June, Burd and the other officers refused to believe them. Instead, they barraged the nations' representatives with queries to gauge their knowledge about the new war and, through that, confirm an already presupposed belief about their violent intentions. Burd, for example, followed up his lengthy speech about the peaceful goals of the Pennsylvania government under the shadow of an armed guard by anxiously demanding "to know what Indians had struck us, or whether they or any other Nation had Just Cause to Complain of us." Looking around at the manned fort walls, the representatives of the Susquehanna Nations simply said, "They know nothing & therefore could say nothing." For a conference, their answer was noticeably curt. Yet that curtness was most likely a product of their surroundings rather than indicative of duplicity.[67]

Really, the Susquehanna Nations could offer little to change popular beliefs. They could either confirm or deny that they interacted with hostile nations, but both answers would only serve to reinforce colonial perceptions. Not only did the fort's officers know that Indigenous representatives from Ohio recently had made their way to the Susquehanna Nations carrying news of the war, but over the previous two years those officers had heard terrifying rumors that Tahaiadoris, a Chenussio Seneca from Genesee in western New York, and Kiashuta, an Ohio Valley Mingo living at Logstown, had promoted a grand alliance of Native peoples to violently remove the British from Native lands.[68] So, when the Susquehanna Nations denied any knowledge of the war, the fort's officers quickly deemed "their answer" as "evasive weak & Frivolous."[69] In sum, the colonial garrison was suspicious, and the Susquehanna Nations, caught in the middle and obviously knowing more than they let on, simply wanted to move beyond rumors of a general war to remain at peace. Distrust lingered in the air.

Despite the clear suspicion and the intimidating posturing of the colonial officers and common soldiers at Fort Augusta, Nutimus and others of the Susquehanna Nations' leaders hoped that they had reconfirmed peaceful coexistence during their conference with Burd. That hope did not last long. Mere days after the Susquehanna Council left the fort, Burd and his officers started receiving a steady stream of reports from trusted Indigenous go-betweens, especially Andrew Montour, that the Native Americans living on "the West Branch of this River" were preparing for war. Some reports suggested that the officers should instantly distrust any Native American from the Northern Susquehanna River Valley who came to the fort because the British could "not Expect to see any more here in a Friendly Manner."[70]

The rumors swirling through official circles reached such a height that important officers such as Colonel Henry Bouquet, who had risen to prominence in both Pennsylvania and the British military through his service in the Seven Years' War, demanded a moratorium on trading ammunition with any Native American, regardless of their professed allegiance. Although "the Indians on this River have not yet Committed any Hostilities against his Majesty's Subjects," James Irvine, the store clerk at Fort Augusta, protested, "the Coll. is pleas'd to look on all that shall supply them with Ammunition as Traitors to their King & Country." Irvine was "at a loss" about what to do. Caught between fact and fiction, he complained, "For should I Supply the Indians with ever so trifling a Quantity of Powder it may be said that I Enabled his Majesty's Enemies to carry on a War against him. On the Contrary should I refuse to let them have any, the Indians may say we forc'd them to take part against us by depriving them of the Means of Subsisting among us." In the end, he opted to act in "a manner as to Occasion no Just Reflections on my Conduct" and therefore would "not let them have anymore Powder." Besides, he thought, "from the best information I can procure a general War with the Indians seems inevitable." The Susquehanna Nations' pronouncement of peace meant little. They should either acquiesce to a presumed dependency or become enemies. For British officers like Bouquet or Irvine, there was no in between.[71]

Dependence was a nonstarter and peace even harder to maintain. Pontiac's War, as this new war has come to be called, resulted in the militarization of Pennsylvania with several counties creating voluntary associations, ranger companies, and garrison troops to support the war effort. Even Governor Hamilton, who professed peace, appropriated enough money to support seven hundred men to fight "against the Incursions of our cruel and barbarous Enemies the Indians." As that general vision of enemies as "the Indians" inferred—he would never have said "war against Europeans" when he meant "war against the French"—these troops could not, nor honestly would not, distinguish friends from enemies when it came to Native peoples. Like Bouquet's orders about trade, the officers and soldiers on the ground believed all of "the Indians" harbored malevolent designs.[72]

Soon, the fears of Pennsylvanians, and what they would do because of them, were all too often expressed by common soldiers, traders, and settlers as well as military officers and fort commanders. These colonists did not have the magical power to hide what they thought. Their fears and their prejudices, often intermixing, influenced their interactions with any and all Native peoples who came near Fort Augusta or elsewhere. Every mundane contact reflected what was going on. When Captain Bull and many like him came to trade or even negotiate at the fort after they professed peace in June, they lived and witnessed the colonists' perceived reality infused with paranoia, and quite correctly worried about their fate. They were in danger of becoming "the Slaves of the White people" if they remained "humble as Dogs."[73]

In July, Nutimus again traveled to Fort Augusta to explain how these daily interactions diminished his position and factionalized the Susquehanna Nations, endangering what he thought they had accomplished that June. He was "now Old," and although he "desires that as our Forefathers were in Antient Friendship" and that they should all work hard to "brighten that Friendship," he also believed "the World in a bad condition" and "does not know what to say." The "times are so bad we don't know how long we may see the Light," he thought. Recognizing his weakened voice, Nutimus could now only promise to request "all whom he has any Influence over" to "hold fast the same Friendship" agreed to a month earlier. That was a statement that reflected the end of the Susquehanna Nations as a confederated body with a concerted voice. All "old Nutimus" could do now was hope "that when your Young Men and us meet one another that we should not be Foolish."[74]

Pennsylvania's "Young Men" were "Foolish" that summer, destroying what was left of Nutimus's influence. Many of the colonial officers leading the new county volunteers had long wished for the destruction of peaceful or allied Native communities. Pontiac's War seemed to unleash their fury. At Fort Allen along the Lehigh River about seventy miles east of Fort Augusta, Captain Nicholaus Wetterholt, commanding the Northampton County militia, boasted that August that if he found any Native American "in the Woods far or near" he would "kill him." Wetterholt made good on that promise when, that same month, he drunkenly ordered the murder of Captain Bull's cousin, a Moravian convert named Zacharias, along with Zacharias's wife and small child, who were making their way home to Great Island on the West Branch. This family had nothing to do with the war, yet they were "in the Woods" and Native American so, according to the stark racial distinctions of far too many colonists, they must be "bad Indians."[75] Faced with such odds, Zacharias tried to defend his family with "his knif," but that only enraged the militiamen. One of the soldiers shot Zacharias, and then Wetterholt and two of his men "kildt the Indian Woman and her boy" as the mother "begged for their lives upon her knees." This was just one of many "insults and robberies for which" Native peoples living along the West Branch of the Susquehanna River "could obtain no redress."[76]

Around the same time that Wetterholt and his men murdered a small family, two militia captains commanding about one hundred men made their way "up the West Branch" to eradicate what they assumed was a nest of "snakes" at "Great Island." They never got that far. Less than thirty miles from Fort Augusta, they encountered heavy fire from an enemy who they "could not see," resulting in the separation of their "party." Feeling "Disappointed," twenty-six men commanded by a frontier trader, George Allen, tried to make their way back to Fort Augusta. Along the way they crossed paths with three Delaware and Nanticoke hunters going home to Great Island, one of whom they knew rather well, so well in fact that this Delaware hunter often went by the name "George Allen, after the George Allen that was with us."[77]

Using that friendship as a ruse, the militiamen "took them prisoners," and then just before they reached Fort Augusta, some of Captain Allen's men "thought proper to kill & scalp" the hunters and steal "their peltry." Although the three Native men begged their "brothers" not to "shoot," and even Captain Allen urged restraint, one of the militiamen, determined to exact "revenge on the first Indian that I saw," convinced five of his friends to form an execution squad, "two men to each prisoner." Sending the prisoners in a line thirty yards in front of them, the soldiers fired and then scalped their "bloodied" corpses. George Allen's namesake fortunately survived. He was shot through the arm and managed to play dead during his scalping, a terrible ordeal. Once the militiamen finished he "started up and ran." His executioners, "surprised at his raising from the dead," did not give chase. He eventually made it all the way to Great Island, telling the people there of his experience and swearing "revenge."[78]

The mourning, loss, and misery of the Susquehanna Nations at Great Island did not end there. Just a few weeks after Zacharias and his family were killed and Delaware George Allen stumbled into the settlement holding up the "skin on his" face with a legging and protecting his "brains" with "cold moss," Colonel John Armstrong led a militia unit from Cumberland County "on the Susquehannah campaign, against the Indians." They marched to Great Island where they "burnt the Delaware and Monsey towns, on the West Branch of the Susquehannah, and destroyed all their corn." Many of the men from Great Island and the surrounding towns were away hunting that day, and the women, children, and elderly (including Nutimus) had fled when they learned of the march against them, but they nonetheless returned to find the smoldering ashes of their homes and the loss of the corn they expected to live on during the winter. All of this was done by their professed "friends" and "brothers," the Pennsylvanians.[79]

From Captain Bull's perspective, the actions of the British colonists must have been infuriating. Despite listening to Nutimus's and Burd's speeches at Fort Augusta in June and appealing to Governor Hamilton, he found no solace in their relationship. Of all of Teedyuscung's sons, Captain Bull followed most closely the path his father had trod in life, although they had a tumultuous relationship at times. From all accounts, he, like his father, cut an imposing and memorable figure. According to one colonist who encountered him, Captain Bull was "the best looking Indian I ever saw. He is quite the fine Gentleman." Yet, he had a difficult past. Like his father, he too was dispossessed by Pennsylvania's land deals with the Haudenosaunee east of the Susquehanna River in the late 1730s and throughout the 1740s. After that childhood trauma (he was about sixteen during the Walking Purchase), he, like his father, relocated to a Moravian mission where he was baptized, taking the Christian name Johann Jacob. Not long thereafter, he married a fellow Christian Delaware, had a family, and stayed close to his father, making a home at Meniolagomekah, a multiethnic Native American town and Moravian mission less than ten miles east of Bethlehem, which was also near his uncle Captain John. Just like his father, the Seven Years' War changed his life. At around the same time his father left Gnadenhutten for Wyoming in 1754, Johann Jacob packed up his belongings to live with some of his relatives, particularly Nutimus, at Nescopeck, a village just southwest of Wyoming. Such a move was not coincidental; it helped establish his father's connections and, through that, his influence.[80]

At Nescopeck, reflective of his father's growing leadership and his new status, Johann abandoned his adopted Christian name for the more prominent, if militaristic, Captain Bull. The name fit the new life he and his father had created. Within a year of his arrival at Nescopeck, Captain Bull joined with his father and many of the other Susquehanna Nations in a war against the British, leading men in Northampton County. Yet, when they sought peace, he was there too. He attended the Easton conferences and demonstrated the same ambivalence toward Six Nations suzerainty and colonial interests as his father, all the while hoping the conferences could achieve security for the future.[81]

Once peace was established at Easton he followed the path of his father again, attempting to demonstrate his "friendship" with the British colonies and, through that, obtain a status that could protect him and his people. Representing his father and using kinship connections, he helped spread the message of peace to the Ohio region. While there, he even acted as a spy for the British, gathering intelligence at Venango where his uncle Captain Peter (or Young Captain Harris) was chief of a group of pro-French Delaware. Captain Bull's experiences, like those of many other Native peoples, highlights how past moments, both large and small, shaped generations, echoing through time.[82]

Despite his efforts to demonstrate his loyalty to the British, Captain Bull's father and cousins were murdered, and he did not have a home. The Pennsylvanians, who had professed their friendship, appeared indifferent if not outright hostile. After Teedyuscung's death, the governor took almost two months to issue a proclamation against Connecticut settlers encroaching on Native American land, disregarding the assassination and failing to offer condolences. Although Pennsylvania officials had acknowledged Teedyuscung's importance and occasionally referred to him as a king, they made minimal effort to honor his passing. Hamilton also did not investigate the murder of Zacharias and his family, nor did he take action when Great Island was destroyed, although he expressed some sadness because he assumed Nutimus must be dead. Despite Pennsylvania officials' verbal commitment to maintaining friendly relations, their actions seemed hollow and insincere. As one Cayuga chief cautioned at Easton in 1758, the Pennsylvanians "only speak from their Mouth and not from their Heart." Captain Bull attended that meeting and perhaps reflected on those words or even that sentiment in this moment. There is no reason to think otherwise.[83]

Reeling from the attacks on their people and their homes, few Native Americans made their way to Fort Augusta in August and September 1763, and those who came to trade were turned away. That stillness worried the fort's officers, who removed the official trade house as well as many of the colonial inhabitants inside the fort's walls. Preparing for the fort's evacuation, James Irvine shipped most of the trade goods in his possession down to Paxton township in Lancaster County, hoping for wagons to move it all safely to Philadelphia.[84] The officers even started punishing soldiers for "misbehavior on Guard" and "Neglect of Duty," a rarity before, and ordered a military tattoo "Beat Every Night at eight o'clock." After a long few months, their fears were confirmed when the fort's lieutenant, Samuel Hunter, learned on October 5 that "the Indians are Universally Joined against us."[85] This time, the rumors were mostly correct.

About the same time Hunter heard the ominous news, Captain Bull and a faction of the Susquehanna Nations marched from the smoldering ashes of Great Island off to war, asserting their independence and attempting to exact revenge. They were not, though, in league with Pontiac, nor really anyone else. They were fighting for their own cause and their own goals. Pontiac's War merely served a purpose, not unlike the motivations for the many other Native nations and peoples who chose to take up arms.[86]

On the morning of October 8, Bull surprised his cousin Zacharias' killers, Captain Wetterholt and his company, at a tavern near Hokendauqua Creek in Allen township, Northampton County, killing the captain, most of the men under his command, and the tavernkeeper. Surprised and frightened, Wetterholt's lieutenant, Jonathan Dodge, a man who often boasted about his ability to kill Indigenous people, and who many Native Americans and some colonists deemed "a most precious scoundrel," sent an urgent message to local notable, Timothy Horsfield. "Pray send me help," Dodge scrawled, "for all my men are killed But one, and Captn. Wetterhold is amost Dead."

In a series of urgent pleas thereafter, Dodge wrote, "Send me help or I am a Dead man," and "Pray send up the Doctor for God sake."[87]

Although Dodge managed to escape, most of his men did not, and Bull's warriors set fire to the tavern. From there, Bull and his men raided some of the neighboring communities of Allen and Whitehall townships, setting homes on fire and killing or taking captive some inhabitants. According to reports received at Fort Augusta, Captain Bull and his men "killed 54 Persons in Northampton County, and Continued Killing and scalping" thereafter.[88] Bull later boasted that he personally killed twenty-six colonists.[89]

Within days, the *Pennsylvania Gazette,* one of the most popular newspapers in the mid-Atlantic colonies, published the "melancholy account" of the attack on the tavern and the subsequent events in the area. The *Gazette* and other city newspapers had been reporting on Pontiac's War for months, but Bull's raids struck a nerve. As a result, the *Gazette* recast Wetterholt's death as heroic, depicting the wounded captain, shot through the gut and "growing very weak," as crawling "to a Window" to shoot "an Indian dead" who "was setting Fire to the House with a Match." In the several columns that followed, the *Gazette* published letters from Northampton County colonists describing the gruesome deaths of women and children, "Houses on Fire," and in general "the deplorable Condition of this Poor Country." Unpromisingly, the report ended, colonists "feared there were many Houses & c. burnt, and Lives lost, that were not then known."[90]

These melodramatic scenes were provided to readers entirely bereft of context. Over the previous several months the *Gazette* had never reported on the fire that killed Teedyuscung and consumed Wyoming in April or of the Susquehanna Nations' subsequent efforts to remain at peace despite it. The *Gazette* also did not report on Wetterholt's murder of Zacharias and his family in August, the execution of Delaware and Nanticoke hunters outside of Fort Augusta, nor the other outrages that precipitated the "melancholy account" of that October in the first place. For a newspaper that seemed to revel in the description of houses on fire and the gruesome deaths of women, children, and other noncombatants, the absence of these stories is telling. Yet, the *Gazette*'s reporting about Bull's raids in Northampton did help push a reluctant colonial legislature to pass a law funding an additional eight hundred men for war.[91]

While the *Gazette* busily constructed what one scholar has described as an "anti-Indian sublime" for its readers, Captain Bull shifted his attention to Wyoming. On October 15, he entered the Connecticut settlement near Wyoming with at least 135 warriors seeking revenge for the death of his father and their "king," and to reclaim what was theirs, but found only a smattering of settlers. After Bull's early October raids, most Connecticut settlers had hastily packed up their belongings and fled east for safety. Forty people, however, remained. Of those forty, Bull and his men killed ten, and besides a few who managed to escape, took the rest captive, burning the settlement to the ground before they headed north to Wyalusing. This new bid for independence and revenge was short-lived. British officers with the help of a Haudenosaunee viceroy, Thomas King, sought to tamp out the Susquehanna Nations' independence, capturing and imprisoning Captain Bull. When they asked Bull why he went to war, though, he refused to give his captors any satisfaction, offering only a smile.[92]

Just like Bull's earlier actions in Northampton County, the destruction of Wyoming shocked and enraged colonists. A few days after Bull attacked Wyoming and headed north to Wyalusing, a company of Pennsylvania militia from Lancaster County, the Paxtang Rangers, arrived at Wyoming to witness the aftermath. They were sent to Wyoming by Reverend John Elder, an influential Presbyterian minister in Paxton township charged by the colonial government to oversee the rangers, to harass the Connecticut settlers, and to "scout a little way into the Enemy's Country." When his rangers arrived at Wyoming they had nothing to do but bury Connecticut's dead.[93] It was not long before these soldiers relayed home what they had witnessed.

On hearing the news of the "melancholy Scene" at Wyoming from his rangers, Elder, who had a fairly short temper to begin with, exploded into a fit of rage. Writing to the governor, Elder castigated "the Savages" and demanded Hamilton act. "Until that Branch [of the Susquehanna River] is cleared of the Enemy," Elder stated, "the frontier Settlements will be in no safety." Elder might have written "Enemy," but who he or the colonists he commanded actually saw as enemies was rather murky. There were many peaceful and neutral Native peoples who still lived on "that Branch."[94]

The editors of the *Pennsylvania Gazette* also ran wild with the story the Paxtang Rangers brought home, depicting a grizzly image for their readers.

Pennsylvania troops, readers learned, had entered Wyoming to find "nine men and a woman, who had been most cruelly butchered, the woman was roasted, and had two Hinges in her Hands, supposed to be put in red hot, and several of the men had Awls thrust into their Eyes, and Spears, arrows, Pitchforks, &c sticking in their Bodies."[95]

Although these Connecticut settlers had been Pennsylvania's enemies just a few months before, envisioned as unseemly invaders and troublemakers who would assuredly instigate another war, they were now, in the *Gazette*'s hands, the unwitting victims of a "Savage" massacre. Perceptions shifted fast as the war and the stories told about what happened at Wyoming hardened racial attitudes in the colony, creating a climate of anger, suspicion, and fear that could and would be turned on any Native community in or near the province. After Wyoming, lines were quickly being drawn in the sand as both white colonists and many Native peoples constructed a vision of the future bereft of, or at the very least significantly removed from, each other.

5

A "Diversity of Interests"

ATTEMPTS TO SEPARATE PEOPLE AND DIVIDE LAND, 1763–1767

PONTIAC'S WAR AND CAPTAIN Bull's destruction of Wyoming, especially the reporting and gossip about them, led to the evacuation of many of Pennsylvania's frontier colonial settlements. They also inflamed the minds of ordinary white colonists against their government and any and all Native peoples. Reeling from the experiences of war or learning secondhand about them, many Pennsylvanians demanded their government take the offensive against their Indigenous enemies, often erroneously blaming Quakers, whom many Pennsylvanians imagined controlled the government (which they did not), for the colony's delayed and meager response to the war. Doing away with all circumspection, enraged colonists also turned their attention toward the many communities of Indigenous Christians, some of whom had peacefully coexisted with their white neighbors for decades and had nothing to do with the war.

This is not to say that such suspicions of *all* Native Americans did not exist before; they most assuredly did. But by 1763, ordinary colonists, especially on the frontier, more eagerly and publicly lumped all Native Americans together as part of the same "Nation" sharing racial characteristics that separated them from white British colonists. In that year, a group of frontiersmen from Paxton (many of whom had ridden to Wyoming as the Paxtang Rangers), upset that Pennsylvania's government refused to countenance the violent extermination of all Indigenous peoples in retribution for the war, angrily asserted their right to do so on their own as "British subjects" facing a single menacing Native American threat. In one petition they sent to the government, which was also widely publicized, they justified violence against Indigenous peoples by asking their fellow subjects to consider "in what nation under the Sun was it ever the custom that when a neighboring Nation took up Arms, not an individual should be touched but only the Persons that offered Hostilities?" Such a rhetorical question, criticism of the government, and justification for violence only worked if both colonists and Native Americans could be viewed as members of two distinct nations. By conflating national and racial difference, these colonists projected a potent vision of separation that pit seemingly unified "British subjects" against a coherent and "savage" enemy nation.[1]

This idea of a clear separation between British Americans and Native Americans was not harbored by frontier colonists alone. Elite land speculators, military officers, colonial officials, imperial managers, and even the king and his advisors saw separation between two supposedly distinct peoples as necessary, even desirable, and, some thought, definitely profitable. Native peoples too, experiencing the trauma of war, the murder of family, and the destruction of their homes, sought separation from "white people." By the mid-1760s, it seemed as if everyone was talking about or making plans for separation. For many British and colonial officials this separation could only be achieved by establishing one clear dividing line on a map separating British from Native American land and people, a perfect cure-all.

There were obvious problems with this binary geopolitical division of peoples demarcated by specific latitudes and longitudes. While the vision of two distinct peoples was useful when promoting and arguing for the necessity of a line of separation in the abstract, it never reflected a semblance of reality. Despite the heated rhetoric, two separate peoples didn't actually exist. Early America was a heterogeneous place composed of a diverse collection of ethnically, culturally, racially, and religiously different peoples. The shear diversity of early America could and would challenge any plan for separation.

Prominent colonial politicians who supported creating some sort of dividing line between two distinct peoples understood this problem. Joseph Galloway, who argued for the necessity of a dividing line, also knew that colonists' "different Religions—tempers and private Interest—their Prejudices against, and Jealousies of, each other—all have, and ever will, from the Nature and Reason of things, conspire to create such a Diversity of Interests, Inclinations, and Decisions, that they never can unite together." Like Galloway, another contemporary observed in 1760 that the diversity of colonists, their "different nations, different manners, different religions, and different languages," mixed like "Fire and Water," mutually destructive. That logic could have been applied across early America, reflecting both British subjects and Native Americans, who were also divided among themselves and jockeying for power.[2]

These were all fair assessments of the North American landscape. Even colonists from Paxton, who described themselves as "British subjects," members of the same nation, simultaneously clung to their particular regional, ethnic, religious, and social differences, which separated them from and put them at odds with other "British subjects." And they articulated these distinctions simultaneously. Their now famous "Declaration and Remonstrance of the Distressed and Bleeding Frontier Inhabitants of the Province of Pennsylvania," which pronounced their rights as "British subjects," was far from a statement of British solidarity and identity. They were, they argued, nothing like those other colonists "in the east." Similarly, colonial politicians, speculators, and imperial officials often used the language of racial difference and the need for national unity to achieve their own ends but were also quick to separate themselves from unruly "white savages" on the frontier who were, a young George Washington thought, "as Ignorant a Set of People as the Indians." Even the separate British colonies were often at odds with one another, which only worsened as the decade progressed.[3]

Native peoples too saw important distinctions among themselves. Delaware, Shawnee, and Haudenosaunee peoples, for instance, may have spoken of themselves as "Indians," but they also described themselves as members of distinct nations with their own interests, their own land, and their own sovereignty, much of which conflicted. Even those distinct national identities could pale in comparison to more intimate clan and kinship ones. The same people who described themselves as "Indians" as well as Delaware, Shawnee, or one of the separate Six Nations also identified as members of the Bear, Turkey, Wolf, Turtle, and other clan divisions, with particular kinship networks and autonomy. From childhood, they learned and internalized their clan belongings and lineages. Stark racial distinctions, then, may have been powerful rhetorical devices pervading public discourse in the latter half of the eighteenth century that could galvanize solidarity and justify violence in moments of perceived danger, but that solidarity was often fleeting and impossible to sustain. A "Diversity of Interests," as Galloway had so astutely observed, was always at play.[4]

Given this reality, actually establishing a policy of separation between two peoples with a clear line on a map was way more difficult to achieve than any one person, nation, or faction of people argued it could be. Nobody involved, whether British colonists or Native Americans, would ever agree between and among themselves over the exact limits of any boundary, nor who had the authority to negotiate it, who would pay for and manage it, and, most importantly, who would benefit.

These were real cleavages that Native nations and peoples, colonial governors, colonial legislators, military officers, frontier agents, speculators, settlers, squatters, and even the king, his ministers, and Parliament contended with as they imagined separation and how to achieve it in the mid-1760s. As they all too often found, any one solution only exacerbated existing tensions and divisions within and between colonial Americans, Native peoples, and the British Empire that could and would erupt in internecine conflict. By the late 1760s, efforts to divide people and land using the logic of two separate peoples let loose a "Diversity of Interests" and set the stage for rebellion and, ultimately, the American Revolution.

In the immediate aftermath of Captain Bull's October 1763 raids, many of Northampton County's colonial residents blamed not Bull but the local Indigenous Christians living in the Moravian mission town of Bethlehem, particularly a Christian Mohican, Renatus. Charging the whole group with conspiring with the enemy, a vocal contingent of colonists demanded action. They wanted Renatus arrested and the rest of the community removed. There was, however, no evidence that Renatus or any of the Native people at Bethlehem were involved. The evidence available, from white witnesses no less, suggested that Renatus was nowhere near the area at the time. Nevertheless, the local sheriff, under intense pressure, arrested Renatus on October 29 and conveyed him to jail to await trial.[5]

Although Renatus was eventually acquitted by an all-white jury, colonists along the frontier, hearing rumors at taverns or reading the accounts of the trial in newspapers and pamphlets, refused to accept the verdict, believing in a grand conspiracy involving prominent government officials, especially Quakers, who, they argued, were in league with Native American "murderers." In the colonists' minds, the colonial government, Renatus, and really all Indigenous Christians, whether at Bethlehem or elsewhere, were responsible for the destruction of the war or were, at the very least, complicit. Belief in such conspiracies reflected pent up animosities, lingering grievances, and racial attitudes that, when combined, defined the Pennsylvania frontier for years to come.[6]

In December 1763, colonists in Lancaster County, known to history as the "Paxton Boys," used a similar conspiratorial logic to justify the violent extermination of the local Christian Conestoga. The Paxton Boys even referenced Renatus when explaining their actions and, in eerily similar language, claimed that that small peaceful community at Conestoga harbored a "murderer," Will Sock, based on equally flimsy evidence.[7] On two separate occasions in December, anywhere from fifty to one hundred mounted men, "equipped for murder," butchered the Conestoga, leaving behind them "men, women and children" who were "shot, scalped, hacked and cut to pieces."[8] Among the few possessions found scattered amid the carnage and debris were wampum belts and a piece of parchment dated April 23, 1701, charting the treaty of peace and friendship between William Penn and the Conestoga that laid the foundation for the Conestoga's town and the future safety of their people.[9]

The Paxton Boys were not done there. Because of the animosity of the colonial inhabitants against Indigenous Christians, especially those in Northampton County, Pennsylvania's governor, now Thomas Penn's nephew John Penn, ordered the removal of those Indigenous people to the city of Philadelphia for protection. It wasn't general humanitarianism that motivated Penn. He knew that if anything happened to the Native peoples most closely associated with his colony, it would ultimately enrage Native communities throughout the Northeast, if not beyond. More problematic still, the Six Nations claimed most of those Christian communities as allied tributaries.[10]

Governor Penn was in the midst of a diplomatic nightmare and facing an insurrection. Fearing for the safety of his city rather than the Native Americans he sought to protect, Penn tried to ship the Indigenous Christians off to New York to live under the safety of the Six Nations, but that colony's governor, Cadwallader Colden, refused to let them pass. Calling Indigenous Christians "rogues and thieves, runaways from the other Nations" that were "not to be trusted," Colden made it clear that they were unwelcome. He was "rather disposed to attack & punish [them], than to support and protect them."[11] The young Penn, once committed to their protection and without New York's approval, had no choice but to provide asylum near the city of Philadelphia. As he feared, though, anger over the idea that the Pennsylvania government protected "known murderers" increased the number of frontier colonists supporting the Paxton Boys. Emboldened by those numbers, over five hundred frontiersmen marched on the city to eradicate the supposed murderers. Some thought this march was the beginning of "a Civil War."[12]

The Paxton Boys, claiming to represent all the frontier counties and the real meaning of being "British subjects," also sought to use their numbers as leverage to force an overhaul of the provincial government to make it more inclusive for white male inhabitants, and therefore more representative of their wants and desires.[13] Racially charged beliefs and grievances against the exclusive nature of the colonial government and its policies—which brought into question the province's unequal land distribution and economic inequality—converged in this moment, making it seem as if the entire government was fundamentally broken, or at least in need of significant repair. The Paxton Boys and those colonists who supported them desired a future where they had a significant say in the colonial government and its policies, as equal British subjects, living within a colony entirely devoid of and outright hostile against what they viewed as a singular enemy Native "Nation." As it would turn out, many of those Paxton Boys and their supporters would see the Northern Susquehanna River Valley and the American Revolution as the answer to their dreams.[14]

Those dreams of the future were fundamentally wrapped up in religion. Many of the Presbyterian ministers on the frontier, including Reverend John Elder, the leader of the Paxtang Rangers, who comprised the core leadership of the Paxton Boys, had long preached a message that castigated the provincial government and eastern elites for failing to support the "Liberty" of the people. They even countenanced extralegal action when that government failed to meet expectations. In one sermon, Elder told his congregants that "liberty does not consist in an Absolute Indifference." All people had to assure liberty's existence by any means necessary, which sometimes meant challenging lawful authority. According to many Presbyterian ministers like Elder, popular action was acceptable and justified. "When man joins himself in civil society with others," one Presbyterian minister argued, "he, as well as every one with him, gives up his rights which he has naturally, to be regulated by the laws made by the society, and to which he consents; at least so far as his own safety, and that of the rest of society, shall require."[15] Obedience to government had limits. Elder also struck a martial air during his sermons. The "fighting parson" often kept his rifle beside him at the pulpit as he preached about the plight of liberty and the need to fight "manfully under the Banner of ye Captain of our Salvation having put on ye whole Armour of God."[16]

Many of the Paxton Boys, particularly their leaders, were Scots-Irish members of Elder's Presbyterian church, and according to contemporaries who met them, a religious lot. They were, as one person called them, "children of Promise or Saints Militant." After the massacre of the Conestoga, one man had a chance encounter with the group. "Suspecting what they had been about," he told them, point blank, that "you have done a very base action" because the Conestoga "were under the protection of government." The Paxton Boys engaged with the man, telling him that "no government" had "a right to protect heathen." Besides, they acted on the authority of a higher power. They followed scripture, particularly God's orders to 'Joshua" to "drive the heathen out of the land." Since their accuser did not "believe in scripture," at least their rendition of it, they had nothing more "to say." From this outsider's perspective, the Paxton Boys "were engaged" in a "holy war," determined "to fulfil the command given to Joshua with the most scrupulous exactness."[17]

The animosity leveled against the Native Americans at Bethlehem, the Conestoga massacre, and the Paxton Boys' professed religious mission highlight how many frontier colonists saw a clear separation between themselves and all Native peoples, challenging official directives. Many of the colonial governors, frontier agents, and imperial officials across the Atlantic disapproved of and tried to distance themselves from these popular actions, which only further alienated white frontiersmen. During meetings with Native peoples and in public pronouncements, these officials often stated their abhorrence of racially motivated violence, promising Indigenous kin swift action that never actually materialized and blaming everything on "imprudent" poor people who were all too often "foolish." Officials well knew that the murder of Native Americans, Christian or not, only increased tensions on the frontier. As one colonial governor explained to imperial officials across the Atlantic, "The whole nation suffers in the opinion of the Indians by a crime committed by a worthless individual."[18] Regardless of elite prognostications but likely exacerbated by their biases, it is readily apparent that a belief in a grand conspiracy of an inadequate government coupled with the necessity of a clear separation between "white people" and "bloody Savages" influenced the violent actions of settlers on the frontier.[19]

White frontier colonists were not alone in seeing the necessity of separation. Native peoples too, experiencing the daily loss of life and land at the hands of enraged colonists, also articulated a desirable future removed from "white people," and like white colonists, religion provided a language to express their feelings. The most famous is the revival inspired by a Delaware prophet, Neolin, who, living in the Ohio region in the 1760s, harnessed the long history of his people's displacement in his religious messages to inspire his followers "to drive the white people out of their country."[20]

After a period of fasting in 1761, Neolin dreamed that he went on a spiritual journey to find the Master of Life, the source of Native American happiness and prosperity. During this important dream, Neolin faced "three roads," two of which ended in "great fire." The easiest road, though, was barred, "now in the possession of the white people," and therefore getting to the master required a spiritual cleansing and climbing a mountain. Once Neolin ascended the mountain, he met the Master of Life, who told Neolin that he was angry with Native Americans for their "addiction to the White man's" ways of living, especially alcohol, and their giving away land. If Neolin and his people wanted to keep their land and its bounty, particularly wild game, and even think of reaching paradise in the afterlife, they must renounce European ways and return to the traditional lives of their ancestors.[21]

Less than a year later the Master of Life gave Neolin a prayer to recite every morning and night that he should spread among his people. Copies of Neolin's "Great Book of Writing," depicted on pieces of deer hide charting his spiritual journey, circulated well beyond the Ohio region and the Delaware people. His message seemed to "spread from village to village," reaching people such as Pontiac in the Illinois Country, as well as those to the east along the Susquehanna River. Pontiac, for example, used Neolin's message to inspire his men during the siege of Fort Detroit, telling them that the Master of Life commanded, "As to those who come to trouble your lands,—drive them out, make war upon them. I do not love them at all."[22]

Neolin's message also justified the forcible removal of white colonists. The Master of Life told Neolin that he made "this Land where ye dwell" for "you and not for others" and demanded to know "whence comes it that ye permit the Whites upon your lands?" The Master of Life had made the white people homes across the ocean, therefore his people in America should "send them back to the lands which I have created for them and let them stay there." This was the "prayer which I give thee in writing to learn by heart and to teach to the Indians and their children."[23] While extremely influential, Neolin was not the only Native American promoting two separate creations that demarcated Indigenous from white land and existence. At Lancaster in 1762, for example, Oneida representative Thomas King wanted Governor Hamilton to "remember that God gave us this Land, and you some other."[24]

The vision of separating peoples erupting across the frontier in the mid-1760s was difficult to achieve and nearly impossible to sustain. The core of the problem, as it had been in the past, was about land—who had access to it, who had sovereign authority over it, and who could reap the rewards from it. The continuing fight over land and sovereignty, then, could shatter visions of two separate peoples in an instant, revealing the "Diversity of Interests" that tore people apart.

The explosiveness of this diversity of interests was readily apparent even as Neolin's message spread and the Paxton Boys marched. The end of the

FIGURE 8. Neolin's "Great Book of Writing," as reproduced by John M'Cullough after his captivity during Pontiac's War, in Archibald Loudon, *A Selection of Some of the Most Interesting Narratives of Outrages Committed by the Indians in Their Wars with the White People* (Carlisle, PA, 1808), 1:274

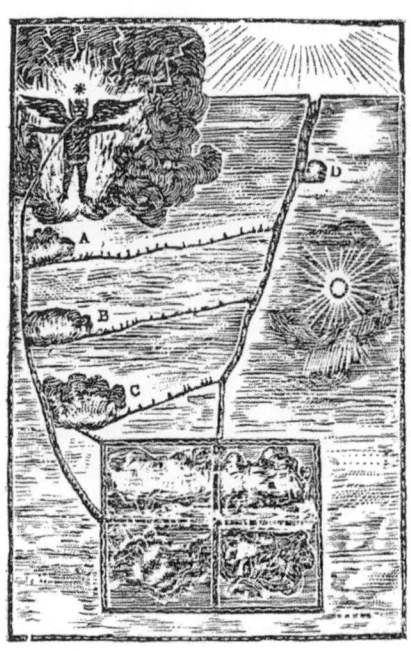

*Mah-tan'-tooh, or the Devil, standing in a flame of fire, with open arms to receive the wicked.

Seven Years' War and the territory the British gained through the Treaty of Paris engendered a great deal of maneuvering in North America. Native nations, rebellious squatters, and avaricious land speculators sought multiple avenues to achieve their interests and enhance their futures. Sometimes those interests aligned, but often they did not, and as a result the various peoples involved fought between and among themselves.

For British colonists, the end of the Seven Years' War precipitated a mad scramble for land. The ink was barely dry on the Treaty of Paris before colonial settlers began staking claims to Indigenous lands with small homesteads and coming to blows with both Native inhabitants and other British subjects to secure those claims. Squatter settlements seemed to materialize across the Northern Susquehanna River Valley as white settlers permeated the land, carving out small farms around Wyoming and north and west of Fort Augusta.[25]

Much like the squatters, colonial elites vigorously competed for extensive sections of the same land. Leveraging their wealth and influence, they collaborated in forming both old and new land companies, strategizing how to partition Britain's recent acquisitions. Among these were the Indiana Company, the Mississippi Company, the Illinois-Wabash Company, the Ohio Company, the Walpole Company, and the Grand Ohio Company. Additionally, military veterans and a group of traders called the "Suffering Traders," who had taken significant losses during the war, devised plans for establishing either new colonies or vast landholdings in the Illinois Country, the Ohio River Valley, and the northern stretches of the Susquehanna River. The Suffering Traders alone aimed to acquire 200,000 acres, a request that paled in comparison to the Mississippi Company's colossal demand for 2.5 million acres. The roster of interested parties in these ventures included governors, legislators, superintendents, politically affiliated trading houses, and even imperial officials across the Atlantic Ocean. Any given list of members also involved a pantheon of what modern Americans consider "founding fathers" such as George Washington, Thomas Jefferson, Patrick Henry, and Benjamin Franklin, and they were the least powerful and connected of the bunch.[26]

While many of these speculators shied away from the racialized rhetoric of common frontiersmen, they too sought clear lines demarcating Native American and British colonial settlement.[27] Couching the justification of their aspirations in the language of beneficent paternalism, speculators made it seem as if new colonies and a new western boundary would protect Native Americans, easing tensions all along the frontier. George Croghan, the deputy superintendent of Indian affairs for the northern district, who speculated in Native American lands in the Illinois Country as well as the Ohio and Susquehanna River Valleys, for instance, tried to convince officials in London that "a natural boundary should be made between them and us," warning that "a general Indian War" would "be a consequence of neglect on our side."[28]

The problem was the exact position of such a boundary. Croghan, like many others speculating in land, thought it should run a westerly course from the headwaters of the Delaware River to the west of the Appalachian

Mountains and the "mouth of the Ohio where it empties into the Mississippi." Privately, Croghan conceded that such a westerly line was absolutely necessary for the land ventures in which he had interests. He even promoted a new colony in the Illinois Country as a means to maintain peace with the Native peoples there. He made it seem as if Native Americans in Illinois, the home of Pontiac, "had not the least objection" to "our forming a Settlement and cultivating Lands." In fact, he argued, the Native people invited "us" to do so.[29]

With a financial stake in many of the speculative companies and facing mounting debts that he could not repay, Croghan urged expediency, writing to anyone with even a modicum of interest that "Indians are of a fickle, uncertain Temper, Wherefore their Offers ought always to be accepted, as soon as possible."[30] The consequences of such a policy be damned—he needed this. Just ten years earlier, some of his own creditors had petitioned the Pennsylvania legislature to pass a special law to extend Croghan's credit and grant him temporary immunity from prosecution for repayment because he was living in "melancholy and deplorable Circumstances" on the frontier to escape arrest. By the early 1760s, that extension was about to expire and his circumstances had only worsened.[31]

Croghan wasn't the sole player attempting to cloak land speculation under a facade of virtuous public service. Joseph Galloway, Croghan's attorney and a Pennsylvania legislator who emphasized the "Diversity of Interests," also acquired shares in the Indiana and Ohio Companies while aligning with the Suffering Traders. Later, he played a role in merging the Indiana and Ohio Company with the Walpole Company, forming the Grand Ohio Company that sought millions of acres of Native American land.[32]

It is unsurprising that Galloway leveraged his political influence to advocate for policies establishing a division line between two distinct peoples. According to "Mr. Croghan's Examination," Galloway asserted that achieving "nothing less than the final Confirmation of this Boundary" was crucial for laying the foundation of solid and lasting peace. He further shepherded legislation aimed at displacing squatters, whom he deemed "wicked" individuals encroaching on Native American land—the very land coveted by the various companies in which he had invested. Despite their mutual animosity, speculators, colonial officials, and squatters were all pursuing the same goal: the acquisition of vast Native American lands.[33]

As squatters persisted and speculators like Croghan and Galloway pushed for a new boundary for "lasting Peace," Native Americans from the Hudson to the Tennessee River found themselves surrounded by white settlers seeking to seize their land. Displeased with the westerly boundary line and the new colonies promoted by land companies, groups like the Nanticoke pledged to safeguard their land "as long as Death would let them live." Additionally, they harbored resentment toward other Native nations, including the Haudenosaunee and Cherokee, whom they believed had aided colonial expansion.[34]

In sum, speculators vied against squatters, squatters and speculators instigated disputes with Native peoples, Native nations fought back while also arguing among themselves, and even the elites battled each other as land companies and colonial governments tried to undermine each other. These divisions only scratch the surface of what was going on after the Treaty of Paris.

Such a "Diversity of Interests" did not bode well for the young twenty-five-year-old British king, George III, who had ascended the throne in 1760 after the death of his grandfather. Inheriting a huge, messy empire, George III faced a dwindling treasury, a fractured people, and another war with Native Americans that had no prospect of ending while Indigenous grievances continued to accumulate. Like many others, he too began thinking of separation as the cure-all. Within three years of his reign he tried to administer that cure.

On October 7, 1763, George III delivered a royal proclamation slamming the door on all his "loving subjects" from settling in regions "not ceded to or purchased by Us" from Native Americans. The proclamation drew a line not to the west but along the Appalachian Mountains, casting a shadow over the ambitious plans of virtually all land companies. The young king emphatically declared it was "Our Royal Will and pleasure, for the present" that the lands of the "several Nations or Tribes of Indians with whom We are connected should not be molested or disturbed." The proclamation also curtailed colonial governments' authority to grant land and privately negotiate for more land, even land east of the line. The proclamation expressed a resolute intent to regulate squatter settlements and trade with Native Americans, anchored by the numerous forts punctuating Britain's extensive frontier. It was a grand, almost romantic notion—albeit a tremendously expensive one.[35]

Yet, it was infectious. Embracing the spirit of that proclamation, the Board of Trade, long responsible for colonial administration and oversight of colonial lawmaking, began considering strategies to centralize all commercial and diplomatic authority under their two superintendents of Indian affairs—Sir William Johnson in the north and John Stuart in the south. The proclamation and restructuring plan together signaled a significant shift from the decentralized and ad-hoc administration of Indigenous relations that had characterized much of the British Empire's history. If colonists were truly part of one nation as "British subjects," this plan treated them as such.[36]

The royal proclamation and the Board of Trade's plan appeared promising at first glance. News of the proclamation, traveling from the Northern Susquehanna River Valley to west of the Appalachian Mountains, brought several Native nations to the negotiation table in pursuit of peace. Facing dwindling supplies and war fatigue, these nations were receptive to peace terms that safeguarded their land and sovereignty while also facilitating fair trade. However, they remained cautious about British intentions and the asserted authority of Onondaga. The apparent unity of Native Americans during Pontiac's War and the foundation of Neolin's vision of a singular Native people did not eliminate these concerns. Many Native nations, therefore, sought to negotiate a separate peace, aiming to achieve a long-sought independence publicly and diplomatically. The royal proclamation and its promise of separation appeared to offer a path toward attaining this independent status. By prohibiting the sale of Indigenous land "not ceded to or purchased by Us," the king's proclamation directly challenged one of the few resources the Haudenosaunee used to assert diplomatic dominance.[37]

Truth be told, the Six Nations' meticulously crafted position as the center of British Native American diplomacy was already diminishing in the eyes of crucial imperial officials in North America. General Jeffery Amherst's strategy of severing costly alliances with Native Americans initiated this decline, a trend that continued under his successor, Thomas Gage, because of Pontiac's War. Gage, the forty-three-year-old son of a viscount, sought retribution against the Mingo and northern Seneca, diverging from the established tradition of overlooking divisions among the Six Nations to bolster the impression of the Grand Council's extensive authority at Onondaga.

Shortly after George III's proclamation and just before the British ministry considered reorganizing diplomacy, Gage instructed Sir William Johnson to secure separate peace agreements with Britain's Native American adversaries. This approach contradicted the established practice of convening all the northern nations in one conference, where the Six Nations would play a significant role. Gage aimed to pit the Six Nations against other nations, intending to "raise up Jealousies of each other and kindle those Suspicions So natural to every Indian." The authority of Onondaga teetered on the brink.[38]

The 1764 plan to grant near-autonomous power over the northern frontier to Johnson, though, did provide a glimmer of hope for the Six Nations. This jurisdiction covered all British possessions north of the Ohio. For nearly thirty years, Johnson, an Irish immigrant who arrived in the colonies a year after the Walking Purchase, had fostered a close relationship with the Six Nations, particularly the Mohawk. He had children with Konwatsitsiaienni (Molly Brant), an influential Canajoharie Mohawk residing at Johnson Hall. Although they never officially married by British standards, the Six Nations recognized their union as such. Unlike Europeans, marriage wasn't a legal arrangement for the Haudenosaunee. Instead, it was a matter of agreement representing the union of not just two individuals but kin groups, forging economic and political alliances and responsibilities. This aspect was crucial, especially since the Haudenosaunee followed a matrilineal descent system that elevated the status and power of women beyond the patrilineal and patriarchal norms of British culture.[39]

And Konwatsitsiaienni's lineage was significant. Her mother and grandmother were important power brokers in the Turtle Clan, whose leading women chose the council chief for the entire Canajoharie Mohawk, who by midcentury led the council fire at Onondaga. Needless to say, Johnson's marriage to Konwatsitsiaienni only raised his status. Johnson's ambition, combined with these kinship connections and Britain's long history of elevating the place of the Six Nations in diplomacy, made Johnson's career. In effect, Johnson's power and his status were fundamentally linked to the authority of the Six Nations in the British Empire, and he worked hard to maintain that position.[40]

In the face of Gage's call for retribution against the Mingo and northern Seneca, as well as his demands for separate peace treaties, Johnson professed his agreement but nonetheless worked to shift blame for the new war away from the Haudenosaunee to Pontiac as well as the Delaware and Shawnee. He also made moves to reassert the supremacy of Onondaga over the Ohio and Northern Susquehanna River Valleys. When he heard that the Board of Trade was seriously considering granting more authority to his department, a plan he had been pushing since at least 1759, he became more forward in his designs, conjoining the approval of that plan with an official recognition of Onondaga's power as the only option to achieve peaceful coexistence along the British Empire's northern frontier. The Six Nations too vocally supported the plan.[41]

The royal proclamation and plans for the reorganization of the empire's Indian Department turned out to be of little practical significance, merely serving as words on paper. While the proclamation hindered the aspirations of adventurous speculators, it failed to alter their priorities or plans. The language used, particularly the phrase "Our Royal Will and pleasure, for the present," suggested that the proclaimed boundary was only temporary. This led to a power struggle within the colonies and England, with various factions seeking to abolish or extend the new boundary. Speculators strategically secured seats in colonial legislatures, luring other established legislators and royal governors to join their cause. They also reached out internationally, leveraging connections in London to expand their influence. While their efforts occasionally showed promise, the unpredictability of transatlantic politics kept speculative plans in a state of perpetual uncertainty. The correspondence of individuals associated with land companies is replete with years of optimistic declarations regarding imminent approval, which were seldom realized. Despite the lack of tangible progress, the anticipation of approval remained a potent force shaping Native American diplomacy for the foreseeable future.[42]

On the ground, the proclamation line was even more ineffectual. It may have deterred speculators from achieving their plans for the time being but it in no way put an end to squatting. All across the frontier, colonial settlers created squatter communities beyond the king's line that irritated Native peoples and speculators alike. Squatter settlements sprung up around Fort Augusta and were creeping up the West Branch. Connecticut settlers also continued to trickle into the lands along the North and East Branches. Speculators, though, were particularly angry at Pennsylvania's colonial government, declaring that it did little to restrict its colonists from squatting on lands beyond "the Limitts prescribed by his Majesty." Despite all the other exaggerations and lies perpetuated by prominent shareholders in land companies, this one was true. The existence of squatters undeterred by the colonial governments flew in the face of the peace agreements that were putting an end to Pontiac's War, thus undermining any ability to establish a new, more westerly boundary as part of the negotiations for peace, which some speculators and officials thought more than possible.[43]

That fault cannot be solely attributed to Pennsylvania or any specific colony. The home government in Britain never allocated sufficient resources to enforce George III's proclamation, and some key imperial officials resisted taking any action. One important official dismissed the king's proclamation as "a very silly" thing. Lord Barrington, responsible for American affairs in the mid-1760s, stated that if the proclamation "be right," then "the maintenance of forts to the westward of that line must be wrong." This lack of commitment aligned with the broader nonpolicy approach of Lord Rockingham during his tenure as prime minister. He was more than reluctant to allocate additional funds for the proclamation's enforcement. Similarly, when William Pitt (Lord Chatham) served as prime minister from 1766 to 1768, his secretary in charge of American affairs, Lord Shelburne, actively worked against the line, advocating for new colonies beyond it.[44]

The Board of Trade's plan to reorganize Native American diplomacy that Johnson and the Haudenosaunee were excited about suffered a similar fate. Initially expected to be implemented, the plan never materialized. Imperial administrators balked at the estimated cost of £20,000 per year. Complaints from Thomas Gage about Johnson's extravagant spending, along with ridicule from colonial governors, further undermined it.

Consequently, Barrington and Shelburne reduced the power and budgets for the superintendents, placing more and more responsibility for Indigenous affairs in the hands of the individual colonial governments. It was not long before Johnson found himself heading an understaffed diplomatic corps within the British military. There were even rumors of eliminating his office entirely. The once-ambitious superintendent, and the Six Nations with him, seemed increasingly inconsequential. The future from Onondaga and Johnson Hall appeared bleak.[45]

All was not lost. The royal proclamation line, both its meager successes and many failures, created an opportunity for Johnson and the Six Nations to reassert their importance within the British Empire. Johnson had much to work with. The western nations detested squatter encroachments and speculative plans, sparking near-constant frontier violence, creating the real possibility of another war before even Pontiac's War had officially ended. Using that prospect to his advantage, Johnson urged imperial administrators to let him negotiate a reconsideration of the king's boundary line with the Haudenosaunee.

According to Johnson, it wasn't the logic of separation that was the problem but the extent of the line that mattered. A new boundary, he argued to the Board of Trade, Thomas Gage, and anyone else who would listen, was the surest means of achieving tranquility. Johnson also knew, if he played it just right, that negotiating a new boundary would endear him to prominent officials with an interest in Indigenous land while at the same time reassert the significance of the Six Nations over the lands and peoples of the northern district and beyond. To be sure, such a plan in no way spoke to the interests of the Susquehanna or Ohio Nations, but it would make Johnson and the Six Nations seem indispensable to the future of the British Empire. It was all smoke and mirrors.[46]

In spring 1765, with General Gage's approval, Johnson convened discussions at Johnson Hall involving the Six Nations, as well as some Ohio and Susquehanna Nations. While the initial purpose was to establish peace and urge the Delaware and Seneca to release British captives, the conference quickly evolved into a platform for the Six Nations to reclaim suzerainty over the Ohio and Northern Susquehanna River Valleys. Johnson also initiated the process of securing a new boundary. Addressing the Six

Nations as "Uncles," the few Delaware present acknowledged their change of stance, recognizing the Haudenosaunee's influence and expressing readiness to embrace the Covenant Chain. The Six Nations, particularly the Mohawk, Oneida, and Onondaga, then took the lead, reprimanding their "Nephews" for warring with their brothers and delaying the delivery of "the Flesh and Blood of the English." With this achieved, the focus shifted to "the last but most important affair," the "settling a boundary between you and the English."[47]

Johnson had already prepared some of the principal Haudenosaunee chiefs for this part of the conference. He "sent a message to some of your Nations some time ago to acquaint you that I should confer with you at this Meeting upon it," and now desired "to know in what manner you would choose to extend" the boundary. He also promised that this new "Division Line" would be final and "no White man shall dare to invade" it. This, he argued, was "the best and surest method of ending" their "disputes" and securing "your property to you beyond a possibility of disturbance." But, he cautioned, the line should be drawn "for the advantage of both White Men and Indians" and should "best agree with the Extent and Encrease of each Province." The population of those colonies nearly doubled every twenty years, therefore such a stipulation laid bare the "Extent" of his desires.[48]

Haudenosaunee representatives were more than happy to oblige, "provided the White People will abide by it." More to the point, they understood the larger imperial audience and hoped that by showing "our good Disposition by our Actions," "it will render us more regarded by the English." After a few days of debate, the Six Nations "agreed together for Ourselves, our Wives and Children to make a Cession to the King," which they thought "shall now please you better." The line would run down the east side of the North and East Branches of the Susquehanna River from Owego (about ten miles from New York's current southern border) to Fort Augusta, and then follow the south side of the West Branch to the Ohio River. From there, the line extended south to the Tennessee River. In effect, the Haudenosaunee ceded much of the Shawnee's territory in the Ohio Valley and even some Cherokee land south of that, while at the same time preserving most of the lands belonging to both the western and eastern Haudenosaunee and their multiethnic "Nephews" living in the Northern Susquehanna River

Valley. To be sure, the new agreement gave the British some of the land around Fort Augusta, which had been a sticking point a few years earlier, but as the Haudenosaunee had made clear many times before, the majority of the Northern Susquehanna River Valley was still off-limits.[49]

The Six Nations' delegates, though, staunchly rejected the notion of a boundary through their territory north of Owego. Johnson, however, had an interest in that land. Just a few years earlier the Canajoharie Mohawk had "gifted" him about 25,000 acres in the area, but the royal proclamation barred such private grants. That could all change with a new line. At the time of this meeting, though, the Haudenosaunee representatives said there were too many difficulties and interested parties involved to strike a line north of Owego. Establishing a boundary there would require a much more delicate negotiation, which in the not too distant future would actually endanger the Northern Susquehanna Valley and the peoples who lived there. In this moment, though, Haudenosaunee delegates hoped this massive land cession to their south would shift attention away from their own territory to that of the western nations, particularly the Shawnee, those "silly people," as Johnson called them, who demanded their own independence and did not attend the conference.[50]

The new boundary agreed to at Johnson Hall in the spring of 1765 was far from final. Johnson may have obtained a piece of "Parchment" affixed with "the Marks" of the Six Nations, but he would also need to get colonial governors, imperial officials, and other interested parties on board to finalize it all. There was, in essence, a lot of politicking left, egos to massage, and interests to address before this new boundary would become official. For some, especially proprietor Thomas Penn and his enemy, the Susquehannah Company, that line would not be official until the Six Nations ceded the lands of the Susquehanna Nations north of the West Branch of the Susquehanna River.[51]

Johnson wasted little time in garnering support after the conference. Soon after, he dispatched letters to Thomas Gage, governors, and the Board of Trade, extolling his successes and urging their agreement to the new boundary. He painted a dire picture, asserting that without approval, maintaining harmony with "the Indians" would be impossible. In his words, he was "confident" that neglecting the approval would lead to a "Rupture more general & infinitely more calamitous than the former." His deputies, especially George Croghan, echoed these sentiments, rallying support from elite men with the capital to shoulder the burden. This formed an extensive network of influential speculators lobbying for the new boundary. Despite these efforts, some important imperial officials remained skeptical. Johnson's boundary negotiation, after all, was not officially sanctioned and challenged the king's proclamation.[52]

Official hesitancy was eventually overwhelmed by violent resistance and rebellion erupting across the British Empire in the mid-1760s, not least of which occurred on the North American frontier. Unsurprisingly, the various interested parties seeking Indigenous land, knowingly and unknowingly, created many of those problems in the first place. Croghan, for instance, buoyed by Johnson's and other speculators' vision for the future of the northern frontier and besieged by debt, sought to open and monopolize trade with the Illinois Country, even though peace, which seemed imminent, was not technically established with all of Britain's Native enemies. Such a trade, according to George III's proclamation, was therefore illegal. But Croghan pressed ahead and contracted with a firm owned by key members of the Suffering Traders, John Baynton, Samuel Wharton, and George Morgan, who were desperate. Trying to exploit a lucrative opportunity, Croghan and the firm ignored the trade's illegality and sent "a number of wagons loaded with Indians goods, and warlike stores" to Fort Pitt en route to the Illinois Country.[53]

News of the trade goods quickly spread throughout the colonial settlements on the frontier, sparking another round of frontier rage. On March 6, 1765, white colonists in Cumberland County who did not see the necessity of establishing goodwill with Native American "enemies," blackened their faces and descended on Croghan's pack trains, confiscating the goods and blowing up several tons of gunpowder. According to some estimates, angry frontiersmen destroyed or confiscated nearly £30,000 worth of goods. In the weeks and months ahead, those "Black Boys," as they would come to be known, set up their own inspection regime, rifling through official mail, harassing traders, and even laying siege to a British fort and kidnapping a British officer. At the same time, white settlers using their own visions of separation continued to murder Native peoples across the frontier. Soon rumors surfaced that the Ohio, Illinois, and Great Lakes Nations were organizing an alliance to attack the British in retribution. Croghan, Wharton's firm, the Black Boys, and other murderous frontiersmen may have worked against and even hated one another, but they all together created a combustible situation on the frontier.[54]

The Susquehanna Nations also faced ongoing challenges: rogue traders, primarily dealing in alcohol, disrupted fair trade. Moreover, despite the royal proclamation and subsequent negotiations, settlers and poachers persisted. In spring 1765, around fifty individuals from Cumberland County, likely militia members from Colonel John Armstrong's "Susquehanna Campaign" two years earlier, passed by Fort Augusta and expressed a keen interest in Great Island beyond the proclamation and Johnson's negotiated line with the Haudenosaunee. These settlers, described as "very inquisitive about Indians," raised concerns, especially since "a Muncey Man" reported that a host of Indigenous families, including Newalike, the Susquehanna Nations' new leader, were also on their way to settle Great Island. Alarmed, an officer at Fort Augusta dispatched a rider to Governor Penn, urging action against potential intruders northwest of the fort. Conflict seemed imminent.[55]

In the end, there was little official effort or ability to stop the colonists or the conflict over land that they would most assuredly instigate. When those inquisitive colonists came to the fort, it was significantly understaffed. The colonial government, faced with dwindling resources and engaged in a protracted factional dispute over military spending and the taxes to fund it, let the pay for militia to staff the provincial forts dry up, leaving a skeleton crew at Fort Augusta. That reality was symptomatic of what was happening throughout British North America. Receiving an endless stream of reports about the lack of funds, racial violence, and squatter settlements, Thomas Gage basically washed his hands of the matter. Pressed by the home government to cut expenses, Gage informed Johnson on Christmas Day 1765 that many of the forts along Britain's expansive frontier would need to be evacuated.[56]

While the forts had been a constant source of tension between the British and almost all the Native communities near them, the royal proclamation made them the only real deterrence to squatters and rogue illegal traders. According to Johnson, "There is no doing without them." As he well knew, without those forts, Indigenous affairs and policing the frontier would further fall to the whims and meager infrastructure of the colonial governments. Riddled by factional politics and controlled by the interests of speculators, both in trade and land, those governments could and would do little. Although the colonial governors made grand pronouncements and promises, colonial weakness and ineptitude was instantly felt. Frequent trespasses, murders, and vigilante actions became the norm on the frontier beyond and around a contested line.[57]

In the Northern Susquehanna River Valley, squatters proved one of the most serious problems. Not only were Connecticut settlers on the move but Pennsylvanians were hacking their initials into trees and building settlements just northwest of Fort Augusta and also near Great Island, beyond "the late purchase." Those settlements elicited such animosity from both the Haudenosaunee and Susquehanna Nations that Johnson had to convene a meeting at Johnson Hall and Pennsylvania's governor had to issue another proclamation against the intruders. Penn also ordered a justice of the peace, Colonel Turbutt Francis, to forcibly evict some of those squatters, especially "Frederick Stump, a German settled beyond the Indian Purchase near to Fort Augusta," who would forever be known to history for his vicious murder of Native peoples a few years later. Governor Penn reported to his uncle Thomas Penn that the "Indians thereabouts had complained" that Stump "settled there, without their leave." What was more, Stump tried to make "the Indians believe that" Penn "had taken money of him for the land." Apparently, Stump claimed that he purchased the land northwest of Fort Augusta from Governor Penn, who gave Stump his "Warrant or Authority for making such settlements." Penn, then, was pleased when Colonel Francis reported that he, "accompanied by some Indians," went to Stump's home, "burnt the house and destroyed all the corn that was growing so that this fellow is entirely routed."[58]

Nevertheless, writing to the Board of Trade, Johnson rightfully argued that such squatters and illegal traders and the violence of white settlers seriously threatened peace along the northern frontier. Nonetheless, he also claimed that the only way to fix the situation was to grant him more power and confirm his new boundary. Even Croghan, who instigated some of that trouble, used settler resistance and violence as evidence for the need for that new boundary, more colonies, and more autonomous power for the superintendents. Prominent speculators too maneuvered to capitalize on the chaos to achieve their own ends.[59]

All of these justifications and interests were intimately connected. Representative of the intrigue behind the scenes, Johnson told the Suffering Traders, particularly Baynton, Wharton, and Morgan, that he had "their Interests & Sufferings much at heart" and would, if the king and his ministers approved his new boundary, assure the acquisition of "a Tract of land as Restitution for the Traders Losses." It would be, he promised, "an Advantagious Grant as a Reimbursement." Interestingly, he also hinted that such an advantage required a different boundary than even the one he had just negotiated with the Haudenosaunee. Although Johnson made that boundary agreement seem somewhat finalized to many imperial officials, he was already maneuvering to alter it.[60]

Since much was left to be settled after the 1765 boundary conference with the Haudenosaunee, especially the line north of Owego, Johnson thought he would most likely be the person to negotiate a final settlement, which would give him the power to alter the entirety of the line. The 1765 negotiation, then, had only been the beginning, and if he had authority from London to finalize it all, he would also have the "power," he told Baynton, Wharton, and Morgan, "to deal with my Friends." In just a few sentences, Johnson solidified his relationship with important backers of the new boundary who, like many others, used their utmost to buttress Johnson's authority. They saw in him a tool to achieve their self-interested dreams, and Johnson knew it and used it.[61]

The home government, facing a depleted treasury, the prospects of yet another war it could not afford, and influential men supporting Johnson's new boundary, started to listen. While they proved more willing to hear out Johnson and his supporters, they also sought avenues to fix the treasury in a way that would allow the home government to follow through with some of the promises made by George III's proclamation. If those initiatives failed, Johnson at least gave them other options to consider.

To fix the treasury, several British prime ministers, starting with George Grenville, wanted to tax the colonies. After all, the colonies gained the most because of the recent wars fought in North America, and according to the information received from British military officers, the colonies had become rich and were overflowing with cash. It was really the only option. Increasing taxes in England, Grenville knew, would not work; British subjects there were already taxed beyond what they had the ability to pay.[62]

The tales of wealth in the colonies, however alluring, were false. Although there may have been prosperous years during the early stages of the Seven Years' War, by 1765 this prosperity had largely disappeared for the majority of colonists. When Parliament passed the Stamp Act in March of that year, taxing printed materials like newspapers, legal documents, dice, and playing cards, colonists from Boston to Savannah resisted. Furious colonists not only rejected the tax but also tore down homes, threatened government officials, closed courts, and asserted that Parliament had no authority over Britain's North American colonies. Because of colonial resistance, the new tax produced little revenue, just over £3,000 for the treasury, mostly from the West Indies, which was a far cry from the anticipated £60,000 envisioned by Grenville and other imperial officials. This outcome highlighted a clear issue: the home government's inability to manage the extensive British Empire after the Seven Years' War. This was further emphasized by a subsequent round of taxation in 1767.[63]

Like Grenville, Britain's secretary of the treasury, Charles Townshend, saw taxing the colonies as the only viable way to fill the empire's depleted coffers. In 1767, he ushered through a slew of taxes on everything from glass and lead to paint and tea. Moreover, part of Townshend's tax scheme would pay for the forts and troops needed to police the king's proclamation line. In the end, though, these taxes resulted in the same kind of colonial resistance as happened with the Stamp Act, and therefore the same outcome for the treasury.[64]

The situation was troubling. The colonies were nearing a state of rebellion, relations with Native Americans were at a low ebb, and nothing, it seemed, worked in imperial officials' favor or the larger interests of the British Empire. It did not take long before some important imperial officials simply wanted to remove themselves entirely from fixing the situation, and many others looked for the cheapest and most shortsighted of remedies (or, as they put it, "the most frugal and reasonable method") to stop the financial bleeding and heal tensions in the empire.[65]

This was the scenario that gave Johnson's "Division Line" life. All of the grandiloquence about a "lasting peace" through a new boundary, and the doggedness with which Johnson and others pursued it, struck a chord with imperial officials scrambling to figure out a way to come out of the 1760s with an empire intact and financially unscathed. In December 1767, about six months after the implementation of Townshend's new taxes, the Board of Trade wrote a report to the king extolling the benefits of a new boundary with new treaties administered by their two colonial superintendents in the north and south, William Johnson and John Stuart. Both superintendents and their deputies, the report argued, should hold separate conferences establishing a western line beyond the one established by the Royal Proclamation of 1763. Separating colonists from Native Americans while at the same time giving angry British subjects more land, imperial administrators hoped, would be the tonic to cure the empire's growing ills.[66]

Britain's financial woes, the interests of speculators, settlers, diplomatic agents, and even "the Indians" came together in the imperial imagination, setting the stage for the largest land grab in American history to that point. But it was just that, imagination. As it turned out, there was no real coming together, a "Diversity of Interests" that pit all of those groups against each other remained, and the future of the Northern Susquehanna River Valley and Britain's North American empire hung with it in the balance.

6

"A Great Run for the Lands on Susquehanna"

THE TREATY OF FORT STANWIX, 1768

AS LETTERS AND INSTRUCTIONS crisscrossed the Atlantic Ocean in the early months of 1768, Sir William Johnson was seriously ill and traveling to New England for fresh air. His illness was the first inkling of something more serious; he would be dead in just six years. Yet, Johnson could not enjoy the healing powers of his convalescence. Lord Shelburne and the Board of Trade finally gave Johnson the authority to establish a new boundary, and therefore he had to go back to Johnson Hall to prepare. Seizing the opportunity, Johnson jettisoned his personal health to plan for a new conference to take place that fall at Fort Stanwix, a British fortress situated on Haudenosaunee land commonly called the Oneida Carry (present-day Rome, New York). And the conference would be large. According to information Johnson and his deputies received, no fewer than three thousand Indigenous people planned to make their way to the fort to finalize a boundary. If this information was to be believed, the conference at Fort Stanwix would be the largest Johnson had ever managed, and accommodating all of these people at this place would be, to say the least, difficult and expensive. Not only would residences need to be built and many apartments in the fort repaired but one week alone would require nearly 150 barrels of pork and flour, not to mention the alcohol and gifts Johnson wanted to use to grease the wheels of negotiation.[1]

He would leave nothing to chance, engineering plans for a constant stream of provisions and gifts to cover what he knew would be a lengthy proceeding. As he told an Albany merchant, he needed to do everything in his power to obtain these goods, "otherwise it must overset the design of

{141}

this Congress, as it cannot be Supposed that Hungry Indians can be kept here, or in any temper without a Bellyfull."² Such preparations were the least of Johnson's problems. He would soon find his planned congress at Fort Stanwix a lightning rod for the "Diversity of Interests" pervading the early American landscape. What was intended as a meeting to help fix the empire further tore it apart.

A lot had changed and still needed to be done since Johnson's negotiation with the Six Nations for a new boundary in 1765, or so he argued. The boundary agreed to then was, in some cases, incomplete. The exact "line to be drawn from the West Branch of Susquehanna" to the Ohio River was unclear, and Johnson and his deputies argued that the line agreed to north of the West Branch to Owego lacked particulars and therefore needed to be identified at the new conference.³ Really, the particulars on that score were clear. At Johnson Hall in 1765, the Six Nations drew a line using the natural boundary that the northern, eastern, and western branches of the Susquehanna River provided, carving the Northern Susquehanna River Valley out from the land deal. There was, then, never any talk of granting the British land between those branches with some sort of northern line jutting off from somewhere on the West Branch. Nevertheless, by 1768 Pennsylvania and Connecticut were racing to claim that northern land. A finalized boundary, if either of those colonies had any say, especially Thomas Penn who had far more influence across the Atlantic than the Susquehannah Company, would need to deviate from the line drawn in 1765. There was also the matter of the boundary north of Owego to Canada. That had not been established yet, and Johnson hoped this new conference at Fort Stanwix would finally settle it.⁴

Johnson's maneuverings were not lost on the Indigenous people who actually lived in the areas that suddenly seemed up for grabs. Hearing rumors that the upcoming conference would change the boundary yet again, some of them made their way to Johnson Hall "complaining about Lands."⁵ By May 1768, it was clear that there would be "much opposition made to it by some of the Nations, on Acct of their Tribes living within them Limits." Irritated, the Delaware and Shawnee threatened to boycott the conference at Fort Stanwix.⁶ What was more, news reached Johnson's deputies that the Spanish as well as those "Crafty Agents of the French" had sent messengers to the southern and western nations, particularly the Delaware and Shawnee, telling them that the upcoming conference was a ruse to gather their people together and murder them all.⁷

Johnson, trying to triage, sent out deputies to Fort Pitt to "get the Temper of the Indians" and prepare the minds of the "Shawnese & Delawares" to agree to a Haudenosaunee cession of lands that "actually belonged to them." Those nations, although he deemed them mere "dependents" of the Six Nations, should, he now conceded, be "considered."⁸ As it turns out, those minds were not the only ones Johnson needed to prepare or convince. As he dispatched deputies to Fort Pitt and planned for provisions and gifts to be sent to Fort Stanwix, he received an inauspicious letter from London that had the potential to derail everything.

In February of that year, King George III created a new cabinet-level position to oversee his vast North American empire, secretary of state for the colonies. The founding minister for that position, Wills Hills, Lord Hillsborough, viewed most colonial initiatives and complaints with suspicion, if not outright hostility. The king created the office to combat colonial truculence and resistance to imperial measures, or so at least Hillsborough believed. British officials in the colonies, whether Johnson or members of the colonial legislatures, Hillsborough thought, should be brought to heel. Their independence had done nothing but bring turmoil to the empire and created the "enourmous expence She at present groans under."⁹ He even contemplated "abolishing the Superintendencies" altogether, a sentiment he also held for some of the colonial legislatures, especially in Massachusetts.¹⁰

Hillsborough saw the upcoming conference at Fort Stanwix as no different. Perhaps, as Benjamin Franklin thought, Hillsborough also feared it. Most of the new secretary's income came from rents on his Irish estates, which, with more land opening in America, made him "terribly afraid of dispeopling Ireland."¹¹ Whatever the motive, Hillsborough wanted to circumscribe the geographic limits of the new boundary and therefore desired Johnson to follow "precise Instructions." The lack of such instructions in the past, Hillsborough mused in a letter to Johnson, all too "frequently embarrass you" and "impedes the exertion of your abilities to that advantage for his Majestys Service." In just one sentence, Hillsborough passively rebuked Johnson for his past conduct, making it seem as if Johnson had consistently failed in his duty to the king because he was left to his own devices without proper management, a sentiment that irritated the ever-ambitious superintendent. Johnson was, to say the least, "not at all pleased."[12]

When it came to the upcoming conference at Fort Stanwix, Hillsborough gave Johnson no leeway to conduct affairs. The boundary, Hillsborough argued, was set by the Haudenosaunee in 1765, and therefore the new conference was a mere formality. Just in case Hillsborough's words did not clearly elucidate his position, he also had "the honour to inclose to you a Map, whereon is delineated the Boundary line proposed by the Board of Trade to be Settled with the Six Nations in conformity to what was agreed upon at the Congress in 1765." Such instructions were important: if Johnson deviated from that boundary at Fort Stanwix, he would still need Hillsborough's approval to make it official. If this letter was any indication of Hillsborough's thoughts, Johnson would need a good excuse to ignore the secretary's "precise Instructions."[13]

Johnson did have a few things going for him. Adhering to Hillsborough's instructions and the Board of Trade's map would never work. The colonial commissioners attending the upcoming conference, especially the Pennsylvanians, would never agree to that boundary, potentially derailing the negotiations and wasting valuable time and money. As Johnson's nephew and deputy agent Guy Johnson explained to Thomas Gage, "The Proprietaries of Pennsylvania are desirous of Extending the boundary beyond that prescribed, so as to Comprehend the Land between the Forks of Susquehanna by a direct Line from the head of the West Branch towards Owegy [Owego]." Moreover, "the White people" already made "encroachments" near that land, and neither they nor the proprietors would be willing to give up "so Valuable a piece of Ground."[14] Those desires could be worked to William Johnson's advantage.

Moreover, Johnson had been prodding the Mohawk and Oneida about establishing the boundary north of Owego for the last three years, and it just so happens they were ready to clarify a boundary now. Since their meeting with Johnson in 1765, squatters had inundated their lands, and New York speculators were drudging up purported purchases made many years earlier to lay claim to vast sections of those same lands. A boundary north of Owego now seemed necessary to deter these encroachments.[15] Using that necessity to his advantage, Johnson argued to Thomas Gage that without the northern line from Owego to Canada, "the Indians will not be secure, & the affair of the Boundary will be defeated." Hillsborough and the Board of Trade, therefore, made "a Mistake" on their map.[16] Johnson could and would use the need to correct that mistake as leverage to renegotiate the boundary everywhere and justify his actions to Hillsborough. Preparations on his end were mostly complete.

Johnson was not the only person preparing for Fort Stanwix. Upon hearing rumors of the upcoming conference, Connecticut's Susquehannah Company, though not invited to Fort Stanwix (Johnson actively excluded the company), planned to capitalize on the purported extension of the boundary to undercut Pennsylvania by physically inhabiting any newly purchased land. Inspiring settlers to make their way to the Northern Susquehanna River Valley, Connecticut newspapers churned out articles by authors attached to the company attacking Pennsylvania's land policies, which, they argued, benefited the proprietors and speculators, creating a country of "land-lords" and "vassals." Connecticut's land policy, in contrast, allowed everyone "some share in the soil, and therefore" they could never be "slave vassals or beggars." Connecticut settlers had a duty to "settle these immense forests" to bring their vision of "liberty" to "those regions."[17] At the same time, the Susquehannah Company dispatched new agents to London to lobby on its behalf. The company also doled out shares "in the Susquehanna Purchase" to prominent Pennsylvania politicians and land speculators such as Joseph Galloway, "in Testimony of the Greatefull Sense This Company have of their kind Services for said Company."[18] Obviously, something was stirring behind the scenes in Pennsylvania to help Connecticut undermine the proprietors. Suffice it to say, the Susquehannah Company and its shareholders "were determined to take possession of" the valley "as soon as the Treaty is over" and that land was "purchased of the Indians."[19]

Never one to be outdone, Thomas Penn was also making moves. Since a significant portion of any new boundary would run through what he saw as the land "within" Pennsylvania but "not purchased," Penn wanted to use the

Fort Stanwix meeting to secure his claim to the land north of the forks and the West Branch of the Susquehanna River to deter Connecticut's Susquehannah Company. In letter after letter, Penn pressed Johnson "to get as much Land for us (between the West branch of Susquehannah & Delaware) as the Indians will consent and prevent any further dealings, between the Six Nations and the people of Connecticut."[20] Penn was especially eager to obtain several promising silver mines in the Northern Susquehanna River Valley, particularly a rather large one he had heard rumors about near Wyoming. Moreover, he had "great faith" that the upcoming boundary negotiation would go his way, and therefore desired his land agents to start laying out "thirty or forty thousand acres of land" encompassing "the good Land at Wyoming and the Mine, for our use."[21] Obtaining that land by purchase was one thing but actually gaining access to it and holding it was quite another.

In that arena Penn had to race the Susquehannah Company, and therefore he too began making plans to populate the Northern Susquehanna River Valley. The negotiations at Fort Stanwix had not even started before Penn instructed his nephew John Penn, then governor of Pennsylvania, to make plans to distribute land in the valley so it would be immediately settled by people "on whom we can depend."[22] Nor would it be hard to find such people. Back in 1765, the day after Johnson started negotiations with the Haudenosaunee for a new boundary, a group of military veterans led by Colonel Turbutt Francis, a veteran of both the Seven Years' War and Pontiac's War and the son of a prominent proprietary official, petitioned Penn for land between the East and West Branches of the Susquehanna River above Fort Augusta, the same area he also traversed evicting squatters like Frederick Stump. Speaking to the proprietor's interests, Francis proposed to "embody" his men "in a compact settlement of some good land at some distance from the inhabited part of the Province, where . . . by their arms, union and increase" they would "become a powerful barrier to the Province."[23] Dusting off that old petition, Penn instructed his nephew, "We have nothing now to desire, but that Coll. Francis may be settled with his people, and that they keep off the people of Connecticut."[24]

Such planning might seem premature, but Thomas Penn had good reason to believe the conference at Fort Stanwix would go his way. In the same letters urging Johnson to extend the boundary north of Fort Augusta or "the forks," Penn promised to return the favor. "I can truly assure [you] that I have been an importunate Solicitor both on account of your own grant, and that of the Indian Boundary," Penn had written to Johnson earlier that winter. Penn knew that Johnson had been trying to get the British government to approve the grant he had received from the Canajoharie Mohawk for years, and Penn promised to use his influence in London to achieve it, especially if, he reminded Johnson, "you will use your best endeavours with the Indians, to grant us Land, as high as they can be brought to agree to, between the West branch of Sasquehannah & the River Delaware."[25] Although Penn and Johnson had a rocky relationship to this point—they were both headstrong, ambitious, and jealous of each other's power—the superintendent was more than happy to accept this quid pro quo. "It was always my Intention to endeavor to obtain that Tract between the Forks of Susquehannah Northward," Johnson wrote to Penn a few months later.[26]

While Penn enticed Johnson to obtain a larger section of the Northern Susquehanna River Valley than the Haudenosaunee had agreed to in 1765, Pennsylvania speculators were also abuzz. Thomas Wharton, near bankruptcy, planned to attend the conference to negotiate a private purchase with the Haudenosaunee on behalf of the Suffering Traders. In addition, according to rumor, Joseph Galloway and his ally John Hughes, who Grenville had appointed as Pennsylvania's stamp distributer, aligned themselves with the governor of New Jersey, William Franklin (Benjamin Franklin's son), to obtain the "Silver Mine at Wyoming, and a lead mine on the West Branch of the Susquehannah." They had already prepared a warrant based on an old deed "near three weeks before" the treaty, and planted agents at Fort Stanwix as well as at Wyoming to "give notice to their Associates that they might" quickly survey the land and submit their official paperwork to legally undercut the proprietors.[27]

Important families like the Shippens and the Allens were similarly getting their ducks in a row. It was, one onlooker noted, a "great Run for the Lands on Susquehannah."[28] In May 1768, Joseph Shippen, onetime officer at Fort Augusta and now Governor Penn's secretary, petitioned the governor on behalf of himself and his friends to "obtain a Grant of Lands in the next purchase" along the West Branch of the Susquehanna River. Although he received a "favourable Answer"—John Penn told him he "could not see the least objection to his granting the Lands we petitioned for"—Shippen also realized that a lot could happen to derail that promise. Just to be sure it all worked out, he also met with Secretary of the Land Office James Tilghman, a recent arrival from Maryland who had married Turbutt Francis's sister. Shippen told Tilghman that he wanted to secure "first Choice" for himself and his partners and that he was worried about the prospect of squatter rights and the existence of previous claims like those of Galloway and Hughes. Shippen was more than delighted when Tilghman responded that those squatters and anyone else with a prior interest would be disregarded. Jubilant, Shippen wrote to his partners, "We shall no doubt have the Preference in the Choice of our Lands."[29]

Nor did Shippen's partners have to worry about Lord Hillsborough's instructions to William Johnson. Thomas Penn tapped Tilghman to go to Fort Stanwix, and Shippen was also lobbying to be "one of the Commissioners from this Government" to "settle the Boundary Line between the Indians and the Colonies." Therefore, while Hillsborough's instructions, which everyone knew and gossiped about, made it seem as if "all the Lands in the Forks of the Susquehanna are to be reserved by the Indians for their hunting and planting grounds," which threw into question "whether the Lands we have in view can be granted to us or not," Shippen assured his friends that either he or Tilghman would use their positions as commissioners to "get this Matter settled at the ensuing Congress in a different Manner, and more to the advantage of the Proprietaries."[30] For Shippen, like many other speculators, the proprietors' interests were the same as his selfish ones.

The aged yet still powerful William Allen also planned on attending the conference as an advisor to Governor Penn, but due to his constant battles with gout, he sent his son John instead, who "has some inclinations" to take "up some lands in the new purchase."[31] To assure his particular interest in that purchase, William Allen wrote to Thomas Penn to remind the proprietor of his obligations to his old friend. Since Allen had been consistently "active and zealous" for the proprietary family, he thought it was only fair that he and his son should get their share and that his political allies should be able to "to take up in the next Purchase upon the common terms 5 or 6,000 acres of land," especially those lands between "the two branches of the Susquehannah."[32] Penn, ever ready to oblige a staunch ally with octopus-like tentacles of interest, assured Allen he would get what he wanted, and Allen sent back his "hearty thanks for your kind offer about taking up some lands in the new purchase." Yet, like Shippen, Allen was not totally happy with mere promises. Penn's offer meant little if the proprietor and his land agents did not confirm the land deeds fast. Allen feared that before he and those in his interest got their portion, "the best lands will be settled by the scum of America, as an hundred familys have lately moved up there on the rumor of a new purchase." Soon, there would be more than "one thousand familys."[33]

Those poorer families who Allen deemed "scum" had little choice but to act illegally to hopefully obtain land in the upcoming purchase in the face of such powerful opponents. William Allen was the chief justice of the province and simultaneously held a seat in the colonial legislature. Allen, like many others vying for legal rights to land in the Susquehanna River Valley, was a member of the colonial elite, a "small Knot" of "Interested favorites" who wanted to create "Monopolies" to secure the land for themselves.[34] Such opprobrium was not mere hyperbole. If we take the plans of Penn for Wyoming and the silver mines, and combine them with the maneuverings of and promises made to Shippen, Allen, and Francis, then most of the good farmable lands that could possibly be legally obtained in the Northern Susquehanna River Valley were already accounted for, and that does not even consider the numerous other speculators making plans for the valley. As one of Thomas Penn's closest political allies in Pennsylvania put it, it seemed as if the mere idea of the land to be gained created a scenario where "officers as well as others who are intrusted by you, [were] attempting to make an Advantage of their Offices and Securing the best [lands] for themselves." The conference had not even begun and speculators were already poised to realize what Shippen called "our scheme." America's "scum" needed to move, and fast.[35]

Facing serious threats to their land, Indigenous people were also preparing. The destruction of the Seven Years' War and Pontiac's War had seriously diminished the Susquehanna Nations and undermined their ability to claim independence from Onondaga, seemingly paving the way for colonial settlement. By the end of those wars, Teedyuscung had been assassinated, Wyoming had been burned to the ground twice, Nescopeck had also been set ablaze, Wyalusing was barely populated, the Montour strongholds on the West Branch were mostly abandoned, and Great Island was in shambles. Many of the people who lived in those places were either dead or had fled to the northern towns of Tioga, Owego, Assinisink, Oquaga, Otseningo, or the Ohio River Valley. According to a rudimentary census taken by George Croghan in 1765, there were no more than 550 Nanticoke, Mohican, Conoy, Munsee, Saponi, and Delaware warriors in the Northern Susquehanna River Valley, and most of them had taken refuge on the northernmost reaches of the North Branch in Haudenosaunee-controlled towns.[36]

Old and established leaders in the Northern Susquehanna River Valley were also gone. Nutimus had died during Pontiac's War, Paxinosa left for the Ohio Valley, and so had Captain Bull. According to popular memory, after his imprisonment during Pontiac's War, Bull left the valley with some Delaware and Shawnee for modern Braxton County, West Virginia. In 1772, so the story goes, angry colonists burned down his town there but Bull survived and fled, living out the last days of his life in Missouri along the Mississippi River and dying of natural causes sometime in the 1790s. Other, perhaps more credible stories indicate that he resettled somewhere just west of the Alleghany Mountains, fought against the Americans during the Revolution, and died in battle in 1781. Neither, however, can be definitively confirmed. Just like that, the historical record can run cold. Regardless of Bull's ultimate fate, his absence, like the absence of many others, meant that the Northern Susquehanna River Valley was a far different place after more than a decade of war.[37]

The southern part of that valley was not entirely depopulated though. With the conclusion of Pontiac's War in 1766, the Susquehanna Nations started trickling back to the East and West Branches. In addition, in that same year, a little over 130 Tuscarora from North Carolina made their way to the valley. New leaders also emerged, such as Kanigut, a Tuscarora chief; Jemmy Nanticoke; Kanak't, a Conoy chief known as Last Night; as well as Delaware, Mohican, and Munsee sachems, Papunhank, Nanhun, and Newalike, respectively. Nevertheless, settlements would need to be rebuilt, fields cleared and planted, and trading patterns and connections recreated. Moreover, history still echoed and past grievances remained, perhaps even more so now.[38]

Because of the demographic situation in the Northern Susquehanna River Valley and the land lust of British colonists, the Haudenosaunee also made moves to further repopulate the valley. Attempting to create a bulwark to preserve their lands and sovereignty, the Grand Council at Onondaga looked to an aging Seneca elder, Osternados, who the British called Seneca George, living on the North Branch of the Susquehanna River at the town of Otseningo (near present-day Binghamton, New York). Since at least 1750, the Grand Council had charged Osternados with looking after the interests of and managing the Haudenosaunee's relationship with the Susquehanna Nations, particularly the Nanticoke and Conoy. Like many others, Osternados attended the conferences at Easton and Lancaster. He was also a regular presence in Philadelphia during the many meetings there. Although Osternados seldom spoke at those meetings, his silence in the public record in no way represented his actual status. During those years he developed a close relationship with one of Pennsylvania's most important diplomatic agents, Conrad Weiser. When Weiser died in 1760, it was Osternados who led the condolence ceremony, symbolically drying colonists' eyes, expressing his feeling of "great loss." In all, he was an important diplomat that mostly worked outside of rather than in the colonial public's eye. By the late 1760s, he was one of the few experienced Haudenosaunee elders left to oversee affairs in the Northern Susquehanna River Valley.[39]

As the upcoming conference at Fort Stanwix approached, Osternados worked hard to repopulate the valley. There were still Nanticoke and Conoy in Maryland, and many Delaware also remained in New Jersey "among the White People." All of them were in the midst of disputes with colonists over land. The Delaware were being pushed out of New Jersey and white Marylanders had completely surrounded the Nanticoke and Conoy, claiming ownership over all of their lands. Like everywhere else in the British Empire, New Jersey and Maryland speculators and settlers produced old and questionable deeds, treaties, and agreements to justify their claims, and squatters were a perennial problem. Speaking to shared grievances, Osternados commiserated with the Indigenous nations there, noting that once colonists "got all their lands" they "become" not only "rich" but "very cross" and "forget their former Obligations." In order to "be out of trouble, and danger from the White People," he suggested that they all move to the

Northern Susquehanna River Valley. "Their people," whether extended clan or kin, Osternados argued, had for at least the last thirty years made their homes there. Therefore, they should "settle together" in that valley on, he was quick to point out, "Six Nation Lands."[40] Heeding that advice, Delaware, Nanticoke, and Conoy made their way to the valley.

By the early months of 1768, the Northern Susquehanna River Valley, from Owego to Great Island, seemed to be getting back to normal. Even the few official traders at Fort Augusta began to see and service more people. Goods flowed from Philadelphia, Harris Ferry, and other terminals, making their way to the fort and then back again loaded with peltry. Yet, as before, the Native peoples who lived in the valley worried about their future. The new norm, after all, had a violent underbelly. Indeed, it seemed as if frontier inhabitants "think it meritorious to murder the Heathen as they call them."[41]

Such racialized violence defined the lives of people on the frontier in the 1760s, and as Indigenous people repopulated the Northern Susquehanna River Valley, that violence continued to rear its ugly head. In January 1768, Newalike, a Munsee sachem who was also "the Chief of the Delawares, and other Indians at Great Island," sent his advisor, Bill Champion, to Philadelphia to complain that "five white men had lately been marking Trees and Surveying land in the Forks of the Susquehanna" northwest of Fort Augusta. If Newalike inherited the mantle of Teedyuscung and Nutimus, which seems likely, the forks were also part of his people's lands. When Newalike tried to stop those intruders, arguing that the land was "as yet not purchased from the Indians," the squatters threatened to kill him. After Champion retold this experience to the governor, John Penn sent Champion home with a message and a wampum belt to present to Newalike professing that Pennsylvania would stop these invasions.[42]

Penn also sent Champion back to Newalike with sorrowful news. Pennsylvania colonists Frederick Stump and his indentured servant John Ironcutter had recently murdered four Native men and two of their wives at the mouth of Middle Creek, south of Great Island, and then traveled up that creek where they butchered their victim's surviving wives and children, including a female infant. In all, ten Mohican, Shawnee, Delaware, Seneca, and Mingo men and women were killed, and at least one of them Stump scalped, which some Native peoples declared "is worse than murdering." Stump and Ironcutter also burned down the small settlement and hid the bodies of the slain in the creek under the ice. In the governor's message to Newalike, Penn expressed sorrow for the loss and promised to take "Steps" to "apprehend the offenders."[43]

This tragic massacre symbolized the precarious nature of life for Indigenous people on the northern frontier. It also strained relationships between Pennsylvania and many Native Americans before the meeting at Fort Stanwix. One of the men Stump had murdered was Kanaghragait, also known as White Mingo or John Cook, an important leader from Tioga, a multiethnic town on the North Branch of the Susquehanna River. White Mingo and the others slain had kin and connections that spanned well beyond Middle Creek and Tioga. White Mingo, for instance, had clan and kin spread throughout the Ohio and Susquehanna River Valleys as well as Seneca country. The Mohican, Delaware, and Shawnee family of John and Cornelius Campbell murdered by Stump had just as far-reaching connections. They had relations at Great Island, Logstown, and Venango and relatives living near the Seneca town of Chemung. Another of the slain, Jonas Griffy, was a Munsee with connections in Stockbridge, Massachusetts, as well as West Jersey. The murders seemed to touch people everywhere.[44]

At Great Island, Newalike and the Susquehanna people there were understandably upset. As one of the Shawnee leaders at Great Island, Shawana Ben, declared, "There are four of my Relations Murdered by Stump, and all I desire is that he may suffer for his wicked Action." If Stump did not suffer, Shawana Ben cautioned, he would take it as a sign that "my Brothers, the English, have let" go of the "Chain of Friendship" and therefore he would "let go, too."[45]

This was a feeling that swept across the Northern Susquehanna River Valley. When a local Indian agent, Thomas McKee, heard of the murders he instantly "went up to Fort Augusta to Spake to ye. Indians on Susquehannah" where he "found them much agitated and Thretening" to "immediately" take their revenge "on the frontier inhabitants." To make matters worse, before McKee could offer any kind of condolence, "four Indians" were "sent from the great Island in Sasquehanna to inform the Western Nations of that unlucky affair."[46] They "reached Ohio" on January 27, and by early

February Thomas McKee's son Alexander, stationed at Fort Pitt, found that the news the Great Island messengers brought had enraged "the Warriors of the different nations" there, who, like the Susquehanna Nations, "say the English are certainly determined to make war on us, or otherwise they would not scalp our people."[47]

The skeleton crew back at Fort Augusta, fearful for the future, tried to keep any more news about Stump's murders from leaking out from the Northern Susquehanna River Valley. Not long after McKee's visit, for example, a Tuscarora hunting party made their way to the fort for trade and respite before they headed further north. Most likely, they sat, drank, ate, and spoke with the members of the Susquehanna Nations who were also there and lived around the fort. Anxious that the hunting party would return home and spread news of the massacre to the other Six Nations before William Johnson or John Penn could triage, the officers decided to forcibly detain them.[48] Not only was that a poor decision sure to alienate more than it helped but the news of the murders traveled regardless. Soon Haudenosaunee messengers made their way to Johnson Hall and Philadelphia. With what information Governor Penn could gather from those meetings, "an Indian War seems inevitable, and it is drawn upon us by the villanny & wickedness of our own people." As he pointed out, "The Indians have for some time past been very uneasy at the white people settling upon their lands," and that uneasiness had turned to bitterness because of Stump, Ironcutter, and many others like them.[49]

It should be no surprise that when Johnson's deputy George Croghan held a conference at Fort Pitt that spring to "get the temper" of the Ohio Nations before the conference at Fort Stanwix, some members of the Susquehanna Nations made it a point to attend, which did not bode well. "Munsies and Mohickons," residing "on the Heads of the West Branch of Susquehanna," likely including kin to some of those slain by Stump, packed themselves into "Fourteen Canoes" to take part in the proceedings and to complain. Trade, they argued, was unequal, prices for their peltry too low, and, worse still, white "Encroachments being made on their Lands" circumscribed their hunting territory and resulted in all too frequent murders. They "do not like it." While Croghan tried to assure those in attendance of British goodwill, and the Pennsylvanians sent by Governor Penn—John

Allen and Joseph Shippen—tried to cover Indigenous grief with gifts and over £1,000 in currency, little had actually been settled at the conference. Suffice it to say, the meeting at Fort Pitt, while useful as an arena to air grievances, did not pave an easy path to Fort Stanwix.[50]

Penn thought the situation so bad that the upcoming conference at Fort Stanwix should be "delayed some time till our affairs are a little better settled with the Indians."[51] Johnson, however, would not postpone the planned fall conference. Too much had already been prearranged, and Johnson thought the gifts from Pennsylvania and continued promises to punish the murderers pacified some of the most important Haudenosaunee leaders who would take part in the proceedings. What the Susquehanna Nations thought, it seemed, didn't matter. Moreover, about twenty boats loaded with perishables and other goods "intended for the Presents to be made by the Cession of Lands to the King" had already arrived at the fort on September 19.[52]

Nevertheless, as Penn feared, the all-too-frequent murders on the frontier and the maneuverings of the French and Spanish delayed many of the Ohio and some of the Susquehanna Nations from attending the congress. As those nations carried their thoughts about the murders as well as the messages from the Spanish and French north into Seneca country on their way to the fort, more nations halted to deliberate. Then the death of a Seneca chief created another delay. Many of the Haudenosaunee, Ohio, and Susquehanna delegates converged "in the Senecas Country" to conduct a condolence ceremony to cover their grief before they moved on to Fort Stanwix, which would take "some days more."[53]

Those "some days" turned into weeks. Apoplectic, Johnson sent out messengers to Seneca country urging expediency. He even offered to dedicate the opening days of the conference to a full condolence ceremony to speed things along. Not only was he worried about the potential impact of the meetings among Ohio Nations, Susquehanna Nations, and Six Nations discussing frontier violence and the messages from the Spanish and French, but nearly a thousand Indigenous people had filtered into Fort Stanwix since Johnson arrived. It did not take long before the "provisions which I had for the Congress is already consumed by the Number of Indians who have been here above three Weeks waiting ye Arrival of the Rest." Johnson did not "know what to do," and he was "distressed."[54] While Johnson could easily procure more supplies, he would still have to justify that added expense to his superiors, especially Lord Hillsborough, who he needed to keep happy. Moreover, Johnson could not know "the temper" of the peoples who would be traveling to Fort Stanwix from Seneca country.[55]

Finally, on October 24, after over a month of waiting and handwringing, everyone arrived. In all, there were just over 3,100 Indigenous people in attendance, mostly Haudenosaunee but also representatives of the Susquehanna and Ohio Nations. Additionally, the Six Nations invited Native Americans from Stockbridge in western Massachusetts who had been living with the Oneida, though they "have but little business here," aside from the loss of at least one relation to Stump. To save money, Johnson wanted to "get rid of them if possible."[56] Commissioners from Virginia and Pennsylvania were also in attendance, as was the governor of New Jersey, William Franklin. Pennsylvania's governor, John Penn, who had arrived three weeks prior, did not stay for the conference. He left just days before the treaty negotiations finally began. There did not seem to be much reason for him to stay. As the governor's legal advisor told Thomas Penn, William Johnson "seemed heartily disposed to do everything in his Power to serve you," therefore "the governor and I took our leave."[57]

There were also representatives of the Suffering Traders and a few New England clergymen who lived with the Oneida in attendance.[58] Much to Johnson's chagrin, the conference had not even started before the Suffering Traders barraged Haudenosaunee delegates with inquiries about land, and the New England clergymen handed Johnson a memorial stating their opposition to any land cession that deviated from the 1765 agreement. The clergy were also busy trying to influence the Oneida "to refuse to make an advantageous Cession." While the missionaries proclaimed that they resisted a further cession to save the land for the creation of Christian missions and schools, Johnson thought they were working on behalf of Connecticut speculators to undermine Pennsylvania.[59]

To ensure a harmonious start, Johnson dedicated the conference's initial days to a condolence ceremony honoring the recently deceased Seneca chief and others lost during and after the wars. Starting a conference this way wasn't new. Typically, the first day of any conference saw variations of this ceremony, where each side presented gifts and strings of wampum. Strings and belts of wampum, made from shell beads that were individually crafted in a cylindrical shape and drilled, had represented both the spoken word and a sacred power for Indigenous people for well over a century. Such items captured and conveyed the history of past negotiations, promises, and alliances, and lent legitimacy to messages and speeches that formed relationships. With each string of wampum, the assembled peoples symbolically cleared each other's eyes, ears, and throats so that everyone might see, hear, and speak clearly again. For the Haudenosaunee, this symbolic cleansing represented the origins of the Six Nations and formed the basis of their diplomatic protocol, establishing the unity undergirding the meetings of the Grand Council Fire at Onondaga and most of the treaties and conferences they attended with Europeans. Such unity was important. Conferences with Europeans were often a contest of wills played out in speeches, the airing of grievances, and ceremonies that could take days if not weeks. Sitting across from each other in the council chamber, both sides needed to project unity and strength. The failure to attend to these diplomatic protocols had the potential to derail any treaty.[60]

Conducting a condolence ceremony, while fairly normal, was perhaps more important than ever now, especially for Johnson. The ceremony offered him an opportunity to reaffirm British unity and goodwill to hopefully mitigate the ill will generated by the murders committed by Stump and Ironcutter, the messages of the Spanish and French, and the arguments of the New England clergy. Adept at navigating Haudenosaunee diplomatic culture, Johnson, "on behalf of His Majesty & all His subjects," wiped "away the Tears from your eyes which you are constantly shedding for your late deceased Chiefs," thereby clearing "your sight so," he importantly added, "you may look cheerfully at your Brethren, who are come from Several Provinces to attend this General Congress ordered by His Majesty to be held by me in order to settle some necessary points between him & you." He made similar statements conjoining condolence with "necessary points" when he symbolically cleared Indigenous ears and throats. At the same time, Johnson offered gifts to help cover their grief. In all, Johnson wanted to project British benevolence while capitalizing on the power and symbolic importance of the ceremony to make the Haudenosaunee "unanimous amongst yourselves" when they considered the necessity of the boundary. For their part, the Haudenosaunee responded with the typical "Yo-hah at the proper places," vocally asserting their assent, ending that day's session.[61]

The next day the Haudenosaunee continued the condolence ceremony to establish unity. First, they bestowed a new name on William Franklin because "the several American Governors had Indian Names, by which they were known to the Indians, the Governor of New Jersey excepted."[62] That naming process was also part of the condolence ceremony, rendering strangers into friends and kin. Names and naming reflected not just a symbolic gesture but incorporated people into a much more important matrix of kinship alliances and obligations.[63] Once accomplished, the Haudenosaunee also cleared the eyes, ears, and throats of the British with words and wampum, and expressed their "thanks to you for the remembrance of our antient ceremonies," which served as the "cement of our union." With this, unity and goodwill were established so that "they may be able to attend the important affairs which were to be transacted," at least within the council chamber.[64]

On October 26, the third day of the conference, Johnson got down to business. Nevertheless, he still faced difficulties. The Haudenosaunee may have projected an image of unity among themselves, their "dependents," and colonial representatives with the opening ceremony but that in no way reflected what was going on outside of the council chamber. Many Haudenosaunee warriors and hunters in attendance harbored long-held grievances, knew what colonists wanted, and outright refused to give up any more land than what was agreed to in 1765. The same could be said of the Susquehanna and the few Ohio Nations' representatives in attendance.

Johnson, hoping to draw on the authority and professed unity of Haudenosaunee elders in the council chamber to appease their discontented members and dependents, urged those elders to consult with their warriors outside of the council chamber after each proposal. He hoped that those warriors would "pay a due regard to your Sachems and Councillors whose sage advice will seldom or never be amiss." To ensure this calculated deference worked in his favor, Johnson doled out gifts to the elders throughout the proceedings and held private conferences with them each night to convince them of the necessity of the new boundary he imagined.[65]

Negotiating the northern boundary around the West Branch of the Susquehanna River and north of Owego was the toughest challenge during the conference. The Oneida strongly opposed any westerly boundary in this area. Meanwhile, Seneca and Cayuga leaders were hesitant, if not outright against it, given their close ties and presence in the valley. The Susquehanna Nations, though present at the treaty conference, were entirely silent on the matter according to the official record. But, then, Johnson treated them as mere dependents and the record reflects that. Despite their silence and the bias of the record, it is doubtful, given their past complaints, that the Susquehanna Nations did not resist any new northern boundary. More than likely they worked outside of the chamber to influence their professed "Uncles."

Regardless of this opposition, on October 28, the fifth day of the gathering, Johnson was ready to offer up his version of the boundary line for the northern frontier, but he would not do it in the council chamber. Instead, he invited the Haudenosaunee elders, particularly the Oneida, to his private quarters. With a map stretched out on the table in front of him, Johnson packaged together his new vision for the boundary north of the West Branch and that from Owego to Canada. Tracing a line starting at the end of the West Branch until it met the edge of the Alleghany Mountains, he followed the crest of the mountains to Owego and then proceeded to chart a westerly course from that town about one hundred miles north, "so as to close it" near Canada Creek. Since the Oneida occupied the territory Johnson wanted around Owego and offered the fiercest resistance, he focused on gaining their approval. If the Oneida agreed to this new northern boundary, Johnson told them, "Mr. Penn" would offer "a large & handsome consideration over and besides his Majesty's Royal Bounty." Gifts and promises of more dominated Johnson's handling of the conference, in and out of council. Moreover, by packaging the two northern boundaries together in the negotiation, Johnson could use Penn's "handsome consideration" for the Northern Susquehanna River Valley to entice the Oneida to agree to a boundary north of Owego.[66]

As was typical with most proceedings of this kind, Haudenosaunee representatives did not instantly agree. Instead, because "this is a great Cession of Land which will require much thought and attention," they went back to their lodgings to "consider the affair in private." But, they also warned, "we cannot be expected to part with what lies at our Doors, besides your people are come already too close to us" and would move ever closer once the boundary line was redrawn, especially after speculators got their share.[67]

That private conversation took the better part of a week. Haudenosaunee warriors and hunters, when they heard of Johnson's proposal, were instantly upset. The crest of the Alleghany Mountains as it extended from the West Branch would create a new northern boundary that would give the British Great Island and most of the other communities, towns, and hunting grounds in the Northern Susquehanna River Valley. No doubt frustrated by Johnson's proposal, they declared "they would not part with any Lands to the Westward," especially those "towards Wioming or Great Island, as they reserved that part of the Country for their Dependents." Perhaps the Susquehanna Nations did have some leverage outside of the council chamber. The Oneida were also unwilling to give away so much land north of Owego.[68]

Taking both arguments against Johnson's boundary into consideration, Haudenosaunee delegates countered with a northern line that basically replicated the 1765 boundary south of Owego. As for north of that town to Canada, which they were willing to negotiate, they proposed a line that moved northeast rather than northwest, protecting many existing Oneida and Mohawk towns and hunting grounds, jeopardizing Johnson's 25,000-acre grant from the Canajoharie as well as a recent purchase of about 127,000 acres near Oriskany from some Oneida. According to their new proposal, even Fort Stanwix would remain on Haudenosaunee land.[69]

Johnson was visibly irritated after he heard this proposal and outright refused to accept it. In a "long and warm speech to the Chiefs," he argued that they must accept *his* proposed northern boundary or reap the consequences. "If they rejected this opportunity now offered them and drew the Line so as to interfere with Grants" he or other interested British colonists attending the conference held, "or approach almost our settlements, he could not see any thing more effectual could thereafter be proposed for preventing encroachments, and the Crown after being already at a very heavy expence on this occasion must find its good intentions and reasonable proposals totally defeated." Moreover, because he packaged the two northern boundaries together, he made it seem as if the failure to agree to one would derail negotiations for both. All the goods, presents, and cash offered for the new boundary, which Johnson strategically placed in plain view during the negotiations, would be off the table. He also sweetened the pot to get what he wanted, promising an additional "five hundred Dollars & a handsome present for each of the chiefs" if they came back with a more "favorable Answer."[70]

Even that didn't work. The Haudenosaunee were "much divided in opinion." Oneida elders told Johnson "that their people positively refused to agree to any other line than they proposed the last night." Game, they argued, was "scarce in their neighbourhood," and therefore they "had come to a Resolution" to keep as much of that northern land as possible to "support their families." Without the Oneida, there would be no deal. Achieving unity in council could cut both ways. Worried that his dreams for the deal would be dashed by what he called "extraordinary" claims, Johnson offered six hundred dollars to each chief desiring they "would so act as to shew their love and respect for the King & friendship for his Subjects." He also promised that with this boundary, "no province should on any pretense invade the line," thus securing their future.[71] This was a promise he had to know he could not keep.

After several days of private meetings, promises, and gift-giving, the Haudenosaunee came up with a northern boundary that Johnson could agree with. Instead of starting the line where the western ridge of the Alleghany Mountains reached the West Branch of the Susquehanna River, they pushed it east to "Tiadaghta Creek" and up that creek until it reached a series of hills called Burnett's Hills. The line would then follow those hills to the North Branch and up that branch to Owego. From there, following a northwesterly course, though not as westerly as Johnson wanted, the line would finally terminate at Canada Creek. This boundary, "although Less than I could wish," was still, as Johnson told Thomas Penn, "a very advantagious Cession." It did after all more than halve the Susquehanna Nations' land in the Northern Susquehanna River Valley.[72]

While Johnson combined the line north of the West Branch with that north of Owego for negotiation with the Haudenosaunee, he separated

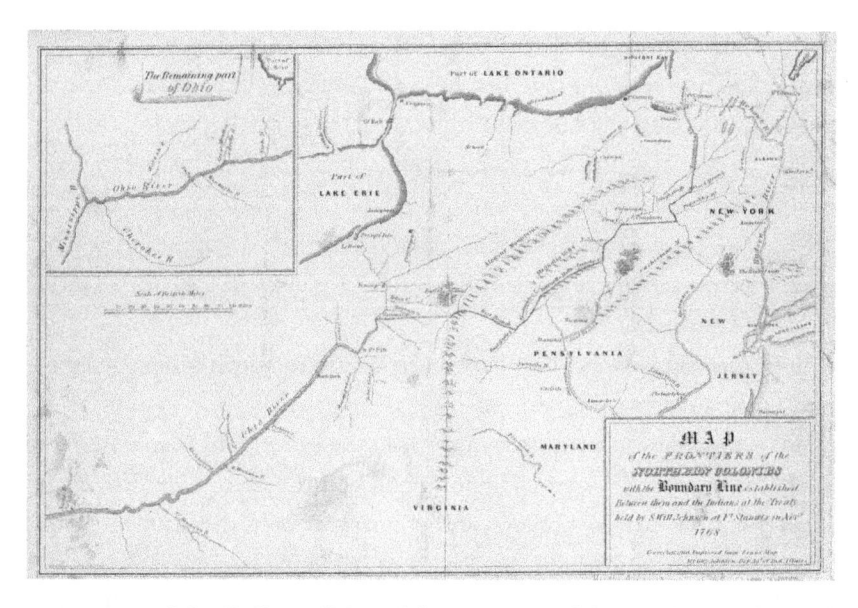

FIGURE 9. John E. Gavit, "Map of the Frontiers of the Northern Colonies," 1850. (New York Public Library Digital Collections)

them out in official documents to the advantage of Thomas Penn. Such a move also challenged Hillsborough's instructions. The boundary negotiation at Fort Stanwix was supposed to be between the Haudenosaunee and the British king (represented by Johnson). The disputes between Pennsylvania and Virginia over land near Fort Pitt, or between Pennsylvania and Connecticut over the Northern Susquehanna River Valley, Hillsborough instructed, should have no place in this conference. Regardless, Johnson carved out the portion of the line that fell within the limits of Thomas Penn's vision of Pennsylvania as a separate deal, with separate documents, which Penn would separately pay for, thus giving Penn ample evidence to establish his land rights. Johnson also exacted an important statement from the Haudenosaunee to contest Connecticut's "Susquehanna Purchase." When the Haudenosaunee agreed to the northern boundary, they went on the written record, stating that although "Lydius of Albany did in the name of" Connecticut "lay claim to Lands in Pennsylvania," those claims were "unjust" and "invalid." Therefore, "We expect that no regard will be paid to them or any such claims now or hereafter, as we have fairly sold them to the proprietors of Pennsylvania to whom alone we shall sell Lands within that Province." Penn, Johnson knew, would be pleased.[73]

In all, the Haudenosaunee ceded to the British millions of acres from the headwaters of the Tennessee River to Canada. Pennsylvania alone gained much from that new boundary, independently paying 10,000 Spanish dollars for land stretching north from the Ohio River and encompassing a significant portion of land in the Northern Susquehanna River Valley. The Fort Stanwix cession included land in all or part of twenty-six of the sixty-seven present-day counties in the state. No land deal to that point even came close to what the proprietors gained at this conference.[74]

Even then, Johnson did not get everything Thomas Penn wanted in the Northern Susquehanna River Valley, but Johnson thought it was more than enough to demonstrate his goodwill. He was right. When Penn learned of the deal and what Johnson did to accomplish it, he was ecstatic. Johnson may not have gotten "the boundary we wished," but Penn commended him for his labors and "the trouble you have taken in this affair." Penn and his "family are obliged to you for your endeavours." He especially liked that Johnson struck a deal "separate from the general deed made to the King," which would "free us" from negotiating the boundary with other British officials and colonies. The Haudenosaunee's vocal recognition of Penn's vast claims against Connecticut was also pleasing.[75] Surely, Penn thought, the Susquehannah Company would not dare to continue their claims, and even if they did, the treaty itself would make any legal argument the company could muster difficult to sustain. Making good on his promises to Johnson, and just two months after he received the news about the cession, Penn "had the pleasure to inform" Johnson that he went to the "Council office to press the finishing of your Grant" for 25,000 acres and that it would now receive the "Great Seal."[76] Happy, both Johnson and Penn upheld their ends of the bargain to acquire Indigenous land.

All was not exactly well, though. The Delaware and Shawnee living in the Ohio Valley refused to acknowledge the legitimacy of the Fort Stanwix cession. While Johnson "considered" them, he did not give them an opportunity to negotiate. Irritated, they "complained much of the Conduct of the Six Nations giving up so much of the Country to the English without asking their Consent."[77] This statement reflected their continued independence.

They also renewed their overtures to the Susquehanna Nations to move west so the nations could use their combined power to resist this deal and the new encroachments it would initiate. The "Worrars Say they May as well Dey Like Men as be Kicked about Like Doggs."[78]

The Ohio Nations were not the only Indigenous people upset by the treaty. The Cherokee, who lived on and claimed sovereignty over much of the southwestern land near the Tennessee River negotiated away by the Haudenosaunee at Fort Stanwix, were also aghast. The Haudenosaunee's cession of their land ran contrary to a similar treaty held in mid-October between the Cherokee and Britain's superintendent for the southern district, John Stuart, as stipulated by the Board of Trade and its map. Even the Haudenosaunee were still divided, as some Seneca and Cayuga ridiculed the sheer scale of land ceded to the British.[79] It seemed, Croghan wrote to Johnson, that there would be "a Warr with us Sonner than" anyone expected.[80]

Lord Hillsborough was likewise displeased. The Fort Stanwix treaty not only exceeded Johnson's instructions but contradicted Stuart's negotiations with the southern Native nations. Hillsborough was angry that Johnson had disregarded "His Majesty's commands you was instructed to adhere," especially since the new boundary would only "produce jealousy and dissatisfaction" and sow more "confusion."[81] Equally miffed, the Board of Trade, under Hillsborough's control, issued a report to King George III condemning the treaty at Fort Stanwix and the "indiscretion of Sir William Johnson." From the board's perspective it seemed as if "the claims and interests of private persons, not stated to, or approved by your Majesty, have been allowed to mix themselves in this Negotiation," creating a boundary "materially different from that directed by your Majesty's Instructions" to Johnson. Therefore, the board thought, the treaty at Fort Stanwix "ought to be rejected." Irritated, Hillsborough sent Johnson a letter demanding he go back to the Six Nations and "settle the Line according to your Instructions."[82]

Despite the bluster of Hillsborough and the Board of Trade, they were in no position to deny the validity of the treaty. Johnson argued that a renegotiation would never work. It would only alienate the Haudenosaunee, and he refused to comply, hoping to wait out this new round of Hillsborough's anger with strident but deferential arguments. He also sent the bill for the treaty, which cost the crown just over £20,000.[83]

His play worked. Just four months later, Hillsborough told Johnson that if the superintendent thought such a renegotiation too difficult to achieve or detrimental to an alliance with the Haudenosaunee, "His Majesty, rather than risk the defeating the important object of establishing a final Boundary Line, will upon your report of this matter, give the necessary directions for the confirmation of it as agreed upon at Fort Stanwix." Hillsborough still held out hope that Johnson would be able to renegotiate, but it was no longer a command. The time and money expended at Fort Stanwix alone was probably enough to dissuade Hillsborough and other crown officials from disowning the treaty and starting again, but they also feared that by not approving the land deed generated by the treaty, Britain would officially undermine the sovereignty and honor of the Haudenosaunee, which was on full display at Fort Stanwix.[84]

Haudenosaunee elders, not Johnson, initiated the cession of Cherokee land near the Tennessee River to demonstrate "our Rights." It was one of the first stipulations of the treaty, and failure to include that land "to the Southward" in the cession would, the Haudenosaunee argued, do "wrong to our Posterity" and therefore be "unworthy those Warriors who fought & conquered it."[85] The Haudenosaunee had been at war with the Cherokee for years, and they wanted the British to recognize that fight, their assumed victory, and their supreme status over any and all Native peoples within their presumed jurisdiction. Johnson had little inclination to deny their request, especially if he wanted continued goodwill to establish the northern boundary. Hillsborough and the Board of Trade were also caught between the same proverbial rock and a hard place. They had little choice but to support the boundary established at Fort Stanwix, fully aware that it had the very real potential to bring future turmoil to the empire.[86]

While Hillsborough and the Board of Trade fretted over the southern border, the northern boundary was similarly controversial. Leaders of Delaware and Mohican communities in the Northern Susquehanna River Valley, Papunhank and Nanhun, disparaged the cession. During a meeting with the Cayuga and Mohawk, they critically asked, "You know that you sold to your white brothers the Wyalusing land, upon which you placed us seven years ago?"[87] Their use of "your white brothers" rather than "our white brothers" highlighted a clear fracture between the Susquehanna Nations and both the Haudenosaunee and the British. Others in the valley were a bit more forceful in their denunciation. Thomas McKee reported that those "Indians he met upon Susquahannah" at and near Fort Augusta "spoke of the Six Nations with great disrespect and resentment and calls them the Slaves of the White people." As a result, some Delaware, Munsee, and Shawnee living in the valley packed up and left for the Ohio region, intending to combine forces to resist British encroachment and secure their future. The Susquehanna Nations' land, again, had been taken, as Teedyuscung railed many years previously, "by fraud" and "deception."[88]

There were still more problems with that northern border beyond just the sheer scope of what the Six Nations had ceded to the British. The boundary established for the Northern Susquehanna River Valley, seemingly so clear-cut in the treaty, and the land deed it created were, in the end, unclear. The exact creek establishing the northern trajectory of the boundary from the West Branch of the Susquehanna River to Owego, the "Tiadaghta" or "Tiadaghton," was not actually well known to the British. Few British maps to that point used the name "Tiadaghta" for any creek in the region, and those that did depicted it as one of only three creaks east of Great Island on the West Branch, especially Lewis Evans's map of the middle colonies published in 1755, which was the base map used during negotiations at Fort Stanwix. The problem, however, was that there are seven creeks, large and small, east of Great Island. Therefore, the Tiadaghta could have been any one of them. It was not until 1770, when William Scull published

FIGURE 10. Detail of Lewis Evans, "A General Map of the Middle British Colonies, in America," 1755. (Library of Congress)

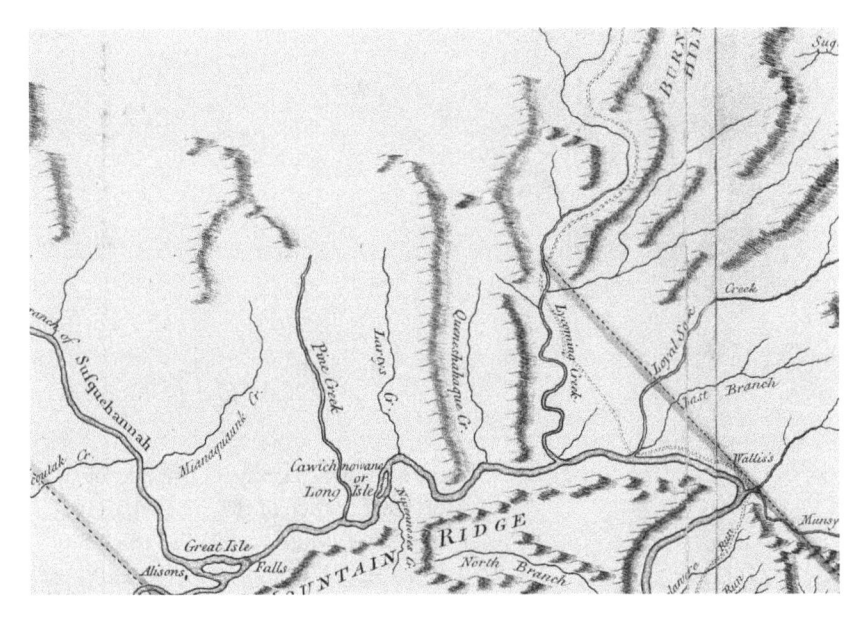

FIGURE 11. Detail of William Scull, "A Map of Pennsylvania," 1775. (Library of Congress)

a new map of Pennsylvania, that all of those creeks were included and their positions widely disseminated and learned, but none of them was labeled "Tiadaghta."

Out of the many creeks east of Great Island, two stood out at the time as having the potential to be "Tiadaghta"—Pine Creek closest to Great Island, and Lycoming Creek further to the east. That distinction mattered. Those two creeks were separated by over twenty miles. More than likely, the Haudenosaunee called Lycoming Creek the Tiadaghta at Fort Stanwix. Of the two creeks, Lycoming was the closest to Burnett's Hills, which was the natural line used in the treaty to connect to Owego. Lycoming Creek ran through those hills and Pine Creek was too far west to make any sense. Moreover, when Conrad Weiser traveled to Onondaga with Haudenosaunee guides in 1736, he followed Lycoming Creek, which the Haudenosaunee called and Weiser documented in his mixed German and English writing as "Dia-daclitu." This not only shares a phonetic similarity with "Tiadaghta" but, as Weiser described, geographic similarities as well.[89]

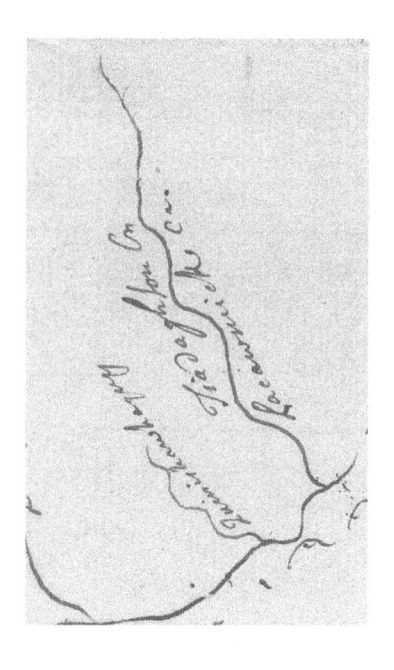

FIGURE 12. Detail of "Draught of the West Branch of the Susquehanna Taken by Captain Patterson," April 1, 1769. (Shippen Family Papers, American Philosophical Society)

The real proof, however, rests with the fact that when Penn's agents went out to survey and draw the new line after Fort Stanwix, the Indigenous people who accompanied them pointed to Lycoming Creek as beginning the natural line north from the West Branch. Even some colonial militia officers, intimate with the geography of the West Branch, noted on their private maps that Lycoming Creek was also the Tiadaghta. In 1769, for example, a Captain Patterson, stationed at Fort Augusta, made that distinction, identifying "Lacowmick" as "Tiadaghton."[90] Yet, despite such historical usage and contemporary clarifications and evidence, speculators and potential settlers fervently contested the idea that what they called Lycoming Creek was the Tiadaghta, preferring instead the more western Pine Creek. That dispute in and of itself would embroil the Northern Susquehanna River Valley in turmoil for the next two decades, significantly influencing the choices both Native peoples and colonists made as they contemplated independence and their place in the American Revolution. There was, then, an important consequence to the Treaty of Fort Stanwix.

7

An Empire Divided

THE CONSEQUENCES OF FORT STANWIX, 1768–1773

THE TREATY OF FORT STANWIX, the confusion it bred, and the scramble for land it initiated happened during a period of extreme turmoil in the British Empire. In many ways, the struggle within and among colonies as well as Native polities over the newly acquired land at Fort Stanwix widened already deep cleavages in colonial society threatening to tear the empire apart. The years after 1768 were not good ones for the British Empire. Colonists up and down North America violently resisted imperial policies, taxes, and the maintenance and ever-increasing existence of British soldiers in their colonies. Even within legislative chambers, rather conservative bodies, colonial politicians made clear and cogent declarations against the right of Parliament to tax the colonies or to fundamentally interfere with their internal affairs. The colonial legislatures, as unrepresentative as most of them were in reality, were nonetheless, legislators argued, supreme.

That vision of colonial sovereignty touched off a constitutional crisis in the empire and an increasing call for colonial unity. Just a year before Fort Stanwix, the legislature in New York gave this constitutional dispute new meaning when it refused to comply with Parliament's Quartering Act, which demanded that each colony provision and house British soldiers in either barracks or public houses. Although these soldiers were supposed to make their way to the frontier as per the Townshend Acts of 1767, many of the soldiers remained in the cities on ministerial orders. Irritated, New York's legislators refused to comply or do anything to accommodate near 1,500 British soldiers because they, not Parliament, controlled the province.

Parliament responded by suspending that colony's legislature in late 1767 and again in 1769.[1]

It did not take long before a powerful and vocal opposition to parliamentary power and imperial overreach took to the streets and legislative chambers throughout the colonies to formalize a colonial-wide resistance. What happened in New York could happen anywhere, especially considering Parliament's efforts to tax the colonies, all of which made British colonists, Boston's Samuel Adams argued, "slaves." Therefore, unity and solidarity among and within the colonies was necessary. In February 1768, the Massachusetts legislature issued its now famous Circular Letter to all the other colonial legislatures to achieve that unity. Requesting that colonial legislatures declare Parliament's actions unconstitutional, the Circular Letter laid down a constitutional gauntlet, one the colonial legislatures could either confirm or deny. Not every colony was initially on board, though. Pennsylvania's assembly waffled on the issue. The factions in that government, ever at odds, acknowledged the merits of the circular but little more.[2]

Lord Hillsborough, as he often did, propelled resistance and colonial unity forward far better than the circular from Massachusetts ever could. When the Massachusetts Circular Letter reached London in April 1768, Hillsborough was incensed, denouncing it as "a most dangerous and factious" document "calculated to inflame the minds" of the king's "good subjects in the colonies, to promote an unwarrantable combination, and to excite and encourage an open opposition to and denial of the authority of Parliament, and to subvert the true principles of the constitution." Issuing his own circular to the colonial governors, Hillsborough demanded that if colonial legislatures considered the "seditious paper" from Massachusetts, the governors should immediately prorogue or dissolve them.[3] When Pennsylvania's legislature learned of Hillsborough's circular, its timidity and factiousness abated. According to William Allen, "Our party matters and internal contentions are in a manner subsided." The "cause of the present Harmony," Allen explained, "is that it is agreed by all partys that this is by no means a proper time to differ among ourselves when our all is at stake from another quarter." Pennsylvania's legislature would take up the cause in spite of Hillsborough's threats.[4]

All was not exactly harmonious. The factions in the assembly may have dropped their disputes as unseasonable, but that did not reflect the temper of the times. Throughout the colonies there were still those who thought resistance not only foolhardy but borderline treasonous, and when they refused to act harmoniously they were targeted by riotous self-styled patriots. Some faced tarring and feathering, a brutal form of ostracization and public shaming. Others found their homes plastered with feces, or, as it was more commonly called, "Hillsborough paint."[5]

There were still deeper schisms among and within the colonies rooted in much older struggles over land and power. Virginians still fought with Pennsylvanians and Native peoples over the Ohio River Valley. Similarly, Connecticut and Pennsylvania were still at odds over land in the Northern Susquehanna River Valley. More important still, systemic economic and social disparities within those colonies remained. Divisions still existed between those with power and those without, those who could legally acquire land and those who could not, and those animosities could not simply be painted over with tar or excrement. More problematic, such chasms only widened because of the Treaty of Fort Stanwix and how everyone involved tried to reap its rewards.

Like his response to the Massachusetts Circular Letter, Hillsborough created a lot but not all of this tension over the land acquired at Fort Stanwix. Still angered by that acquisition and irritated with colonial resistance to parliamentary power, Hillsborough tried to stop the settlement of land in the new boundary, complaining that "every day discovers more and more the fatal policy of departing from the line prescribed by the Proclamation of 1763."[6] A new war with Native Americans, he thought, was imminent, adding to the empire's woes. To avert that war, Hillsborough directed Virginia's governor to void any surveys and refuse any applications for land in the newly acquired territories, especially those in the Ohio River Valley and out near the Tennessee River. Such a directive potentially denied the aspirations of Virginia speculators in the Ohio Company whose shareholders included such revolutionary luminaries as George Washington, Patrick Henry, and

Thomas Jefferson. It also officially cut off the speculative ventures of Benjamin Franklin, Joseph Galloway, and the Suffering Traders.[7]

It was not just Hillsborough's directives that exacerbated tensions among and within the colonies. Because Johnson carved out Pennsylvania's purchase from the overall land acquisition at Fort Stanwix, Hillsborough had no real authority to circumvent Thomas Penn or speculators in Pennsylvania from capitalizing on the land gained by the treaty. In reality, without police power, Hillsborough's directives to any governor were mere words, easily disregarded. Virginia's governor simply ignored Hillsborough. Jurisdictional disputes between colonies, then, would continue unabated. Nor did Hillsborough have the political clout or patience to make his words the official policy of the empire, giving speculators the upper hand.[8]

To challenge Hillsborough, Virginia's Ohio Company aligned itself with speculators in Pennsylvania, New York, New Jersey, and London, establishing the Grand Ohio Company. Pooling their interests together, that new conglomeration applied for 20 million acres for a mere £10,604 to create a new colony west of the Ohio River called Vandalia. Hillsborough had a lot to do with the sheer scale of what the company requested. Pretending he was cowed, Hillsborough encouraged the company to make such a large land request, secretly hoping to use the size of the request as justification to reject the proposal. And that is exactly what he did. When the Grand Ohio Company submitted its proposal, Hillsborough used the Board of Trade to deny it, arguing the proposal took too much away from the Native nations who lived there. "Let the savages enjoy their deserts in quiet," he argued. Besides, "Were they driven from their forests the peltry trade would decrease."[9]

Hillsborough, though, was dealing with influential opponents. The Americans holding shares in the company included Virginia and Pennsylvania speculators as well as Governor William Franklin, Sir William Johnson, George Croghan, and, unsurprisingly, the leaders of the Suffering Traders, Samuel and Thomas Wharton. The Grand Ohio Company also included influential shareholders in London such as Thomas and Richard Walpole, the wealthy and politically connected nephews of Robert Walpole, the Earl of Orford and late prime minister. Harnessing that influence, the company appealed to the king's Privy Council, which overrode Hillsborough's rejection and approved the land grant. Irritated and embarrassed, Hillsborough resigned. In the end, the speculators won, and that victory included far more than just the approval of the Grand Ohio Company's schemes. That company's success was symptomatic of what was happening everywhere, driving a wedge in the colonies over land, power, and political interest.[10]

In Pennsylvania, a small circle of influential men controlled access to the land gained at Fort Stanwix, which they called the "New Purchase." It was a striking irony. At a time when the colonial government counseled unity against Parliament, it also created and supported policies that exacerbated very real and lasting divisions in the colony that, if they continued unchecked, could throw the province and the empire into further turmoil. In sum, when legislators like William Allen or Joseph Galloway harmoniously asserted their stance to guard "Our Rights" against Parliament or Hillsborough, that "our" was narrowly defined and harkened back to a time when the desires of elite colonists could shape public policy with little popular or imperial oversight and direction, especially when it came to land.[11] As events soon proved, that was not a position or a reality that spoke to or alleviated the grievances of the bulk of the colonial population. In fact, it was entirely at odds with what a majority of colonists wanted.

What happened in the Northern Susquehanna River Valley after the treaty at Fort Stanwix encapsulates the problems threatening the future of the British Empire. Almost immediately after that treaty, Pennsylvania officials, not exactly acting "harmoniously," hurried out to the Northern Susquehanna River Valley to survey proprietary manor lands and investigate potentially lucrative mines in the New Purchase. While Thomas Penn appreciated the assiduity of his officials in quickly annexing that land for his use, he also fixated on stopping the advancement of Connecticut settlers in the Wyoming territory and beyond. If they further occupied the valley before Pennsylvania gained a foothold, Penn could never capitalize on what he gained at Fort Stanwix. Since at least January of the previous year, Penn had made it clear to officials that if a treaty at Fort Stanwix extended Pennsylvania's jurisdiction north and west, he wanted to quickly settle the land with a group of Pennsylvania militia officers led by Turbutt Francis to "keep off the people of Connecticut."[12] Nor did he care how his officials achieved it. "Grant them large Tracts," he wrote his nephew, the governor, John Penn; it didn't matter if he granted those soldiers "tracts of five thousand Acres each" as long as it was done quickly "to oppose these intruders, so as to drive them off."[13]

Thomas Penn's fixation on Connecticut settlers created confusion and his officials' haste to "drive them off" intertwined with their personal connections and promises made to friends and family, opening the door to rampant corruption. The other problem was that Penn did not send clear instructions to his officials about when or how to sell land in the New Purchase, which put the members of his Board of Property, legally tasked with selling land, at odds, especially with Secretary of the Land Office James Tilghman and Receiver-General Edmund Physick.

Secretary Tilghman, tacitly backed by the proprietor, had already promised large sections to prominent speculators, especially his brother-in-law Turbutt Francis. Physick, on the other hand, charged with maintaining proprietary account books, rent rolls, and quitrents, resisted opening the land to "jobbers" and "monopolies" who brought little to the proprietary treasury. Speculators were often exempt from paying quitrents and rarely, if ever, paid full price for the land they acquired. Tilghman and Physick, because of their divergent goals, fought over when to open the office to the public, how to process applications, if down payments should be demanded, and how many acres any individual could purchase.[14]

Physick, trying to strike before Tilghman established a policy for the land office's opening, proposed a strategy to the Board of Property to assure a semblance of equal access to the New Purchase. His plan would also bring instant cash and future quitrents, reviving a depleting proprietary treasury. Physick wanted to appoint new government surveyors to establish several clearly demarcated districts from which any potential buyer would have to choose. Such a move would delay opening the land office for several months since it would require the selection and appointment of surveyors and for them to survey the districts. Meanwhile, the Board of Property would publish advertisements in the newspapers, which would then give inhabitants time to liquidate assets for ready money for a *mandatory* down payment and to prepare for a journey to the land office in Philadelphia. Once the land office opened after that delay, Physick proposed to limit applicants from obtaining more than three hundred acres of land in any district and pushed for a lottery system where applicants would write their names on strips of paper and place them in a large trunk. After a few days, a member of the land office would commission a young man to shake the trunk and pull out names to establish the order of applications, hopefully mitigating one speculator from purchasing several three-hundred-acre lots by submitting numerous applications or using proxies. Physick also demanded down payments for any purchase so that even if the trunk system failed and one speculator received a bunch of tracts, they would still have to pay a significant sum down, which, he thought, would deter their efforts to game the system, assuring that, as he explained to others, "the Appliers were real Purchasers & not Jobbers." Crude as it may seem, it was the only way Physick could envision fairness.[15]

Relating his thoughts to Thomas Penn, Physick justified his proposal for selling land in the New Purchase by focusing on the benefits of catering to farmers. In a long letter to Penn, Physick argued that "many hundred of people in this Province were ready to receive grants from you, and being farmers, would undoubtedly settle the Lands in a very short time on any sudden emergency."[16] From Physick's point of view, farmers would actually inhabit the land, ward off Connecticut settlers, and pay their quitrents. Physick also warned Penn that those farmers would never have a chance to acquire land, and the proprietor would never be able to reap the rewards of their settlements, if the land office didn't change its regular procedures, which all too often favored those with connections.[17]

He was right. In the past, the land office had opened in Philadelphia, and people lined up to register their names, the dates of their appearances, and the location of the land they desired (often issuing several applications at once). The secretary of the land office sent these applications in order of appearance to the surveyor general, who then instructed a district surveyor to prepare a survey. Many of these local surveyors farmed the work out to someone else or, in some cases, accepted the work of surveyors hired by the applicants. Once surveyed and approved by the district surveyor, the surveyor general warranted the land, and then an applicant had six months to pay the receiver-general for the official land patent. In short, the system favored those with inside information about when exactly the land office would open because the order of appearance to start the process mattered most.[18]

Moreover, speculative acquisitions came with near zero financial risk. Purchasers rarely, if ever, paid money down, and when they did it was never more than a few shillings. Therefore, if they could not sell their acquisition before the money for the patent came due, they could simply default on their speculation and hand the land back to the proprietor. According to one disgruntled official writing to Thomas Penn, such a policy "really encouraged men, who were neither able nor had any Design to pay for Lands to take up as many three hundred Acres as they could find Seven Shillings to enter them with; in hopes of selling them again to others." If their speculation didn't work out, they could "desert them at last with the Loss only of Seven Shillings, or perhaps Surveying Fees, & thus the Land fall back into your Hands to be granted again." In the process, the proprietors would lose "all the intermediate Interest & Quit Rent."[19]

Such arguments in favor of changing procedures did not persuade Secretary Tilghman. Only having Penn's urgent letters about quickly settling Colonel Francis and his associates to go by and beholden to speculators vying to acquire the best lands in the New Purchase, Tilghman argued for an immediate opening of the land office without down payment or, critically, public advertisement. According to Surveyor General John Lukens, Tilghman countered Physick's proposal with the old "application Scheme without the payment of any Money Down, and urged the Necessity of going into it immediately that the land might be granted to persons who would settle the same (without paying any money down) & thereby prevent the Settlement of a number of New Englanders who it was said was on their way to Settle at Wioming & the forks of Susquehanna."[20] In effect, Tilghman argued necessity trumped Physick's vision of equal access. The majority of members of the Board of Property, which included the old governor James Hamilton and others connected or related to prominent speculators, used the same "reason of necessity" and sided with Tilghman.[21]

With the Board of Property's approval, Tilghman quickly got to work. He opened the land office "late in the Evening" on Sunday, February 3, 1769, without any public advertisement. Obviously, news of the date and time of the opening had already spread "from the Mouth of one Man to another" in the city, especially among speculators. More corrupt still, Physick learned that "some particular persons in this City" had prearranged their purchases with other members of the Board of Property and would "receive large Grants of large Quantities of the best Lands, and that some have already desired the Surveyors to hold themselves in readiness to survey for them." It was clear "who it will suit best and who worst to have the office suddenly opened." Without a delay or publishing a general advertisement, "the design of getting the Country settled vanished, and we soon found the Office open to none but Favourites."[22]

The process of doling out land to "Favourites" was swift. A number of "Gentlemen" went to the land office that late Sunday night, "entered their Applications," and "hurried the Surveyors from Town to make their Surveys, taking the Precaution of imploying Persons to go with them to see their surveys made to the best Advantage" and "to discover more good lands."[23] Irritated, Surveyor General Lukens railed that the land office was "immediately opened" and "a Number of Applications was Entered and have been so from time to time & Sent up for Large Tracts of Land without any Intention I believe of making many Settlers thereon."[24] Equally miffed, William Smith, an Anglican minister and proprietary ally, complained that it seemed as if "when favors are to be bestowed they are all shared among a small knot of particular Connexions."[25]

Such descriptions of what happened reflected reality. Near midnight on February 3, twenty-four officers, or at least a few of them led by Francis, made their way to the land office controlled by Francis's brother-in-law and applied for and received nearly twenty thousand acres in the Northern Susquehanna River Valley. Moreover, despite those soldiers' initial proposal of settling together in a "compact settlement," those same officers received lands scattered throughout the valley, particularly along the West Branch. The officers, it seems, wanted all of the good lands along that river and its tributary creeks and had little interest in becoming "a powerful barrier to the Province."[26] According to land office records and a map the officers made of the West Branch highlighting their acquisition, Francis and his associates took up most of the rich alluvial land available east of Lycoming Creek. Nor did many of those officers actually settle on that land,

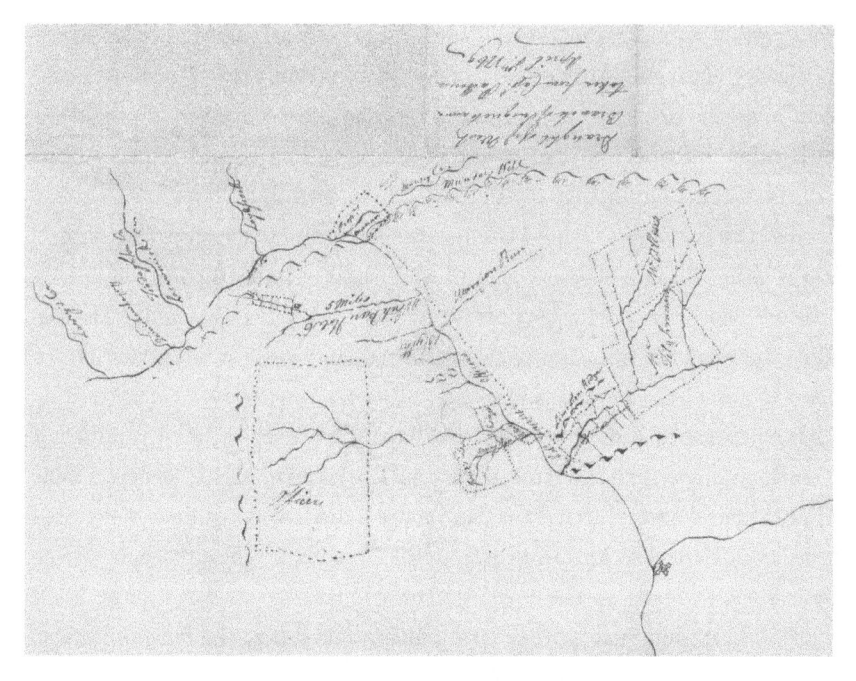

FIGURE 13. "Draught of the West Branch of the Susquehanna Taken by Captain Patterson," April 1, 1769. (Shippen Family Papers, American Philosophical Society)

preferring to sell parcels immediately to speculators or to hold on to the land and sell it to colonists at several times the initial purchase price.[27]

Most of the good land left in the Northern Susquehanna River Valley east of Lycoming Creek was either already set aside as proprietary manor lands or gobbled up by eleven "Gentlemen" who started applying for "Special Grants" directly after the officers took their portion. Unsurprisingly, Tilghman did not close the office after Francis's men applied but kept it open to prominent speculators, and he did this for nearly two months. Between February 4 and April 1, those speculators received forty thousand acres in the New Purchase. Francis, Tilghman's brother-in-law, received an additional 2,500 acres "on the West Branch of the River Susquehanna." Besides Francis, several prominent merchants and proprietary officeholders, including the secretary of the land office himself, joined in the speculative bonanza. Tilghman actually submitted and approved his own applications for 5,500 acres of land "on the West branch of Susquehanna next after the Officers of the Pennsylvania Regiment."[28] Once he approved his own grants, he started processing and approving the applications of his friends. The first ones he approved were for William Allen's sons, Andrew and John, who received ten thousand acres spread strategically along portions of the East and West Branches. Illustrative of the "monopolies" created after Fort Stanwix, not long after Tilghman approved their applications, the Allen brothers sold them to another merchant land speculator, Samuel Purviance, who was most likely next in line at the land office on February 4. It seems that deal occurred while they were all lounging in the land office itself. A similar deal was struck between Francis and Presbyterian minister and proprietary ally Francis Alison for 1,500 acres on the West Branch, near present-day Lock Haven. Alison applied for the land and quickly signed it over to Turbutt Francis. Some of that land is now part of the current town of Turbotville, a fitting nomenclature.[29]

Out of all of the speculators vying for land, Samuel Purviance was easily the biggest winner. According to one witness, "The grant to Mr. Purviance has surprised many."[30] Rightly so. Purviance, though politically connected in proprietary circles and on the proprietors' payroll, was not the most socially significant Philadelphian. Yet he was ambitious. Using word-of-mouth information as well as a crucial friendship with Tilghman and the Allen brothers, Purviance rushed to the land office and walked away with 16,000 of the 40,000 acres of "Special Grants" issued between February 4 and April 1, a cool 40 percent. His acquisitions covered the land north and west of Muncy Creek past Loyalsock Creek on the West Branch, as well as the lands surrounding Wyoming on the East Branch. By the end of the decade, he and his brother held claims to over 300,000 acres throughout British North America.[31]

And yet there were still other prominent officials trying to monopolize lands in Pennsylvania's New Purchase. George Croghan capitalized on the private opening of the land office, receiving 5,000 acres of "Special Grants." Some didn't even need to worry themselves about the land office opening. The Shippens, for instance, ignored the opening in February because they already had the governor's approval for land north of Fort Augusta and disparate lots along the West Branch. Joseph Shippen Jr. collaborated with

Pennsylvania officers who had served in the previous two wars, such as his old commander at Fort Augusta and brother-in-law James Burd, to petition the governor for 100,000 acres of "such *good* Land as we should chuse."[32] Suffice it to say, between February 3 and April 1, Physick complained, "not even a Foot" of land "was granted to a Farmer."[33]

To assure this "small knot" of "Favourites" obtained clear title to the land they desired, Tilghman significantly delayed opening the land office to the general public. Surveying and granting warrants for "Gentlemen" took time. To guard against overlapping claims, on February 23, twenty days after opening the office to "Favourites," Tilghman finally published an advertisement notifying the public that the land office would "officially" open on April 3. Although Tilghman justified the delay by arguing it would provide the back inhabitants time to prepare, others, especially Physick, understood it as a postponement to establish the claims started in early February. Moreover, unlike the gentlemen speculators, the general public had to pay five pounds per hundred acres, one penny per acre quitrent per annum, with the stipulation that "no person will be allowed to take up more than three hundred Acres without special Licence of the proprietaries or the Governor."[34]

Frontier inhabitants who heard about what happened in the New Purchase were, unsurprisingly, angry. After traveling about Pennsylvania's frontier, William Smith informed Thomas Penn that Tilghman's policies created "Monopolies" which "have run in so narrow a Channel among a few Interested Favorites, that they have raised great Clamor."[35] Similarly, Edmund Physick, who traveled to Lancaster County and Cumberland County to collect quitrents, "was greatly affected with the Complaints of the people." According to him, inhabitants "remembered an Advertisement published a few Years" before "wherein the Proprietaries expressed their great Abhorrence of Monopolies." Due to these seemingly official sentiments and Tilghman's advertisement on February 23, those frontier inhabitants could not understand why "Military Officers and other private Gentlemen" were able to purchase much more than the three hundred acres allowed to everyone else.[36]

In a petition to the governor on March 27, sixty-three "Back-Inhabitants" articulated that feeling. "Having long labored under the great difficulty of a long tedious Indian War, being Frontiers and straitly bounded, enjoying but small Tracts of land & mostly Barrening Ground," they thought that "providence hath opened a Door for the relief of the poor people by a late purchase made from the Indian Tribes." That purchase at Fort Stanwix "imparted to us great Joy to think, we had relief so nigh at hand." The joy vanished, however, after they learned that "the whole of the best of the said purchase betwixt Military Officers and other private Gentlemen is wholly taken up." To make matters worse, those "Gentlemen" were already advertising lands for sale "that we are not of ability to buy" due to "the rate they will sell the land." They hoped the governor would "take our deplorable condition under your most wise consideration" as "none of us is endeavoring for more than one tract in said Purchase and is ready and willing to make the Honourable Proprietors restitution for said Lands."[37]

When Thomas Penn learned of this petition, he was aghast, but he did not respond as the petitioners hoped. To Physick, who related the feelings of the back inhabitants and their petition to the proprietor, Penn curtly replied, "I think with Mr. Tilghman."[38] Besides, "the people have no cause to complain" because there was no "Rule of not giving a patent for more than 300 Acres." He could not "see any foundation" for their petition. Penn obviously forgot his earlier public proclamations against monopolies. Nevertheless, after he relieved himself of his astonishment, he softened a bit and instructed Physick to "let Mr. Tilghman know I would now have grants made only to settlers."[39] Given that Penn sent this letter in late summer 1769, such a directive was a bit too late.

Meanwhile, the application process Tilghman implemented to sell land to the general public in April lent itself to abuse as well as fraud, again giving advantage to speculators. When Tilghman opened the office, he begrudgingly took Physick's advice and adopted the lottery/trunk system and limited applications to three hundred acres. While that *might* have worked if Tilghman had limited one piece of paper per applicant and demanded a significant down payment, he did not, and therefore speculators got around the limitation by hiring proxies or writing down the names of friends and associates who would assign the land over later. It was the established norm to use proxies. Just a month before the office opened to the public, Edward Shippen Sr. pointed out to his son that Richard Peters commonly took "up Lands in my Name and afterwards got me to make them over to him." Therefore, he implied, the same scheme could work again.[40]

The elder Shippen knew the system well. When the office opened on April 3 to "the public," he and his son acquired 6,900 acres from at least twenty-four applicants, all but 600 of those acres located in the Northern Susquehanna River Valley.[41] The Shippens were not alone. John Cox, for instance, a prominent merchant in Philadelphia, used fifteen proxies, including his brother and young son, to obtain 4,500 acres of land along the West Branch, particularly around Lycoming Creek, Great Island, and Fishing Creek, much of which was beyond the boundary established at Fort Stanwix.[42] Frustrated, Physick complained to Thomas Penn that speculators acquired numerous three-hundred-acre tracts using this method.[43]

Some speculators used even more underhanded ways to get land in the New Purchase after the office opened to the public. Take, for instance, the shadowy dealings of Samuel Wallis, a land agent for prosperous merchants Abel James and Henry Drinker, who were also working with Joseph Galloway (though Galloway would later deny having any involvement). After the land office opened to the public in April, Wallis had seemingly legal claims to over ten thousand acres stretching along the West Branch from Muncy to Pine Creek, much of which conflicted with the officers' tracts, "Special Grants," and Penn's manor lands, not to mention the actual boundary agreed to with the Haudenosaunee at Fort Stanwix, clogging up the legal system for well over a decade.[44]

Over the previous ten years or so, Wallis had perfected a scheme whereby he would fill out an application for land in one area, submit a survey without topographical features to lazy or indolent deputy surveyors, then use their approval to patent land in a completely different area, often for more acres. He applied the same method for lands in the New Purchase. For example, Wallis used a vague survey to transform an application for 700 acres of land near the town of Bedford into a patent of 3,200 acres of land about seventy miles away in the New Purchase. More important still, Wallis used questionable patents like this one to sell or lease thousands of acres along the West Branch of the Susquehanna River to unsuspecting settlers, instigating a series of ejectment suits brought by proprietary officials and other speculators that bounced around the court system between 1770 and 1785.

In the end, Wallis lost most, but not all, of these court cases, and therefore so too did the people who purchased or leased land from him. As James Tilghman tried to warn potential purchasers of the Wallis tracts, "Those patents are fraudulent & good for nothing."[45]

If the "Back-Inhabitants" who petitioned Governor John Penn in March 1769 were irritated, they must have been furious by this point. Out of fifty-eight known signatories, thirty-four applied for land in the New Purchase when it opened to the public in April. Only seven of these applicants were granted land, receiving a total of 2,521 acres, far less than they had requested. For perspective, these thirty-one applicants sought just over half the land Samuel Purviance received in February but only obtained 15 percent of his grant. Additionally, despite the lottery/trunk system's intent to distribute remaining land fairly, it did not work as expected—Joseph Shippen and his father secured over twice the land acquired by these thirty-one applicants.[46]

The ramifications of such a reality were clear. Some of the dejected petitioners, as well as others who felt similarly, called it quits and supported Connecticut's claim to the Northern Susquehanna River Valley. For example, one petitioner, Lazarus Stewart, a ringleader of the infamous Paxton Boys, applied for three hundred acres on the East Branch of the Susquehanna River when Tilghman's office opened in April. His application, however, clashed with two other speculators who received "special grants." Disaffected, Stewart aligned himself with Connecticut's Susquehannah Company, staking claim to land on the East Branch under its auspices and wreaking havoc in the valley for the next several years on the company's behalf. He was like many other petitioners whose land applications were disregarded because they were either never pulled from the trunk or conflicted with those of powerful claimants.[47]

Not every dejected petitioner cum land applicant joined the Susquehannah Company. Some simply settled for smaller parcels of land purchased at inflated prices from speculators, especially Wallis. Still others abandoned the colonial government entirely and settled illegally beyond Tiadaghta or Lycoming Creek, creating communities and eventually their own government that attracted still other colonists, especially those who purchased small parcels of hardscrabble land from speculators, thus setting the stage for a dispute among settlers, the proprietary government, and a host of Native American polities still reeling from the outcome of the Treaty of Fort Stanwix. Out of the fifty-eight known signers to the March 1769 petition, at least thirteen of them or their immediate family members ended up squatting on land beyond Lycoming Creek. Of those thirteen, eleven applied for land in the New Purchase when the office opened in April.[48] As Physick warned Thomas Penn, the advantage given to speculators "with the intent to defraud honest men of the chance" of obtaining land had "certainly brought very unhappy Effects on your Affairs."[49]

Penn, finally realizing he had a problem on his hands two years later, tried to counteract these issues by selling or leasing parcels on his manor lands along the West Branch for a fraction of their value and decreasing quitrents. Nevertheless, the damage had been done. Pennsylvania's frontier settlers who joined Connecticut proved a serious threat. "If we had only the people of Connecticut to deal with," John Penn thought, it would "be very easy." But, instead, "the greatest danger is from the Pennsylvanians themselves who have through this whole affair given them [the Susquehannah Company] every possible encouragement."[50] By the early 1770s, the Northern Susquehanna River Valley had become a warzone between Connecticut and Pennsylvania, as both sides mustered posses, constructed rudimentary forts, and killed or jailed officials and ordinary farmers. In the spring of 1770, Penn sent news to his father Richard Penn that "our people have at last been obliged entirely to abandon their possessions & give up the whole country to these lawless invaders, who are carrying on Settlements on the West Branch of the Susquehanna."[51]

Pennsylvania's settlers had valid reasons to flee. Lazarus Stewart, who protested the land office in March and was denied land in the New Purchase, joined forces with a prominent Connecticut settler, Zebulon Butler. Both wore "white Cockades" symbolizing their allegiance to Connecticut and attacked Pennsylvania settlements in the Susquehanna River Valley. They captured people, subjecting them to torture for psychological effect. On one occasion, Stewart and other ex-Pennsylvania frontiersmen backing Connecticut took nine Pennsylvania land claimants as prisoners. Confined in Fort Wyoming, the prisoners faced starvation unless they left the territory. To display their resolve, Stewart and his posse "killed one poor fellow by ill treatment & then stript his body & threw it into a small room among the rest of the prisoners where they left it to rot."[52]

Those settlers siding with Pennsylvania, then, found even legitimate land claims difficult to hold, and some asserted that they would not pay for them or their quitrents until the Pennsylvania government assured "quiet and certain possession" of the land.[53] Moreover, the inability of Pennsylvania's officials to assert the law of the province against Connecticut led those loyal Pennsylvania colonists to castigate the proprietary government's inadequacies "as scarce to be paralleled in the History of any Civilized Country."[54]

At the same time that Pennsylvania officials scrambled to figure out a way to remove Connecticut claimants backed by many ordinary Pennsylvanians, Virginia made matters worse and laid claim to land near Fort Pitt by right of conquest. Virginia's governor, Lord Dunmore, acting "ungentlemanlike," refused to deal amicably with Pennsylvania officials. Similar to circumstances with Connecticut, contested land with Virginia in the New Purchase became a warzone, or, as one contemporary called it, an "asylum of the lawless." Both Virginia and Pennsylvania established overlapping counties in the area, sold land to settlers, appointed county officials, and then violently harassed one another. The dispute between Pennsylvania and Virginia, and the actions of their respective people on the ground, also threatened and ultimately resulted in "a general War" with some of the Ohio Nations, who, because of Connecticut settlers and Pennsylvania squatters, were growing in number with the inclusion of irritated members of the Susquehanna Nations. In addition, Pennsylvania's southern border with Maryland was in dispute again, and much to the Penns' dismay, they were fighting legal actions against Hurst & Company, a firm laying claim to large sections of Philadelphia's Northern Liberties as well as proprietary manor lands in York County.[55]

Large portions of land occupied and legally owned by Pennsylvanians now seemed insecure, and the Pennsylvania government could do little about it. That does not mean Thomas Penn did not try. The proprietor, expending large sums of money for lawyers and defensive operations on the ground, much of which he could not recoup without the quitrents from inhabitants occupying the lands under dispute, believed only King George III could end his troubles with other colonies, thus strengthening the bond between the proprietary colony and the British government.[56] The timing of that reliance could not have been worse considering the growing imperial dispute over the authority of Parliament.

Nor were these the only problems Pennsylvania's government faced on the frontier. While Governor John Penn complained that "we have been attacked on three sides of the Province already," and claimed it was the New Englanders settling the "West Branch of the Susquehanna," his own colonists also pushed beyond the boundary of the New Purchase, potentially damaging a tenuous peace with the Haudenosaunee and Susquehanna Nations. Pennsylvania speculators had sent surveyors beyond the purchase line on the West Branch, and Pennsylvania settlers, unassociated with Connecticut, occupied that same territory. This was a terrible and costly repercussion of poor policy.[57]

It should be remembered that at Fort Stanwix, "a chief & Warrior from each Nation" communicated "the final resolves of all the Nations." With a map in front of them and pushed to create a new boundary by Sir William Johnson, the Six Nation delegates had traced a line from "the mouth of the Cherokee River [Tennessee River], then along to the South East side of the Ohio to Kittanning" along to "the Head of the West Branch of Susquehanna," limiting the northwest boundary of Pennsylvania to the east side of "Tiadaghta Creek." With this, the Haudenosaunee made clear "that no further attempts shall be made on our Lands, but that this Line be considered as final." In 1769, proprietary surveyors went out to demarcate that boundary and a dispute arose over which creek, Lycoming or Pine, was, as stipulated in the treaty, the Tiadaghta.[58]

Thomas Penn, hoping to continue the goodwill of the Haudenosaunee, officially declared Lycoming Creek the northern boundary. It was important to Penn that he had the Haudenosaunee and their proclaimed dependencies on his side.[59] Penn and his officials relied on the Haudenosaunee to continue firm in their argument that Connecticut's claim to the Northern Susquehanna River Valley hinged on "a fraudulent Grant obtained by a private Company in Connecticut from the Six Nation Indians in the year

1754." Although proprietary officials had "evidence" that the Haudenosaunee "condemned" this "deed," especially the treaty minutes from Fort Stanwix, they needed the Haudenosaunee to maintain that position to win the argument.[60]

Such a goal was easier said than done. In August 1769, just a few miles below Fort Augusta, Peter Read, a "wicked person," murdered the son of Osternados (Seneca George) for no apparent reason other than Osternados's son and his friends were fishing on the banks of the Susquehanna River.[61] This incident, combined with the murders committed by Frederick Stump and John Ironcutter several months earlier, as well as the constant encroachment of squatters on Native American land, seriously undermined Penn's relationship with the Haudenosaunee and a host of other Indigenous nations. As Johnson explained to Governor Penn, "the murder of Seneca George's Son on the Susquehanna" would "not be easily or soon forgotten," especially since "the disposition I have discovered in the different Nations who I have lately seen appears very unfavorable at this time." On Pennsylvania's frontier, Johnson complained, it seemed as if that colony's settlers were "under no Government, as at present they can neither be restrained from settling or brought to punishment tho' guilty of many irregularities towards the Indians."[62] Pennsylvania officials, cognizant that "this is a matter of the utmost Consequence [for] the Settlement of our New Purchase," urged Johnson to "quiet the minds" of the Native Americans by assuring them "that this Government Possesses the most sincere and steady Intentions to redress their Injuries at all times, and to preserve public Faith with them to the utmost of its Power."[63]

Penn's assurances were pathetic. Frederick Stump and John Ironcutter, for example, aided by about eighty frontier inhabitants, escaped from jail later that same year, undermining Penn's guarantee to "bring the murderer[s] to Exemplary Punishment."[64] If the government could not punish two murderers, how could it stop numerous settlers from encroaching on Native American land? According to George Croghan, the Delaware and Shawnee "aperehend themselves Insulted" and viewed the frequent murders and Stump's rescue as part of a "Desine" for their land. To make matters worse, Croghan thought, "thire is No prospect of this Government being able to give them thet Satisfaction which Might Convince them" otherwise because "the perbetraters of itt is Not Likely to be brought to Justus." The "weakness of government" was apparent to everyone.[65]

This fact became clearer as Pennsylvanians continued to settle land beyond Lycoming Creek despite the proprietors' stated commitment to a northwest boundary on the eastern edge of that creek. Some of those squatters may have even been members or kin of the mob who rescued Stump and Ironcutter from jail. Of the nearly eighty or so men who rescued Stump, colonial officials identified twenty-six. Of those, eight shared surnames with the known squatters west of Lycoming Creek, one of whom, Francis Clark, almost instantly got into a tussle with a Native American from Great Island. Given the fact that the squatters west of Lycoming migrated with extended families and over fifty of Stump's rescuers are still unknown, it is reasonable to assume that the Irwins, Roddys, Fergusons, Bairds, and Clarks who settled in the disputed territory and shared surnames with the rescuers were in some way connected to or even participated in Stump's escape, but we will never know for sure.[66]

Regardless, the settlement of so many people beyond the line infuriated both the Native peoples who lived there and the Haudenosaunee who brokered the deal in the first place. Angry, the Canajoharie Mohawk "Chiefs Warriors & c." accused "the Governor of Pensilvania" of ignoring the Fort Stanwix Treaty's "Easterly line." They "hope[d] that Mr. Penn will act the Honest Man." "Otherwise," they warned, "he will give great umbrage to the whole Confederacy."[67] The Ohio and Susquehanna Nations were also upset, remarking that while they "are not desirous of making War," they would "when the same appears necessary." That necessity, they argued, seemed clear enough. "At the Treaty of Fort Stanwix," an Ohio speaker named Conoquieson pointed out, "you then told us as you had done before" that "we should pass our time in peace" and "that care should be taken to prevent any Person from imposing on us." Yet "it is now worse than it was before."[68]

Fed up, Newalike, Shawana Ben, and others "of the several different Nations, namely the Six Nations, Shawanese, Delawares, Mohickons, Nanticokes and Conoys," traveled "from the West Branch of the Susquehanna" with a Cayuga messenger to Philadelphia in September 1771. They made their way to the city because from their "Home we were looking towards Wyoming, and observed the people of New-England were come to live there." They wanted to know why and, more importantly, "what they meant by this?" Looking east from their home they must have spied a host of white people similar to the "New-Englandmen" settling all around them, so much so that Shawana Ben noted that he and many others of the Susquehanna Nations wanted to "remove from the Place where we live, the Great Island" to move west to the Ohio region, which Penn knew was not a good omen, especially since the Susquehanna Nations at this meeting called the West Branch of the Susquehanna River "*Mingo* Country," suggesting a clear association of the Susquehanna Nations and their lands with the Ohio Nations instead of the Six Nations at Onondaga.[69]

Such warnings and requests did little. The governor, for example, followed up the speeches by Shawana Ben and other Native peoples from the West Branch by blaming all of the mischief on Connecticut while also trying to reaffirm Haudenosaunee supremacy in the region. Ignoring the statements about moving to the Ohio region or their calling the area Mingo country, Penn told the Susquehanna Nations to stay and to "consult your Uncles, the Six Nations, when you find any inclination to remove." They, he argued, rather than the Ohio Nations or even their own leaders, "will give you good advice." He then handed out some gifts and sent them on their way, promising little because he could not "do anything in that matter without your uncles, the Six Nations, present in Council."[70]

Meanwhile, Pennsylvania squatters continued to make their way to the West Branch beyond Lycoming Creek, pushing west of even Pine Creek to settle around Great Island with little deterrence from the colonial government. By 1773, two years after the meeting in Philadelphia, still nothing had been done to remove or even deter the squatters there, and Newalike and Shawana Ben moved to the Ohio region. Frustrated by the movement of so many of the Susquehanna Nations out of the Northern Susquehanna River Valley, the Cayuga, speaking for the Six Nations and their "dependents," demanded Governor Penn travel to *them* for a meeting at Shamokin about the problems with the "boundary line."[71]

Replying to the Cayuga and a host of other complaints, John Penn, claiming he could not travel to Shamokin because of business with the

"Great King," finally swore to enforce the boundary at Tiadaghta, or Lycoming Creek, promising that "none of my People will ever trouble my Brothers the Indians" again.[72] Spurred to action, Penn called together the provincial council, relating that "he had received information that several Families had lately seated themselves on Lands on the North side of the West Branch of Susquehanna, beyond the Boundaries of the last purchase." Penn urged swift action because "the making of settlements on the Indians' Lands would create great uneasinesses among them, and if not immediately removed and prevented for the future, might be attended with Fatal Consequences." Several days later, on September 20, 1773, Penn "ordered to be published in all the public Papers, and also a number of Printed Copies to be made and dispersed thro' the back Counties" a proclamation declaring "that if any Person or Persons" settled "upon any Lands within the Boundaries of this Province, not purchased of the Indians," they "shall forfeit and pay for every such offence the sum of Five hundred Pounds, and suffer twelve Month's Imprisonment, without Bail or Main-Prize." Therefore, anyone "settled or Residing on any lands beyond the Boundary Line of the Last Indian Purchase" should "immediately evacuate their illegal Settlements, and depart and remove themselves from the said Lands without Delay, on pain of being prosecuted with the utmost rigour of the Law."[73]

Governor Penn's strongly worded proclamation did little. About two months after the governor's edict, one proprietary official and local sheriff, William Cooke, sent to evict "the peopel then Living" beyond Lycoming Creek because "there seemed to be an Uneasiness amongst the Indians" on "account of the white people Living on their Land," reported that he found over "fourty Improvements made between Licoming and Great Island." He "would have found more Settlers there" if not for a recent "Disturbance that happened Betwixt the White People and the Indians." As Cooke found out, the Susquehanna Nations resisted the squatters' encroachment and many of the white families were "flying away from the Indians" when the sheriff arrived.[74]

One of those squatters, John Walker, who claimed about three hundred acres at the mouth of Pine Creek, fled south of the Susquehanna River, taking refuge in a "Stockade fort at Henry Antes." He was not alone. Captain Thomas Robinson, who made a trip out to the West Branch around the same time as Cooke, noted that he "found the inhabitants of that Country collected & inclosed within stockade forts" on "the Southern shore" because of their "fear of the Indians." Still other squatters "went off when they heard" proprietary officials were making their way to the West Branch to remove them.[75]

Evicting these squatters, however, proved difficult. Sheriff Cooke, for instance, working with what information he could about the squatters, actually made a "Return of their Names to Court." With those few names in hand, the grand jury of Northumberland County ruled against the squatters, but nothing actually came of it. A defendant, by simply refusing to attend court, could derail the entire legal process. The government, in effect, could not deter these encroachments, and many of the squatters returned to their illegal settlements within a few months.[76] Perhaps more worried about the Susquehannah Company's settlers at Wyoming, the Pennsylvania government made a half-hearted effort to enforce the new boundary beyond Lycoming Creek.

What Pennsylvania officials did not know or perhaps failed to see was that those colonists squatting on the West Branch were a significant threat to the future of the colony and the larger interests of the British Empire. While those squatters were not connected to the Susquehannah Company, they did defy both proprietary and imperial restrictions, not to mention the sovereignty of several Native nations. By 1774 or early 1775, they had even set themselves up as a people outside of the British Empire, forming their own independent squatter government at odds with the imperial and colonial governing structures that claimed to rule them. Such a scenario was part and parcel of a revolutionary situation sweeping the colonies in the mid-1770s that neither the imperial or colonial governments, try as they did, could contain or resist.

8

"A Spirit of Liberty and Patriotism Pervaded the People"

THE CREATION OF A SQUATTER REPUBLIC IN THE NORTHERN SUSQUEHANNA RIVER VALLEY AND THE BEGINNING OF THE AMERICAN REVOLUTION, 1773–1776

WITHIN A YEAR OF Sheriff William Cooke's attempt to evict squatters west of Lycoming Creek in 1773, not only did the squatters who fled return but at least another one hundred colonists joined them. By 1775, even more settlers had arrived beyond the line on the West Branch. That summer, an itinerant Presbyterian minister, Philip Vickers Fithian, traveled to the Northern Susquehanna River Valley and was shocked to find his sermons attended by at least 140 families who lived beyond Lycoming Creek where the "New Purchase ends and the Indian land begins."[1] Fithian was not exaggerating. Between 1773 and 1775, over two hundred squatter families took up residence west of Lycoming Creek, occupying a swath of land roughly twenty-five miles long and two miles wide, and still more came thereafter.[2]

The consistent migration of so many colonists to the West Branch, squatting on Native American land beyond the new boundary, was quite simply an act of defiance. The aftermath of the Treaty of Fort Stanwix triggered pent-up animosities and lingering grievances that had roiled Pennsylvania for decades. The New Purchase did not, as many colonists hoped, open "a Door for the relief of the poor people." Instead, it opened a door to speculators, slamming it shut for most everybody else. Seriously irritated with how land, resources, and power were allocated in their colony and the larger British Empire, and outright dismissive of, if not hostile against, Native

American sovereignty and rights, ordinary colonists flocked to the West Branch where they not only illegally staked their claim to small plots of land but also collected together to protect their interests, establishing an independent yet interdependent squatter republic that they tellingly called "Fair Play."[3]

It was, for all intents and purposes, a rudimentary republic, without a constitution, even written laws, but a republic nonetheless. The Fair Play government, organized as a tribunal, gained its legitimacy by rooting itself in popular sovereignty, boasting annual elections, a mandatory rotation of officeholders, and a franchise that included any white male who improved land in the territory recognized as valid by their neighbors and the tribunal. Moreover, its elected officials jealously protected their republic from colonial officials, speculators, and even unruly settlers by upholding community needs over those of individuals, often with a heavy hand. Their squatter republic was everything average colonists had professed they wanted for years and flew in the face of the governing powers that had claimed to rule them for decades.[4]

Nevertheless, their squatter republic was precarious. Despite their efforts to protect their community from the prying eyes and interests of "outsiders" and "enemies," Native Americans moved against them. Rightfully detesting squatter encroachments, the Haudenosaunee as well as the Susquehanna and Ohio Nations wanted the Fair Play settlers gone. So too did Pennsylvania speculators, who were actively angling to purchase the land out from under them. As the prospects of another war in the Northern Susquehanna River Valley loomed, both imperial and proprietary officials sought to remove those squatters, but more often than not, officials and speculators were one in the same, which was a significant source of Fair Play discontent and the reason for the republic in the first place. All were "our enemies," the Fair Play settlers later argued.[5]

Although new, small, and contending with powerful opponents, the Fair Play settlers were not exactly isolated or alone in their defiance. Their republic came to fruition during a tumultuous and revolutionary time. The still larger colonial resistance to imperial policy, which had been steadily growing since at least 1765 with the Stamp Act, came to a head in the mid-1770s, ultimately resulting in a bid for American independence and another destructive war that would envelop and shape the future of the Northern Susquehanna River Valley. For their part, the squatter republic settlers drew important parallels between their resistance and that larger struggle, "cheerfully" supporting what they began to see as "our Common Cause" with a common goal to eradicate "our enemies." Land "jobbers," a "Moneyed interest," and "savage enemies" beware.[6]

That feeling for many colonists who had no seeming connection to the Fair Play republic was mutual. The evolving colonial resistance, which was rapidly turning into a revolution, *could* fulfill *all* of their republican dreams, or so some colonists thought. How a collection of colonial settlers came to create a small squatter republic that became part and parcel of the American Revolution reveals much about the meaning of that revolution for not just those Fair Play settlers but for the many other colonists who found common cause with them as well as the Native peoples and speculators they thought stood in their way. While in the beginning, the Fair Play settlers merely followed the growing resistance, using it to their advantage, what they built there in the Northern Susquehanna River Valley had consequences that directly influenced, even shaped, the common cause as the Revolution progressed and the memory of it for generations to come.[7]

After the Treaty of Fort Stanwix, a steady wave of colonial settlers, most of whom hailed from Pennsylvania's most western counties, made their way to the West Branch of the Susquehanna River beyond the boundary line of Lycoming Creek. While a diverse bunch, composed of English, German, and Scots-Irish, Anglican, Lutheran, Reformed, and Presbyterian, the majority of the settlers, nearly 50 percent, were Scots-Irish Presbyterians arriving mostly from Lancaster, Berks, Cumberland, and York Counties. There were also a host of settlers arriving from as far away as New Jersey.[8]

The predominance of Presbyterians on the West Branch was the reason for Fithian's journey to the area in 1775. Since at least 1772, "settlers upon the W. Branch" had been petitioning the Presbytery of Donegal for a minister and, finally, the Presbytery sent Fithian. He would not stay. He was mostly appalled by what he experienced and could not envision a life beyond the line. The living situation of the people left much to be desired, the bugs relentless, the terrain difficult to maneuver, and the people crude. He was also constantly fearful of Native Americans who seemed to be everywhere. There were some aspects of life there that he enjoyed. The settlers, at least one of them, had a library filled with the most recent pamphlets and newspapers from Philadelphia, which enlivened Fithian. Moreover, his sermons were well attended. The people came out en masse to hear him preach. Nevertheless, he still left as quickly as he came. Despite his quick sojourn, the Presbyterians on the West Branch were not left to themselves. Within a year another minister, John Kincaid, arrived, establishing a church and schoolhouse at the base of Pine Creek.[9]

Given such efforts to establish a Presbyterian church and the demographic predominance of the Scots-Irish, the Presbyterian religion surely influenced that community's development and outlook, especially as the settlers began constructing their republic. In the eighteenth century, the Presbyterian religion was more than just a collection of churches, ministers, elders, and lay people but a way of life centered on the construction and protection of community. Churches and ministers played a vital role in emphasizing the social responsibilities within community life, where an individual's rights were intertwined with the public good. Presbyterian churches particularly highlighted a doctrine rooted in community solidarity, prioritizing the collective over individual interests in their teachings and organization. In those churches, the clergy served as role models, illustrating the significance of law and governance in sustaining a united community. While focusing on God's law as a guiding principle for congregants, many Presbyterian ministers extended their teachings to include the importance of civil society, discussing concepts like the state of nature and natural law. These discussions, while seemingly beyond religious realms, reinforced the core values of community, law, and governance inherent in Presbyterianism.[10]

Presbyterian ministers also pushed the theme of community and law to extremes in North America and Pennsylvania in particular, due to perceived instability and lack of significant social organization. Pennsylvanians' geographic mobility, settlement patterns, and religious heterogeneity proved the need, at least from a clerical perspective, for community and order. After midcentury, apparent challenges to community, church, and, to some extent, the patriarchal family also inspired ministers to reaffirm the relationship of individuals to the wider community. "Every man," ministers argued, "is bound by the law of nature, not only to preserve his own life, liberty and property; but also that of others." The reason for this reciprocal obligation of individuals in society, according to Presbyterian clergyman John Goodlet, was simple: "There is a natural relation between all mankind constituted by our glorious Creator, an universal brotherhood or fraternity." Therefore, he argued, "every one by the law of nature is every one's neighbor, and every one's brother, and consequently ought to be his *helper* and *keeper;* that is, he ought to use all lawful means to preserve his life, property and freedom, as well as his own." Communities tied people together, and law assured adherence to mutual social obligations. No one individual's needs, in this sense, was greater than the needs of the larger community—a powerful message that could justify the construction of an interdependent squatter republic at odds with both the provincial government and the special interests of prominent individuals that government promoted.[11]

While the ethnic-religious makeup of the community mattered, where these squatters on the West Branch came from was equally consequential. The majority of inhabitants who squatted on land beyond Lycoming Creek migrated from Pennsylvania's frontier counties, a concentration of which came from Lancaster County, particularly from the area around the townships of Paxton, Derry, and Donegal near modern-day Harrisburg.[12] That area had given birth to the Paxton Boys. While the Paxton Boys were popular in the area, that does not mean every frontier settler joined their "holy war."[13] Yet, it is clear by the petitions from that same area, as well as the other areas squatters on the West Branch came from such as York and Cumberland Counties, the overarching sentiments of the Paxton Boys against "a particular set of men, deeply concerned in the government" and "the singular regards they have always shown to the savages" had wide currency.[14] The settlers confirmed their position on these sentiments by denying the just claims of Native Americans, the wishes of the proprietors, the proclamations of the governor, and a grand jury presentment when they continued to occupy territory beyond Lycoming Creek.

Their motivations for defying both Native Americans and proprietary officials can also be extrapolated by comparing the March 1769 petition of the "back-inhabitants" after the fiasco of the land office opening in February 1769 to "none but Favourites" with the way settlers occupied land beyond the boundary of the New Purchase.[15] In that petition, inhabitants railed against the preference the land office had given to gentlemen and land speculators who monopolized the land to the detriment of "the poor." Squatters beyond the boundary adhered to the principles expressed in that petition; fewer than a handful of squatters there claimed more than three hundred acres, and those few outliers were for five hundred acres.[16] Moreover, their improvements were modest. Most of the settlers built small cabins and cleared few acres, rarely more than two to four acres each spring. Some were even more modest. Alexander Irwin, for example, who squatted on land just west of Lycoming Creek only cleared about a quarter of an acre where he planted potatoes he got from his neighbor, as well as some "Salad and Onions."[17]

For all of these squatters, the land beyond the New Purchase offered a fresh start, an opportunity to break free from impediments they believed government officials and prominent gentlemen had placed in their way. As the squatters pointed out, "Necessity forc'd" them to "settle on those Lands" to "support their families," which they could not do "by Reason of such Large Tracts of Lands in the Hands of a few."[18] Put simply by another settler, "we ware poor" and therefore "moved to this then back country."[19] John Walker, for instance, sold his small farm in Derry, Lancaster County, to purchase land from a speculator in the New Purchase for several times that land's initial value, leaving him in considerable debt. Unfortunately, the land he purchased proved unprofitable and isolating. His family, also looking for land in the New Purchase, could not acquire land near him. Within just a year or so he abandoned his small parcel to squat on fewer than three hundred acres well beyond the Fort Stanwix boundary near the mouth of Pine Creek. His brother Benjamin went with him, becoming his neighbor. Symbolizing his aspirations, John Walker dubbed his new illegal settlement "Good Hope."[20]

Others had a longer history of moving to better their circumstances with dismal results. The Dunn family, for instance, started off in Maryland around 1762 on a small plot of land that could not sustain a growing family. William Dunn and his wife had their first child, James, on March 27 of that year, and within six months of his birth moved to York County, Pennsylvania, most likely leasing land with William's father or brother, both named James. After the lease ended, they left, deciding to squat on land for a few years along the Juniata River, but that too proved precarious if not dangerous. Cobbling together a little savings, the Dunns made their way to Philadelphia in April 1769, hoping to purchase three hundred acres of New Purchase land in the Ohio Valley, which the land office denied. A year later, William Dunn and his small family headed out to the West Branch of the Susquehanna River with his two brothers James and John, where William took odd jobs protecting surveying parties to the south of the West Branch while he personally staked claim to Native American land to the north of it around Great Island.[21]

While such evidence could be used to support the popular view of self-reliant, individualistic frontiersmen akin to Laura Ingalls Wilder's *Little House on the Prairie*, the families who squatted beyond Tiadaghta Creek constructed an interdependent community of small farm families that upheld mutual social obligations. As they said in their 1769 petition, they were looking for land "sufficient [enough] for a number of families to settle together" for "support." That self-proclaimed "design" influenced the communities created beyond the "purchase line."[22] Pooling their meager resources, tools, and manpower together, they helped each other clear small plots of land and build cabins. For instance, George Woods, William McMeen, Thomas Ferguson, and others, all neighbors who squatted beyond Lycoming Creek, worked together to build their homes as well as clear, fence, and plant a few acres of corn. Similarly, the McClure brothers and their neighbors "assisted" each other to "make a Considerable Improvement." On William McClure's land, that "Improvement" included planting "a quantity of Potatoes" and building a small "house" that they "covered with clapboard." They also "made better than one Thousand rails and built part of them in a fence."[23]

These were common descriptions of life and settlement beyond the Fort Stanwix line. John Boyd helped his neighbor William Luckey raise "part of a house." Thomas Mahhaffey "assisted" his neighbor James Chambers "Build a House" and clear about four acres of land for wheat. Thomas Ferguson similarly "assisted Henery Dougharty to raise a House," and then William Luckey helped Dougherty drive his cattle to a clear spot of land. John McElvaine "with Others of the Neighbouring Settlers" helped James Alexander construct a "Dwelling House" and clear about three acres of land.[24] These moments were so central and memorable that Benjamin Walker, who moved to Pine Creek with his father and uncle (also named Benjamin) in 1773, remembered much later in life that when he was "young" he often joined "with divers others of the neighboring inhabitants" to help build homes and clear fields.[25]

The squatters beyond the line also busily constructed communal spaces and practices. John Jackson donated a portion of his squatter claim on Pine Creek to Presbyterian minister John Kincaid, and the neighbors came together to build a schoolhouse for their children. James Richardson sowed timothy seed, a perennial bunchgrass used for hay, for his and his neighbors' cattle, neighbors helped James Parr build a storehouse, Abraham De-Witt built and operated a tavern where much of the community gathered, and William McElhatton constructed a distillery where neighbors brought their grain to make alcohol.[26] Unsurprisingly, ten of the squatters mentioned in the paragraphs above applied for and failed to receive land in the New Purchase. Of those ten, seven applied for land situated close to each other. If it had all worked out when the land office opened in April 1769, the McLure brothers, as well as Chambers, McMeen, Parr, Woods, and Alexander, would have been near neighbors with legal claims.[27]

In essence, it was not just access to land but the construction of community that mattered to these squatters. They probably did not separate those two goals; they were mutually reinforcing. For poorer folk, the land meant nothing without the help of friends and kin who could volunteer their time, energy, and tools to reap its rewards. Interested squatters beyond Lycoming Creek even sought the approval of their potential neighbors to settle there. When William King wanted land beyond the line in 1775, for example, he went to his potential neighbors to make sure "they would accept me as a neighbor."[28] Similarly, when Alexander Irwin squatted on some "Indian

Land" at the mouth of Lycoming Creek, he made sure that he "was allowed by all the Neighbors to be the first Improver."[29]

As the squatter settlement grew, the community they were constructing became more precarious. Accordingly, the settlers who lived there entered into "a mutual compact among themselves" to ensure current and future squatters upheld community goals and would unite against common "enemies," forming their own republic that they called Fair Play. Everything they did was illegal, but they nonetheless tried to give it the veneer of legitimacy by embracing popular sovereignty. While there are no extant written laws or minutes of their government, a series of court cases in county district courts as well as the state supreme court after the Revolutionary War provide ample evidence of how the Fair Play government operated.[30]

The Fair Play system was quite simple in its construction. Settlers of the area gathered annually at a number of places, whether DeWitt's tavern or a local home doubling as a crude fort, and elected three men to form a tribunal (on a rotation to assure a revolving polity that reflected the larger community), which contemporaries called the "Fair-Play men." Largely representative of the ethnic composition of the area, the Scots-Irish often held the majority of the seats on the tribunal but never total control because the Fair Play system required unanimity. Both German and English settlers were elected to the tribunal. Perhaps just as representative of their motivations for creating and serving on the tribunal, of the known Fair-Play men, at least fourteen applied for land in the New Purchase but only two of them gained legal title.[31]

This squatter tribunal, established by popular consent, spoke for the community by arbitrating disputes between neighbors, approving land claims, and settling boundaries. According to one early compiler of Pennsylvania's laws, the Fair-Play men decided "all controversies" and "from their decision there was no appeal, and there could be no resistance." There was "no resistance" because the community "in mass" enforced the tribunal's decisions.[32]

To settle in the area, an individual not only had to get approval from neighbors but needed to take evidence of that endorsement to the tribunal and make a "solemn engagement to submit in all respects to the law of this land."³³ Such a process of obtaining "unanimous agreement" of the "Fair-Play Men and the Neighbors of the Settlement" bound the community together to uphold community will as expressed by the tribunal.³⁴ In short, individuals either embraced the rules of the community or were forced out. It was as much an exclusive experiment as it was an inclusive one.

In 1775, for example, Robert Arthur and his small family made their way to the Fair Play district and, without asking for their neighbor's approval or taking their squatter claim to the tribunal, constructed a cabin. That proved problematic because the Arthur family settled on land that another squatter, William Paul, had already claimed and had approved by the tribunal. To protect "his land," Paul "applied to the Fair-play men," who ordered the Arthur family to immediately abandon their home. Defying the tribunal, Arthur refused to leave. Irritated that "Arthur still lived on the land and would not go off, although the Fair-play men had decided against him," community members collected together and "proceeded to Arthur's cabin." When they arrived, they found Arthur "with his rifle" and Arthur's wife brandishing "a bayonet on a stick," threatening "death to the first person who would enter the house." That did not stop those gathered. Thomas Kemplen, "our captain," dashed "at the door, burst it open and instantly seized Arthur by the neck. We [then] pulled down the cabin, threw it into the river, lashed two canoes together and put Arthur and his family and his goods into them and sent them down the river." Casting off offenders reinforced the importance and strength of the community and its exclusive welfare.³⁵

The known "laws" of the Fair-Play men also reflected that importance. One "resolution" of the tribunal "which they agreed to enforce as the law of the place" declared that "if any person was absent from his settlement for six weeks he should forfeit his right." If individuals tried to place tenants on the land in their absence without prior approval, the Fair-Play men divested that right and gave it to the tenants or someone else who wanted it. For example, James Hughes, who made a small improvement near Pine Creek in 1773 and whose older brother served on the tribunal, left the area the next year to visit his father in the township of Donegal, Lancaster County, where he died due to an unknown illness. Just two years after Hughes's death, Henry Dougherty appeared before the tribunal and applied for land and "was advised by the Fair Play Men to settle on the premises which Hughes had left; this he did, and built a cabin."[36]

Not long thereafter, Hughes's younger brother John made his way to the area and claimed Dougherty's property "in right of his brother." When Dougherty refused to leave, John Hughes violently "took possession of the cabin." Undeterred, Dougherty took his case to the Fair-Play men. The tribunal and the community, following their own resolution, sided with Dougherty. With that ruling in hand, Dougherty, supported by his neighbors, marched on the property where "an affray ensued, in which Hughes was beaten off" and Dougherty was "left in possession." While dramatic and violent, the "law of the place" was nonetheless upheld. Dougherty remained on the property and "continued to improve, built an house and stable, and cleared about ten acres."[37] The Fair Play tribunal did make exceptions to the absentee rule for those individuals acting on behalf of the community through military service. As one settler remembered, "If a man went into the army, the Fair-play men protected his property."[38]

Not only did such rules against absentees reflect settlers' abhorrence of landlords, but since land ownership made a settler part of the squatter republic with the right to vote and hold office in the tribunal, it only made sense that anyone who would not permanently join that community and fight on its behalf should be excluded. To put this principle in perspective, it was the established norm in Pennsylvania for prominent politicians to be placed on election tickets or appointed to judicial positions for counties in which they owned land but did not actually reside. The political careers of Joseph Galloway and William Allen and his sons, who all mostly lived in the city of Philadelphia but held offices in Bucks and Northampton Counties, are an important reminder of that fact. The Fair Play resolve, then, challenged notions of representation and the relationship between the government and the governed as practiced by the colonial government and derided by common people.[39]

The Fair Play republic, therefore, was thoughtfully created and expressive of popular ideas about government and its purposes. Far from just three men meeting at a tavern or under a tree, the tribunal set procedures for witnesses; logged evidence of payment for sold improvements; stored

"Articles of Writing" between parties; and set rules to regulate land sales, leases, and even the lending of farm equipment and work animals.[40] It must have been difficult and tedious work.

Without legal surveys, individual squatter claims rested on rudimentary descriptions of the natural landscape and the existence and word of neighbors. For example, Thomas Henry described his claim to two hundred acres as "on Larrys Creek about a half a mile from the West Branch of Susquehannah beginning at a forked Black Oak Tree standing on the west bank of Larrys Creek thence running westerly to the first hill or rising ground & adjoining Captain Simpson Coals Improvement then to extend up Shugar Tree Run." Another settler simply stated that his claim was bounded to the north by a rock, "known by the name of the great rock." To make matters more difficult, some squatter claims changed hands several times in the space of a few years. Still others were disputed as two or more parties laid claim to sections of the same land.[41]

Arbitrating such disputes required an intimate knowledge of the area, its settlers, and previous transactions. One dispute, for example, involved no less than five sales and a lease agreement sanctioned by the tribunal, as well as two unsanctioned sales by the lessee, all of which took place over the span of two years. The lessee, William McLlhatton, most likely tried to take advantage of the illegal nature of the settlement to make some quick cash. Claiming his lease agreement for three hundred acres as his own improvement, McLlhatton sold pieces of it to interested settlers. As he told the Fair Play tribunal once he was caught, if the purchaser "would be such a fool as to give him forty or fifty pounds for Nothing He McLlhatton would be a greater fool for not taking it." Needless to say, McLlhatton knew he did not have "any right," and besides, both the "Neighbors and Fair-Play Men" knew the exact boundaries of the land under dispute as well as the history of ownership. They easily decided the case against McLlhatton and the people who bought land from him.[42]

The tribunal also adjudicated criminal and moral cases, meting out draconian punishments that at the same time revealed how they understood the purpose of government. Two cases are illustrative. In one case, the tribunal heard a complaint from a local Native American from Great Island that a squatter, Francis Clark, stole his dog. Acting swiftly, the tribunal had

Clark arrested and tried. While seemingly a minor crime, the tribunal took it seriously, convicting Clark and ordering that he be publicly flogged. The severity of the punishment most likely related to the potential impact of the crime on the broader community. Settlers in the area had already fled once because of a dispute with the Susquehanna Nations and likely did not want that to happen again.[43] The punishment, however, did not appease the local Native American, who, either from pity or disliking Clark's encroachment, perhaps both, asked that the tribunal remit the sentence if Clark "would abandon the land where he had settled." The tribunal complied and Clark left the territory, not returning until 1795.[44]

The tribunal similarly charged and convicted Presbyterian minister and schoolmaster John Kincaid with domestic abuse. Apparently, Kincaid liked strong drink and had a penchant for beating his wife and kids. Once convicted, the Fair-Play men forced him to ride the rail, a ritualistic and violent form of punishment known as "rough music." Typically, this punishment commenced with a cacophony of noise made by riotous but organized community members banging pots and pans, shouting, and blowing trumpets or playing other instruments as they marched to an offender's home. Once there, they forcibly entered the home and placed the offender on a fence rail, parading them throughout the community as onlookers shouted insults and threw garbage, stones, and anything else handy at the offender. The ritual often ended with violent physical punishment such as tarring and feathering or a public whipping. Even if the gathered community did not carry out this final punishment, the threat of violence was always there and equally as terrifying.[45]

Such actions of the Fair Play settlers also reflected wider popular trends in the middle colonies, where colonists used rough music to control unruly men to maintain community values. These values often revolved around the accepted boundaries of patriarchal behavior that defined the very fabric of the community. Moreover, the increased use of rough music in the eighteenth century coincided with a weakening of legitimate channels to regulate these boundaries, such as courts and churches. That weakening was the product of a diversity of religious belonging, the logistical inadequacies of the colonial legal system, and the anglicization of a bench and bar that deviated from popular values by protecting the individual aspirations of patriarchal heads of household, often turning a blind eye to domestic abuse. Obviously, the Fair Play settlement reflected that trend as there was no "legal" government nor state-sanctioned church in the area. Therefore, as happened elsewhere, the use of rough music reflected popular efforts to place the interests of the wider community and their social values and expectations against that of John Kincaid, the male head of household.[46] More revealing still is the fact that the Fair Play tribunal, an elected extralegal government that could not operate without widespread acceptance, convicted a minister and chose such a punishment.

Dealing with troublemakers within the community was one thing but there were also, Fair Play settlers came to believe, enemies all around them. While they occupied Indigenous lands and constructed their republic, there were increasing and near constant rumors that Native Americans were mobilizing against them. The extant writings of any one settler in the area often includes statements such as James Carson's, who "continued in possession of the Land until drove off by the Indians." Although Newalike and Shawana Ben had left for the Ohio region a few years earlier, still others, such as the leader of the Nanticoke, Jacob Asquash, remained. There were also Tuscarora, Shawnee, Delaware, Tutelo, and Conoy living in the area, and the Ohio Nations as well as the Haudenosaunee still laid claim to the West Branch. Proprietary officials were likewise lurking about to evict the squatters, and even some proprietary surveyors made their way to the area with their chains, compasses, and logbooks. Everything the Fair Play settlers built was under threat, producing a feeling of desperation if not anger. Some of the official proclamations against their illegal settlement even threatened public execution if they did not leave.[47]

The mounting threats to the Fair Play republic and its efforts to combat them, however, came at an auspicious time. By the mid-1770s, the dispute between the colonies and the British government had come to a fever pitch. The organization of colonial resistance that that dispute inspired significantly shaped the future of the squatter republic created on the West Branch. For many of the people living there, the budding imperial resistance offered an opportunity to legitimize their claims and their fight against perceived enemies both within and without.

In the larger British Atlantic world, colonial opposition to imperial policy was at a low ebb when the settlers started making their way to the West Branch. The Townshend duties' partial repeal in 1770 had eased tensions, but the remaining duty on tea kept some resistance alive. In 1773, colonists swiftly opposed the Tea Act, granting the East India Company a monopoly over North American tea trade, leading to widespread protests along the eastern seaboard, particularly in Boston. The Bostonian response—dumping tea into the harbor—sparked imperial retaliation through the Coercive Acts of 1774. These acts, including the Boston Port Bill, the Administration of Justice Act, and the Massachusetts Government Act, were met with further resistance. At the same time, Parliament also passed the Quebec Act, expanding Quebec's jurisdiction over western territories gained from the French. This law introduced an executive-style government, depriving colonists of representation in self-elected assemblies, setting a concerning precedent for the future of British rule. The combination of the Coercive Acts with the Quebec Act seemed to prove the existence of a despotic plot "calculated for enslaving these Colonies."[48]

Almost immediately after news of these acts reached America, colonial North Americans clamored for a new kind of concerted resistance. In the past, colonial resistance hinged on individual colonies that often acted independently, and therefore it was sporadically and ineffectually carried out. In order to assure a continent-wide effort and demonstrate colonial solidarity, several colonies called for the formation of a continental congress. Pennsylvanians, especially outside the legislative chamber of the assembly, joined the chorus. On June 15, over 1,200 colonists met on Pennsylvania's statehouse yard to proclaim their support for a continental congress and a popular system to elect representatives to it. Just a few days later, nearly eight thousand people met in the city and made a similar declaration. The Pennsylvania Assembly, fearing such popular gatherings would set "up a power to control" what it considered legitimate institutions, condemned those public meetings as attempting to set "up anarchy above order; IT IS THE BEGINNING OF REPUBLICANISM." The legislators needed to "nip this pernicious weed in the bud, before it has taken too deep root."[49]

Joseph Galloway, who had risen to Speaker of the assembly and was the leader of a legislative majority, feared and detested both Parliament's new policies and this popular clamor. He no more wanted popular forces to dictate Pennsylvania's public policy than he wanted Parliament to pass laws affecting the province, and he actively resisted both. Whatever happened, he would not give ground to Parliament or the "mad people" in his colony who wanted the province to be "managed by the very Dregs" of society. If those "Dregs" got their way, it should be noted, he would be on the chopping block quite literally. It was around this time that Galloway awoke one morning to find a box on his doorstep containing a noose and a message telling him to "hang yourself or we shall do it for you."[50] While that threat may have "fix[ed] me in my former resolutions," as Galloway later boasted, he was in no position to stem the tide. A continental congress would happen and popular clamor would exist regardless of his prognostications. The only thing Galloway could do as Speaker was undermine the popular election of delegates to the congress from his colony. Ignoring the meetings on the statehouse yard, Galloway chose delegates to the Continental Congress from members of the assembly, and obviously he was one of those chosen. What the settlers on the West Branch thought about this moment remains unknown.[51]

Nevertheless, the settlers did agree there needed to be a general congress, and in early September that necessity was realized as fifty-six delegates hailing from twelve of the thirteen colonies made their way to Philadelphia, convening a new and now semi-official Continental Congress. In what was certainly a jab at Galloway, the new congress elected to meet at Carpenters' Hall, a focal point of popular resistance in the city, rather than the Pennsylvania State House, the home of the more conservative Pennsylvania legislature. If Galloway was worried by what this move meant, he had good reason. The Continental Congress forever changed politics in Pennsylvania and elsewhere. That congress addressed salient issues related to the resistance effort by declaring colonial rights as British subjects and providing a concerted plan of opposition to imperial measures. Its most important accomplishment proved the creation of the Continental Association, which propelled resistance forward and undermined the authority of traditional political leaders like Galloway in one fell swoop. It also elevated the grievances and status of political outsiders such as those living in the Fair Play republic.[52]

Signed by all members of the Continental Congress, even Joseph Galloway, who opposed the measure from the beginning, the association bound all colonists in mainland North America to resist British policies through economic sanctions. Starting on December 1, 1774, the Continental Congress outlawed the importation of certain goods from Great Britain, and in September 1775 a full embargo of British trade took place. Congress deemed such action necessary, not only because of the Coercive Acts but because the Quebec Act took away the "western Frontiers of these Colonies, establishing an arbitrary Government therein" that would discourage "the Settlement of British Subjects in that wide-extended Country." The Quebec Act proved that the British government was "wicked," highlighting the importance of western land in the matrix of colonial grievances as projected by the new congress.[53]

To enforce the association, the Continental Congress called for the creation of new committees "to be chosen in every County, City, and Town" throughout the colonies. What was more, Congress granted these new committees the authority to regulate the use of scarce articles such as wool, set "reasonable prices" for manufactured goods, and enforce the prohibition on British trade. The committees could also actively "discourage every Species of Extravagance and Dissipation, especially all Horse-racing, and all Kinds of Gaming, Cock-fighting, Exhibitions of Shows, Plays, and other expensive Diversions and Entertainments." The public and private rights of people within the colonies, Congress declared, needed to be policed by the committees. Even mourning the dead needed to be monitored. Congress dictated that "on the Death of any Relation, or Friend, none of us, or any of our Families, will go into any farther Mourning Dress than a black Crape or Riband on the Arm or Hat for Gentleman, and a black Riband and Necklace for Ladies, and we will discontinue the giving of Gloves and Scarfs at Funerals." Those funerary accoutrements often visibly reflected the power of elite colonial notables, which, considering the new authority granted to ordinary people through the resistance effort, could no longer be countenanced by the Continental Congress. It may have constantly declared itself "his Majesty's most dutiful and loyal Subjects," but Congress nonetheless actively regulated and diminished displays of monarchical culture in the colonies using the new committees.[54]

The association and the committees it created meant much more than just abiding by and enforcing trade restrictions and policing monarchical "Extravagance and Dissipation"; it also required the committees to ensure that the colonists under their jurisdictions actively tried to "improve themselves in the military art."[55] By asking colonists to support a potential war with Britain, the chance of which was made real after the outbreak of actual fighting at Lexington and Concord in April 1775, Congress solidified a scenario where the committees could delineate friends from foes, thus providing a semblance of collective identity wrapped up in the resistance movement. Like enforcing trade regulations, the committees throughout the colonies canvased their districts, compiling lists of military "Associators" and "Non-Associators."[56] Such a move brought many more people under the watchful eye of the committees, thus increasing their coercive strength.

Although the Fair Play settlers made no clear declarations against imperial policies like the Coercive Acts, they "Cheerfully" joined the Continental Congress's resistance efforts. For them, Congress promised inclusion in a new kind of government based "on the authority of the people" that would represent their vision of a properly functioning government and their squatter claims to Native American land against those of "jobbers" and "monopolies."[57] Congress's creation of the association, especially the committees to enforce it, played no small part in that rationale and ultimate decision.

The association's committees provided a welcoming opportunity for the Fair Play settlers to bind themselves to a seemingly national cause that lent legitimacy to their claims, grievances, and ideas about government and its purposes. In the towns and counties throughout Pennsylvania, inhabitants instantly set about to establish elections to form committees. To ensure widespread representation, county committees operated and were elected at the town level instead of at the county seats—the usual place for colonial elections. York County's committee, for example, structured representation to ensure "that there is at least one of that Body in each Township of the County."[58] Northumberland County, which was created in 1772 for Pennsylvania's new northern boundary after Fort Stanwix, similarly structured its county committee, creating local town branches comprising three to five representatives each. The Northumberland County committee even incorporated the territory beyond Lycoming Creek into Bald Eagle township, granting representation on the committee to the Fair Play republic. Inclusion in the county committee gave the citizens of that republic a say in the continental resistance effort while making them privy to news and information from the city of Philadelphia.[59]

The rise of the committees' power and influence during the mid-1770s furthered the process of inclusion of the Fair Play republic into the resistance effort while giving quasi-legitimacy to the very ideas that defined it. By late 1775, the committees throughout Pennsylvania became the de facto government. Acting as the "Guardians" of the "public welfare," the committees had "the whole Executive & Legislative authority in their hands."[60] In September of that year, Pennsylvania's county committees published proclamations stating that they provided "the reality of justice" and therefore could decide who did and did not act "consistent with the peace and welfare of society." Anyone whom the committees judged dangerous to the public welfare had no right "to the protection of a community or society" and therefore would be "deemed a foe to the rights of British America and unworthy of those blessings" of government.[61] The committees were, one critic said, "Usurping Powers."[62] In short, the committees did far more than enforce the association. They were central to the transition of a resistance effort into a revolution.

The Fair Play settlers used that expansive authority to their advantage, transferring power from the tribunal to the town committee. In the records it is difficult to decipher where the authority of the Fair Play tribunal ended and the committee's power began. That confusion mostly has to do with the fact that the Fair Play settlers elected members of their tribunal as the three representatives to the town committee, such as William Dunn, John Walker, Alexander Hamilton, and Thomas Hughes. Like the tribunal had done, the town committee declared themselves "the most competent judges of the circumstances of the people of that township," set about mobilizing men and resources for war, and used the authority of the committee to regulate the public and at times private lives of "the people."[63]

While the Fair Play republic's town committee spent some of its time approving the election returns for military officers, it also, like the tribunal, functioned as a court. The town committee issued its own "Special

Warrants," granted bail, exacted fines, and imprisoned neighbors. It hauled people before it for breaking the sabbath in an "unchristian and Scandalous manner" and abusing servants, vowing to "suppress such like practices to the utmost of their power." The committee also imprisoned people for "refusing to associate and Bear arms," and used the power delegated by Congress to regulate the economy for the benefit of "the poor."[64]

This latter action reveals much about how the Fair Play republic's committee members understood the purpose of government and the goals of the Revolution. During one town committee meeting, the local inhabitants presented a petition complaining that some people, especially colonists living just outside of the Fair Play settlement, refused to sell grain for a fair market price, going so far as to threaten to hoard the grain or sell it outside the area unless inhabitants paid what they asked. While these grain farmers adhered to a laissez-faire vision of the economy, the Fair Play settlers and committee did not. Since "a great number of the inhabitants of the township will suffer if such a practice is allowed to go on," the town committee resolved that they would "seize" and "take by force" the grain of anyone who refused a fair price or attempted to sell it out of the area before "the poor is supplied."[65] By regulating profits, the committee made clear that it understood the economy as a public phenomenon that the government could shape and regulate, a position and power that politicians and jurists claimed for the state and used to justify regulatory policies well into the nineteenth century.[66]

This does not mean frontier settlers in the Fair Play republic disapproved of profit, far from it. They simply believed profit should not be gained to the detriment of the broader community. They were, after all, perfectly willing to pay what they considered a "fair price" for the seized goods. This resolve, like the earlier rulings of the Fair Play tribunal, brings to light a frontier value system that relegated the desires of individuals in a community and demonstrates their understanding of how government, if properly functioning, upheld those community values. That, in and of itself, was the very essence of a society and government adhering to fair play.

Representation in the revolutionary committees also offered an opportunity for this small squatter republic to attach itself to "the general cause," further committing its settlers to the Revolution. Not only had they resisted the proprietary colony and the empire but they saw commonality with the revolutionary cause. This especially became true as talk of American independence increased throughout Pennsylvania by the beginning of 1776. For most of the early 1770s, independence existed on the margins of the resistance movement, rarely capturing the attention of more than a few people. By the first months of 1776, that had fundamentally changed. Thomas Paine, a member of Philadelphia's city committee, which served as an organizational and messaging hub for the various local committees, issued a clarion call for American independence in January with his popularly consumed pamphlet *Common Sense*. Soon, "a terrible wordy war" on "the subject of Independence" consumed the province as newspaper articles and pamphlets shot from the presses branding the British king tyrannical and the colonial government an oligarchy filled with "*unworthy persons*" who treated their offices "as their own property, and deemed it an inheritance to their children." Similarly, Pennsylvania's charter, which buttressed both proprietary power and the authority of the colonial legislature, came under severe criticism. Angry Pennsylvanians derided it as "defective," an "imperfect thing," and a "wretched mangled constitution" that gave "advantage to the profligate and corrupt."[67]

By May, Philadelphia's city committee was fully on board with a complete break with both the colonial government and the British Empire. Sending runners bearing a message to the counties, the city committee instructed the county committees to come together to declare their support for independence and with it the power to create a new government for Pennsylvania based solely "on the authority of the people."[68] Everyone needed to act, the committee's circular letter implored, because the current government, "prejudiced in favour of old and established forms" and "influenced by self-interest," was working to "influence" all "whom they can" to undermine "*American* freedom." Calling on "that class of men which are most to be depended on in times of danger," a nod to the lower and middling sorts who made up the membership of the many committees, the city committee declared it "absolutely necessary for us to unite with firmness" for the "safety and happiness of the Province."[69]

Such a message directly spoke to the Fair Play wing of the Northumberland County Committee, which seized on this moment, gathering the squatter community together to proclaim their approval of American independence and a new government that would share their values. Those squatters may have resisted the proprietary and imperial governments, but a new independent government based on the values promoted by Congress and the revolutionary committees augured something else entirely. After all, the grievances leveled by the Pennsylvania press and the Philadelphia committee's circular in the spring of 1776 had also been articulated by the people who comprised the Fair Play republic. As a result, American independence on the West Branch was a popular initiative. Many years later, Anna Jackson, a nonagenarian widow of a well-known Fair Play tribunal member and sister-in-law to a committee member, noted, "I remember well the day indipendence was declared on the plains of Pine Creek, seeing such numbers flocking there." "Indipendence," she recollected, was "all the talk."[70] The memory of independence on the West Branch lived strong, even carrying through in various permutations to this day.

According to popular legend, on July 4, 1776, the citizens of the Fair Play republic gathered under the shade of an elm tree (improperly nicknamed the "Tiadaghton Elm" in the twentieth century) just north of where Pine Creek meets the northwest branch of the Susquehanna River, and signed a document declaring "themselves and the country free and independent of Great Britain."[71] Whether the gathered Fair Play settlers drew up a declaration of independence, discussed the merits of independence, or just made a general pronouncement is in the end unknown; what is clear, though, is that this small community hitched its fate to the success of American independence, the toppling of the old regime, and the creation of a new government for Pennsylvania.

Animosity toward Pennsylvania's colonial government and "the gentlemen" and "monopolizers" who benefited from it had motivated colonial migration to and settlement of land outside the established boundary of the province. The May 1776 circular letter of the Philadelphia committee to the county committees urging independence spoke to those grievances, promising redemption from "tyranny" with a new government based on popular sovereignty. The letter declared that supporting independence meant Pennsylvanians would no longer have to endure the "the unjust claims of haughty and absolute Proprietaries" and "all of their dependants," which was on full display in the aftermath of Fort Stanwix.[72] Such a message gave a glimmer of hope that, as thirty-nine settlers living beyond Lycoming Creek articulated, independence and the new government it would create would guarantee their rights to the land against avaricious gentlemen and "Land Jobbers." As those same settlers declared, a new government based on popular sovereignty would "never suffer any man or any set of men to take such undue Advantages to Ruin many for the Advantage of the few."[73] "The Poor distress'd People," through the Revolution, would finally triumph over a "Set of men" with connections and "hard money."[74]

The new state constitution that came out of that moment enshrined those beliefs, declaring to the world that "a set of men" who represented "a few" should never have complete power over the "many." Even here, though, in this revolutionary logic promising so much, the definition of the "many" was narrowly defined. The Fair Play settlers thought as much, stating that they supported the new state constitution because it elevated them, the "poor distress'd people," to a coequal status with other white Pennsylvanians. Yet, that revolutionary elevation did not include the "Cruel and Savage Enemy" who also threatened their illegal land claims. That squatters on Native American land pointed to the dispossession of Native peoples in the list of reasons to support the new state of Pennsylvania is not at all surprising.[75]

In the buildup to American independence, patriot printers spilled gallons of ink to galvanize support by not only using the specter of an exclusive proprietary government but by also utilizing the popularly imagined threat of "Indian savages" whom the British purportedly encouraged to "ravage our frontiers, and murder, after their inhuman manner, our defenceless wives and children." The British, according to patriot publicists, had a penchant for stirring up racial others. Not only did the British persuade supposedly homicidal Native Americans to massacre settlers but the British "enticed" "our Negro slaves" to "rebel against their masters, and . . . murder them," and even "the King of England's own slaves, the Hanovarians," similarly depicted as racial others, were being brought over to the colonies to commit heinous crimes. Enemies were everywhere. All Americans could do, according to vocal patriots in the popular press, was either "fight or die."[76]

Like the patriot press, Philadelphia's city committee drew on this threat of racial others to "incite such of the good people as are friends to liberty." In the same circular letter urging the committees throughout the province to support independence and the new state it would create to resist the machinations of the "haughty and absolute Proprietaries" and "their dependants," the committee asked their compatriots to "recollect the horrors of the late *Indian* war" and "shudder." If the people did not act now in support of independence, "fire, sword, desolation, and death in the most infernal forms will be presented to our view; parents and children weltering in their blood; infants torn with savage brutality from their mothers' wombs, and made the food of dogs!!!" Worse still, the circular declared that the proprietary government and the British crown supported these "horrid ravages" to make them all "slaves." Therefore, "Liberty and slavery is before you; take, then, your choice."[77]

Given that the struggle for land on the Pennsylvania frontier was consistently punctuated by racialized violence, the rhetoric of the patriot press and committees in the months leading up to American independence spoke to the Fair Play squatters and shaped their understanding of patriotic service. Mustering in droves, they promised "every thing in Their Power to support the present Contest, not only against the British Army, but also against a Cruel and Savage Enemy on our Frontiers."[78] Later, some of them did not even refer to the War for Independence as the Revolutionary War; instead, they called it "the late unhappy Indian War."[79] Imbibing the language of the times, the Fair Play settlers thought their "stand" was guided by "devine providence" because it prevented "the encroachments and depradations of the savages" on a newly independent America. God, these squatters argued, supported the removal of Native American threats to white settlement.[80]

In effect, the squatters on the West Branch had been mobilized by revolutionary propaganda that played to their alienation, especially their hatred of land speculators and corrupt politicians, and to their prejudices against Native Americans. And we know the Fair Play settlers were aware of this public dialogue. When Philip Vickers Fithian traveled to the West Branch in 1775, he instantly "fixed" on the library of one of the leading men in the area that included oppositional newspapers and pamphlets published in

Philadelphia. According to Fithian's observations, the settlers there were far from isolated from the larger imperial conflict but were rather engaged with a powerful and all-encompassing revolutionary message, which was obviously furthered through the creation of the committees and their circulars. The message shooting from the press and those circulars fundamentally shaped the memory of the American Revolution and those squatters' place in it for generations to come. For many squatters on the West Branch, they *were* the American Revolution.[81]

Over eighty years after those early days of revolution and on the eve of yet another American war that would decide the future of the young republic, John Hamilton, a Christian missionary tasked with proselytizing to Native peoples but also the son of Robert Hamilton, who served on the Fair Play tribunal and fought in the Revolutionary War, described his father's patriotism and love of country by effortlessly conjoining his father's support for American independence with his father's hatred of Native Americans. In a revealing paragraph, the son related that his father was "one among others of his neighbors who held a meeting on the banks of Pine Creek on the Fourth of July 1776 and passed resolutions declaring themselves and the country free and independent of Great Britain," the "remarkable coincidence of this with the national declaration made it remembered." John Hamilton followed up this proof of his father's patriotism in the very next sentence by stating, "I have often heard my father say that in those exciting times he had a great desire to kill an Indian." This last sentiment, he admitted, was shocking since "such a desire was far from being in harmony with his naturally amiable disposition . . . for he was an exemplary Christian!" Nevertheless, the son quibbled, "it must be remembered a spirit of liberty and patriotism pervaded the people." For the son, his father's participation in the Pine Creek declaration of independence and his desire to "kill an Indian" were equally important and mutually reinforcing in any understanding of his father's dedication to "liberty and patriotism," the lifeblood of the Revolution. That symbiosis, offered as a kind of disclaimer by the son of a Fair Play settler, nonetheless fueled the American Revolution in the Northern Susquehanna River Valley. As it would turn out, what happened in that valley because of that symbiosis would shape the war and the very meaning of the American Revolution itself.[82]

9

"The Title of Savages"

THE REVOLUTIONARY WAR IN THE NORTHERN SUSQUEHANNA RIVER VALLEY, 1776–1783

DESPITE PATRIOT PROPAGANDA AND fears, the Northern Susquehanna River Valley was relatively peaceful during the first few years of the Revolutionary War. By the time war with Britain broke out, many but not all of the Susquehanna Nations had temporarily left the valley for other quarters, dispersing in a wide arc north and west for safety. Along the East Branch, the towns associated with Moravian missions such as Friedenshutten and Sheshequin near Wyalusing packed up and headed west to the Tuscarawas River in modern-day Ohio, establishing new missions like Gnadenhutten, Salem, and Shoenbrunn. Other Delaware and Shawnee communities in the valley also headed in that direction. Shawana Ben and Newalike, for instance, had left the West Branch for the Ohio region just a few years earlier. Moreover, the Ohio Delaware and Shawnee had been actively recruiting the Susquehanna Nations to join them for years. As squatters inundated their land on the West Branch, it seemed more than ever that strength in numbers would secure their future.[1]

Their move west also reflected the fractured relationship between some of the Susquehanna Nations and the Haudenosaunee after Fort Stanwix. Not only did they start calling the West Branch "*Mingo* Country" but when they moved west, migrating members of the Susquehanna Nations moved to areas that the Haudenosaunee had little control over, such as the area around the Tuscarawas where the Wyandot, or Wendat, an Iroquois-speaking people popularly known as the Huron, claimed sovereignty and set aside land for these newcomers. According to White Eyes, a prominent

Delaware war captain and chief, "my Uncles the Wiandots have bound themselves the Shawanese Tawaas and Delawares together and have made us as one People and have also given me that Tract of Country." Speaking on behalf of the Delaware, White Eyes told commissioners from the Continental Congress that his people would remain neutral during the Revolutionary War as long as Americans recognized that those "Lands belong to us" and "you will not permit any of your foolish People to sit down upon it." That, he said, "I cannot suffer."[2]

The Ohio Valley was not the only place the Susquehanna Nations went. Many of the Munsee, Mohican, Nanticoke, Conoy, Tutelo, and even some Delaware and Shawnee temporarily (or so they thought) moved north to Haudenosaunee towns such as Tioga, Oquaga, Otsentigno, and Chemung. Still others, though, remained. Just south of Tioga, a large and vibrant multiethnic community thrived at what was known as Queen Esther's Town, which boasted some seventy homes, vast corn and wheat fields, and grazing grounds. Further south on the West Branch, a community of Delaware, Shawnee, and Mohican people still lived on Great Island amid the Fair Play settlers. There was also a Munsee village just west of Great Island near Bald Eagle Creek, named after Chief Woapalanne, who the British and colonists commonly called Chief Bald Eagle. The mere existence of these remaining Native peoples, though, seemed to terrify the white inhabitants beyond Lycoming Creek, who believed "that they *will be* disturb'd by the Indians" and therefore would "greatly suffer" if not "immediately supplyed with a sufficient quantity of Ammunition to defend themselves."[3]

Despite those stated fears, the Continental Congress had successfully used negotiators to achieve Native American neutrality.[4] On June 16, 1775, Congress established regional commissioners of Indian affairs to oversee diplomacy with Indigenous people. Their job was not too difficult to accomplish initially. Up north, the Haudenosaunee and Susquehanna Nations who lived with them saw neutrality as in their best interest. Siding with either the British or Americans too early could be disastrous, lest they gamble their lives and land on supporting a loser. Trying to strike a middle ground, the Haudenosaunee's Grand Council refused to "join on either side of such a contest, for we love you both—old England and new."[5] They were "firmly resolved to maintain peace" during this "family affair" and would "sit still and see you fight it out."[6]

There were, however, clear divisions and factions who contested the viability of such a neutral stance, seeing either the Americans or the British as "double dealers" who "we despise," but at least to begin with, neutrality was mostly upheld. Indigenous proclamations of neutrality came with stipulations, however, requiring both British and Americans to recognize Indigenous rights and their sovereign authority, articulating their own independence. Yet, sovereignty and for whom was under question in these years, opening up new avenues for both Native peoples and white colonists to try to achieve independence, autonomy, and survival in the Northern Susquehanna River Valley. In the end, neutrality did not hold and it would be all-out war there, the reverberations of which would be felt well-beyond the valley.[7]

As Indigenous people proclaimed their independence, sovereignty, and neutrality, the Fair Play republic mobilized for war in support of "our Common Cause." Between 1775 and 1776, the Northumberland County Committee of Safety organized four battalions, each composed of around eight companies of roughly sixty men. Most of the Fair Play squatters who volunteered served in the Second Battalion in either the Fifth Company commanded by Captain Cookson Long, called "Cookey" by his men, or in the Eighth Company under Captain Henry Antes, both of whom were members of the Fair Play tribunal. The importance of the tribunal for the Fair Play community was ultimately reflected in who the soldiers chose as their officers. Those militias had to be representative as the Revolution required such popular acceptance to succeed, and therefore not only did the common soldiers gain the right to vote for their officers but they used that right to vote for Fair Play tribunal members as their captains, lieutenants, and ensigns.[8]

As elsewhere, familial ties and forged connections between community members mattered for the mobilization of men for war. When Cookson Long volunteered, so too did his young thirteen-year-old son George. The

Longs' family friends, the Dunns, also volunteered together. James Dunn, then fourteen years old, joined Long's company alongside his father, William. The Walker family, who were likewise friends of the Longs and Dunns, volunteered as well, joining Antes's company. John Walker, a member of the tribunal, and his young sons Benjamin, Henry, and Joseph, served together at different points in the war. Like those three families, Henry Hill, Robert Covenhoven, and Covenhoven's siblings, who had all been close friends for several years, volunteered together in the "Company Commanded by Cookson Long."[9] Such connections not only helped inspire fathers, sons, brothers, and friends to volunteer together, but those connections and shared experiences during the war led many of both companies to reenlist, especially when patriot fears narrowed in on Native Americans.

The Fair Play settlers' first taste of military life was more marching than actual fighting. Since the Northern Susquehanna River Valley was then "quiet," Cookson Long marched his battalion east to join the overall commander of the Continental Army, General George Washington, at Trenton and Princeton, New Jersey. Although they arrived just after the famous battles fought there, Long's troops volunteered to serve beyond their three-month enlistments, fought the British at Ash Swamp, and continued to guard supplies and process prisoners just outside of Washington's encampment at Morristown. When their enlistment ended late in April they were discharged and marched home to the West Branch.[10]

Much to the dismay of General Washington, this early and rather uneventful service would be the last time most of the soldiers from the Fair Play republic marched east, though not for lack of trying to convince them to return. Washington, Congress, and even Pennsylvania's new Supreme Executive Council (SEC) constantly tried to get those settlers to help in the eastern theater, but the Fair Play squatters refused. When President of the SEC Thomas Wharton, along with Washington, requested reinforcements from Northumberland County to fend off what they thought was a general British invasion of Philadelphia, that county's lieutenant, Colonel Samuel Hunter, in charge of mustering troops for the war effort and stationed at Fort Augusta, could do little. "The Generality of the Inhabitants," he explained, "does not think it prudent to let any out of the County at this present call for the Militia, when the Frontiers is like to suffer by a cruel savage enemy."[11] Nevertheless, Hunter wanted to make clear, the settlers were patriots willing to show "their attachment to the American cause" by defending that frontier, which many of them thought and later claimed was a central aspect of the war and the future of the American republic.[12]

The poor response to Washington's and Wharton's call to arms had a lot to do with rumors swirling through the Northern Susquehanna River Valley of an impending Native American attack. Near the end of 1776, the rather small multiethnic community of Delaware, Shawnee, and Mohican people still living on Great Island packed up their belongings, cut down their corn, and headed north to live with the Haudenosaunee at Tioga and neighboring towns, the usual sign that war was in the offing.[13] If that move did not prove inauspicious, Job Chillaway, a Delaware interpreter who remained in the valley, informed Captain Antes that the Susquehanna Nations in conjunction with the Ohio Nations and the Seneca were preparing to attack the settlements on the West Branch. The mere thought of a new "Indian War," one soldier explained after Chillaway's warning, sent many of the Fair Play settlers flying to different homes "making little forts" on the West Branch, such as Fort Antes, Fort Horn, Fort Reid, and Fort Kelly, all situated near Great Island. There was even an attempt to erect a fort at the base of Lycoming Creek.[14]

Then, in late 1777, an unidentified number of Native Americans confirmed settler fears when they attacked a small cluster of homes near Loyalsock Creek. Around the same time, another group of Native Americans overwhelmed six men and women milking cows near Pine Creek. Similarly, three men who ventured out of Fort Horn quickly found themselves surrounded and fired upon. On December 23, "near the Mouth of Pine Creek," settlers discovered another "two men kill'd & scalped."[15] Although few in number, these attacks were part and parcel of an effort by just some of the Susquehanna Nations to showcase their power and, hopefully, remove the squatters from their land.

Those squatters could not see or refused to recognize the reason for these attacks. It was a sort of collective amnesia. Besieged squatters combined these attacks with the larger "Cause," seeing in these violent encounters the beginning of a general "Indian War" provoked by the British. It was proof, Samuel Hunter thought, of a concerted effort of all Indigenous people incited by the British to remove white people from the land to undermine American independence.[16]

Yet, he and the settlers did not know what to do. Nothing they did worked. Antes, recently promoted to the rank of lieutenant colonel, traveled to Fort Augusta to "consult what was best to be done." He and Hunter both agreed that Cookson Long, also a newly promoted lieutenant colonel and "an Excellent Good, Woods man," should gather all of the volunteers along the West Branch and "use all means to come up with them savages." Nevertheless, "for all the scouts" Long "kept out, there was another of the Inhabitants kill'd and scalped." Apparently, Long's men pursued "Eleven Indians" but "could not come up with them." Frustrated, "they turned back to their familys, which is suffering at this inclement season of the year, as they are afraid to live in their own Houses." These small and short encounters in 1777 terrified the valley's inhabitants, throwing everything into "confusion."[17]

Those attacks also further militarized the Fair Play republic. Fully imbibing a revolutionary language deeply steeped in racialized visions of the war, Henry Hill, who had been discharged at Morristown, volunteered again when he reached Fort Augusta, "protecting the inhabitants from a cruel and bloodthirsty enemy."[18] Many shared that sentiment. William Campbell, just fifteen years old, "was driven into Fort Kelly with my father's family by the Indians" that winter, and it was there that he and his father decided to volunteer "our Services for the defence of the Fort and our Country."[19] Benjamin Walker stated bluntly that "the cause" of his continued service rested on the fact that "his father living there, and suffering the loss not only of property but of life by savage barbarity."[20] It seemed, Colonel Hunter relayed to state officials in Philadelphia, that "the Indians," which he described as a "cruel savage enemy," had entered the war on the side of the British.[21]

That was certainly how the settlers and the patriot press saw and wanted to present things to reinvigorate the war effort. The war was not going well for the Americans in 1777. That July, the British under General John Burgoyne marched from Montreal and captured Fort Ticonderoga. New York City had also been in British control since the previous summer, and General William Howe, the commander in chief of the British Army, was poised to invade Philadelphia, the American capital, which he accomplished that

September. The situation seemed dire. Congress and Pennsylvania's new state government, fearful for the future, fled to Lancaster and York Counties, and Washington's bedraggled, ill-equipped, and underfed army at Valley Forge was the only thing standing in the way of their annihilation. To make matters worse, American enthusiasm for the war had ebbed. According to John Adams, nothing could be done without inciting "the Passions of Men." The "public may be clearly convinced that a War is just," he wrote his wife, Abigail, "yet, until their Passions are excited, will carry it languidly on." To win the war, he argued, patriot leaders needed to capitalize on the people's "prejudices" and their "Anger" to foment a renewed "Hatred of the English."[22]

Those prejudices had been long in the making and easily nurtured. The patriot press, under its own duress because of the war, churned out articles attacking Britain, but they focused a lot of their ire on Britain's use of "murderous savages." In that the British gave them plenty to work with. British General John Burgoyne, for instance, attempting to split the American colonies in the north, issued a widely circulated proclamation threatening to "give Stretch to the Indian Forces under my Direction, and they amount to Thousands, to overtake the hardened Enemies of Great-Britain and America."[23] Even the new secretary of state for the colonies, Lord George Germain, boasted in February 1777 that "all the Indians upon the Continent are united in a solemn League to oppose any encroachments upon their hunting Grounds, and in support of His Majesty's Government."[24] It was all exaggeration. Burgoyne, for instance, was fortunate to raise four hundred Native peoples for his campaign, but the bombast mattered nonetheless. When a Wyandot warrior who may have been aligned to the British killed and scalped a young woman, Jane McCrea, whose fiancé was a loyalist officer marching with Burgoyne, the patriot press went wild. Burgoyne's proclamation combined with McCrea's death created a near perfect storm.[25]

Every patriot newspaper covered her death. In Pennsylvania alone, the *Pennsylvania Packet, Pennsylvania Gazette, Pennsylvania Journal, Pennsylvania Evening Post,* and the German *Der Wöchentliche Pennsylvanische Staatsbote,* ran the same story. It was proof, patriot printers proclaimed, that "the barbarous savages, having received full liberty from the more barbarous Britain, to murder and scalp all before them, without regard to age or sex." McCrea was "killed and scalped in cold blood" while "another woman" suffered the same fate and several more people were "inhumanly butchered." One man, both the *Pennsylvania Evening Post* and *Staatsbote* reported, "had both his hands cut off." That Native Americans murdered white women and noncombatants, even those remaining loyal to Britain, was proof of their "barbarity." There was no line Native peoples would not cross, and the British were at fault.[26]

Within just a few days of that reporting, more garrulous stories of atrocities populated the pages of popular patriot newspapers. Two little girls "gathering raspberries," one letter in the *Pennsylvania Journal* recounted, "were killed and scalped." That story ran everywhere too. Such stories led to the same conclusion and one seemingly insurmountable exaggeration perceived as truth, that "the Indians daily scalp men, women and children" instigated by the British. There was "little difference between" British "regulars and Indians," another newspaper proclaimed. The Native Americans were the mere "mercenaries of Britain" who "lie in wait to murder," to "get a scalp, whether it be from a soldier or an innocent babe."[27] "Oh America!" one letter to the press begged, "be aroused." Britain was inspiring "our enemies, who, devil like, delight in the most barbarous acts of cruelty" and "have an insatiable thirst for human blood."[28]

Whether these monstrous vampiric stories were true or not made little difference. They all served a particular purpose, proving beyond a shadow of a doubt, that, as the Declaration of Independence proclaimed to the world, the king "has endeavoured to bring on the Inhabitants of our Frontiers, the merciless Indian Savages, whose known Rule of Warfare, is an undistinguished Destruction, of all Ages, Sexes, and Conditions."[29] Echoing that refrain, patriot newspaper editors curated their stories to provide "another specimen of the tender mercies of the King of Britain in his hiring the Savages to murder us." When Americans read their newspapers, they learned of lurid events emphasizing murdered women and children by Britain's "savages," which played to their prejudices and their fears. As John Adams hoped, American "passions" were "excited."[30]

The stories circulating during late 1777 and early 1778 missed the mark on the actual situation. While clashes did occur between white settlers and Native Americans in the Northern Susquehanna River Valley and upstate

New York, these conflicts did not signal the start of an overall "Indian War" in the region. Native peoples were deeply divided over the ongoing war and their roles in it. The once-united front of the Haudenosaunee, for instance, was fractured. Sir William Johnson, a key figure in British-Indian relations, had passed away in 1774, leaving a significant gap in Britain's diplomatic efforts. His successor and nephew, Guy Johnson, struggled to maintain stability, and the Six Nations were clearly at odds. While some, like the Seneca, Cayuga, and Mohawk, leaned toward the British, others like the Oneida and Tuscarora did not. The latter felt neglected by British officials and had strong ties to New England missionaries supporting the American cause. The Onondaga, responsible for the ceremonial council fire, attempted to balance these conflicting interests to preserve unity.[31]

But even these divisions between the Six Nations do not adequately represent the fracturing of the Haudenosaunee; it cut much deeper than that. Like Native communities elsewhere, the separate nations were divided internally, and as the war progressed it began to upend the Native nations' political ties and structures. The different clans and kinship groups that made up each nation started going their own way, guided by influential war captains rather than civil chiefs. In many clans, the war captains took on leadership authority without any official call to arms or even discussion and negotiation with clan matrons and chiefs. The world seemed topsy-turvy. The "True Chiefs have lost" much of their authority "since the Commencement of the Rebellion," Guy Johnson reported.[32] According to a chief from Onondaga, Tenhoghskweaghta, "Times are altered with us Indians. Formerly the warriors were governed by the wisdom of their uncles the Sachems but now they take their own way and dispose of themselves without consulting the Sachems." Even his own nation had split, with clans going this way and that. In short, many had simply "forsaken our Council Fire." Then, in late 1777, after a serious bout with disease and factionalism, the central council fire in Onondaga, the fire that never dies, was extinguished.[33]

Ultimately, the Americans and British helped create these divisions. Although both started off the war trying to achieve Native American neutrality, that quickly gave way to constant pressure on Native peoples to choose sides. Despite patriot propaganda that whipped up colonists about

Britain's use of "those Hereditary Enemies of America," the Americans also meddled with the internal politics of Indigenous communities, offered "money and goods" to achieve their support, and tried to create "client" chiefs that they could control.[34] Americans, for example, made much of the fact that the British had a clear hand in elevating the power of a Mohawk war captain, Thayendanegea, more commonly known as Joseph Brant, a protégé of Sir William Johnson and, more importantly, the brother of Konwatsitsiaienni (Molly Brant), an influential clan matron who sided with the British.[35] Yet, at the same time, American officials and commanders did the same thing. As early as 1776 they tried to counteract Britain's influence with the Haudenosaunee by attempting to manipulate the choice of chiefs at the Grand Council Fire at Onondaga. When smallpox broke out there late that year, killing nearly ninety people including three chiefs, the Americans scrambled to put together a condolence ceremony to "replace those Sachems" with others in their interest.[36]

Meddling could only go so far, and in most cases only worked because Native peoples were making their own choices when it came to the war and their futures. Joseph Brant, for instance, traveled to London in 1775 where he met with people on "both sides of the question." After hearing everyone out, Brant "plainly discovered" that "all" the "Americans aimed at was to be sole Masters of the Continent of America, an Event so destructive to the Liberty of the Indians & their Country." Others came to a similar conclusion without traveling to London and hearing a rather one-sided discussion. Some Onondaga, Cayuga, Mohawk, and Seneca war captains who had actually met with American diplomats feared the "subjection & Slavery they must be exposed to if the Rebels got the better as their Behaviour towards them for many years past clearly point out."[37]

The long, sordid history of American expansion clearly still rankled many Haudenosaunee leaders and undermined the very rationale Americans used to justify the war against Britain. Turning patriot rhetoric on its head, one Mohawk captain stated to American commissioners, "You say you are uncertain of holding your possessions, and that you do not know who may enjoy the product of your labor" because of the "great King," but "you" at the same time take "land from us, without any reward, not so much as a single pipe."[38] Similarly, the Native peoples still living along "the West

Branch of Susquehanna where there are some settlements of Delaware" were equally irritated with American encroachments and willing to offer the British "their services."[39]

While some war captains decided to go to war against the Americans relatively early on in the conflict, there were still others who remained undecided. Even Joseph Brant and his British allies had to admit that past experiences coupled with new fears, animosities, and irritations were not enough to convince everyone to "take up the hatchet" against the Americans. There were still a "great many" chiefs and war captains who wanted to remain "Friends to both King & Americans."[40] There were also Haudenosaunee Nations who openly supported the Americans. Many but not all of the Oneida and Tuscarora sided with the Americans.[41] For the Haudenosaunee, the Revolutionary War was turning into an internecine conflict. At the Oneida town of Oriska in August 1777, for example, not only did British and American forces collide but the Haudenosaunee Nations who went to war fought and killed one another. In the coming years, Haudenosaunee warriors initiated a series of raids and reprisals against each other from the Mohawk to the Genesee Rivers, burning towns, destroying crops, and confiscating property.[42]

The Delaware and Shawnee also faced internal divisions during the American Revolution, with factions advocating neutrality, support for the Americans, or opposition. Not long before the Revolution, the Delaware established the Lupwaaeenoawk, a Great Council of "wise men" representing the Turtle, Turkey, and Wolf divisions. The head chief, typically from the Turtle division, was White Eyes, influenced to some extent by American intervention. While the Delaware initially aimed for neutrality under White Eyes, discord quickly emerged. White Eyes and Captain John Killbuck Jr. of the Turkey division leaned toward the Americans, while Captain Pipe, leader of the larger Wolf division, believed the Americans only wanted to seize their lands. Pipe, supported by Newalike, a recent Munsee emigrant from Great Island and leader of a group of Susquehanna Nations refugees, counseled war against the Americans. Nevertheless, White Eyes managed to contain Pipe and his faction.[43]

Yet, Americans often fueled arguments that strengthened the pro-British factions in Native communities. Patriot rhetoric about "savage murderers" stirred American enthusiasm for the war but also animosity against all Native peoples. When Captain White Eyes, a recently promoted U.S. colonel guiding troops to Detroit, was "treacherously put to death" by American soldiers in November 1778, it heightened tensions. Fearing repercussions, Colonel George Morgan concealed the details from White Eyes' son, attributing his father's death to smallpox. Regardless, White Eyes' death upset the balance of power in the Delaware Great Council. Soon after, more Delaware captains, aligning with Pipe, marched with Ottawa, Chippewa, Shawnee, and Mingo warriors against the Americans.[44]

In essence, the Americans made Native American entrance into the war on the side of the British a sort of self-fulfilling prophecy. Patriot suspicions influenced their behavior toward Native Americans, which ultimately alienated the very peoples they wanted aligned to them, or at the very least to remain neutral.[45] One of the "most leading" Seneca war chiefs, Sayenqueraghta, who fought to keep the Seneca neutral, detested this disconnect between patriot professions of peace and the reality his people experienced, coming to believe that "the Rebels, notwithstanding their fair Speeches, wish for nothing more than to extirpate us from the Earth," to "possess our Lands, the Desire of attaining which we are convinced is the Cause of the present War."[46] By 1778, Sayenqueraghta, along with many of the war captains from the Cayuga and Mohawk, as well as a few captains representing discontented Onondaga, Oneida, and Tuscarora clans, after "mature deliberation" decided to "take up the hatchet" against the Americans to stave off "subjection & Slavery."[47] Both sides, then, fought for liberty.

Of particular importance for the Seneca, Cayuga, Susquehanna, and a faction of the Ohio Nations was an offensive to secure the Northern Susquehanna River Valley. Not only did they detest settler encroachment there, but those same Fair Play settlers had constructed rudimentary forts on Indigenous land at strategic locations commanding the Wyalusing and Sheshequin paths, which threatened Tioga, Owego, and Onondaga and cut off easy travel between the two main branches of the Susquehanna River and the well-trodden routes of warriors, diplomats, and hunters to and from the Ohio Valley. Although the different valleys, regions, and Indigenous peoples can seem separate, and sometimes they were, they were also intimately connected. The Northern Susquehanna Valley was in many ways not only a home and valuable farm and hunting ground but a gateway connecting all of those nations, a position Native peoples had articulated to colonial officials for decades.[48]

Between May and June 1778, a combination of loyalist rangers and Seneca, Cayuga, Delaware, and Shawnee warriors, as well as a detachment of Nanticoke and Conoy, descended on the Northern Susquehanna Valley. It is as if the entire history of that valley came home to roost. Most of the settlers of the Fair Play republic, according to reports received by Colonel Samuel Hunter at Fort Augusta, again "evacuated their habitations and Assembled in different places," such as Fort Horn, Fort Antes, and Fort Kelly "above Lycoming." Those forts, though, provided little protection. They may have held against the raids conducted in 1777 but they could not stand against the consistent and coordinated attacks in the spring of 1778.[49]

In early May of that year, Fort Kelly fell. According to Cookson Long's son George, the garrison held out for a few weeks, constantly skirmishing with Native Americans where "many of our men were killed & wounded." After the last skirmish, Long volunteered to bury the dead, but that burial crew was "instantly surrounded." Coming on "with increased numbers," Native American warriors "took & destroyed our cattle & horses & laid waste the country about the fort."[50] The inhabitants inside the fort had little choice but to flee to either Fort Horn or Fort Antes.

Within a few days, the settlers who had gathered at Fort Horn experienced a similar reality. Fearing for their safety after the fall of Fort Kelly, the settlers at Fort Horn sent four men on a mission to Fort Antes to get flatboats to convey what little goods and supplies they had to safer quarters. On their way back with the boats, "a body of Indians concealed in the bushes" along the shoreline fired at the four men. One of the survivors, John Hamilton, "ran for dear life" to Fort Horn to sound the alarm, and then all of the settlers fled downriver to Antes, which quickly became the last fort on the West Branch "above Lycoming." According to Anna Jackson, who fled with her family to Fort Antes, there were so many inhabitants inside the fort that "the people got large timbers" and expanded the fort's walls so that it was "large enuff for tents for their families, and the men to exercise within." They "ware all involvd," she remembered. But as the fort grew, so too did the danger. To account for those inevitably "lost" during the night—settlers often left the fort using the cover of darkness to scavenge for food—the settlers initiated a "roll called over every morning each man answering to his name." According to Anna Jackson, the several silences during those morning calls sent shockwaves through the fort's community.[51]

By the beginning of June, the anti-American factions of the Haudenosaunee, Ohio, and Susquehanna Nations had near total control of the area north of the West Branch of the Susquehanna River and west of Lycoming Creek. Most of the squatters who lived there had fled either to Fort Antes south of the West Branch or to further east, hastily erecting crude fortifications around a few homes near Muncy Creek, some sixteen miles east of Lycoming Creek. According to Samuel Hunter at Fort Augusta, it seemed as if every available white male inhabitant from the Fair Play district had volunteered in some capacity. Besides the militia proper, men "above ye age of fifty three and under Eighteen" were "stationed at such little Forts as they are erecting for the preservation of the Women & Children."[52] Many of them had no weapons and few provisions to "defend it," though.[53]

After the evacuation of Fort Horn, the area was relatively quiet. At Fort Antes, Jackson remembered, "the Indians did not attack the fort, or burn and destroy property." They seemed to be just "walking around."[54] Samuel Hunter heard similar reports. "There has no Damages been done since the 24th of last month by the Indians," but "they have been frequently seen by Our People a Cross the River opposite Antis's Mill & at ye Great Island."[55] The settlers holed up in makeshift forts at Muncy or south of the West Branch at Fort Antes were close to starvation, however, and wanted to go home to retrieve their cattle and goods and to reap the crops growing in the fields. It was, Hunter pointed out, "a Melancholy situation" and "really Distressing to see the inhabitants flying away and leaving their all," especially because "the generality of the setlers is poor they cannot subsist long."[56] Hunter believed that this was the Native Americans' plan. They would, he argued, wait until "about the time of Harvest" with starvation and desperation at its height and then attack, which would require "all the Militia of this county to Guard against," and "so by this means they would lose all their Crops, which would ruien this poor Infant county."[57]

Exasperated, some settlers thought it would be wise to secretly make their way across the West Branch in small groups to capitalize on the quiet and conduct an early harvest. On June 10, for example, several families, including six men, two women, and eight children, ignored the warnings of military commanders, loaded up their wagons, and headed home, but they quickly found their path blocked by Native American warriors who vigorously defended the northern boundary of their land at Lycoming Creek. Within a quarter mile of that creek, "the Indians fired at them" and then ran on the wagons, surrounded them, and only a young man and woman escaped. The next day, the militia "went down & found the bodies" of men, women, and children "Tomahawk'd, Stab'd, and Scalp'd."[58] These spring attacks on the West Branch were only the first wave of a concerted effort by Indigenous people to reclaim the Northern Susquehanna River Valley and push the interlopers east.

The second wave of attacks came a few weeks later. On June 30, Seneca leaders Sayenqueraghta and Cornplanter, and a Cayuga leader, Fish Carrier, commanded 465 Seneca, Cayuga, and Susquehanna warriors alongside Major John Butler and 110 loyalist rangers in an advance on Wyoming, quickly overwhelming two of the three forts in the area. Only Forty Fort, which immediately guarded the Wyoming settlement, refused to surrender. Holed up inside, Colonel Zebulon Butler's sixty Continental soldiers and over four hundred militia under the command of Colonel Nathan Dennison braced for an attack, which never came. Yet, Native American and loyalist troops were there in force and waiting.[59]

On July 3, Butler, against better judgment but facing popular pressure, led his combined forces outside of the fort into a trap. Once he sallied out of the fort, the combined forces against the Americans seemed to descend on all sides. Although he managed to escape by fleeing west, less than 15 percent of his men survived and Forty Fort quickly surrendered. One of Butler's men killed was Lazarus Stewart, a "notorious" outlaw supporting Connecticut and a revolution to upend the colonial establishment, who was also a member of the Paxtang Rangers during Pontiac's War, a ringleader of the Paxton Boys that slaughtered the Conestoga and marched on Philadelphia, a petitioner against Pennsylvania's land policy in 1768 with some of the Fair-Play men, and, just like them, a person who tried but failed to acquire land in the Northern Susquehanna River Valley when Pennsylvania's land office opened to the public after Fort Stanwix. The past, as it often does, reverberates, shaping large and small moments alike.[60]

Victorious, Native and British leaders promised safety and security for the American noncombatants and their property, but the loyalist rangers and Native American warriors had other ideas. They decimated the area, burning the fields and nearly a thousand homes (or so reported), and driving off or killing all of the cattle. According to some purported eyewitnesses, many of the homes burned had families inside, which both Sayenqueraghta and John Butler vigorously denied.[61] Whether true or not, such stories of atrocities traveled fast.

It did not take long before the war in the Northern Susquehanna River Valley became a key moment in American visions of the Revolution. Due to the severity of the attack and the history of the area, the Battle of Wyoming captured the attention of the American public, particularly through the reporting about it by the patriot press. For Americans, what happened there became known as the "Wyoming Massacre," where, as the *Pennsylvania Evening Post* reported, "a large body of Indians, Tories, and some British Troops" committed "the most horrid murders on defenceless farmers, women and children, and also laying waste and destroying the plantations of the inhabitants."[62]

Patriot printers also quickly used what happened in the area to justify American independence and the war to secure it. In that same reporting on the "Wyoming Massacre" by the *Evening Post*, the editor opined, "Thus, while our defenceless wives and children are cut off by merciless savages, and our country laid waste and destroyed," the *"humane* King of Britain" sues for peace. Around the same time as the Battle of Wyoming, a group of British negotiators headed by the Earl of Carlisle offered the Continental Congress peace terms that included a recognition of American self-rule and even representation in Parliament. Americans, however, the editor of the *Evening Post* argued, should not be so easily subdued because of what happened at Wyoming: "Let this fresh act of his [the king's] cruelty and wickedness stimulate every good man to support, with redoubled vigor, that INDEPENDENCE which nature, necessity, and reason have dictated to us."[63]

Wyoming was not an isolated incident in the Northern Susquehanna River Valley. Over the next month, Haudenosaunee, Susquehanna, and Ohio war captains coordinated a series of devastating attacks on the remaining settlements on the West Branch. Writing from Fort Augusta less than a week later, Samuel Hunter reported to Pennsylvania's president, Thomas Wharton, "I suppose before this comes to hand you will be informed of the Carnage which happened at Wioming." But, he was quick to point out, "the Inhabitants of the West Branch of the Susquehannah have suffered almost as much." As a result, Hunter reported, "both branches are almost evacuated, and from all appearances the Towns of Northumberland & Sunbury will be the Frontier in less than twenty-four hours."[64]

It took longer than twenty-four hours, but Hunter was right about the ultimate outcome. A few days after the Battle of Wyoming, there were several more attacks near Muncy Creek to, settlers tellingly remembered, "take the land away from the whites."[65] The patriot press might have viewed Native American's as mere tools of the crown but longer-held grievances continued to motivate their actions. The land, after all, was theirs.

In response to these attacks, which were popularly remembered, Fair Play member Robert Covenhoven, along with his wife, Mercy, and Rachel Silverthorn, whose husband died defending Fort Washington in the fall of 1776, volunteered to ride through the disparate "little forts," the refugee homes of the Fair Play republic, to warn its settlers of the dire situation and urge their removal. Colonel Hunter too sent out two battalions to Great Island to help cover an evacuation. He also issued orders to Colonel Antes to abandon his fort and remove the settlers there to Fort Augusta. All of this resulted in the mass evacuation of what was left of the Fair Play republic, which patriot settlers called and has later been remembered as the "Big" or "Great Runaway."[66] By July 12, the many families holed up at Fort Antes or in fortifications along Muncy Creek deserted the West Branch. Some fled to as far away as New Jersey, but many took shelter at Fort Augusta. They were "too poor" to go anywhere else.[67]

According to Robert Covenhoven, who witnessed the runaway, "such a sight I never saw in my life." The "whole convoy from all the forts above" Muncy Creek packed themselves in "boats, canoes, hog-troughs, rafts hastily made of dry sticks, every sort of floating article had been put in requisition." They were "crowded with women, children, and plunder." The "men of the settlement," however, "came down in single file on each side of the river to guard the women and children" all the way to Fort Augusta, "leaving the entire range of farms along the West Branch to the ravages of the Indians." There were so many people fleeing along the river that Anna Jackson described it rather poetically, stating that "you may as well try to count the raindrops in a cloud as to try to count them."[68]

Witnessing the onslaught of refugees, William Maclay, visiting Fort Augusta, was beside himself: "I never in my Life saw such Scenes of distress. The River and the Roads leading down it were covered with men, women and children, flying for their lives, without any Property at all, and none who had not left the greatest part behind; In short, Northumberland County is broken up." It would not be long, he thought, before all of the inhabitants from Fort Augusta to the town of Paxton would soon need to evacuate to the interior. "For God's Sake, for the Sake of the Country," he wrote to the SEC, "let Col. Hunter be reinforced at Sunbury!" The larger war effort to achieve American independence, from Maclay's perspective, depended on securing the Northern Susquehanna River Valley.[69]

Just because the Fair Play settlers fled east does not mean they abandoned their hopes to one day return to their illegal claims on Indigenous land. Far from it. Like Maclay, these settlers believed that since patriotic service meant fighting Native Americans, it only made sense that the state government should muster its newfound power to help them "maintain our ground." Anything less than the "immediate exertions of Government for our support," nearly fifty refugee settlers at Fort Augusta proclaimed, would "bee very injurious to our Common Cause." Taking their side, Hunter told Pennsylvania officials that the state should support these refugees because "they have stood in defence of their liberty & Country," and that proved their "readiness to turn out upon all occasions when call'd upon in defence of the common cause." That "common cause," as both the refugees and Hunter pointed out, had a decidedly local twist, encapsulating the fears, animosities, and experiences of the Northern Susquehanna River Valley. It was as if visions of the Revolution, though understood as far-reaching, could not be viewed beyond geographically confined local parameters.[70]

Regardless of the settlers' motives, they desperately needed the state's help. The influx of "the poor" to Fort Augusta strained already limited provisions. According to Hunter, when settlers started arriving in July, Fort Augusta had maybe a month's rations of beef and pork left. Within a few weeks, the number of people living in the fort reached such a height that they constructed another rudimentary fort in what is now the borough of Northumberland, just across the river from Fort Augusta. To make matters worse, the settlers who fled to Augusta or the surrounding area would miss another harvest season, and they did not have the arms or ammunition to mount a defense. The public stock was extremely low: Hunter counted only sixty muskets, and few of the settlers had arms of their own. One need only remember the poor Arthur family, who had one rifle and a bayonet on a stick, to understand the predicament of settlers at Fort Augusta. And then some of those who did have arms, Hunter complained, were selling them off or bartering them for food and supplies. If they did not get help soon, Hunter warned, it was "doubtful whether To-morrow's sun will rise on them freemen, Captives or in eternity."[71]

The state responded as best as it could. The SEC sent funds to purchase provisions and ordered nearly 200 stands of arms, 100 rifles, 250 pounds of gunpowder, and 500 pounds of lead from public stores in Lancaster and Northampton Counties to be sent to the beleaguered settlers at Fort Augusta. The SEC also ordered a militia regiment under Colonel Thomas Hartley to finish building and garrison a new fort near Muncy Creek to help take back the West Branch.[72]

When Colonel Hartley arrived at Fort Augusta on August 1, he found the situation far more dire than he imagined or was told. He had few troops, most of his men were stationed at Wyoming because of popular pressure, and the two hundred or so militia already at Fort Augusta were poorly armed and provisioned. Before he could even think of constructing a fort in Muncy, he would need to shore up defenses across the West Branch and provide protection to selected reapers sent into the fields to cut and gather crops. "Four fifths of the Inhabitants fled with such Effects as they could carry from the Country," he told state officials, and "unless I can support four or five Posts between the Great Island and fishing Creek, I fear few women will return again to their former Habitations," and therefore "many of the men" would only return under guard. "A most extraordinary panic seems to have struck the People."[73]

Hartley, an ambitious and boastful thirty-two-year-old lawyer from York County, did inspire some confidence when he arrived at Fort Augusta. He had a decidedly backcountry lilt when talking about the war and his ability to protect "women and children" while he decimated the "barbarians" and "savages." Within a few days of his arrival, one correspondent related that "the spirit of the people seems to be returning to them." Those who fled farther east started trickling back to Fort Augusta hoping that Hartley's efforts would allow them to "get Back to their Homes."[74]

Despite that confidence, Hartley had no better success than the Northumberland County militia. Although he eventually "laid out a small Fort" near Muncy Creek; was reinforced by militia from the neighboring counties, which allowed him to establish a line of guards along the southern portion of the West Branch; and even helped arm the area's volunteers, it amounted to little. "Lurking partys of Indians" were "constantly seen about us," he complained, and at night those parties captured or killed "our Centenals." The morning hours were no better. About twenty Munsee and Mohican warriors under the command of Woapalanne (Chief Bald Eagle) used the fog of morning to attack "a reaping party of about 14," all "armed" and also under guard near Loyalsock Creek. Woapalanne's warriors "kill'd & scalp'd" two, "mortally wounded" another, and took a few prisoners. The small detachment Hartley sent as a guard could do little, and Woapalanne's forces simply "retired to the mountains." Although "few men were lost in the above attack," Hartley wrote to the Board of War, "yet we may observe & infer that too much caution cannot be used in a war with these savages."[75]

Defense of the Northern Susquehanna River Valley seemed impossible. As Hartley argued, "Indians are daily appearing," and their "attacks upon the Frontiers are really become serious." Native nations could quickly dispatch small parties to push off any settlers or even militia venturing out of their crude forts to harvest grain or gather cattle. "The Indians have gained so much plunder & have met with so little opposition" that Hartley worried they would be "induced to pay another visit to these Frontiers" in "some sort of Force." He expected to "soon have some of the Barbarians to attack the settlements." In this situation, "it may be said that these Forts are of but little Security to the Inhabitants."[76]

Colonel Zebulon Butler, who had returned to Wyoming, had a comparable experience. Within two days of his return he saw four "small parties of Indians" shadowing his men. Yet, "what number there is about is uncertain." From his perspective nothing could be done unless the Americans took the offensive and "advance as far up the river" as possible. "I think," he wrote Hartley, an offensive maneuver would "be a means of keeping the Savages from murdering & robing the Inhabitants of these Frontiers." That was a near-constant refrain. Letters, dispatches, and even later memories of soldiers garrisoned in the forts in the Susquehanna River Valley are filled with such visions of an all-encompassing Native American enemy bent on murdering innocent civilians, particularly women and children, for no apparent reason, or, as they constantly argued, "unprovoked." Butler, Hartley, the settlers, Congress, and the state government seemed to forget in an instant that much of that valley remained Indigenous land and that the Americans were invading. But the war had demolished circumspection. All that remained, from the perspective of many frontiersmen, politicians, and commanders on the ground, were patriots on one side and Britain's "barbarians" or "savages" on the other.[77]

That reorientation of the situation had significant implications for the future, as the colonists in the Northern Susquehanna River Valley faced limited options. They had to decide between completely abandoning their mostly illegal claims or intensifying their defense of these settlements as an integral part of the war effort. Abandoning their homes without a fight was not an option. Petitioners to the SEC, including Henry Hill, Robert Covenhoven, and seventy others, argued that such an action would be a surrender of their hard-fought "stand against a Cruel and Savage Enemy," conducted "in full faith & Confidence" in state officials, the "fathers and Guardians of the People." Another fifty petitioners "from the West Branch of Susquehannah" detailed the loss of "near fifty murdered and made Captives" and being "Driven By the Indians from our habitations." Despite these challenges, they remained united for their common defense. They strongly believed that continuing to defend their homes demonstrated their support for American independence, which they believed essential for securing legal ownership of their "Considerable improvements." Anything less, they declared, would be "Injurious to the Interest and welfare" of the people who associated early in the conflict, undermining the rationale for the "present Contest" and "our Common Cause."[78]

Remaining on the defensive would not work either. For the fortifications Hartley was constructing to provide any kind of safety, he told both the Board of War and the SEC, would require more men and the payment of those men already in service to keep them active, many of whom had not been paid in four or five months and they were "poor indeed" and "complain." He also needed money to provision the garrisons and the many inhabitants taking refuge therein. Moreover, the forts had few pieces of artillery, and he needed those as well.[79]

Neither the state nor the Continental Congress had the money to provide these things. Inflation ran rampant and scarcity of goods of all kinds threatened the lives of Americans everywhere and the war effort. "We are sorry to inform you," the SEC wrote to Hartley, that "we, at present, see no probability of our being able to procure the Cannon which you mention." Nor could they send anything else. "The distress for want of money cannot be relieved at present." Congress was equally strapped. That body wanted fortifications but could not "admit of any expence in erecting them." In sum, Hartley, like commanders all across the frontier, had to make do. That was no easy task. There were at least 650 soldiers in actual service along the West Branch, and many of them and their families "who has lost their all" were in such "distress" that the commissary was nearly depleted. What was more, many of their enlistments were due to expire the next month. Their adherence to the "Common Cause" was in danger.[80]

According to the officers on the northern frontier, the only viable solution was to go on the offensive. Such activity, they argued, would inspire people's confidence and restore some much-needed morale. Since at least early July, General John Armstrong, stationed in Carlisle, had been trying to convince Congress, the Board of War, and the SEC of "the Expedience of redressing these barbarous Murders by carrying War into the Indian Country." After he received news that Hartley had arrived at Fort Augusta, Armstrong expanded on his plans for a northern expedition, envisioning a coordinated attack emanating from Fort Pitt, Fort Augusta, Wyoming, and

Fort Stanwix. He particularly thought Hartley should round up volunteers to march north to the Native American town of Tioga where he would link up with Colonel Zebulon Butler from Wyoming and they would both march against "the Seneca Towns as the first mark, leaving all the inferior Tribes to be subdued by traverse marches, or by detachment on the return, or at least their Villages & produce destroyed."[81]

Hartley and Samuel Hunter liked Armstrong's plan. According to Hunter, "Col. Hartly has stationed" his men "to the best advantage for the good of the Country, but all cannot keep the savages from doing mischief, and it will be the case until there is regular expeditions Carry'd on against their Towns, which I hope may be soon." Vice President of the SEC George Bryan agreed. To "enter the Indian Country & attack them at home," he argued, "is the only mode of protecting the Country to any purpose." The Indigenous people, he thought, needed to "be chastized."[82]

The grand coordinated attack that Armstrong and others imagined never happened. Delays and miscommunication hampered everything. Moreover, besides some state and congressional officials like Bryan, enthusiasm for a northern expedition was far from popular in the political councils of the state and Congress. Neither had the money nor supplies to support such an effort without diverting what little George Washington had for the eastern theater. And then there was the reality of Native American allegiance. Despite what western commanders wanted and the press churned out, all information pointed to the fact that, as even General Armstrong conceded, "the whole of the Indians tribes have not yet taken up the Hatchet against us," and therefore an invasion into their country might actually have an adverse effect by galvanizing Native American resistance. Nevertheless, the reluctance of state officials and Congress quickly produced cries of abandonment and exorbitant rhetoric about murderous "savages" by frontier settlers—a dangerous situation for new democratic governments claiming to derive their authority from a narrowly defined "people."[83]

Stuck in Northumberland with exasperated settlers, Hartley believed he had few options but to follow through with his portion of the northern expedition. If he did not take the offensive, he argued, "hundreds of Families will" become "Paupers." After nearly two months of waiting for instructions, Hartley set out with about 250 volunteers, of which many of the Fair

Play settlers joined, on a two-week raid up Lycoming Creek indiscriminately looting and burning Indigenous villages. As he later justified to the SEC, "Anxious for the welfare & safety of these Frontiers, I wished if possible to drive the Savages to a greater distance; By acting on the Defensive only, this could not be effected." Moreover, "the times of the Militia were soon expired," and therefore he was "induced" to "push an Expedition to Tioga & its neighbourhood."[84]

Hartley's expedition turned out to be a tortuous march. It had barely begun before "we met with great Rains & prodigious swamps, Mountains, Defiles & Rocks" that "impeded" his soldiers' progress. To make matters worse they had to swim "the River Lycoming upwards of 20 times." That delay gave the multiethnic Indigenous communities at Tioga and the surrounding area time to evacuate north, some of whom still clung to neutrality. For the most part, Hartley and his men only "discovered" what they imagined as the "Haunts and Lurking Places of the savage Murderers who had desolated our Frontier" and the "Huts where they had dressed and dried the scalps of the helpless women & Children who had fell in their hands." Hartley's account of events is filled with such melodrama, which certainly reflected what his men thought and what some state and congressional officials wanted to hear. Those few people whom he and his men actually encountered, such as the Indigenous people they found at a town just south of Tioga, were women, children, and the elderly. Hartley's men rounded them up as prisoners while they also set fire to the Native towns. At one point, Hartley's advanced guard of nineteen men fired on a small group of fleeing Indigenous people. Proudly, Hartley recalled that his guard "had the first fire" and "killed and scalped" the leader.[85]

Hartley and his men were clearly bent on exacting revenge. When they got to Tioga, which was also mostly abandoned, they burned it and moved northeast along the Susquehanna River toward the town of Chemung. Along that march they found two "tories," a term Americans used to describe colonists who remained loyal to Britain. Hartley instantly asked them "how many Indians there were at the Indian Camp" at Chemung, but the loyalists "would not tell." To get the information he wanted, Henry Hill, a Fair Play squatter who volunteered to join the expedition, gleefully explained that "Col. Hartley then put a rope around their necks and ordered his soldiers to draw them up on the limbs of a tree." After they struggled in the air, Hartley ordered them down and "the Tories lost their stubbornness and told us that there were 500 Indians and British at the Indian camp."[86] Now believing he was outnumbered, Hartley moved his expedition back to Tioga to resume a march to the East Branch. Along the way, Hartley and his men "burnt" Queen Esther's Town, which consisted of about seventy houses as well as a large home described as a "castle." From there, they destroyed and plundered "all the settlements on this side" of the river, which were also abandoned.[87]

Refusing to go any farther, "we pushed our good Fortune as far as we dare," Hartley reported, he conducted a forced march south toward Wyoming. Hartley's march roused some kind of Native American resistance even among those Native Americans who had tried to remain neutral, most likely those who fled the towns around Tioga. About fifty miles from Wyoming Hartley found his rear guard under "heavy attack." Conceiving that "we had no alternative but Conquest or Death," he ordered his men into two battle lines and "advanced on the Enemy on all sides." After a short engagement of "some minutes," the pursuing Native Americans "fled with the utmost Haste." It was, he boasted, a magnificent victory, especially since he estimated that the Native Americans had "a large Body" of men, perhaps "threble the number" of his "Little army." Nevertheless, "the Great God of Battles protected us in the day of Danger," he later wrote to Congress. Puffed up with pride, Hartley declared that the Native Americans "received such a Beating as prevented them from giving us any further trouble during our March to Wioming." Despite his bragging, Hartley soon found his position at Wyoming untenable. When a few of his men left the garrison "to go in search of Potatoes" because they were starving, they were quickly surrounded, "kill'd & scalped."[88]

Capitalizing on the perception of victory, Hartley left Wyoming and paraded through the settlements along the East and West Branches of the Susquehanna River on his way to Fort Muncy with sixty head of cattle and horses that he had looted from Tioga and Queen Esther's town, and showed off "Indian scalps," including one of "a very important Indian Chief." He also dragged behind him some loyalist prisoners. It seems the Indigenous prisoners taken during the march north (if they were taken as prisoners at all) did not make it south; perhaps they were reduced to the "Indian scalps" Hartley and his men showed off.[89] Those were not the only "trophies" taken. Hartley's volunteers also sought evidence of their successful vengeance. Robert Covenhoven, for example, kept "two knives which he prized very highly," especially "his hunting knife," which had a six-inch blade and a black wood handle about five inches long on which he "filed twelve or thirteen notches and each notch represented an Indian killed by him." Later, he would be remembered, even lionized, as "a great Indian Killer."[90]

Triumphant, Hartley and his men declared their mission a success. He even sent off messengers in all directions boasting of his victories and his strength. One of those messages he directed to the Seneca at Chemung, condemning their purported murder of "women and children" and threatening to "desolate" their country "by Fire and Sword."[91] He also sent reports to the SEC and Congress that he and his men had successfully "turned back the Barbarians from Deluging our Country with the Blood of Helpless Mothers & Infants."[92] Hartley's reports were written as if designed for the patriot press. And they were. In the coming days, newspapers in Boston, New York, Pennsylvania, and Maryland reprinted Hartley's reports "by order of Congress."[93] It did not take long before patriot editors glorified this "gallant officer and his little corps" for their "successful exertions against the Indians and Tories."[94]

Hartley's campaign of destruction to the north was only the first of many such forays. At nearly the same time as his march up Lycoming Creek, the Fourth Pennsylvania Regiment under Zebulon Butler, which according to Armstrong was supposed to hook up with Hartley at Tioga, entered the large multiethnic town of Oquaga on the North Branch, found it mostly abandoned of warriors, and burned it to the ground while they murdered small children "by running them through with bayonets and holding them up to see how they would twist and turn."[95] Pleased by these raids, the SEC unanimously passed a vote of thanks "for the brave and prudent course in covering the North Western frontiers of this State and repelling the savages and other enemies." The SEC also recognized the common soldiers, wanting them informed "that the Council is highly sensible of the difficulties and hardships of the duty which they have performed, and the zeal which they have shown during the last campaign."[96]

The "zeal" of these expeditions, while well-received by the American public, had the opposite effect of what Hartley and others imagined. Not all of the Haudenosaunee or even the Susquehanna Nations had made up their minds about going to war. But that began to change. One Seneca chief, Great Tree, for example, who had recently met with General Washington and declared he would convince his people to remain neutral, returned home to find his "whole People in Arms." American assaults and Hartley's threatening message only confirmed "a Rumour being circulated that the Americans were about to invade them." As a result, Great Tree took up arms "determined to Chastize the Enemy that Dared to penetrate their Country." Moreover, Great Tree was "Joined" not only by other Haudenosaunee Nations "as far as the Onandagos" but also "those of the Several Settlements upon the Susquehanna," especially near "the Teyoga Branch," the refugee home of many of the Susquehanna Nations that Hartley had just burned to the ground.[97]

Even Hartley had to follow up his reports about defeating the "barbarians" with the dire news of Native American enthusiasm for the war. To Congress, he reported that "the Indians are numerous as well as Tories." Within a few months, he argued, they would envelope his meager forces on the West Branch, and he urged Congress, as well as the state of Pennsylvania, to fund a larger expedition into Haudenosaunee country to crush "all villainous Indians & Tories from the different Tribes and states." The SEC agreed and sent requests to Congress and George Washington to mount a military offensive against the Haudenosaunee and their tributaries on the Pennsylvania and New York frontiers.[98]

The outcome of their requests was a scorched-earth campaign up the Susquehanna River by General John Sullivan and his second in command, General James Clinton, in the summer and fall of 1779. As they had done before, the Fair Play squatters on the West Branch enthusiastically supported this effort and volunteered to join Sullivan, acting as "spies," scouts, guards, and guides. This campaign was strictly punitive and reflective of the vengeful mood of American soldiers and the populace at large. Sullivan's forces invaded and destroyed nearly forty abandoned Native American villages east of the Genesee River as well as the livestock and vast fruit and vegetable fields the Native peoples depended on for their survival during the coming year. Those few Native Americans who they encountered and killed became morbid trophies for some of the American officers. After one of the only pitched battles during the campaign at Newtown, just northwest of Chemung, American soldiers, instead of following the retreating enemy, attacked vegetable fields and abandoned homes and searched for Native American corpses that they "skinned" from "their hips down" to create "boot legs" of human flesh.[99]

Inflicting few battlefield casualties, that campaign nonetheless succeeded in displacing the Haudenosaunee and Susquehanna Nations, depriving them of sustenance, which resulted in a refugee crisis that exacted massive fatalities from starvation, disease, and exposure during one of the most severe winters experienced in several years.[100] The Sullivan campaign, as it has come to be known, altered the landscape forever. It may not have ended the war with the Haudenosaunee or Susquehanna Nations—in fact it only reinvigorated their resistance—but it viscerally removed Native communities from lands and homes they had lived in and hunted on for generations.[101]

Ultimately, that was the goal. Earlier that September, Washington stated his "wish" to Sullivan that he make "the destruction of their settlements so final and complete, as to put it out of their power to derive the smallest succor from them."[102] That Sullivan did. By October, more than five thousand Indigenous people had fled Sullivan's army to Fort Niagara, the majority representing the Haudenosaunee and Susquehanna Nations, which now had "no Homes to go to," adding to the thousands of Native peoples and loyalist refugees who already depended on the British garrison for subsistence.[103]

Sullivan's campaign up the Susquehanna River also marked a general reimagining of the war for independence as a war of conquest. That view of the war had always been there, especially in the Fair Play republic, but with Sullivan's publicized success, it gained wider currency. When the soldiers returned from their campaign, triumphantly marching into Easton, Pennsylvania, they were fêted as "Hero[es]," "true patriots and brave soldiers" for their "complete conquest of so fertile a part of the western world." In a sermon by their chaplain, Presbyterian minister Israel Evans, which was subsequently published and distributed for free to Sullivan's men, the minister linked their efforts to a new future for "the United States." Everything from the Northern Susquehanna River Valley to nearly Niagara, he proclaimed, was now free of the "bloody savages" so that "all these lands" could be "inhabited by the independent Citizens of America." Sullivan's soldiers had secured the "futurity" of the "patriotic youth" who could now live on that land and remember with pride their fathers' "courage and love of freedom" when they "defeated the savage and tory bands." Evans could do nothing more than "congratulate posterity on this addition of immense wealth and extensive territory to the United States."[104] Indigenous land, as it often did, captured the American public's imagination. Poems, portraits, and songs, days of fasting and thanksgiving, all started to envision the war as opening up a vast landscape to freedom-loving patriots. As one popular poem began in 1779, "*Fame* before the vista flies, Rising to the western skies."[105]

After Sullivan's campaign, Americans clamored for similar military actions along the frontier. Previous calls to focus on an all-encompassing "Savage enemy" had been tempered by state and congressional authorities advocating for conciliation that recognized the complexity of Native American allegiances. Commanders like George Morgan and Daniel Brodhead supported these arguments, emphasizing the diversity of allegiances, particularly among the Delaware communities in the Ohio Country. However, by late 1779, the political landscape had changed significantly. Many congressmen and state officials who had opposed aggressive raids into "Indian Country" were no longer in office or had shifted their stance. Morgan resigned in disgust that spring, and the following year Brodhead was relieved of command at Fort Pitt. With little opposition and growing political and popular support, militia commanders and zealous continental officers urgently proclaimed the need to wage "war in too our Savidge enemy's Cuntrey." Revolutionary politicians couldn't even "conseave the pleasure it would give me to see it dun," that same writer concluded.[106]

In response, Pennsylvania issued new scalp bounties and approved plans to violently enter the Ohio Country where some of the Susquehanna Nations had fled just before the war. As with Sullivan's campaign, retaliatory expeditions in Ohio influenced many Delaware, Shawnee, and Mingo communities to abandon neutrality to resist the invaders. That too created a vicious cycle. Indigenous resistance only increased popular calls by Americans for their destruction.[107]

The war against the "Savidge enemy" and the enthusiasm to continue it seemed to be never-ending and became a central part of the war effort. This change was especially apparent by the end of 1781 as the war with Britain neared its end. That October, British major general Lord Cornwallis and his seven-thousand-man army surrendered to American forces and their French allies at Yorktown, Virginia, crippling the British war effort in North America and resulting in a general ceasefire. Despite all of that, Americans, whose "hearts" had been "hardened" by the "many barbarities of Britons and their allies," particularly the "murders by the savages," were still screaming "from mountain to mountain . . . Retaliate, Retaliate, Retaliate!"[108] Astonished, George Croghan's son found that "the Country taulks of Nothing but killing Indians, & taking possession of their lands."[109]

Refugee settlers at Fort Augusta certainly felt that way, complaining that the surrender at Yorktown brought them little solace as they were still under "the power and mercy of a merciless enemy." Small detachments of Haudenosaunee, Mingo, Delaware, Shawnee, Munsee, Nanticoke, and Conoy from the north and west continued to resist white settlement in the Northern Susquehanna River Valley. Securing the Revolution, according to frontier settlers at Fort Augusta, required state and congressional authorities to support the cause with a "sufficient force willing to drive" Native Americans "off" the land "and to extirpate them from the face of the earth."[110]

Extirpate they tried, and they did so indiscriminately. In March 1782, a full five months after Yorktown, a detachment of Pennsylvania militia under the command of David Williamson entered into Moravian mission towns around Gnadenhutten on the Tuscarawaras, rounded up nearly one hundred Christian pacifist Native Americans, and voted to "kill them" all. The Indigenous people were bound, sorted by sex (the children sent with the women), and placed in two buildings that the Americans "called the Slaughter Houses." One by one, militiamen brought the bound prisoners out of the buildings like cattle and bludgeoned them with a mallet before the soldiers scalped them. Midway through the mass execution, the soldiers did away with the mallet—they complained their arms were sore—entered the buildings with tomahawks, and killed and scalped the rest while the waiting captives sang hymns.[111] "Many of the children," one American officer, General James Irvine, reported, "were killed in their wretched mothers' arms." "Whether this was right or wrong," he went on, "I do not pretend to determine," but, he relayed to his wife, the contagion was spreading. Around the same time as the Gnaddenhutten massacre, a group of Pennsylvania militia near Fort Pitt slaughtered "some friendly Indians, who were not only under our protection but several actually had commissions in our service." There was "no reasoning" with these "people."[112]

As American troops violently entered into "Indian Country" and even attacked their Native allies, the British and Americans started formal negotiations in Paris to establish peace, leaving many Native peoples in the lurch. When news of these negotiations reached Fort Niagara, a crucial gathering place, refugee camp, and supply depot for both the British and their Native allies in the north, Frederick Haldimand, the governor of Quebec, ordered a cessation of hostilities, going so far as to demand Britain's Native allies discontinue their attacks on American positions. Such a ceasefire, from the perspective of Britain's Indigenous allies, seemed one-sided. Americans, regardless of the Paris negotiations and the ceasefire, continued to enter and stake claim to Native lands, indiscriminately killing Native peoples in their way. In the fall of 1782, for instance, American soldiers pushed across the Ohio River and attacked a Shawnee village at Standing Stone while the Native men were away hunting, killing the women and children and burning down the town. Then the officers started surveying the land.[113]

Furious that Americans disregarded the cessation of hostilities and attacked their "nephews," the Haudenosaunee pleaded with Governor Haldimand to aid them in resuming the war. After all, they were allies, and the British promised that "the King will always consider and reward them" for their support of "His and *their own* Rights." The Delaware too wanted to "retaliate."[114] The king and his ministers were uninterested. Lord Shelburne, the new prime minister, stated simply that "these Indians" should be left to "the Americans" who "knew best how to tame their savage natures."[115] At Fort Niagara, then, Haldimand had little choice but to refuse Native requests and only offered protection by stationing soldiers at Fort Oswego and near Native American homes west of the Genesee River. He would not even supply them with shoes, never mind provisions for war, which he did not really want to give them anyway. "Depending on the King's Provisions," he argued, only continued their "Habits of Indolence which must ever keep them poor and dependent."[116]

Exasperated with this situation, Seneca chief Sayenqueraghta argued with British officials, declaring that continuing the war was necessary. Inactivity would only give the Americans free reign to destroy them. Besides, the Americans "gave us great good Reason to be revenged on them for their Cruelties to us and our Friends, and if we had the means of publishing to the World the many Acts of Treachery and Cruelty committed by them on our Women and Children, it would appear that the title of Savages wou'd with much greater justice be applied to them than to us." Britain's refusal to support them, Joseph Brant thought, put his people "between two Hells." They had "gone too far that way already against the Rebels" to stop now and be abandoned by their allies. Yet, abandoned they were, and peace with vengeful Americans bent on conquest would not come easy. As it would turn out, the future of the Northern Susquehanna River Valley was an integral part of that American vision of conquest, or what many Americans began to see as the Revolution's "Value."[117]

Aftermath

ESTABLISHING THE REVOLUTION'S "VALUE" IN A "RISING EMPIRE" OF LIBERTY

THROUGHOUT THE DAY AND well into the night of April 16, 1783, citizens in Philadelphia were celebrating. "A general joy diffused itself throughout the city," one newspaper reported. State officials raised Pennsylvania's state flag above the Market Street wharf, bells situated throughout the city rang, and a "vast concourse of people" milled about in front of the courthouse as the "sheriff accompanied by the magistrates of this city" ascended the steps to read a proclamation issued by the state of Pennsylvania informing the public of the final "cessation of hostilities." The Continental Congress had recently ratified the Treaty of Paris ending the war with Britain and securing American independence. The sheriff could barely get through a reading of that proclamation as the crowd repeatedly interrupted him with "shouts" to express "their satisfaction." According to Thomas Paine, the famed author of *Common Sense*, "'the times that tried men's souls' are over, and the greatest and completest revolution the world ever knew, is gloriously and happily accomplished." That same night, Charles Willson Peale, the renowned painter of revolutionary portraits, "entertained the citizens with an agreeable display of luminous figures, descriptive and emblematical of our rising empire."[1]

But what was this American Empire and what had peace accomplished? These were questions that no celebration in Philadelphia could adequately answer, especially on the frontier. Thomas Paine and the citizens of the city might have thought that since the "scenes of war are closed," everyone could go "home" to bask in "happier times," but such a feeling of finality remained elusive for many. The Haudenosaunee and Susquehanna Nations were still refugees. Many were living in squalid camps along a narrow eight-mile stretch of land from Fort Niagara to Lewiston, while still others continued to fight for their survival against American invasion. For them, there were few homes to go back to and peace, as the British and Americans saw it, meant destruction. American frontier settlers were also critical of the situation. As one frontier correspondent asked, what has been "gained by Peace?"[2]

In the same newspapers reporting on the city of Philadelphia's happy celebration of a "rising empire" were also severe criticisms leveled by frontier settlers who found it "hard that all the rest of the world should enjoy peace, while the families of the western country are murdered daily." As these settlers explained things, Britain's "savage mercenaries" had not laid down their arms; "they continue to make war on the frontiers." To accomplish peace, to establish this "rising empire," then, Fair Play settlers at Fort Augusta proclaimed, required that "these savages" should not "reign for ever." It was "high time," they argued, "to subject and drive them from our frontiers." Those Fair Play settlers seeking refuge in Fort Augusta remained a vocal contingent counseling a continuation of the war for their independence, providing the public with a vision of the Revolution as more than just independence from Great Britain but the complete conquest of Native peoples to assure the future security and happiness of that revolution's proponents.[3]

Such sentiments struck a chord with others in Pennsylvania. Within a week of the happy gathering near the city of Philadelphia's courthouse and the refugees at Fort Augusta's plea, the *Freeman's Journal* started running a series of editorials "to induce our governments to take effectual steps to chastise and repress" the "animals, vulgarly called Indians." Hopefully, the editor, Francis Bailey, opined, "they will see that the nature of an Indian is fierce and cruel, and that an extirpation of them would be useful to the world, and honourable to those who can effect it."[4]

While Bailey's editorials did not speak to every American—in fact their reception revealed clear divisions in American society—they were nevertheless expressive of what the Fair Play squatters on the "the Unpurchased Lands" beyond Lycoming Creek believed and wanted to see done. According to a petition to the SEC, those settlers were still "scattered through the interior parts of this State," taking "Refuge" and living off the generosity of neighbors, kin, and strangers due to what they saw as the "Barbaritys & Distresses of a Cruel Savage enemy." They too wanted to look forward to "the day and hour we are Bless'd with peace, which we earnestly hope the day is not farr off, When we hope & purpose Returning to our respective places." Given the "distresses & Calamities that has Befell us" and the "great number of men we have produced to the standing army and militia from time to time, Besides the remainder being along a frontier & Defending against the savages," they "Humbly Conceived" the state should militarily secure and thereby legitimize their claim to Indigenous land.[5]

Highlighting their commitment, twenty-seven of the thirty-nine signers of that petition had clear records of service in the war, which was surely calculated. That documented number, however, is probably too low as many defined their Revolutionary War credentials as being "bisey with the best of there Neighboiers in Procting there Lives & Property from the Savages."[6] In short, their "suffering" and their "service" proved their "Desire and Real Intentions" to "Support Government" and "our Common Cause," therefore entitling them to Native American land.[7]

Such entitlement was rooted in how they viewed the purpose and the promises of the Revolution. Not only did the patriot press, politicians, and committees justify American independence as a means to protect, as the Declaration of Independence states, "our Frontiers" from "merciless Indian savages," but during the war Americans had increasingly described their efforts as opening up a bountiful land for American prosperity.[8] By the end of the war with Britain, it seemed as if "the whole world" looked "on that W[estern] Country with a wishful eye."[9]

There were, though, still problems that American independence and the Revolutionary War to secure it had not decisively solved. That "wishful eye" for Indigenous land, like it had always done, brought with it the old specter of "Land Jobbing," which also threatened the Fair Play squatters' vision of the Revolution they fought to achieve. From their perspective, they had struggled against "merciless Indian savages" and the British Empire to produce a future where, they argued and their own state constitution declared, no "man or any set of men" could "take such undue Advantages to Ruin many for the Advantage of a few." Yet, despite those promises, "we are most

Exceedingly alarmed on being Informed that a Set of men has made application to the proper offices for the very lands we have improved & long Injoy'd." These "engrossers" too were "our enemies," they told state officials.[10]

In this belief they were not alone. In the same newspapers calling for the "extermination" of Indigenous people, writers railed against the "whispering and laughing" of "gentlemen" who had concocted a "well laid scheme" to "be as rich as Nabobs." If these "pretended proprietors," who were actually "men of bad or tory principals," got their way, accomplishing "base plots," they would "rob" the people "of their lands" and thereby undermine a revolution achieved by "the blood" of "real" patriots, the "true friends to independency," who had risked their lives to take "all lands" from "the savages by force of arms." Eradicating Native peoples and resisting the machinations of "pretended proprietors" went hand in hand.[11] On the West Branch of the Susquehanna River those were the twin pillars that propped up the Fair Play squatters' republic, their embrace of American independence, and eventually what they thought it meant to be citizens of a new state in a new republic. Only by accomplishing both could their vision of independence be complete; only then could they celebrate America's "rising empire."[12]

In accomplishing the first part of their desires, they had crucial allies in Congress, its "Indian Department," and Pennsylvania's state government. Philosophically, some revolutionary politicians, but certainly not all, did not exactly see eye to eye with frontiersmen and their constant requests for Indigenous extermination. After all, if "All Men Are Created Equal" as the Declaration of Independence asserts, then it should follow "as a necessary and final conclusion" that Native Americans should also have rights.[13] But other circumstances seemed to supersede such humanitarian conclusions, creating a semblance of parity between the goals of revolutionary politicians and frontier settlers.

The reason for that parity is certainly complex, involving a host of economic issues that shaped the political world of the founding. The Revolutionary War had put both Congress and the individual states in massive debt. The citizens of those states had little to contribute, and the soldiers who won the war had been paid with near-worthless paper currency and "depreciation certificates," which were essentially interest-bearing IOUs. In January 1781, Pennsylvania's Continental soldiers, irritated by the lack of pay, provisions, and housing, mutinied and marched on Pennsylvania's state government in Philadelphia. Although both sides came to an agreement, the underlining grievances remained two years later when news of the Treaty of Paris reached America. The solution to this lingering predicament, many politicians thought, lay in western land, which citizen soldiers could receive in lieu of enlistment bounties or redeem with their "depreciation certificates." Not only would such a plan placate angry soldiers but it could also alleviate the states' colossal war debt. In Pennsylvania, depreciation certificates and other government securities comprised nearly three-quarters of that debt. The main problem was that Pennsylvania and the other states did not actually have enough legally purchased land to accomplish such a policy. Therefore, acquiring Indigenous lands without increasing the debt became integral to the peace, harmony, and financial security of the young republic.[14]

Needless to say, neither Congress nor the state governments could pay for western land using the usual means of expensive treaties with Native peoples. Instead, a "special committee on Indian affairs" reported to Congress in October 1783 that since Native peoples had been the "aggressors in the war, without even a pretence of provocation," they had brought on their own "ruin." Rather than holding new negotiations, Congress should simply inform those nations that since they had caused a "vast expense to the United States," who *had* to carry war "into their own country, which they abandoned in dismay," Native peoples now needed to cede away their land as "compensation for the expences which the United States have incurred by their wanton barbarity."[15]

Even this proposition, the special committee explained, was a mere gesture. "Great Britain" through the Treaty of Paris "has ceded" those lands to the United States, which now inherited most of that vast North American empire east of the Mississippi River. The problem, however, as the special committee well knew, was that neither the British nor the Americans even considered the opinions or sovereignty of their Native American allies when they negotiated a peace in Paris. Without Indigenous representation, the British and Americans agreed to a land cession that nearly doubled the size of the young United States, which many Indigenous peoples could not understand. "Thunderstruck," the Haudenosaunee argued that they were a "free people subject to no Power upon Earth," and therefore the British king could not "cede to America what was not his own to give."[16] To get around this point and belittling Indigenous independence and sovereign status, Congress's special committee simply argued that since "the Indians" were "determined to join their arms to those of Great Britain," they should then "share their fortunes." But, the committee argued, Americans were a "generous people," and would "be kind to them" and "provide" for them land beyond white settlement to "*contain* and support them."[17]

This report merely echoed the thoughts of many members of Congress and Pennsylvania's state officials who thought the Treaty of Paris made American ownership of Native American land a foregone conclusion. According to the president of Pennsylvania, John Dickinson, the famous Pennsylvania farmer, the lands ceded to America at Paris were final. The "back country with all the forts is thereby ceded to us." Therefore, if "any Indians" disagreed and continued to assert their rights, America should "instantly turn upon them our armies that have conquered the king of Great Britain" and "extirpate them from the Land where they were born."[18] To his surveyor general, John Lukens, who was already demarcating "Lots" of Indigenous land for sale within the newly presumed boundary of the state, Dickinson advised that "if any Indians converse with you on this Business, you may assure them that those lands are within the Boundary of Pennsylvania." The "king of Great Britain has ceded and finally relinquished them, and we have full power to maintain our title by force of arms."[19] Native Americans were a conquered people, or so revolutionaries wanted to believe.

Subjection, conquest, empire—these were the words in vogue about Native Americans and their lands throughout the newly independent United States after the Treaty of Paris, but as those same people who used those words understood, the states and Congress were in no position to actually realize them by force of arms. Such a scenario would require resources and manpower that neither had on hand. As Congress's special committee put it, "The public finances do not admit of any considerable expenditure to extinguish Indian claims upon such lands." Patriot politicians might have threatened war, but it was all posturing and bravado. Behind the scenes, underneath the veneer of militant rhetoric, patriot politicians concocted plans hinging on "Skill and Delicacy" to "reconcile" Native peoples to "the idea" that they were "members of" and "dependent on" the states in which they now lived per the Treaty of Paris. Accomplishing the goals of the Revolutionary War would not only take place on the field of battle but also through the use of calculated threats and coercive diplomacy.[20]

According to James Duane, a member of the special committee and a prominent New York speculator who had the ear of New York's governor, George Clinton, when Americans "treated" with Indigenous nations to establish peace and obtain their land, they should no longer "adopt the disgraceful system of pensioning, courting and flattering" them "as great and mighty nations" as had been done in the colonial past. Old forms needed to be done away with. "Neither Belts nor strings" should be exchanged "in any Communication," he counseled. Americans should not deign to call them "nations" or even "Brethren, Sachems and Warriors." Adopting Native diplomatic "forms" and using such distinctions, he argued, would only "confirm their former Ideas of Independence," or, what was worse, suggest "Equality," which would make Native peoples "Tyrants." Instead, all the nuance, specific negotiations, and diplomatic protocols that had existed for decades should be jettisoned for an approach that "taught" all Indigenous people that they were "dependent," thereby "humbling" them to recognize that they "had weakened and destroyed themselves."[21]

As for the Six Nations, Duane's real focus because he held speculative claims to their land, they needed to feel that "their importance had long since ceased." If the Haudenosaunee were not humbled and subjected, Duane concluded, "this Revolution in my Eyes will have lost more than half its' Value." His understanding of the Revolution's "Value," or rather who should be the beneficiaries of it, was obviously relative, rooted in the class, social standing, and interests of its user. The Fair Play squatters, while they agreed with Duane about "humbling" Native peoples to take their lands, certainly thought differently about who should benefit from that part of the Revolution's value. Superficially, many Americans might have been on the same page, but that could quickly fall apart with any level of scrutiny.[22]

Regardless of this disconnect, realizing the Revolution's value hinged on the outcome of a negotiation between the Haudenosaunee and Congress to be held at Fort Stanwix in October 1784. At first, achieving a settlement seemed easier said than done. Scarcely had Congress started planning for the meeting than disputes arose between Americans over sovereignty, interest, and power. New York State declared its right to conduct its own separate negotiation with the Haudenosaunee, denying the authority of Congress to meddle with what Governor Clinton and other New York officials saw as a state affair. The Haudenosaunee, they argued, were not independent nations but dependencies of the state and therefore outside the jurisdiction of Congress.[23]

Congress obviously disagreed, and that disagreement mattered for the future of the young United States. There should be, many in Congress argued, a unified diplomatic voice emanating from Congress whether dealing with European or Native nations. The failure to achieve that diplomatic voice could, they thought, spell disaster for the union, undermining American interests at home and abroad. Both Britain and France were already using the discordant and independent voices of the individual states as grounds to circumscribe American trade and status on a European stage. That would only worsen if Congress could not achieve unanimity at home.[24]

The Articles of Confederation, the main governing document that brought the new states together, ratified in February 1781, proved problematic in achieving such a unified diplomatic voice. That document might have vested in Congress the authority to direct diplomacy with sovereign nations, but after the Revolutionary War many Americans vigorously denied Native sovereignty. Therefore, other stipulations in the Articles opened avenues for the individual states to challenge congressional authority. Those same articles, after all, preserved the power of the individual states over "Indians" deemed "dependent" or "members of any of the states," which New Yorkers tried to wield as a scythe to sever congressional authority. The Haudenosaunee, New Yorkers argued, were dependent, not sovereign peoples.[25]

Yet, the long history of diplomacy, extending as it did back to colonial claims, recognized Haudenosaunee land and sovereignty well beyond the presumed confines of New York, and therefore Congress could call on other states to recognize its authority. Pennsylvania, for instance, embraced the proposed congressional treaty at Fort Stanwix, effectively recognizing Congress's diplomatic authority to "treat" with Native peoples there. Not only was there a history of recognizing Haudenosaunee sovereignty, but in its history of jurisdictional disputes with other colonies, Pennsylvania had consistently drawn on the power of others to settle them. It only made sense, then, that Pennsylvanians would turn to Congress.

Moreover, Pennsylvania's relationship with Congress, though rocky for a few years, had only served to benefit the new state. In 1782, for instance, Congress ruled in favor of Pennsylvania in its dispute with Connecticut over the Northern Susquehanna River Valley. From Pennsylvania's perspective, Congress would continue to back its claims, especially since Congress made it clear that it would not make much of a fuss about individual states conducting their own land negotiations at Fort Stanwix as long as they were "properly transacted at the same time with, and in subordination to the General Treaty." Moreover, that Pennsylvania, who had a history with the Haudenosaunee and claimed *their* land, accepted congressional authority at Fort Stanwix also served to buttress Congress's claims of diplomatic supremacy.[26]

New York's Governor Clinton was not so easily swayed that Congress would mediate matters to the benefit of his state, and he rushed his own negotiators to Fort Stanwix in September to conduct a treaty before Congress could act. The Haudenosaunee delegates who met there that September were clearly unimpressed with this divided approach, seeing in it a political fracture they could use to preserve their own independence, sovereignty, and land. According to Joseph Brant, who made his way to Fort Stanwix that September, New Yorkers might claim their sovereign right to negotiate, but it seemed strange "that there should be two separate bodies to manage these Affairs," creating "some Difficulty in our Minds." Therefore, since both New York and Congress claimed to hold the same authority and could not agree among themselves, he personally would deal with neither. Nor, he argued, did any of the Haudenosaunee delegates have the authority "to stipulate any particular Cession of Lands" with New York.[27]

Demonstrating an acute understanding of not only the Treaty of Paris but the Articles of Confederation, Brant and the other delegates also articulated that since the Haudenosaunee were an independent and sovereign people, not dependencies of any state, Congress had the superior claim to negotiate. "It was the voice of our Chiefs and their Confederates," he argued to New York's delegates, "that we should first meet Commissioners of the whole 13 States," and only "*after that,* if any matters should remain between us and any particular State that we should *then* attend to them." New York, in sum, was subordinate to Congress. Moreover, since New York claimed much of the Haudenosaunee's land via the Treaty of Paris and were at odds with Congress, many of the Native delegates preferred to deal with Congress anyway, hoping for fairer treatment.[28]

That may have been an astute political argument rooted in a keen understanding of both "antient customs" and the constitutional language undergirding the new confederation of the United States, but that understanding meant little, and any faith in Congress was misplaced. Congressional commissioners may have pinned their authority on the sovereign status of the Haudenosaunee in their constitutional battles with New York but they were no more willing than New Yorkers to recognize that same Native sovereignty in reality. When congressional commissioners arrived at Fort Stanwix, wampum belts and conciliatory speeches quickly gave way to blunt demands and demeaning rhetoric. American commissioners even degraded the condolence ceremony, a key component of treaties in the past, as "curious indeed." The congressional commissioners simply wanted to get down to business, establishing new boundaries on their terms and theirs alone.[29]

This was especially apparent after the Haudenosaunee at Fort Stanwix proposed a boundary line to congressional and state representatives that was much in keeping with that of the Fort Stanwix treaty of 1768. It was a standard negotiating tactic the Haudenosaunee utilized at treaties, starting far short of what they knew white officials wanted and negotiating from there. American commissioners had no patience for that, resorting to threats and demands that "made the Indians stare."[30]

Congressional and state commissioners dismissed the Haudenosaunee proposal as a "farce," calculated "to cede a great [part] of the State of Pennsylvania long ago purchased."[31] Arthur Lee, Oliver Wolcott, and Richard Butler, on behalf of Congress, refused to accept anything less than what was granted by the king through the Treaty of Paris. The Americans were entitled to the whole "by the right of conquest." This was not up for debate or negotiation, they argued. The Haudenosaunee were a "Subdued people." "We shall now, therefore declare to you the condition, on which alone you can be received into the peace and protection of the United States," the congressional commissioners concluded. Pleased, one of Pennsylvania's representatives scribbled in his journal that the commissioners used "a language by no means accommodating or flattering; quite unlike what they [the Haudenosaunee] used to receive."[32] Such coercive diplomacy, like the war, merely continued popular calls for conquest.

For their part, the Haudenosaunee tried to resist at Fort Stanwix by continuing to assert their independence. Aaron Hill, a vocal defender of Haudenosaunee rights and a Mohawk war captain, refused to accept the status congressional officers accorded him and his people. In a forceful speech, Hill declared, "We are free, and independent, and at present under no influence." American commissioners must, he argued, deal with the Six Nations as such, especially their "Warriors," who were still "strong." Whether his people supported the "Great King" in the past, which the commissioners wielded as a weapon of dispossession, did not matter in 1784. He argued that King George III, through the Treaty of Paris, "broke the chain" linking the Haudenosaunee with the British, and therefore "left us to ourselves," which only confirmed that the Haudenosaunee were "free and independent."[33]

In effect, Hill threw American arguments rationalizing their own independence from the "Great King" back at them. Strikingly similar to what he argued, Americans stated in the Declaration of Independence no less, that that same king had "abdicated his Government here, by declaring us out of his Protection." He had, like Hill claimed, broken the chain connecting them together. In the end, American commissioners refused to accord the same respect for Hill's justification for independence as they demanded of their own. Instead, they deemed "ridiculous" his "assumed all importance." The fact that he tried to compare "himself at least with the American potentates" was laughable, or so one of Pennsylvania's representatives thought.[34]

American delegates found it far easier to ridicule and revile Haudenosaunee delegates at Fort Stanwix than their British predecessors ever could. The strength of the Haudenosaunee in the past rested on the presumed power that unity within and between the Six Nations signified to British agents and colonial officers. In the fall of 1784, that strength through unity had long since passed. Because of the war, the Haudenosaunee had lost nearly one-third of their population, and many of their leaders had died. More than that, the divisions engendered by the war fractured their union.

The Six Nations had become a collection of culturally connected but politically isolated peoples by the time of Fort Stanwix. Not only were those Haudenosaunee who aligned with either the British or the Americans at odds but so too were those who sided with Britain and now charged King George III with "throwing us away." According to American commissioners, there were clear fissures and "private animosities" that precluded a united front among those who supported Joseph Brant, Deserontyon, Sayenqueraghta, and Cornplanter, all British allies during the war.[35]

In the end, the Haudenosaunee could do little at Fort Stanwix to deter American visions of "peace" and their designs for Indigenous land. The Americans, though also fractured, were far more unified in their purpose. Through militant intimidation, alcohol, and eventually holding Indigenous leaders hostage, American commissioners "compelled" the Haudenosaunee to acquiesce to their demands for "peace." Even Captain Aaron Hill had no choice but to publicly accept American terms, though he tried to resist their implications.

Feeling coerced, Hill desperately tried to get a message to his people around Fort Niagara. At one point, he "begged" a New York sutler stopping at Fort Stanwix on his way to Fort Niagara to tell Britain's deputy superintendent, who could relate Hill's news to his people, "not to think hard of whatever they should do" or sign at this place. The Six Nations "were obliged to comply with whatever the commissioners dictated. That in short, they were prisoners, and moreover that he with five others were to remain as Hostages." Hill could barely relay his message before one of the commissioners, "jealous of their speaking," broke up the conversation and "took" him "away abruptly." The sutler, realizing "it was dangerous to be seen in conversation with an Indian," left the fort.[36] While the sutler eventually relayed Hill's message at Niagara, it did not deter the commissioners from getting what they wanted. The Haudenosaunee delegates agreed to Congress's demands, and congressional representatives "raked up the council fire."[37]

Those smoldering ashes did not end the negotiations at Fort Stanwix, only Congress's part in them. Pennsylvania's commissioners were still waiting in the wings, ready to step in and ride the coattails of intimidation. Holding a one-sided negotiation over the course of two days, Pennsylvania's commissioners secured the signatures of thirteen representatives of the Six Nations to a deed renouncing "any Right Title Interest" to "all that part of the said Commonwealth not yet purchased of the Indians within the acknowledged Limits of the same."[38] The deed also stipulated that the Six Nations were to "be forever ban[ned] and excluded" from the land ceded. In return, the Pennsylvanians offered a meager $4,000 "in goods," which "many of our young Warriors" found "inadequate." According to Hockushakwego, a Seneca chief known to the Americans as Whole Face, the "Reward we received for the Lands" amounted to little more than "one pair of Mokosons a piece."[39]

Despondent, Cornplanter, on behalf of a faction of the Seneca as well as many of the Susquehanna Nations who called much of the land ceded their home, tried to negotiate, hoping to hold onto what was left of "the river Susquehanna." "We Indians love our lands," he said, and he "begged" Pennsylvania's commissioners "to take pity on my nation and not buy it forever." But, ultimately, he was "unable to contend, at that time." The Pennsylvanians "were determined to have the land." Under duress, he complained, "I agreed," and the Pennsylvanians "now got the most of our lands, and have taken the game upon the same."[40] Matching Conrplanter's sadness and anger with their jubilance, Pennsylvania's commissioners boasted that everything was "concluded to our great satisfaction, credit, and to the advantage of the state."[41] The Northern Susquehanna River Valley, which Teedyuscung, his sons, and the many others who came after them fought so hard to keep, and that white settlers and speculators had coveted since at least the 1740s, enveloping "this country in blood," was now, Americans believed, "subdued."[42]

Even the New Yorkers, who had been excluded from the treaty at Fort Stanwix due to their earlier truculence, won out. In a series of land deals after Fort Stanwix, Governor Clinton went after Haudenosaunee land within his presumed jurisdiction. Like the Pennsylvanians had done, even America's Indigenous allies, the Oneida and Tuscarora, did not escape New York's land hunger. The importance of alliances crumbled in the minds of Americans after the Treaty of Paris. Within less than five years after that treaty, the Oneida were confined to small reservations in what is now upstate New York. The Onondaga and Cayuga suffered a similar fate. Combined, the reservations of the Oneida, Onondaga, and Cayuga equated to no more than 4 percent of their prewar territory. The Seneca too removed to small and disparately located reservations that amounted to only a fraction of their prewar lands. The Tuscarora, who had made much of the Northern Susquehanna River Valley their home, retained little.[43]

With such a future clear, many Haudenosaunee Nations and peoples abandoned in dismay their lands now claimed by the United States. The Mohawk under Joseph Brant left Canajoharie and resettled over three hundred miles away on a six-mile tract of land granted to them by the British west of Lake Ontario around the Grand River. That site quickly became a focal point for other Indigenous refugees. Less than a year after Fort Stanwix, it boasted nearly two thousand inhabitants. Another faction of Mohawk led by Deserontyon, at odds with Brant, established a competing settlement in Canada at the Bay of Quinte. Even the American-allied Tuscarora deemed it better to leave what little land they retained than fight it out with land-hungry Americans. Most either left to live near the British at Niagara or joined a growing group of Haudenosaunee refugees representing each of the other Six Nations moving to Brant's new settlement at Grand River. In effect, separated by growing settler populations and an international border, there were two if not three Haudenosaunee confederacies claiming to inherit and represent the former power and prestige of the Six Nations' council fire at Onondaga.[44]

Peace with the Americans had been even more disastrous for the Susquehanna Nations. It seemed the culmination of a history of hardship and displacement, at least that is how Way-Way, a Nanticoke woman who once lived "on the Susquehanna," remembered it. Her mother and grandmother were originally from Maryland, one of many Nanticoke families "put upon the Susquehanna by the Six Nations." They lived for a time southwest of Wyoming but after the "Six Nations sold" that land at Fort Stanwix in 1768, the "Nanticokes got nothing." Her family then moved to a town just north of Tioga where she was born. Not long thereafter her parents died and she was adopted into a new family. Then, while still just a "little girl" during the American Revolution, "the white men" came and "destroyed our crops & drove us off." Most likely because of Thomas Hartley's expedition up Lycoming Creek, Way-Way and her family fled, perhaps to the Genesee River near Avon, New York, and its sulfur springs, or, as she remembered it, the "bad smelling water." And then John Sullivan's campaign and the starvation it bred drove them further to Fort Niagara, leaving them to eke out a meager subsistence in crude huts and dugouts in the earth around the fort. Such accommodations were a death sentence to many Native peoples during the brutal winter of 1779–80. When winter finally ended that spring, work crews from the British fort carted around quicklime and dirt to cover whole Native families who had frozen to death and were left to rot.[45]

While Way-Way and her family survived that winter and the war, they still had no place to go. After the Fort Stanwix treaty of 1784, they tried to return to the Northern Susquehanna River Valley "where my folks had once lived" but quickly found that white Americans "lived there" now. All her adopted mother could do was point at "our corn fields" and cry, "They have been destroyed, but why can't we come back here to live where our people have been buried?" History had repeated itself. Even worse than what happened at Fort Stanwix in 1768, white officials did not negotiate or even consult with the Nanticoke and other Susquehanna Nations at that same fort in 1784. They were, Americans believed, "inferior Tribes," tributaries of the Haudenosaunee. Therefore, the dispossession of the Six Nations in 1784 meant the dispossession of the Susquehanna Nations as well. Way-Way and her family, with few choices left, roamed about for two years and finally settled with a host of other refugees at Grand River.[46]

Way-Way's story is emblematic of the long, tortuous diaspora of the Susquehanna Nations accelerated by the American Revolution. Many of the Susquehanna Delaware who removed to Ohio Territory before and during the Revolutionary War also removed again, trekking west to what is now the state of Indiana after the Treaty of Fort Macintosh in January 1785, when American commissioners used the same coercive tactics they had perfected with the Haudenosaunee to formalize dispossession. The Shawnee who left the Susquehanna Valley experienced a similar reality when they were yet again forced from their homes along the Ohio River by the American governments and their settlers after the Treaty of Fort Finney in January 1786, as well as another destructive war for their independence and their land in the early 1790s.[47]

Those of the Susquehanna Nations who moved north just before the war suffered similarly. The multiethnic settlement at Tioga, for instance, which in the mid-1770s was the home of Delaware, Munsee, Mohican, Saponi, Tutelo, Nanticoke, and Conoy refugees from the East and West Branches of the Susquehanna River, had few Indigenous people left after the Revolutionary War and the Treaty of Fort Stanwix. When one inquisitive American arrived in 1788, he noted that there were only "a few scattered [Native American] cabins along the river banks."[48] While war ravaged the multiethnic communities in the Northern Susquehanna River Valley, those who survived fled to other quarters. Many of the Munsee and Mohican people from the valley followed the Seneca, moving with them to new reservations and eventually merging with them in 1791. Others followed Joseph Brant to Grand River. According to a British census commissioned by Quebec's Governor Frederick Haldimand in 1785, of the 1,843 Indigenous people living at the Grand River settlement in that year, nearly 500 of them were a combination of Delaware, Tutelo, Nanticoke, or Conoy, as well as other Susquehanna Nations that British officials described as coming from "Oquaga," a refugee home on the North Branch for the Susquehanna Nations during the war.[49]

There were also fifteen "Montours" at Grand River, members of a mixed Munsee, Delaware, Haudenosaunee, and French family whose female decedents once led prominent and vibrant communities such as that at Queen Esther's Town (Esther Montour) just south of Tioga, as well as at Otstonwackin (Madam Montour) and Wenschpochkechung (Margaret Montour) on the West Branch. The latter two Montour towns extended from Loyalsock Creek to Pine Creek on the West Branch, land that the Fair Play squatters demanded of their government in recognition of their patriotic "service" and their "suffering" during the Revolutionary War. Such an outcome was, those squatters believed, the promise of independence and a destructive eight-year "Indian war."[50]

Nevertheless, while state and congressional leaders were eager to dispossess Native Americans like the Montours, Way-Way, and their families, it was far from certain whether those same patriot leaders would recognize squatter claims to Indigenous lands when all was said and done. In order to achieve their vision of independence, then, the Fair Play squatters had to wade into a divisive debate over the American Revolution's "Value," and to them and many others, the very meaning of the Revolution itself.

They, after all, had stated their commitment to the Revolution and even the state of Pennsylvania during the early years of the conflict, transferred the Fair Play tribunal's authority into the new extralegal committees commissioned by Congress and the state, and, as they and their allies said, consistently "stood in defence of their liberty & Country" because of what they believed that revolution promised.[51]

Although the state government had already set aside "donation" lands to fulfill enlistment bounties and redeem rapidly depreciating IOUs given to common soldiers and officers alike, it was by no means a foregone conclusion that with the widely trumpeted "conquest" of Native Americans the state government would listen to or even care about frontier settlers like those on the West Branch. In fact, since Cornwallis's surrender at Yorktown, it did not seem as if many state politicians cared at all.

American soldiers on the frontier, as elsewhere, simply returned home "without cloths, without money, & without friends and rendered by their wounds & infirmities totally destitute of the means of subsistence." Preying on that destitution, American speculators offered soldiers pennies on the dollar for their certificates and other land bounties, hoping to reap massive profits. As one soldier put it, "I never received anything for my military services other than certificates, which I traded for little or no value." By the mid-1780s, Pennsylvania's veterans were so poor that those who owned homes and land were being foreclosed on because of their inability to pay their debts and taxes. For many, the Revolution's promise seemed a chimera, a cruel ploy to mobilize them for war only to be forgotten thereafter.[52]

It makes sense, then, that many soldiers sold away their meager and worthless pay. To be sure, they could have traded in those bounties and certificates for land, but they would still have to muster up the money to pay for surveys, warrants, materials, and tools, and then have to expend immense labor and time for only the prospect of future subsistence. The immediate future was far bleaker and more uncertain. With families to feed and clothe, debts to settle, taxes to pay, and lacking an adequate income, many soldiers had no choice but to sell their certificates. David Ramsay, one of the first historians of the Revolution and a revolutionary himself, recalled that "the war-worn soldier, who received at the close of the contest only an obligation for the payment of his hard-earned dues, was, from necessity, often obliged to transfer his rights for an insignificant sum." If this was allowed to continue, "the monied man" would win the day and the Revolution and its value would be defined by his calculus and his alone. Unsurprisingly, many soldiers felt "cheated."[53]

Terrified by this reality, the Fair Play squatters beseeched Pennsylvania's government to counter the predatory proceedings of speculators. They wanted their state, which they said they had wholeheartedly supported since its creation, to ignore the influence of "those who have already distinguish'd themselves by Land Jobbing" and their offers of "hard money." If the state did not help them, they pleaded, it would be "the Finishing Stroke of Ruin." This petition reads much like the one some of those same squatters had sent to the colonial government more than a decade before, railing against the combination of interest, money, and power. The Revolution, they hoped, would alter the response to such grievances. After all, the Fair Play squatters only wanted time and patience. As the settlers explained things, although they could not pay for their land *now,* they were willing "as soon as in our power, to Comply with the Terms of the Land Office."[54] They, in effect, supported the Revolution and the state it fashioned, but their words evoked both desperation and skepticism about what they had helped create.

The timing of their petition could not have been better. By the mid-1780s, popular politics had swung more favorably in the direction of soldiers and settlers on the frontier rather than just on the Indigenous land they and speculators coveted. The securities speculation bonanza that consumed the country, which pulled in the likes of revolutionary luminaries such as Abigail Adams as well as key politicians directing the state of Pennsylvania, while still steady, resulted in a popular backlash and calls for the state governments to do something. In Pennsylvania, at least for a minority of vocal state politicians, the fate of the Fair Play settlers became a cause in and of itself; those settlers seemed a visceral example of the problem plaguing the future of the young republic. The state the revolutionaries had created, after all, was supposed to be different from the colony that preceded it.[55]

That was certainly how Pennsylvania's state commissioners and some of the other state representatives at the Treaty of Fort Stanwix in 1784 saw it. One of them, Griffith Evans, secretary to the commissioners, was obsessed with the idea of settler "suffering" in the defense "of their possessions," which was "done at the price of their lives." The "savages" and their British "abettors," he thought, had "inflicted on them the most unheard of cruelties and murderous barbarities," and therefore the settlers deserved state notice and action in recognition of their "meritorious share of fortitude." He even rationalized their hatred of and violence against any and all Native Americans, noting it was little "wonder" that "their vengeance" would "never subside."[56]

Having some kind of allies or even sympathizers at Fort Stanwix mattered. According to the state's land laws, passed just before the 1784 treaty, any territory gained beyond the land purchased from the Haudenosaunee way back in 1768 would be sold at public auction for "thirty pounds for every hundred acres." Auction goers could even purchase up to a thousand acres of contiguous land using both "gold and silver, and certificates." In essence, since the Fair Play settlement on the West Branch existed outside the boundaries of the 1768 purchase, that land would be auctioned off to mitigate the state debt as soon as the state acquired it from Indigenous people. From the perspective of Fair Play settlers, that meant speculators with hard money and hoarding certificates had the upper-hand and could buy Fair Play improvements for pennies on the dollar. However, if at the new Fort Stanwix meeting those improvements could be somehow included within the boundary of the old 1768 purchase, it could potentially save their land from public auction and provide a firmer but by no means certain basis to assert what they saw as their legal rights to the land. The nebulous nature of Tiadaghton Creek at the 1768 Fort Stanwix treaty and the deed it created helped make that dream a reality, and it was put in motion at the 1784 Fort Stanwix treaty itself.[57]

At that gathering, Pennsylvania's commissioners did not end their negotiation with the Haudenosaunee after the Six Nations agreed to cede to the state much of what the British king had parted with at the Treaty of Paris. Instead, with a "charge from the state," the commissioners specifically asked the Haudenosaunee which creek, Lycoming or Pine, was in fact known to them as Tiadaghton Creek.[58] According to an addendum filed with the SEC a few days after the initial report, the state commissioners badgered the Haudenosaunee with this question more than once, which obviously irritated Captain Aaron Hill, who responded, "We have already answered you and again repeat it, it is the same you call Pine Creek, being the largest emptying into the West Branch of the Susquehanna." With that, the commissioners reported that the "six nations publicly declared Pine creek to be" the same as "Tiadaughton Creek on the West Branch of Susquehanna mentioned in the Deed of 1768."[59] According to the final coerced agreement at Fort Stanwix, then, Pine Creek rather than Lycoming Creek was the "Tiadaghta," which meant that much of the Fair Play settlement was now part of the old 1768 purchase rather than the new.

That clarification, however, did not offer complete security for the squatters who claimed land there. The Fair Play territory might have been saved from the immediate threat of the auction block, but it could still be purchased at the state's land office by interested speculators. Without available capital, the settlers themselves could be easily swept aside by those with the wherewithal to pay for surveys, warrants, and patents. The Fair Play settlers' only real security was direct state intervention on their behalf. Here, again, the future of the Fair Play district got caught up in the rancorous politics of revolutionary Pennsylvania.

Pennsylvania's state leaders were, at best, fractured over what to do with the war debt and western land, whether it resided in the old purchase or the new. Lines were being drawn in the sand because politicians, like the citizens they represented, had wildly different views about what constituted the Revolution's "Value" or even the "Public's Welfare" and "Benefit." Politicians fought over war certificates, state debts, taxes, and anything else that would either add or detract from the power and interest of the "monied man." And most of those issues were intimately intertwined.[60] Although the state by the mid-1780s had two prominent political parties who did not work well together and fundamentally disagreed when it came to the future of the state's "democratic" constitution established in 1776 (called Constitutionalists and Republicans), issues revolving around certificates and land and the value of the American Revolution didn't follow strict party divisions.[61]

Members of both parties speculated in government securities and both wanted to realize their full worth, including the accrued interest. That, however, would require some politicking, since achieving that goal would require increasing taxes on the state's citizens, many of whom sold their certificates to politically connected speculators in the first place. The future of democracy in the 1776 state constitution was not really an issue when it came to the value of the Revolution from either party's perspective. If a significant number of members from both parties' plans were realized, the certificates American soldiers had received for their service and sold away would instantly hold a higher value and thus allow speculators to monopolize access to new land, taking advantage of many of the state's citizens in the process.[62]

The state's president, John Dickinson, a member of the state's Republican Party who was opposed to the state constitution, but who also did not speculate in certificates, instantly saw in these plans the destruction of the basic principles of the Revolution and the government it created. The problem, he argued, was twofold. Speculation in government securities had put "a very large number of certificates" purchased for a "trifling" sum in the hands of a few, who, if allowed to obtain the interest, would accumulate "great wealth" at the expense of "others" who "will be proportionably depressed." Not only would ordinary citizens have to pay higher taxes but those with meager incomes, "who mean only to form moderate settlements for themselves and their children," would be removed from "their lands," remanding "these and unquestionably many widows and orphans" to the "mercy" of the "possessors of certificates." In fact, he stated, "a dealer in land" who speculated in government securities could buy a whole "township cheaper, than" just one poor family who sold those same certificates could "get a small plantation." Therefore, he argued, not only should the legislature refuse to adopt measures to pay the interest on those certificates but it should make "some alterations" to the laws regarding the sale of land in the state. From Dickinson's perspective, seized Indigenous lands provided an opportunity of "immense importance to the good people of Pennsylvania, and their posterity," and therefore the government should make sure the laws guiding access to "vacant" land were written "upon such an equitable establishment." In essence, he argued the Revolution's value needed to be more widely enjoyed.[63]

Dickinson was asking *a lot* considering the political climate. Many of the state's legislators were actively speculating in government securities and stood to make a hefty profit. The leader of the plan to fund the interest on the certificates, Charles Pettit, for example, was a member of the Constitutionalist Party supporting the 1776 constitution and aligned against Dickinson. Pettit also stood to make nearly £6,000 annually in just interest if what he called "My funding Plan" succeeded. Behind the scenes, Pettit worked tirelessly to gain allies in the legislature, whether they supported the state's democratic constitution or not.[64]

Although the Constitutionalist Party had a significant number of members in the legislature and Pettit had many of the rival Republican Party on board, he still needed to gain adherents to his funding scheme. Political parties in the 1780s were not solid and did not always or even mostly vote according to party wishes. They were often fractured along regional, ethnic, and even religious lines when it came to any policy that did not directly relate to the future of the state constitution. Even then it was not a foregone conclusion.[65]

One of the largest voting blocs in the assembly came from the frontier counties who achieved equal representation in the state legislature through the state's revolutionary constitution, and therefore, like Pettit, overwhelming supported it. Yet, their support for the constitution did not translate into a backing for every agenda their fellow Constitutionalists threw out there. Like their constituents, frontier representatives not only wanted access to western lands but also new laws to secure their constituents' squatter rights (what they called preemption rights). Many of the people the frontier legislators represented, after all, were squatters or others who had tenuous claims to the lands they settled. Pettit's scheme, as originally conceived, would undermine those same people's access to the land, especially any preemption rights. Without promises, frontier legislators would never support Pettit's funding plan. As a result, the bipartisan speculators led by Pettit in the assembly proposed a compromise. If the representatives from the frontier counties voted to fund the full value and interest of government securities, the speculators would secure votes to alter the land laws to recognize *some* preemption rights to western land. In the end, it worked, and Pettit's funding bill passed.[66]

The Fair Play squatters were important beneficiaries of this political and financial arrangement, reflective of the status they had achieved during the

Revolutionary War. In fact, their claims were the only ones the Pennsylvania legislature explicitly identified as worthy of recognition. Five of the eight short paragraphs making up a new law to revise "the acts for opening the Land-Office" had to do directly with the Fair Play district, and those paragraphs had a profound impact on the area's future. Because of "their resolute stand and sufferings during the late war," declared one of the laws Pettit's compromise created, "all and every person, or persons, and their legal representatives, who has, or heretofore settled, on the north side of the West Branch of Susquehanna, between Lycomick or Lycoming Creek on the east, and Tyadaghton, or Pine Creek, on the west... shall be allowed a right of pre-emption to their respective possessions." The law also limited claims to that area to three hundred acres, effectively denying the land to ambitious speculators. Not every Fair Play squatter had the wherewithal to purchase their preemptions, and some had moved away during the war, starting new lives elsewhere, but many others had dreams of returning and benefited from the new law.[67]

This law was also a crucial step in fully including the Fair Play squatter republic and its values into the new republican state. To be sure, the Fair Play settlers had consistently proclaimed their support of the state, but they could have just as easily resorted to insurgency like many other rural Pennsylvanians did in this period if state law did not swing their way.[68] But, in the end, it did. First and foremost, the law effectively prevented land-jobbers from monopolizing the lands of the district, a central request of the Fair Play settlers. According to preemption applications, surveys, and tax records after implementation of the new land law, few inhabitants claimed or owned more than three hundred acres west of Lycoming Creek.[69] In Pine Creek Township, for example, tax lists in 1787 show that only 7 out of 86 householders owned over 300 acres, and those householders did not own much more. Similarly, in Lycoming Township, only 5 of 107 householders owned more than 300 acres, and the largest landholder owned 500. Clearly, the values enshrined by the Fair Play tribunal and its citizens, particularly its abhorrence of absentee landholders, continued to hold sway in the valley.[70]

The preemption law, however, did not eradicate conflict; there were still conflicting land claims between squatters and between them and speculators armed with old warrants and surveys, but the way the state decided these disputes further incorporated the Fair Play republic and its vision of what the Revolution promised into the state. To settle land conflicts in the Fair Play territory, county courts as well as the state supreme court heard out parties and gathered witnesses. In their statements, plaintiffs, defendants, and witnesses demonstrated the legitimacy of their and their neighbors' claims by explaining the rules that guided "fair play" and the decisions of the Fair Play tribunal, such as those against absentee landownership or the rule protecting the claims of those who had served in the Revolutionary War. While state judges would not go so far as to "say the *Fair play men* could make a law," they did recognize that the community, by mutual compact, had the authority to "bind themselves," and therefore used "fair play" rules and decisions in their charges to the juries, thus forever incorporating the Fair Play government into the history of the common law courts and, through them, the state.[71]

There were still other ways that the Fair Play settlers included their ideas into the new state. After the land law granting their preemption rights, of the six representatives to the state assembly from Northumberland County (which now officially included the Fair Play district), the Fair Play settlers managed to elect two known members of their tribunal. Three tribunal members also became the elected judges of the county, one of whom was the presiding judge for the entire county. They also elected Fair-Play men as justices of the peace as well as sheriff. Tribunal members additionally served the towns they erected as constables, overseers, supervisors, and jury members.[72] It was in these ways that "Fair Play" did not "entirely cease" but continued as "law has taken its place." Their "stand and their suffering" during the war made their dreams possible, marking the end of the American Revolution for settlers on that small corner of the West Branch of the Susquehanna River.[73]

Just because the Revolution and the small squatter republic were over does not mean the prejudices, animosities, and hatreds they inspired died with them. The Revolutionary War and the memory of suffering could never be erased by treaties or even the attainment of land and offices. Native peoples, many of whom detested the coerced peace and boundary established at Fort Stanwix in 1784, resisted. They also continued to hunt and trade in the valley. For many Native peoples, their livelihood depended on those lands and that trade. Their continued existence, though, infuriated the white citizens who claimed those same lands as the fruits of a victory obtained with so much blood. Memories of the past died hard in the valley and could easily erupt into racial violence involving and supported by the majority of the white community.

That is exactly what happened in the spring of 1790 on the banks of Pine Creek, not that far from where the Fair Play settlers declared their independence. In that year, two Seneca men, "one of whom was a Chief" of "the Great Turtle Tribe" and the other was about to take "the place" of "the Great King," made their way to the West Branch and erected a small hunting cabin as they had done for many years before, hoping to obtain enough game and furs to trade with one of the few storekeepers in the town of Pine Creek. After one of those long days hunting, they meandered out from their cabin to the local tavern, sharing space and perhaps stories and toasts with the white clientele. But that shared public space was in no way safe. It just so happened that the night those two Seneca men went to the tavern, the Walker brothers—Benjamin, Henry, and Joseph—known to be hard-drinking and violent members of the community, were also in attendance. All three had served in the Revolutionary War in some capacity alongside their father, John Walker, who was one of the first squatters in the area, a member of the Fair Play tribunal as well as the revolutionary town committee, and who died during the war in what settlers called the "Lee Massacre." The brothers' hatred of Native Americans had crystalized during that war and continued to shape their lives and memories thereafter. As late as the 1830s, Benjamin Walker could still be found railing against the way his father had died by "savage barbarity."[74]

On that spring night in 1790, the existence of two Seneca at the local tavern triggered something awful within the brothers. After the Native imbibers left the tavern, the Walker brothers and their friend, Samuel Doyle, followed them back to their hunting cabin where they butchered the two men, shooting the elder Seneca in the head and hacking to death the other. They then hid the bodies of their victims in Pine Creek by weighing them down with stones. The bodies resurfaced days later, sparking fear in the local community and both a state and federal investigation. Supposedly, according to later justifications of the murders, the elder Seneca got drunk at the tavern and claimed that he had killed the Walker brothers' father and that their old man had died like a coward. It should be noted that the tavern-goers that night never heard that particular story or boasting. While later generations in the nineteenth century needed that part of the story to rationalize the Walkers' violence, the community at the time did not, at least initially.[75]

After hearing of the murders, the community living on the West Branch quickly justified the violence as the result of the war and their collective "suffering." According to one man who "craved" the "preservation" of the brothers' "lives," they were "induced" to kill "the two Indians" because the elder of the two Seneca "vanted of his taking twenty-three scalps" during the war, though the elder Seneca did not, according to this petitioner and many more witnesses, identify the Walker brothers' father as one of them. The elder Seneca's involvement in the war on the West Branch itself apparently justified the murders. It was only after the murders and a rather shoddy investigation that it was learned that "one of the scalp'd persons" from the Lee Massacre was "yet alive" and willing to testify that the elder Seneca had "scalp'd her at the same time their father, John Walker was killed & scalp'd." That was a passive and specious connection to John Walker's death, but revenge killing, no matter how baseless, was acceptable, even justified, by the local inhabitants.[76]

When state and federal officials, pushed to action by the new president of the United States, George Washington, who was facing another war with the Shawnee and trying to avert the resumption of war with the Haudenosaunee, particularly the Seneca, tried to capture the Walker brothers and thereby "vindicate the laws of our country," the West Branch community rallied. They hid the perpetrators, shielding them from prosecution. Not only did that community hide the Walker brothers from both state and federal authorities but when the brothers' accomplice, Samuel Doyle, was found, confined, and tried, the local court and a jury composed of that now extinct Fair Play republic's citizens refused to convict, acquitting Doyle of all charges. Such an outcome made it abundantly clear that, one irritated federal official complained to President Washington, "the bulk of the frontier inhabitants consider the killing of Indians in time of peace, to be no crime," demonstrating the exclusive nature and complicated legacy of "fair play" and the Revolution that squatter republic helped secure. The Walker brothers were never punished for their crimes, living out the last days of their lives in Indiana while receiving pensions for their service during the Revolutionary War.[77]

The story of the American Revolution and its aftermath in the Northern Susquehanna River Valley reveals both the possibilities and limitations of that revolution. Ordinary white farmers along the West Branch of the Susquehanna River, empowered by the Revolution, integrated their white squatter republic into the emerging republican state. These Fair Play settlers not only secured title to their squatter claims, an extremely difficult feat in the colonial period, but some also ascended to leadership positions at both state and local levels. This transformation showcased the radical potential of a revolution rooted in popular sovereignty, where citizens, deemed "equal," possessed original sovereignty.[78] However, these advancements were not universally attainable, and many possibilities were built on the dispossession of Native nations and peoples who had also fought for their land and liberty.

This part of the Revolution in the Northern Susquehanna River Valley, though, has been long forgotten, distorted by time and memory, obscuring its complex meaning and legacy. Today, if you were to take a short ride along Route 220, which hugs much of the West Branch of the Susquehanna River, you might be struck by not only the narrowness of the land, encased as it is between a river, creeks, and mountains, but the rather fantastic settler-centric memory of its "founding." Numerous state historical markers currently dot that route, marking the professed origins of the area, especially those places significant to the Fair Play settlers and their revolutionary experience. The place of Native peoples in that story, however, has been relegated, removed to a far more distant and disconnected past, or what is worse, explained away as obstacles, shadowy enemies standing in the way of American progress.

There is, most famously, the two historical markers honoring the Tiadaghton Elm at the base of Pine Creek commissioned in the 1930s and 1940s, where, those placards claim, the "Fair Play men," those "pioneer settlers of the West Branch resolved independence from Britain." "Pioneer" is a complicated term, but at its root is just another word for "first," and those "first" settlers' connection to the birth of the United States helps establish a foundational fiction for the area itself. Surely, the "Fair Play men" were not "first," unless, that is, history starts with European American settlement. The text of the markers aside, even the name of them, "Tiadaghton Elm," is a creative fiction that purposefully muddies history.[79] It was only in 1784, after all, that the Haudenosaunee pointed to Pine Creek as Tiadaghta, and then only begrudgingly. But, just as in 1784, designating a random tree at the base of Pine Creek the Tiadaghton Elm serves a larger purpose. It forever justifies those "pioneer" settlers' possession of the land by not only ignoring how Pine Creek became the Tiadaghta but also erasing the coexisting history of Native American sovereignty there and their subsequent dispossession because of those "first" settlers and the Revolution those settlers helped realize. In the process, settlers can be recast as innocents, and the memory of Indigenous resilience and resistance can be reoriented as examples of unprovoked settler "suffering" at the hands of "Indian" enemies.

The historical markers for the Tiadaghton Elm, therefore, prioritize a contextual memory of white settlers that helps inform the many other sites of memory in the area that valorize the revolutionary founding and the settler "suffering" that made it possible. Two markers honor Fort Muncy, for example, where one of the placards claim a "famed Indian fighter and hero" of the American Revolution was "killed in an ambush by the Indians." There are also markers for Fort Antes, "abandoned during the Great Runaway: burned by Indians." The place where the Walker brothers' father was killed is now the site of a state historical marker labeled the "Lee Massacre." If you drive through Williamsport, Pennsylvania, you might also come across a plaque encased in a large stone near Lycoming Creek marking the "Plum Tree Massacre" commissioned by the Daughters of the American Revolution in 1901, immortalizing the deaths of a small group of Fair Play squatters trying to conduct an early harvest in the summer of 1779 on Indigenous land, which, in 2016, the *Williamsport Sun-Gazette* dubbed an "Ambush of Innocents."[80]

There are still more, such as the state historical marker denoting the Fair Play settlers' "westernmost defense" or the signs marking the beginning of the "Great Runaway" instigated by "Indians." Such memorialization of the past represents a continuity of the logic the Fair Play republic's "pioneer settlers" used to justify their possessions during the Revolution, tunneling a vision of this area's origins, its "firsts," to a settler rather than Native American past, serving to prove an American indigeneity, a sort of double dispossession for Indigenous peoples that erased a much more complicated and contingent past and present.

Such a collective memory that has become "history" in the Northern Susquehanna River Valley is not isolated or peculiar. Numerous towns, rivers, highways, and other topographical features in the United States are now the home to similar foundational fictions. Popularly named and remembered "bloody creeks" and "bloody runs," places of "ambush" and "massacre," as well as "founder's pond[s]," "founder's creek[s]," "first" white homesteads and settlements, even "first" white births, pervade the modern landscape, from east to west, north to south, providing a way to remember American history through settler eyes without including Indigenous ones. Each remembrance of those "first" sites, though, does not really address history, only its distorted memory, and therefore demands a retelling that represents a far more complicated if ugly past that could and should invite a critical evaluation of the present it created. The history of the Northern Susquehanna River Valley told here is part of that retelling, historicizing more than just an interesting local story but a profoundly American one.[81]

NOTES

Abbreviations

ALC	American Loyalist Claims, British National Archives
APS	American Philosophical Society
BNA	British National Archives
BSFP	Burd-Shippen Family Papers, Pennsylvania Historical and Museum Commission
BSP	Burd-Shippen Papers, American Philosophical Society
CO	Colonial Office Records, British National Archives
CR	*Colonial Records*
DCHSNY	*Documents of the Senate of the State of New York*
DRCHSNY	*Documents Relative to the Colonial History of the State of New York*
EAID	*Early American Indian Documents*
HSP	Historical Society of Pennsylvania
NA	National Archives
PA	*Pennsylvania Archives*
PBF	Franklin, *Papers of Benjamin Franklin*
PFP	Penn Family Papers, Historical Society of Pennsylvania
PHMC	Pennsylvania Historical and Museum Commission
PSWJ	Johnson, *Papers of Sir William Johnson*
RLO	Records of the Land Office, Pennsylvania Historical and Museum Commission
RWP	Revolutionary War Pension Files, National Archives
SCP	*Susquehannah Company Papers*
SFP	Shippen Family Papers

TPP   Thomas Penn Papers, Penn Family Papers, Historical Society of Pennsylvania

Introduction

1. John Adams to Abigail Adams, July 3, 1776, Adams Family Papers: An Electronic Archive, Massachusetts Historical Society, https://www.masshist.org/digitaladams/archive/doc?id=L17760703jasecond.
2. Visiting Independence Hall, National Park Service, https://www.nps.gov/inde/planyourvisit/independencehall.htm.
3. Thank you to President of the Jersey Shore Historical Society Tina Cooney and the organizer of the ceremony, Linda Lehman, for spending perhaps more time than they wished explaining the history of the ceremony and its meaning for the community. See also "Tiadaghton Elm Ceremony Reenacted in Jersey Shore," *Williamsport Sun-Gazette*, July 5, 2014, https://www.sungazette.com/news/top-news/2014/07/tiadaghton-elm-ceremony-reenacted-in-jersey-shore/.
4. *Lock Haven Express*, March 15, 1949; Lou Bernard, "The Tiadaghton Declaration," *Lock Haven Express*, July 4, 2020, https://www.lockhaven.com/news/health-and-home/2020/07/the-tiadaghton-declaration/.
5. John Hamilton to George C. Whiting, November 29, 1858, RWP, W. 7668; Anna Jackson to George C. Whiting, December 16, 1858, RWP, W. 7668.
6. *PA*, 2:3:518–22.
7. *PA*, 2:3:217–18. See also *PA*, 2:3:449–52.
8. Declaration of Independence, July 4, 1776.
9. *PA*, 2:3:451–52.
10. See, for example, Brooking, *From Empire to Revolution;* Kars, *Breaking Loose Together;* Holton, *Forced Founders;* McConville, *These Daring Disturbers of the Public Peace;* Taylor, *The Divided Ground;* and Pearl, "Such a Spirit of Innovation."
11. Jensen, "The American People and the American Revolution," 9; Pearl, *Conceived in Crisis,* 19–21.
12. John Hamilton to George C. Whiting, November 29, 1858, RWP, W. 7668; Anna Jackson to George C. Whiting, December 16, 1858, RWP, W. 7668.
13. Deposition of Elenore Colden, June 21, 1785, Preemption Applications, RLO, LO 7.5.
14. *PA*, 2:3:451–52; *Pennsylvania Journal*, August 28, 1782.
15. *EAID*, 19:299–301. See also Silver, *Our Savage Neighbors,* 288.
16. The events in the Northern Susquehanna River Valley told here contribute to the contextualization of what scholars refer to as "settler colonialism," showcasing its theoretical utility while also emphasizing the contingency, diversity, and human agency that should characterize its scholarly application. While this book's narrative aligns with the overarching framework of settler colonialism's "logic of elimination," it underscores that settler colonialism is not a rigid, universally applicable structure easily transposed across diverse locations like Australia and America. Instead, it

comprises distinct processes influenced by specific temporal, spatial, and human factors. Moreover, although the American Revolution is viewed here as a pivotal moment in the settler colonialism process in the United States, it is essential to recognize that it did not dictate the trajectory of the future. As demonstrated by scholars like Pekka Hämäläinen, Native peoples and nations continued to resist, contest, and reshape the United States' settler colonial ambitions well into the nineteenth century. For an excellent and thought-provoking forum on settler colonialism in Early American history, see *William and Mary Quarterly*, 3rd series, 76, no. 3 (2019): 361–450. See especially the introduction to that forum by Jeffrey Ostler and Nancy Shoemaker as well as essays by Allan Greer, Stephanie E. Smallwood, and Jeffrey Ostler. See also Wolfe, "Settler Colonialism and the Elimination of the Native"; Wolfe, *Settler Colonialism and the Transformation of Anthropology*; Richter, "His Own, Their Own"; and Hämäläinen, *Indigenous Continent*.

17. Sayenqueraghta quoted in Taylor, *The Divided Ground*, 102, 112; *EAID*, 18:319; William Johnson quoted in Griffin, *American Leviathan*, 34.
18. For the embrace of settler fears to win the war, particularly those regarding Native Americans, see Parkinson, *The Common Cause*. For the effort to secure sovereign authority, see Pearl, *Conceived in Crisis*, 167–204. For the importance of establishing jurisdictional boundaries, especially those that would encompass Native American land, see Spero, *Frontier Country*, 242–43, and Blaakman, "Speculation Nation," 171–89.
19. *EAID*, 18:319; "Anecdotes of Joseph Brant," Claus Family Papers, vol. 2, M.G. 19, F1, Public Archives, Ottawa, Ontario, Canada.
20. *John Hughes v. Henry Dougherty*, October 1791, *Reports of Cases Ruled and Adjudged in the Courts of Pennsylvania*, 1:498.
21. Merrell, "Shamokin," 22n14; Newman, "The 'Four Nations of Indians upon the Susquehanna.'"
22. *CR*, 6:116.
23. Moravian missionary quoted in Merrell, *Into the American Woods*, 51.
24. Smith, *Laws of the Commonwealth of Pennsylvania*, 195.

1. "The Foundation of Our Uneasiness"

1. Wallace, *Conrad Weiser*, 49. See also Calloway, *The Chiefs Now in This City*.
2. Merrell, *The Lancaster Treaty of 1744*, 74–75.
3. *PA*, 1:1:643–44.
4. Conrad Weiser, Journal, 1745, quoted in Wallace, *Conrad Weiser*, 219.
5. *CR*, 5:389.
6. James Logan to John Penn quoted in Wallace, *Conrad Weiser*, 44. For the number of warriors see page 201.
7. *Correspondence between William Penn and James Logan*, 88.
8. *CR*, 5:400.

9. *The Baptismal Register of Fort Duquesne*, 18.
10. Wallace, *Conrad Weiser*, 230.
11. Shannon, *Iroquois Diplomacy*, 122–23, 127–28.
12. Hutson, *Pennsylvania Politics*, 6–40.
13. Mackraby, "Philadelphia Society before the Revolution," 3:276–87; *PA*, 8:5:3810; Lemon, *Best Poor Man's Country*, 55.
14. William Penn to James Harrison, October 4, 1685, Nash, *Quakers and Politics*, 100.
15. Thomas Penn to Richard Hockley, February 2, 1754, Letters of Thomas Penn, PFP, reel 8.
16. James Burd to Lynford Lardner, June 21, 1762, BSFP, MG-30, reel 2, folder 35.
17. James Burd to Unknown, August 20, 1764, BSFP, MG-30, reel 2, folder 36.
18. Edward Shippen to Edward Shippen Jr., September 30, 1749, BSFP, MG-30, reel 2, folder 1.
19. Cohen, "William Allen," 44; Keith, *The Provincial Councilors of Pennsylvania*, 141; Futhey and Cope, *History of Chester County, Pennsylvania*, 148; "Extract from Logan Manuscripts," in Gordon, *History of Pennsylvania*, 611; Huston, *An Essay on the History and Nature of Original Titles*, 231.
20. Huston, *An Essay on the History and Nature of Original Titles*, 231.
21. Cohen, "William Allen," 69–75; "William Allen," in Horle et al., eds., *Lawmaking and Legislators*, 3:233.
22. "William Allen," 3:233.
23. Richter, "Onas, the Long Knife," 212–13.
24. Ibid.
25. Griffin, *The People with No Name*, 1–8; Pearl, *Conceived in Crisis*, 50.
26. *PA*, 8:4:3329–31.
27. Fogelman, *Hopeful Journeys*, 5–6.
28. Mittelberger, *Journey to Pennsylvania*, 118–19.
29. Smith, *Colonists in Bondage*, 297–300.
30. Simler, "Tenancy in Colonial Pennsylvania"; Simler, "The Landless Worker"; Marietta, "The Distribution of Wealth in Eighteenth-Century America."
31. Mackraby, "Philadelphia Society before the Revolution," 3:276–87; Smith, "Best Poor Man's Country?" xiii.
32. Nash, "Poverty and Politics in Early American History," 9.
33. Moraley, *The Infortunate*, 73–75; Lemon, *Best Poor Man's Country*, 68.
34. Pearl, *Conceived in Crisis*, 25–26.
35. Petition, December 1727, Miscellaneous Collection, box 4a, HSP; Moraley, *The Infortunate*, 73–75; William Allen to Evan Patterson, November 5, 1753, William Allen Letter Book, SFP, HSP; James Logan to Settiplace Bellers, August 10, 1741; Logan and James Steel to Proprietors, n.d., quoted in Schwartz, *"Mixed Multitude,"* 200, 93.
36. James Logan to Proprietors, April 17, 1731, Official Correspondence, PFP.
37. Munger, *Pennsylvania Land Records*, 17, 67, 84.
38. *The Statutes at Large of Pennsylvania*, 5:205–6.

39. Webb, "The Peaceable Kingdom," 180–89.
40. The best description of the layers of confusion when it came to land ownership in early America is McConville, *These Daring Disturbers of the Public Peace*, 11–27; Blackstone, *Commentaries*, 104–5.
41. *American Magazine*, March 1741, 114.
42. Ibid.
43. Ibid.
44. Francis Higginson, *New Englands Plantation*, 316, quoted in Cronon, *Changes in the Land*, 55.
45. *American Magazine*, March 1741, 114. Not all colonists adhered to a vision of property as private nor Native peoples as usufruct; see Greer, *Property and Dispossession*, 27–64, 241–70, 271–310.
46. Cronon, *Changes in the Land*, 50–55; Richter, *Facing East from Indian Country*, 53–59.
47. Cronon, *Changes in the Land*, 50–55; Richter, *Facing East from Indian Country*, 53–59.
48. Richter, *Facing East from Indian Country*, 174–75; Calloway, *The Indian World of George Washington*, 42.
49. Jordan, "Incorporation and Colonization," 36–37; Vest, "An Odyssey among the Iroquois."
50. Jennings, *The Ambiguous Iroquois Empire*; Starna, "Retrospecting the Origins of the League of Iroquois"; Richter, "War and Culture," 528–59; Jordan, "Incorporation and Colonization."
51. Vest, "An Odyssey among the Iroquois," 126–27.
52. Ibid., 124–34; Wallace, *Conrad Weiser*, 350.
53. Newman, "The 'Four Nations of Indians upon the Susquehanna.'"
54. James Logan to John Penn, n.d., quoted in Merritt, *At the Crossroads*, 39.
55. Speech of Ackowanothio quoted in Wallace, *Conrad Weiser*, 529.
56. Croghan and Wainwright, "George Croghan's Journal," 438.
57. Henry Bouquet to "Major Levingston," February 6, 1762, Bouquet, *The Papers of Col. Henry Bouquet*, 2:67.
58. James Logan to Settiplace Bellers, August 10, 1741, quoted in Schwartz, *"Mixed Multitude,"* 200.
59. Cronon, *Changes in the Land*, 127–51; Anderson, "King Philip's Herds"; Anderson, *Creatures of Empire*, 171–72, 175–208.
60. Croghan and Wainwright, "George Croghan's Journal," 420, 433.
61. Ibid.
62. *CR*, 7:333.
63. Ibid.
64. Ibid., 5:389; 7:333.
65. Ibid., 5:389–400.
66. Richard Peters to Thomas Penn, September 11, 1749, TPP, vol. 10, reel 9.
67. *Universal Magazine of Knowledge and Pleasure*, November 1749, 233; Wallace, *Conrad Weiser*, 279–80.

68. Witham Marshe, "Journal of the Treaty Held with the Six Nations," June–July 1744, in Merrell, *The Lancaster Treaty of 1744*, 111.
69. *CR*, 5:389.
70. Ibid., 5:389, 394.
71. Ibid., 5:394.
72. Ibid.

2. "Very Uneasy and Displeas'd"

1. *CR*, 5:406.
2. Wallace, *Conrad Weiser*, 296.
3. *CR*, 5:442; Calloway, *The Indian World of George Washington*, 55; Hirsch, "The Celebrated Madame Montour," 81–112.
4. *CR*, 5:442.
5. Wallace, *Conrad Weiser*, 295; Silver, *Our Savage Neighbors*, 182–83; *CR*, 5:442.
6. Richard Peters to Council, July 10, 1750, quoted in Wallace, *Conrad Weiser*, 297.
7. Richard Peters to Conrad Weiser, October 3, 1750, Peters, "Some Selections from the 'Peters Papers,'" 456.
8. "A Treaty, Held at the Town of Lancaster, in Pennsylvania," June 1744, Merrell, *The Lancaster Treaty of 1744*, 74–75; Richard Peters to Thomas Penn, October 24, 1748, Wallace, *Conrad Weiser*, 270.
9. *CR*, 5:400, 401, 447.
10. Preston, *The Texture of Contact*, 135–44.
11. *CR*, 5:389–404.
12. Schutt, *Peoples of the River Valleys*, 94–123; Merritt, *At the Crossroads*, 22–23; Campbell, *Speculators in Empire*, 34; Calloway, *The Indian World of George Washington*, 47–48.
13. *DRCHSNY*, 10:206; *CR*, 5:438–39.
14. Merrell, *Into the American Woods*, 221–22; Schutt, *Peoples of the River Valleys*, 103–4; Brown, "'Is It Not Our Land?'" 143–200.
15. *CR*, 5:439; Brown, "'Is It Not Our Land?'" 143–200.
16. Hinderaker, "Declaring Independence," 110–12.
17. Conrad Weiser, *Conrad Weiser's Journal of a Tour to the Ohio, August 11–October 2, 1748*, ed. Reuben Gold Thwaites (Cleveland, OH: Arthur H. Clark, 1904), 40.
18. *CR*, 5:635.
19. Calloway, *The Indian World of George Washington*, 5, 37.
20. *CR*, 5:489–90.
21. Ibid.
22. Ibid. For Tattenhick as Teedyuscung, see Grumet, *The Munsee Indians*, 380n10. Tattenhick could also be a different spelling of Teedyuscung. Timothy Horsfield, for instance, documented Teedyuscung's name in 1756 as "King Tatteneskund." See "King

Teedyuscung's Message to the Governor," July 18, 1756, Timothy Horsfield Papers, 1733–71, APS.
23. Wallace, *King of the Delawares*, 2, 18–21.
24. Ibid.
25. Weslager, *The Delaware Indians*, 209–10; Zeisberger, "David Zeisberger's History of the Northern American Indians," 92.
26. Wallace, *King of the Delawares*, 18–30.
27. Ibid., 21; *PSWJ*, 3:779.
28. Calloway, *The Indian World of George Washington*, 5; Schutt, *Peoples of the River Valleys*, 85–86; Jennings, *Ambiguous Iroquois Empire*, 330–31; Harper, "Making History."
29. Harper, "Making History"; Schutt, *Peoples of the River Valleys*, 85.
30. Harper, "Making History," 225–27; Jennings, *The Ambiguous Iroquois Empire*, 331–32.
31. Harper, "Making History," 225–27.
32. Wallace, *King of the Delawares*, 24–26; Harper, "Making History," 220–24; Merritt, *At the Crossroads*, 46–49; Jennings, *The Ambiguous Iroquois Empire*, 333.
33. *PSWJ*, 3:767; Schutt, *Peoples of the River Valleys*, 74–81.
34. Merritt, *At the Crossroads*, 50–86.
35. *CR*, 4:83–84; Shannon, *Iroquois Diplomacy*, 106–9; Jennings, *The Ambiguous Iroquois Empire*, 309–16, 322–23; Harper, "Making History," 223.
36. Thomas Penn quoted in Wallace, *Indians in Pennsylvania*, 142.
37. Jennings, *The Ambiguous Iroquois Empire*, 344–45. For currency conversion and its purchasing power, see Historic Currency, BNA, https://www.nationalarchives.gov.uk/currency-converter/#.
38. Schutt, *Peoples of the River Valleys*, 89–90; Merrell, *Into the American Woods*, 174–75; Jennings, *The Ambiguous Iroquois Empire*, 342–45.
39. *CR*, 4:578–80.
40. Conrad Weiser quoted in Wallace, "Conrad Weiser and the Delawares," 148; White, *The Middle Ground*, 225; Merritt, *At the Crossroads*, 220; Schutt, *Peoples of the River Valleys*, 91–93.
41. Schutt, *Peoples of the River Valleys*, 94–123; Merritt, *At the Crossroads*, 129–37; Harper, "Delawares and Pennsylvanians after the Walking Purchase."
42. Wallace, *King of the Delawares*, 39–40.
43. Weslager, "Delaware Indian Name Giving and Modern Practice," 135–38; Merritt, *At the Crossroads*, 57; White, "'Although I Am Dead, I Am Not Entirely Dead.'"
44. "King Teedyuscung's Message to the Governor," July 18, 1756, Timothy Horsfield Papers, 1733–71, APS.
45. Merritt, *At the Crossroads*, 100.
46. Wallace, *King of the Delawares*, 31–55, 278n1.
47. *PSWJ*, 3:779. For translation of "Minquas," see Minderhout, *Native Americans in the Susquehanna River Valley*, 79.
48. *CR*, 7:297.

49. *PA*, 4:2:323; *CR*, 7:216.
50. Jennings, *The Ambiguous Iroquois Empire*, 345–46.
51. For use of "Haudenosaunee frontier" or "Iroquoian frontier" rather than simply "Pennsylvania frontier" or "American frontier," which presupposes the legitimacy of imperial claims, see Preston, *The Texture of Contact*, 13–14.
52. Schutt, *Peoples of the River Valleys*, 106–7; Anderson, *Crucible of War*, 17–32; Hinderaker, *Elusive Empires*, 136–39.
53. Starna, "The Diplomatic Career of Canasatego," 162–63.
54. Shannon, *Iroquois Diplomacy*, 132.
55. *CR*, 6:216.

3. "Bird on a Bow"

1. *PA*, 4:2:512–14.
2. Shannon, *Indians and Colonists at the Crossroads of Empire*, 161–65.
3. *PA*, 1:2:167; 4:2:699.
4. Jennings, *The Ambiguous Iroquois Empire*, 336.
5. *CR*, 6:113.
6. *PA*, 4:2:699–700; Shannon, *Indians and Colonists at the Crossroads of Empire*, 161–65; Waddell, "Thomas and Richard Penn Return Albany Purchase Land to the Six Nations."
7. Shannon, *Indians and Colonists at the Crossroads of Empire*, 168.
8. William Allen to Evan Patterson, April 20, December 23, 1754, William Allen Letter Book, SFP, HSP.
9. Ibid.
10. Merritt, *At the Crossroads*, 183.
11. Ibid.; William Allen to Evan Patterson, November 5, 1753, William Allen Letter Book, SFP, HSP.
12. *PA*, 1:2:144.
13. *CR*, 6:647; White, *The Middle Ground*, 238; Merritt, *At the Crossroads*, 180–83.
14. *EAID*, 3:424–25.
15. Ibid.; Calloway, *World Turned Upside Down*, 133–34.
16. McConnell, *A Country Between*, 107–10; Brown, "'Is It Not Our Land?'" 82n16; Schutt, *Peoples of the River Valleys*, 103–4.
17. Merritt, *At the Crossroads*, 176–77; Anderson, *Crucible of War*, 158–65.
18. Trask, "Pennsylvania and the Albany Congress"; Calloway, *The Indian World of George Washington*, 106.
19. *EAID*, 3:424; *PA*, 4:2:268–69; Merrell, *Into the American Woods*, 222–24; Anderson, *Crucible of War*, 158–65; White, *The Middle Ground*, 236–40; Richter, *Trade, Land, Power*, 157; Brown, "'Is It Not Our Land?'" 143–200, 256–97; Smith, *An Account of the Remarkable Occurrences*, 47.
20. Schutt, *Peoples of the River Valleys*, 43–46.

21. *PSWJ*, 3:783.
22. Wallace, *King of the Delawares*, 68–86.
23. *EAID*, 3:7; *CR*, 6:590.
24. *CR*, 6:641, 690; Wallace, *King of the Delawares*, 72–73.
25. *CR*, 6:591.
26. Ibid., 6:590, 752; Hunter, "The Upper Susquehanna in the French and Indian War," 156. For the Brodhead estate, see Harper, "Delawares and Pennsylvanians after the Walking Purchase," 168.
27. *CR*, 6:768.
28. Thomas Barton to William Smith, November 2, 1755, *Papers Relating to the History of the Church in Pennsylvania*, 559.
29. Wallace, *King of the Delawares*, 69–71.
30. Calloway, *The Indian World of George Washington*, 113.
31. *DRCHSNY*, 2:418–19.
32. *CR*, 6:514; *DRCHSNY*, 2:418–19.
33. *PSWJ*, 9:335; Thomson, *Enquiry into the Causes of the Alienation of the Delaware and Shawanese Indians*, 83.
34. *CR*, 7:51, 71.
35. Ibid., 7:80.
36. Ibid., 7, 61.
37. Thomson, *Enquiry into the Causes of the Alienation of the Delaware and Shawanese Indians*, 84
38. Thomson, *Enquiry into the Causes of the Alienation of the Delaware and Shawanese Indians*, 84; *CR*, 7:66–67.
39. Thomson, *Enquiry into the Causes of the Alienation of the Delaware and Shawanese Indians*, 83.
40. *CR*, 7:53, 324; Thomson, *Enquiry into the Causes of the Alienation of the Delaware and Shawanese Indians*, 83; Merrell, "'I Desire All That I Have Said,'" 802.
41. Thomson, *Enquiry into the Causes of the Alienation of the Delaware and Shawanese Indians*, 83; *CR*, 7:53, 66–67; 6:738; James Grant and John Fiske, "Teedyuscung," in *Appletons' Cyclopaedia of American Biography* (New York, 1889), 6:58; Wallace, *King of the Delawares*, 279n1.
42. Wallace, *King of the Delawares*, 196.
43. Thomson, *Enquiry into the Causes of the Alienation of the Delaware and Shawanese Indians*, 84–85.
44. *DRCHSNY*, 7:59.
45. *CR*, 7:218.
46. Thomson, *Enquiry into the Causes of the Alienation of the Delaware and Shawanese Indians*, 86–87.
47. *EAID*, 3:7–8.
48. Jennings, *Empire of Fortune*, 266; Thomson, *Enquiry into the Causes of the Alienation of the Delaware and Shawanese Indians*, 87.

49. William Allen to David Barclay & Sons, December 17, 1755, William Allen Letter Book, SFP, HSP.
50. Dowd, *War under Heaven*, 48; Calloway, *The Indian World of George Washington*, 114, 118; Adam Stephen to George Washington, November 7, 1755, Founders Online, NA, https://founders.archives.gov/documents/Washington/02-02-02-0163.
51. CR, 7:73–76, 140; Merritt, *At the Crossroads*, 207–8; EAID, 3:383.
52. Wallace, *King of the Delawares*, 96–97.
53. PA, 1:2:725.
54. For an excellent explanation of the forging of such alliances as "politico-genesis," see Newman, "The 'Four Nations of Indians upon the Susquehanna.'"
55. Thomson, *Enquiry into the Causes of the Alienation of the Delaware and Shawanese Indians*, 84–87.
56. Shannon, *Iroquois Diplomacy*, 156–57; Calloway, *The Indian World of George Washington*, 161.
57. CR, 8:246.
58. "Benjamin Chew's Journal of a Journey to Easton," 1758, *Indian Treaties Printed by Benjamin Franklin*, 312–14.
59. EAID, 3:427–66.
60. Ibid., 3:285.
61. CR, 8:246; EAID, 3:427–66.
62. CR, 7:431–33.
63. Ibid., 8:30.
64. PSWJ, 3:766–67.
65. CR, 8:203.
66. Ibid.; Wallace, *King of the Delawares*, 179.
67. CR, 7:431–33.
68. Ibid.
69. DCHSNY, 2:420.
70. SCP, 2:13.
71. *Indian Treaties Printed by Benjamin Franklin*, 243; EAID, 3:427–66.
72. PSWJ, 3:788.

4. Hearts and Mouths

1. CR, 8:32–44.
2. Ibid. For Teedyuscung as "The Healer," see Oscar Jewell Harvey, *A History of Wilkes-Barre* (Wilkes-Barre, PA: Raeder Press, 1909), 377, and Wallace, *King of the Delawares*, 278.
3. CR, 7:522, 8:43.
4. Ibid., 8:594.
5. Croghan and Wainwright, "George Croghan's Journal," 388

6. Anderson, *Crucible of War*, 404–6, 455; White, *The Middle Ground*, 256–61.
7. Jeffery Amherst quoted in Middleton, *Pontiac's War*, 18, 24; Weslager, *The Delaware Indians*, 244–45.
8. Croghan and Wainwright, "George Croghan's Journal," 410.
9. *PSWJ*, 10:891.
10. *CR*, 7:54, 80.
11. Robert Hunter Morris, September 1756, Gratz Collection, HSP.
12. *PSWJ*, 2:814; Merritt, *At the Crossroads*, 237–38.
13. *PA*, 1:2:665–66; emphasis added.
14. Hunter, *Forts on the Pennsylvania Frontier*, 481–95, 508–30.
15. Merritt, *At the Crossroads*, 237–39; William Denny to Thomas McKee, May 1, 1757, J. I. Mombert, *Authentic History of Lancaster County* (Lancaster, PA, 1869), 177–78; Merrell, "Shamokin," 20–21, 29–37.
16. Captain Joseph Shippen, Journal, Fort Augusta, Shamokin, 1757–1758, SFP, vol. 6, HSP.
17. Ibid.
18. Lieutenant Caleb Graydon to James Burd, May 20, 1761, SFP, vol. 5, HSP.
19. *Pennsylvania Gazette*, September 13, 1759.
20. *PSWJ*, 4:240–46.
21. Ibid.; Calloway, *The Indian World of George Washington*, 154; Schutt, *Peoples of the River Valleys*, 20.
22. Shippen, Journal, SFP, vol. 6, HSP.
23. "Conference with the Indians at Shamokin or Augusta Meeting Minutes," 1763, Gratz Collection, HSP.
24. Samuel Hunter, Diary, Fort Augusta, June–November 1760, BSP.
25. James Burd, Diary, Fort Augusta, 1760, BSP.
26. "Provisions Account at Fort Augusta," 1762; Samuel Hunter to James Burd, May 23, 1758; "Return of Provisions at Fort Augusta," 1760; "Abstract of Rations Issued to Fort Augusta," July 1, 1762; "Memorandum of Goods Wanted at Fort Augusta," 1762; "Inventory of Necessaries at Fort Augusta," n.d.; "Return of Ordinance and Stores at Fort Augusta," August 1, 1760, BSP.
27. James Irvine to Benedict Dorsey, July 20, 1762, BSP.
28. James Irvine to Commissioners of Indian Affairs, June 30, 1763, Gratz Collection, HSP.
29. "Conference with the Indians at Shamokin or Augusta," July 17, 1763, Gratz Collection, HSP.
30. James Irvine to Benedict Dorsey, July 20, 1762, BSP.
31. Ibid.
32. Lieutenant Caleb Graydon, Journal, Fort Augusta, BSP, 973.2 D54; "Conference with the Indians at Shamokin or Augusta," July 17, 1763, Gratz Collection, HSP.
33. James Burd, Diary, BSP, 973.2 D54.
34. *CR*, 8:773–74.
35. Ibid., 8:642.

36. Ibid.
37. Ibid., 8:753.
38. Ibid., 8:752; Friendly Association Minutes, 1760–64, Cox-Parrish-Wharton Family Papers, HSP.
39. *CR*, 8:774.
40. Ibid., 8:753–55.
41. Ibid., 8:739.
42. Ibid., 8:748, 766–67.
43. Spero, *Frontier Country*, 1–5.
44. *CR*, 8:749; Moyer, *Wild Yankees*, 13–23.
45. Moyer, *Wild Yankees*, 13–23; Wallace, *King of the Delawares*, 252–58.
46. *CR*, 8:595.
47. *SCP*, 2:130; *CR*, 8:595.
48. *CR*, 8:223, 749–65; 9:6–8.
49. Ibid. For the importance of council fires, see Richter, *Facing East from Indian Country*, 135.
50. *Memorials of the Moravian Church*, 1:275.
51. *SCP*, 2:191–93, 196–98, 202–4; Spero, *Frontier Country*, 200.
52. *SCP*, 2:122–23.
53. Ibid.
54. Moyer, *Wild Yankees*, 13–26.
55. *PSWJ*, 10:671.
56. Wallace, *King of the Delawares*, 258–61.
57. Ibid.; Moyer, *Wild Yankees*, 22–23; Merritt, *At the Crossroads*, 260–61.
58. Merritt, *At the Crossroads*, 261–62, 276–77.
59. *CR*, 9:27.
60. *SCP*, 2:257.
61. Samuel Hunter, Diary, Fort Augusta, BSP, 973.2 D54.
62. Ibid.
63. Woolman, *The Journal and Essays of John Woolman*, 256–57; Dowd, *War under Heaven*, 88–89; Middleton, *Pontiac's War*, 83–99.
64. Dowd, *War under Heaven*, 54–89; Middleton, *Pontiac's War*, 47–64.
65. Kenny and Jordan, "Journal of James Kenny," 192; Croghan and Wainwright, "George Croghan's Journal," 438.
66. James Irvine to John Reynell and Others Commissioners for Indian Affairs, June 12, 30, 1763, Gratz Collection, HSP.
67. James Irvine to John Reynell and Others, June 26, 1763, Gratz Collection, HSP.
68. Middleton, *Pontiac's War*, 35.
69. James Irvine to John Reynell and Others, June 26, 1763, Gratz Collection, HSP.
70. Samuel Hunter, Diary, Fort Augusta, June 1763; Lieutenant Caleb Graydon, Diary, July 1763, BSP.

71. James Irvine to John Reynell and Others, June 30, 1763, Gratz Collection, HSP.
72. *PA*, 4:3:209.
73. James Burd, Diary, Fort Augusta; Samuel Hunter, Diary, Fort Augusta, BSP; *PSWJ*, 7:315.
74. "Conference with the Indians at Shamokin or Augusta," July 17, 1763, Gratz Collection, HSP.
75. Jacob Wetterholt to Timothy Horsfield, August 18, 1763, quoted in Merritt, *At the Crossroads*, 274–77.
76. Woolman, *The Journal and Essays of John Woolman*, 256–57.
77. Samuel Hunter, Diary, Fort Augusta, August 26, 1763, BSP; Archibald Loudon, *A Selection of Some of the Most Interesting Narratives of Outrages Committed by the Indians in Their Wars with the White People* (Carlisle, PA, 1811), 1:176–77.
78. Samuel Hunter, Diary, Fort Augusta, August 26, 1763, BSP; Loudon, *A Selection of Some of the Most Interesting Narratives of Outrages Committed by the Indians*, 2:187–88.
79. Smith, *An Account of the Remarkable Occurrences*, 60; Wallace, *King of the Delawares*, 263.
80. Merritt, *At the Crossroads*, 274–75.
81. Ibid.; Wallace, *King of the Delawares*, 210–11.
82. Wallace, *King of the Delawares*, 207–10.
83. *CR*, 8:212; "Conference with the Indians at Shamokin or Augusta," July 17, 1763, Gratz Collection, HSP.
84. James Irvine to John Reynell and Other Indian Commissioners for Indian Affairs, August 3, 1763, Gratz Collection, HSP.
85. Sipe, *The Indian Wars of Pennsylvania*, 456; Samuel Hunter, Diary, Fort Augusta, BSP.
86. Dowd, *War under Heaven*, 82.
87. Jonathan Dodge to Timothy Horsfield, October 8, 1763, Timothy Horsfield Papers, 1733–71, APS.
88. Lieutenant Caleb Graydon, Journal, Fort Augusta, BSP.
89. Wallace, *King of the Delawares*, 264.
90. *Pennsylvania Gazette*, October 13, 1763.
91. See, for example, Mickley, *Brief Account of Murders by the Indians*, 32–33.
92. For the "anti-Indian Sublime," see Silver, *Our Savage Neighbors*, xx, 83–90. For Bull's capture, see Wallace, *King of the Delawares*, 264.
93. Kenny, *Peaceable Kingdom Lost*, 128.
94. *SCP*, 2:277–78.
95. *Pennsylvania Gazette*, October 27, 1763.

5. A "Diversity of Interests"

1. *CR*, 9:138–42; Merritt, *At the Crossroads*, 264–308.
2. Joseph Galloway quoted in Bradburn, *Citizenship Revolution*, 8; Burnaby, *Travels through the Middle Settlements*, 86.

3. *Paxton Papers*, 101–4; Benjamin Franklin, *A Narrative of the Late Massacres*, January 30, 1764, Founders Online, NA, https://founders.archives.gov/documents/Franklin/01-11-02-0012; Calloway, *The Indian World of George Washington*, 38.
4. Weslager, *The Delaware Indians*, 44; Jennings, *The Ambiguous Iroquois Empire*, 25–39; Richter, *Ordeal of the Longhouse*, 20–22.
5. Marietta and Rowe, *Troubled Experiment*, 172–73.
6. Silver, *Our Savage Neighbors*, 62–64; Merritt, *At the Crossroads*, 277–79.
7. Landsman, "Religion, Expansion, and Migration," 114; Lazarus Stewart, "Narrative of Lazarus Stewart," in *Historical Collections of the State of Pennsylvania*, 280; Pearl, *Conceived in Crisis*, 102–11.
8. *Paxton Papers*, 29.
9. Kenny, *Peaceable Kingdom Lost*, 136.
10. Pearl, *Conceived in Crisis*, 109.
11. CR, 9:120; PA, 1:4:157.
12. Kenny, *Peaceable Kingdom Lost*, 146.
13. Pearl, *Conceived in Crisis*, 109.
14. *Paxton Papers*, 48.
15. John Elder, "A Booklet of Notes for Sermons and Prayers," Elder Collection, MG 070, Dauphin County Historical Society; Goodlet, *A Vindication of the Associate Synod*, 11.
16. Elder, "A Booklet of Notes for Sermons and Prayers"; *Annals of the American Pulpit*, 77.
17. Anonymous letter, February 29, 1764, *Register of Pennsylvania*, 12:10.
18. Campbell, *Speculators in Empire*, 113.
19. Silver, *Our Savage Neighbors*, 78, 83, 126–27.
20. Loudon, *A Selection of Some of the Most Interesting Narratives of Outrages Committed by the Indians*, 1:273–74.
21. Navarre, *Journal of Pontiac's Conspiracy*, 22–32; Heckewelder, *History, Manners, Customs of the Indian Nations*, 292; Richter, *Facing East from Indian Country*, 196; Dowd, *War under Heaven*, 104–5; Cave, "The Delaware Prophet Neolin."
22. Navarre, *Journal of Pontiac's Conspiracy*, 22–32.
23. Ibid.
24. CR, 8:748.
25. Ibid., 9:327–28.
26. Marshall, "Empire and Opportunity in Britain"; Holton, *Forced Founders*, 3–38.
27. Franklin, *A Narrative of the Late Massacres*.
28. DRCHSNY, 602–7.
29. Ibid.; PSWJ, 4:888; Campbell, "An Adverse Patron," 131; Shirai, "The Indian Trade in Colonial Pennsylvania," 158.
30. PBF, 13:171.
31. PA, 8:5:4161–65.
32. Campbell, *Speculators in Empire*, 118, 128, 181–82.
33. PBF, 15:21; Owens, *Red Dreams, White Nightmares*, 37–38.

34. "Nanticokes Answer to the Deputys," August 12, 1767, William L. Clements Library, University of Michigan, Ann Arbor, Digital Collection, https://clements.umich.edu/exhibit/american-encounters/nah-case-8/choptank-tribes-statement-1767/.
35. King George III, *A Proclamation* (London, 1763), Gilder Lehrman Collection, https://www.gilderlehrman.org/sites/default/files/inline-pdfs/t-05214.pdf.
36. Marshall, "Colonial Protest and Imperial Retrenchment"; "Remarks on the Plan Regulating the Indian Trade," September–October 1766, Founders Online, NA, https://founders.archives.gov/documents/Franklin/01-13-02-0159; Dowd, *War under Heaven*, 182–83; Richter, "Native Americans, the Plan of 1764, and a British Empire That Never Was."
37. Dowd, *War under Heaven*, 177–79; Campbell, *Speculators in Empire*, 73–75; Calloway, *Scratch of a Pen*, 95–100.
38. *PSWJ*, 4:278–80.
39. Merritt, *At the Crossroads*, 136; Taylor, *The Divided Ground*, 47–48.
40. Taylor, *The Divided Ground*, 47–48.
41. Middleton, *Pontiac's War*, 139–42; Richter, "Native Americans, the Plan of 1764, and a British Empire That Never Was."
42. Campbell, *Speculators in Empire*, 67–108; *PBF*, 13:414, 15:275, 17:8, 18:74.
43. Henry Moore to Shelburne, November 11, 1766, *DRCHSNY*, 7:877–78.
44. Rockingham, *Memoirs of the Marquis of Rockingham*, 1:353; Lord Barrington quoted in Dowd, *War under Heaven*, 235; Calloway, *Scratch of a Pen*, 94; Griffin, *American Leviathan*, 24–27.
45. Campbell, *Speculators in Empire*, 108–13.
46. *DRCHSNY*, 7:746–49, 766; Campbell, *Speculators in Empire*, 108–13.
47. *DRCHSNY*, 7:718–30; McCusker and Menard, *The Economy of British America*, 54.
48. *DRCHSNY*, 7:718–30.
49. Ibid.
50. Ibid.
51. Ibid.
52. Campbell, *Speculators in Empire*, 129–38.
53. Smith, *An Account of the Remarkable Occurrences*, 109; Pearl, *Conceived in Crisis*, 111–13.
54. "The Address of the Inhabitants of Cumberland County to the Governor," March 1765, Bouquet, *The Papers of Col. Henry Bouquet*, 6:777–79; Spero, *Frontier Rebels*, 53–96; Pearl, *Conceived in Crisis*, 111–15.
55. *PA*, 1:4:218.
56. Campbell, *Speculators in Empire*, 110.
57. William Johnson to Lords of Trade, January 16, 1765, CO 5/66, 197; Pearl, *Conceived in Crisis*, 113–14; Merritt, *At the Crossroads*, 296–308; Silver, *Our Savage Neighbors*, 146–60.
58. *CR*, 9:327–28; John Penn to Thomas Penn, September 12, 1766, TPP, vol. 10, reel 9.
59. *PSWJ*, 6:22; *DRCHSNY*, 7:871; *PSWJ*, 6:22, 5:700–702.
60. *PSWJ*, 5:16–17.

61. Ibid.
62. Gould, *The Persistence of Empire*, 38, 104–5.
63. Nash, "Up from the Bottom in Franklin's Philadelphia"; Carter et al., *Historical Statistics of the United States, Earliest Times to the Present*, vol. 5, "Imperial Taxes Collected under Several British Laws: 1765–1774," table Eg420–424.
64. Griffin, *The Townshend Moment*, 114–64.
65. Board of Trade quoted in Griffin, *American Leviathan*, 24.
66. DRCHSNY, 7:1003–5; CR, 9:403; Board of Trade to William Petty, December 23, 1767, *Colonial and State Records of North Carolina*, 536–38; Campbell, *Speculators in Empire*, 121.

6. "A Great Run for the Lands on Susquehanna"

1. *PSWJ*, 12:488–89.
2. Ibid., 12:607–8.
3. Ibid., 12:525–26.
4. Ibid., 12:493, 527.
5. Ibid., 12:490.
6. Ibid., 12:550.
7. Ibid., 6:464
8. Ibid., 12:474, 476.
9. *DRCHSNY*, 8:35–36.
10. *PSWJ*, 12:512.
11. *PBF*, 13:414.
12. *SCP*, 3:31–32.
13. *DRCHSNY*, 8:35–36.
14. *PSWJ*, 12:526.
15. Ibid., 12:529–43.
16. Ibid., 12:553.
17. *Connecticut Courant*, June 29, 1767; *SCP*, 2:333–34.
18. *SCP*, 2:323.
19. John Penn to Thomas Penn, November 6, 1768, TPP, vol. 10, reel 9.
20. *SCP*, 2:323.
21. *SCP*, 3:23.
22. Ibid., 3:23–24.
23. *PA*, 5:1:334.
24. *SCP*, 3:64.
25. *SCP*, 2:324–25.
26. *SCP*, 3:24–25.
27. William Allen to Thomas Penn, December 4, 1768, TPP, vol. 10, reel 9.

28. William Smith to Thomas Penn, 1768, TPP, vol. 10, reel 9.
29. Joseph Shippen to David Jameson, June 20, 1768, Joseph Shippen Letterbook, 1763–1773, SFP, APS.
30. Ibid.
31. William Allen to Thomas Penn, October 12, 1768, TPP, vol. 10, reel 9.
32. William Allen to Thomas Penn, March 8, 1767, PFP, reel 9; William Allen to Thomas Penn, September 23, 1768, TPP, vol. 10, reel 9.
33. William Allen to Thomas Penn, October 12, 1768, TPP, vol. 10, reel 9.
34. William Smith to Thomas Penn, 1768, TPP, vol. 10, reel 9.
35. Richard Hockley to Thomas Penn, February 9, 1768, TPP, vol. 10, reel 9; Joseph Shippen to David Jameson, June 20, 1768, Joseph Shippen Letterbook, SFP, APS.
36. George Croghan, "List of the Different Nations and Tribes of Indians in the Northern District of North America, with the Number of Their Fighting Men," 1765, in *Early Western Travels*, 167.
37. Alexander S. Withers, *Chronicles of Border Warfare; or, A History of the Settlement by the Whites, of North-Western Virginia: And of the Indian Wars and Massacres, in That Section of the State; with Reflections, Anecdotes, & c.* (Clarksburg, VA, 1831), 136; Ken Sullivan, "Captain Bull," in *The West Virginia Encyclopedia* (Charleston: West Virginia Humanities Council, 2006), 111.
38. CR, 9:328–32, 617; DRCHSNY, 7:883.
39. Merrell, *Into the American Woods*, 313.
40. PSWJ, 12:258.
41. John Penn to Thomas Penn, March 30, 1768, TPP, vol. 10, reel 9.
42. CR, 9:426.
43. Ibid.; Rowe, "The Frederick Stump Affair"; Spero, *Frontier Country*, 187–93; Ries, "'The Rage of Opposing Government'"; PSWJ, 6:101.
44. CR, 9:470; Ries, "'The Rage of Opposing Government,'" 23.
45. CR, 9:480.
46. PSWJ, 6:108, 110–11.
47. Ibid., 6:102.
48. Ibid., 6:115.
49. John Penn to Thomas Penn, January 21, 1768, TPP, vol. 10, reel 9.
50. EAID, 3:731, 733, 742.
51. John Penn to Thomas Penn, March 30, 1768, TPP, vol. 10, reel 9.
52. DRCHSNY, 8:104–5.
53. Ibid.
54. PSWJ, 12:608.
55. DRCHSNY, 8:104–5.
56. PSWJ, 12:600.
57. Benjamin Chew to Thomas Penn, November 13, 1768, TPP, vol. 10, reel 9.
58. DRCHSNY, 8:111–34.

59. *PSWJ*, 6:464.
60. Schutt, *Peoples of the River Valleys*, 11; Shannon, *Iroquois Diplomacy*, 84.
61. *DRCHSNY*, 8:114–16.
62. Ibid.
63. Shannon, *Iroquois Diplomacy*, 86.
64. *DRCHSNY*, 8:114–16.
65. Ibid., 8:115.
66. Ibid., 8:121.
67. Ibid., 8:121–22.
68. Ibid., 8:123.
69. Ibid. For Johnson's previous purchase of Oneida land, see *PSWJ*, 12:656–58.
70. *DRCHSNY*, 8:124.
71. Ibid., 8:124–25.
72. *PSWJ*, 6:472.
73. *DRCHSNY*, 8:133.
74. McCrea, *Pennsylvania Land Applications*, iii–vi.
75. *PSWJ*, 12:695.
76. Ibid., 12:725.
77. Ibid., 7:184.
78. Ibid., 7:182.
79. Schutt, *Peoples of the River Valleys*, 140.
80. *PSWJ*, 7:182.
81. *DRCHSNY*, 8:144–45.
82. Ibid., 8:158, 145.
83. Ibid., 8:110–11, 144–45, 150–52; *PSWJ*, 6:568–69.
84. *DRCHSNY*, 8:166.
85. Ibid., 8:121.
86. Ibid., 8:150–52.
87. Schutt, *Peoples of the River Valleys*, 137.
88. *PSWJ*, 7:316.
89. Conrad Weiser, Journal, quoted in Wallace, *Conrad Weiser*, 81.
90. "Draught of the West Branch of the Susquehanna Taken by Captain Patterson," April 1, 1769, SFP, APS.

7. An Empire Divided

1. Greene, *The Constitutional Origins of the American Revolution*, 154; Jensen, *Founding of a Nation*, 252–57.
2. Jensen, *Founding of a Nation*, 288–96.
3. Hillsborough Circular, CO, 5:241.

4. William Allen to Thomas Penn, October 12, 1768, TPP, vol. 10, reel 9.
5. Taylor, *American Revolutions*, 108.
6. *DRCHSNY*, 8:302.
7. Taylor, *American Revolutions*, 55–89.
8. Ibid.
9. Ibid., 77–78; "Report of the Lords Commissioners for Trade and Plantations, on the Petition of the Honorable Thomas Walpole and his Associates, for a Grant of Lands on the River Ohio, in North America," in *The Works of Benjamin Franklin*, ed. Jared Sparks (Chicago, 1882), 4:303.
10. Edelson, *The New Map of Empire*, 189–90; Taylor, *American Revolutions*, 77–78.
11. William Allen to Thomas Penn, October 12, 1768, TPP, vol. 10, reel 9.
12. *SCP*, 3:64.
13. Ibid., 3:81.
14. Edmund Physick to Thomas Penn, April 19, 1769, TPP, vol. 10, reel 9.
15. Ibid.; William Smith to Thomas Penn, 1768/69, TPP, vol. 10, reel 9.
16. *SCP*, 3:68.
17. Edmund Physick to Thomas Penn, April 19, 1769, TPP, vol. 10, reel 9.
18. The best and clearest description of the application process is in Maxey, "The Honorable Proprietaries v. Samuel Wallis."
19. For a description of past procedures, see William Smith to Thomas Penn, 1769, TPP, vol. 10, reel 9.
20. *SCP*, 3:78.
21. Edmund Physick to Thomas Penn, February 4, 1769, TPP, vol. 10, reel 9.
22. Edmund Physick to Thomas Penn, February 4, April 19, 1769, TPP, vol. 10, reel 9.
23. Ibid.
24. *SCP*, 3:79.
25. William Smith to Thomas Penn, 1769, TPP, vol. 10, reel 9.
26. *PA*, 5:1:334.
27. "New Purchase Register: Officer's Tracts Listing and Index," RLO, RG-17, series 17.43; "Draught of the West Branch of the Susquehanna Taken by Captain Patterson," April 1, 1769, SFP, APS.
28. Huston, *An Essay on the History and Nature of Original Titles*, 319.
29. See "New Purchase Register: Officer's Tracts Listing and Index," RLO, RG-17, series 17.43.
30. William Smith to Thomas Penn, 1769, TPP, vol. 10, reel 9.
31. Bell, "Samuel Purviance, Jr.," 438.
32. *SCP*, 3:xvii.
33. Ibid., 3:185.
34. Copied Surveys, 1681–1912, RLO, RG-17, series 17.114, Survey Code D-56–205; William Smith to Thomas Penn, 1769, TPP, vol. 10, reel 9; *SCP*, 3:80; Nelson, "The Greening of the West Branch," 52.

35. William Smith to Thomas Penn, 1768/69, TPP, vol. 10, reel 9.
36. Edmund Physick to Thomas Penn, April 19, 1769, TPP, vol. 10, reel 9.
37. Ibid.; "Petition from March 27, 1769," PFP, series VI: Physick Manuscripts, 1676–1811, vol. 3, Letterbook, 189.
38. SCP, 3:120.
39. Ibid., 3:144–45.
40. Edward Shippen to Joseph Shippen, March 3, 1769, SFP, APS.
41. New Purchase Register, 1769, N-41, 276, 302, 310, 341, 482, 500, 521, 585, 698, 813, 1044, 1245, 1307, 1462, 2409, 3136, 3137, 3175, 3176, 3178, 3179, 3181, RLO, RG-17, series 17.43.
42. New Purchase Register, 1769, N-120, 149, 186, 228, 394, 775, 909, 1666, 1732, 3798, 3799, 3800, 3814, 3815, 3823, RLO, RG-17, series 17.43.
43. Edmund Physick to Thomas Penn, September 29, 1769, TPP, vol. 10, reel 9.
44. Maxey, "The Honorable Proprietaries v. Samuel Wallis."
45. Edmund Physick to Thomas Penn, March 13, September 28, 1770; Thomas and John Penn v. Samuel Wallis, Notes on Case of, TPP, reel 9; SCP, 4:119. For a breakdown of Wallis's activities, see Maxey, "The Honorable Proprietaries v. Samuel Wallis."
46. New Purchase Register, 1769, NP-1340, 1629, 2130, 619, 1603, 2706, 571, 518, 1971, 355, 1383, 831, 1745, 2172, 582, 938, 1881, 2210, 410, 540, 1217, 329, 2638, 1094, 1372, 627, 882, 176, 1010, 161, 2391, 176, 226, 1005, 171, 445, 1001, 2161, 958, RLO, RG-17, series 17.43; Copied Surveys, 1681–1912, RLO, RG-17, series 17.114, Survey Codes C-23–283, A-71–100, A-8–195, D-57–377, A-58–223, D-57–254, C-136–33.
47. New Purchase Register, 1769, NP-176, 1010, RLO, RG-17, series 17.43; John Penn to Thomas Penn, January 1, 1770, TPP, reel 9.
48. I use "at least" because our understanding of individual squatters past Lycoming Creek is incomplete. We rely on preemption applications filed by squatters post-1785 to buy their improvements from Pennsylvania. These applications identify the applicant, their neighbors, and witnesses who affirmed their improvements, offering insight into the settlers. However, they don't encompass all squatters. Marcus Gallo, who studied these applications, suggests they probably cover only about half of the squatters in that area. See preemption applications for James Alexander, John Alexander, William Clark, Samuel Cook, Thomas Forster, John Gallagher, Alexander Irwin, John McCormick, and William McClure, Preemption Application, 1785, RLO, LO 7.5. See Gallo, "'Fair Play Has Entirely Ceased, and Law Has Taken Its Place,'" 410.
49. Edmund Physick to Thomas Penn, June 14, 1770, TPP, reel 9. See also Physick to Penn, 1769, SCP, 3:185.
50. Edmund Physick to Thomas Penn, June 14, 1770, TPP, reel 9.
51. SCP, 4:67.
52. Ibid.
53. Ibid., 5:370.
54. PA, 8:7042.
55. SCP, 6:233–34; Frederick Haldimand to Lord Dartmouth, November 3, 1773, Documents of the American Revolution, 6:238; PSWJ, 6:1182.

56. Edmund Physick to Thomas Penn, September 28, 1770, TPP, reel 9.
57. *SCP,* 6:158.
58. *DRCHSNY,* 8:125.
59. Shannon, *Indians and Colonists at the Crossroads of Empire,* 108–9.
60. *SCP,* 6:163.
61. *PSWJ,* 7:63–64.
62. *SCP,* 3:165; *PSWJ,* 8:640.
63. *PSWJ,* 7:64; 12:421.
64. Ibid., 12:420.
65. Ibid., 6:128–29. For the "weakness of government" in Pennsylvania, see Pearl, *Conceived in Crisis,* 130–39.
66. For the names of the rescuers, see Oyer and Terminer Papers, 1768, RG-33, PHMC. See also Ries, "'The Rage of Opposing Government,'" 32. For the names of the squatters beyond Lycoming Creek, see Preemption Application, 1785, RLO, RG-17, series 17.14, reel LO 7.5.
67. *PSWJ,* 12:888.
68. Ibid., 9:373.
69. *CR,* 9:438–41, 773–75.
70. Ibid.
71. *PSWJ,* 8:883.
72. Ibid.
73. *CR,* 10:94–95.
74. *PA,* 1:12:286.
75. Ibid.; Deposition of Captain Thomas Robinson, June 7, 1785, Preemption Application, 1785, RLO, RG-17, series 17.14, reel LO 7.5, PHMC; Deposition of William Cooke, September 23, 1785, Preemption Application, 1785, RLO, RG-17, series 17.14, reel LO 7.5.
76. *PA,* 1:12:286.

8. "A Spirit of Liberty and Patriotism Pervaded the People"

1. "Fithian's Journal," July 1775, Linn, *History of Centre and Clinton Counties,* 471–72. Using land applications after a 1784 law that gave settlers to the area preemption rights, Marcus Gallo has corroborated Fithian's observation. See Gallo, "'Fair Play Has Entirely Ceased, and Law Has Taken Its Place,'" 410.
2. Preemption Warrant Applications, 1785, RLO, LO 7.5, PHMC.
3. *PA,* 2:3:518–22.
4. Smith, *Laws of the Commonwealth of Pennsylvania,* 195.
5. *PA,* 2:3:518–22.
6. Ibid., 2:3:217–18. See also ibid., 2:3:449–52.
7. For a thorough explanation of the "Common Cause" and its use of perceived "enemies" to support it, further explored below, see Parkinson, *The Common Cause.*

8. Wolf, *Fair Play Settlers*, 16–17.
9. "Fithian's Journal," 470–73; Wolf, *Fair Play Settlers*, 16–17.
10. See Pearl, "'Our God, and Our Guns'"; Pearl, "Pulpits of Revolution"; and Pearl, *Conceived in Crisis*, 103–4.
11. Goodlet, *A Vindication of the Associate Synod*, 8–11; Davies, *A Sermon on Man's Primitive State*; Davies, *Religion and Public Spirit*; Montgomery, *A Letter, from a Clergyman in Town*; Williams, *The Essential Rights and Liberties of Protestants*. See also Broderick, "Pulpit, Physics, and Politics."
12. Wolf, *Fair Play Settlers*, 19–20; Nelson, "The Greening of the West Branch," 52–61.
13. Anonymous letter, February 29, 1764, *Register of Pennsylvania*, 12:10.
14. John Elder to Colonel Joseph Shippen, February 1, 1764, Parkman, *The Conspiracy of Pontiac*, appendix E, 2:347. See also petitions sent to the assembly between March 23 and May 25, 1764, *PA*, 8:7:5581–5610.
15. Edmund Physick to Thomas Penn, February 4, April 19, 1769, TPP, reel 9.
16. Nelson, "The Greening of the West Branch," 59; Wolf, *Fair Play Settlers*, 34–35.
17. Preemption Application of Alexander Erwin, October 1785, RLO, LO 7.5.
18. *PA*, 2:3:449–50.
19. Robert Hamilton to the Pennsylvania Legislature, February 15, 1829, RWP, W. 7668.
20. Nelson, "The Greening of the West Branch," 59.
21. James Dunn, Pension Application, RWP, W. 19.199; William Dunn, New Purchase Register, 1769, NP-1963, RLO, RG-17, series 17.43.
22. Edmund Physick to Thomas Penn, April 19, 1769, TPP, reel 9.
23. See Warrant Applications of George Woods, William Luckey, William Walker, James Chambers, Andrew Kinkead, James Richardson, James Vancampin, Henry Dougharty, Preemption Application, 1785, RLO, LO 7.5, and Deposition of William Luckey, September 23, 1785, Preemption Application, 1785, RLO, LO 7.5. See also "Deposition of Eleanor Colden, June 7, 1797, *McKinney v. Proctor*," *Now and Then* 12, no. 9 (1959): 221–22.
24. Deposition of John McElvaine, September 6, 1785, Preemption Application, 1785, RLO, LO 7.5.
25. Deposition of Benjamin Walker, September 7, 1785, Preemption Application, 1785, RLO, LO 7.5.
26. Ibid.
27. New Purchase Register, 1769, NP-33, 63, 443, 486, 1444, 2432, 3562, 1385, 1860, 2296, RLO, RG-17, series 17.43, PHMC.
28. Deposition of William King, March 15, 1801, *Huff v. Satcha*, in Linn, "Indian Land and Its Fair-Play Settlers," 422.
29. Deposition of James Irwin, May 21, 1785, Preemption Application of Alexander Irwin, 1785, RLO, LO 7.5.
30. Smith, *Laws of the Commonwealth of Pennsylvania*, 195.
31. New Purchase Register, 1769, NP-313, 347, 486, 984, 1095, 1115, 2047, 2702, 2799, 3186, 3187, 3200, 3665, 3847, RLO, RG-17, series 17.43.

32. Smith, *Laws of the Commonwealth of Pennsylvania*, 195.
33. Ibid.
34. "Deposition of Eleanor Colden, June 7, 1797," 221–22.
35. Deposition of William King, March 15, 1801, *Huff v. Satcha*, in Linn, "Indian Land and Its Fair-Play Settlers," 423–24.
36. *John Hughes v. Henry Dougherty*, October 1791, *Reports of Cases Ruled and Adjudged in the Courts of Pennsylvania*, 1:497.
37. Ibid.
38. Deposition of Bratton Caldwell, May 1799, *Greer v. Tharp*, in Linn, "Indian Land and its Fair-Play Settlers," 422.
39. See, for example, *Sweeny v. Toner*, October 1791, Smith, *Laws of the Commonwealth of Pennsylvania*, 196.
40. "Deposition of Eleanor Colden, June 7, 1797," 221–22.
41. Preemption Application of Thomas Henry, August 1785, RLO, LO 7.5; Deposition of Elenore Colden, June 21, 1785, Preemption Application, 1785, RLO, LO 7.5.
42. "Deposition of Eleanor Colden, June 7, 1797," 221–22.
43. *PA*, 1:12:286.
44. Meginness, *Otzinachson*, 470; Wolf, *Fair Play Settlers*, 41–42; Gallo, "'Fair Play Has Entirely Ceased, and Law Has Taken Its Place,'" 417–18.
45. Humphrey, "Crowd and Court," 109.
46. McConville, "The Rise of Rough Music," 87–100.
47. Deposition of James Carson, June 10, 1785, Preemption Application, 1785, RLO, RG-17, series 12.14, reel LO 7.5; Deposition of Captain Thomas Robinson, June 7, 1785, Preemption Application, 1785, RLO, RG-17, series 17.14, reel LO 7.5; Deposition of William Cooke, September 23, 1785, Preemption Application, 1785, RLO, RG-17, series 17.14, reel LO 7.5; Smith, *Laws of the Commonwealth of Pennsylvania*, 124.
48. "The Association Entered into by the American Continental Congress in Behalf of All the Colonies," October 20, 1774, Founders Online, NA, https://founders.archives.gov/documents/Jefferson/01-01-02-0094.
49. *Rivington's New-York Gazetteer*, July 28, 1774.
50. *PBF*, 19:330; Memorial of Joseph Galloway, ALC, series II, AO 13/102.
51. Memorial of Joseph Galloway, ALC, series II, AO 13/102.
52. Irvin, *Clothed in Robes of Sovereignty*, 27, 20–24.
53. "The Association Entered into by the American Continental Congress in Behalf of All the Colonies."
54. Ibid.; Bullock and McIntyre, "The Handsome Tokens of a Funeral."
55. *Articles of Association in Pennsylvania, for the Defence of American Liberty*, 1–2.
56. *Extracts from the Votes and Proceedings of the Committee of Observation of Lancaster*, 1
57. *PA*, 2:3:449; Philadelphia Committee to the Committees of the Several Counties in the Province, May 21, 1776, *American Archives*, 4:6:520–21.
58. *Pennsylvania Gazette*, December 28, 1774.
59. Linn, *History of Centre and Clinton Counties*, 473.

60. *Pennsylvania Journal,* May 22, June 12, 1776; Allen, "Diary of James Allen," 2:187.
61. *Pennsylvania Packet,* September 25, 1775.
62. Memorial of Reverend Daniel Batwell, ALC, series II, AO 13/70B.
63. Northumberland Committee of Safety Minutes, 28–29, AM.277, HSP.
64. Ibid., 29–31.
65. Ibid.
66. For the importance of these ideas for the new American states, see Handlin and Handlin, *Commonwealth;* Hartz, *The Liberal Tradition in America;* Novak and Pincus, "Revolutionary State Formation"; Gerstle, *Liberty and Coercion,* 17–88; Murphy, *Building the Empire State;* and Pearl, *Conceived in Crisis.*
67. Joseph Reed to Charles Pettit, March 30, 1776, Reed, *Life and Correspondence of Joseph Reed,* 1:182; *Pennsylvania Packet,* April 22, April 29, June 10, 1776; *Pennsylvania Gazette,* May 15, 1776; *Pennsylvania Evening Post,* March 9, 1776.
68. For the role of the Philadelphia City Committee, see Ryerson, *The Revolution Is Now Begun,* 75–120.
69. Philadelphia Committee to the Committees of the Several Counties in the Province, May 21, 1776, *American Archives,* 4:6:520–21.
70. Anna Jackson to George C. Whiting, December 16, 1858, RWP, W. 7668.
71. John Hamilton to George C. Whiting, November 29, 1858, RWP, W. 7668; *Lock Haven Express,* March 15, 1949; Lou Bernard, "The Tiadaghton Declaration," *Lock Haven Express,* July 4, 2020, https://www.lockhaven.com/news/health-and-home/2020/07/the-tiadaghton-declaration/.
72. Philadelphia Committee to the Committees of the Several Counties in the Province, May 21, 1776, *American Archives,* 4:6:520–21.
73. *PA,* 2:3:449–50.
74. Ibid., 2:3:451–52.
75. Ibid.
76. *Pennsylvania Journal,* February 28, 1776. In his book, *The Common Cause,* Robert G. Parkinson shows how Patriots purposefully used this racially charged imagery of "enemies" to motivate colonists to mobilize for war and support American independence. Parkinson, *The Common Cause,* 185–263. See also Parkinson, *Thirteen Clocks.*
77. Philadelphia Committee to the Committees of the Several Counties in the Province, May 21, 1776, *American Archives,* 4:6:520–21.
78. *PA,* 2:3:451–52.
79. Deposition of Elenore Colden, June 21, 1785, Preemption Application, 1785, RLO, LO 7.5.
80. Robert Hamilton to the Pennsylvania Legislature, February 15, 1829, RWP, W. 7668.
81. "Fithian's Journal," 72.
82. John Hamilton to George C. Whiting, November 29, 1858, RWP, W. 7668.

9. "The Title of Savages"

1. Weslager, *The Delaware Indians*, 282–95; Schutt, *Peoples of the River Valleys*, 129–49.
2. "At a Meeting of the Commissioners for Indian Affairs as Well [as] Those Appointed by Congress," October 9, 1775, *Report of a Treaty with the Western Indians*, 86–87.
3. *PA*, 1:4:788; emphasis added.
4. Taylor, *The Divided Ground*, 81–86.
5. Oneidas, Speech, March 1775, quoted in Graymont, *The Iroquois in the American Revolution*, 58.
6. *DRCHSNY*, 8:611, 622.
7. Taylor, *The Divided Ground*, 84–85; Shannon, *Iroquois Diplomacy*, 83, 187–89.
8. Northumberland County Revolutionary War Militia: Upper Division Associators, January 24, 1776, PHMC, https://www.phmc.PA.gov/Archives/Research-Online/Pages/Revolutionary-War-Militia-Northumberland.aspx; Snyder, "The Militia of Northumberland County During the Revolution."
9. Robert Covenhoven, RWP, S. 12574.
10. Henry Hill, RWP, W. 2.800.
11. *PA*, 1:6:176.
12. Ibid., 1:5:762.
13. Meginness, *Otzinachson*, 477.
14. Meginness, *History of Lycoming County*, 126; *PA*, 1:6:565.
15. *PA*, 1:6:175–76.
16. Ibid.
17. Ibid.
18. Henry Hill, RWP, W. 2.800.
19. William Campbell, RWP, S. 3130.
20. Benjamin Walker, RWP, W. 14088.
21. *PA*, 1:6:176.
22. John Adams to Abigail Adams, April 28, 1777, Adams Family Papers: An Electronic Archive, Massachusetts Historical Society, https://www.masshist.org/digitaladams/archive/doc?id=L17770428ja.
23. Parkinson, *The Common Cause*, 329–40; Burgoyne's proclamation quoted on 330.
24. Germain quoted in Calloway, *The American Revolution in Indian Country*, 63.
25. The best analysis of the press during these years is in Parkinson, *The Common Cause*, 329–40.
26. *Pennsylvania Evening Post, Pennsylvania Packet, Pennsylvania Gazette, Der Wöchentliche Pennsylvanische Staatsbote*, all August 5, 1777.
27. *Pennsylvania Journal*, August 13, 1777.
28. *Pennsylvania Journal*, August 20, 1777.
29. Declaration of Independence, July 4, 1776.
30. *Pennsylvania Journal*, July 16, 1777.
31. Shannon, *Iroquois Diplomacy*, 178.

32. Guy Johnson quoted in Calloway, *The American Revolution in Indian Country*, 143.
33. Tenhoghskweaghta quoted in ibid., 59, 33.
34. Ibid., 60; Parkinson, *Thirteen Clocks*, 79.
35. Graymont, *The Iroquois in the American Revolution*, 159.
36. Ibid., 113.
37. "Anecdotes of Joseph Brant," Claus Family Papers, vol. 2, M.G. 19, F1, Public Archives, Canada.
38. *DRCHSNY*, 8:623, 626.
39. "Observations of Joseph Brant," Claus Family Papers, vol. 2, M.G. 19, F1, Public Archives, Canada.
40. Ibid.
41. George Washington to Commissioners of Indians Affairs, March 13, 1778, Washington, *Papers of George Washington*, Revolutionary War Series, 14:167–68, https://rotunda.upress.virginia.edu/founders/GEWN-03-14-02-0133.
42. Shannon, *Iroquois Diplomacy*, 188–90.
43. Weslager, *The Delaware Indians*, 306–8; Heckewelder and Du Ponceau, "Biographical Sketches," 392; Grimes, "The Emergence and Decline of the Delaware Indian Nation," 120, 136–37, 145–48.
44. Weslager, *The Delaware Indians*, 306–8; Grimes, "The Emergence and Decline of the Delaware Indian Nation," 120, 136–37, 145–48.
45. Taylor, *The Divided Ground*, 81–93.
46. Sayenqueraghta quoted in ibid., 102, 112.
47. "Observations of Joseph Brant," Claus Family Papers, vol. 2, M.G. 19, F1, Public Archives, Canada; Mintz, *Seeds of Empire*, 45; General Frederick Haldimand quoted in Graymont, *The Iroquois in the American Revolution*, 159.
48. Graymont, *The Iroquois in the American Revolution*, 157–91; Dowd, *A Spirited Resistance*, 75–78.
49. *CR*, 6:570.
50. George Long, RWP, W. 9139.
51. Anna Jackson to George C. Whiting, December 16, 1858, RWP, W. 7668.
52. *PA*, 1:6:571.
53. Ibid., 1:6:573.
54. Anna Jackson to George C. Whiting, December 16, 1758, RWP, W. 7668.
55. *PA*, 1:6:571.
56. Ibid., 1:6:564.
57. Ibid., 1:6:573.
58. Ibid., 1:6:589–91.
59. Parkinson, *The Common Cause*, 411–12; Moyer, *Wild Yankees*, 31–32.
60. Parkinson, *The Common Cause*, 411–12; Meier, "'Devoted to Hardships, Danger, and Devastation,'" 65; Mancall, *Valley of Opportunity*, 137–38; Moyer, *Wild Yankees*, 31–32.
61. Parkinson, *The Common Cause*, 412.
62. *Pennsylvania Evening Post*, July 16, 1778.

63. Ibid.
64. *PA*, 1:6:636–37.
65. Sanderson, "Recollections of His Great Grandfather, Robert Covenhoven," 16.
66. Russell, "The Big Runaway of 1778."
67. *PA*, 1:6:570, 631–32, 647.
68. Robert Covenhoven, RWP, S. 12574; Anna Jackson to George C. Whiting, December 16, 1758, RWP, W. 7668.
69. *PA*, 1:6:634.
70. Ibid., 2:3:188–89; 1:6:631–32.
71. Ibid., 1:6:478–636.
72. Ibid., 1:6:563–64.
73. Ibid., 1:6:674.
74. Ibid., 1:6:687.
75. Ibid., 1:6:687, 689.
76. Ibid., 1:6:692.
77. Ibid., 1:6:692, 690; 2:3:217–18.
78. Ibid., 2:3:215–18, 449.
79. Ibid., 1:6:694.
80. Ibid., 1:6:705.
81. Ibid., 1:6:661, 680.
82. Ibid., 1:6:711, 639.
83. Ibid., 1:6:661.
84. Ibid., 1:6:731, 1:7:3.
85. Ibid., 1:7:5–9.
86. Henry Hill, RWP, W. 2.800.
87. *PA*, 1:7:8–9.
88. Ibid., 1:7:5–9.
89. Ibid., 1:6:638–39, 705, 773–74, 644; 1:7:3–6.
90. Sanderson, "Recollections of His Great Grandfather, Robert Covenhoven," 16; *Harrisburg Telegraph*, January 13, 1894.
91. Thomas Hartley to the Senecas, October 1, 1778, quoted in Graymont, *The Iroquois in the American Revolution*, 181.
92. *PA*, 1:6:638–39, 705, 773–74, 644; 1:7:3–6.
93. *Pennsylvania Packet*, October 17, 1778; *Independent Ledger*, November 2, 1778; *New York Gazette*, November 2, 1778.
94. *Pennsylvania Packet*, December 10, 1778.
95. Samuel Preston, "Journey to Harmony," quoted in Calloway, *The American Revolution in Indian Country*, 125.
96. *CR*, 11:640.
97. *PA*, 1:7:11.
98. Ibid., 1:7:3–6.

99. Lieutenant William Barton, Journal, 1779, *Journals of the Military Expedition of Major General John Sullivan*, 8.
100. Shannon, *Iroquois Diplomacy*, 191–92.
101. Koehler, "Hostile Nations."
102. George Washington to Major General John Sullivan, September 15, 1779, Washington, *Papers of George Washington*, Revolutionary War Series, 22:432, https://rotunda.upress.virginia.edu/founders/GEWN-03-22-02-0357.
103. Calloway, *The American Revolution in Indian Country*, 135–37.
104. Evans, *A Discourse, Delivered at Easton*, 19–22.
105. *United States Magazine*, January–October 1779, 6.
106. James Potter to George Bryan, July 25, 1778, *PA*, 1:6:666.
107. Dowd, *A Spirited Resistance*, 65–89; Calloway, *The American Revolution in Indian Country*, 158–81.
108. *Pennsylvania Packet*, November 7, 1782.
109. William Croghan to Barnard Gratz and Michael Gratz, April 26, 1782, quoted in Silver, *Our Savage Neighbors*, 276.
110. *Pennsylvania Journal*, August 28, 1782.
111. Silver, *Our Savage Neighbors*, 270–71.
112. James Irvine to Anne Callender Irvine, April 12, 1782, *Washington-Irvine Correspondence*, 343.
113. White, *The Middle Ground*, 410–11.
114. Taylor, *Divided Ground*, 105–6; emphasis added.
115. *The Parliamentary History of England*, 410.
116. Calloway, *The American Revolution in Indian Country*, 148–49.
117. Graymont, *The Iroquois in the American Revolution*, 256; *EAID*, 19:299–301.

Aftermath

1. *Pennsylvania Journal*, April 23, 1783; *Freeman's Journal*, April 23, 1783.
2. *Pennsylvania Journal*, April 23, 1783; *Freeman's Journal*, April 23, 1783.
3. *Pennsylvania Journal*, April 23, 1783; *Freeman's Journal*, April 23, 1783.
4. *Freeman's Journal*, April 30, 1783.
5. *PA*, 2:3:451–52.
6. Witness Statement of John McCormick, November 9, 1834, in Robert King, RWP, R. 5965.
7. *PA*, 2:3:451–52.
8. Declaration of Independence, July 4, 1776.
9. Charles DeWitt to George Clinton, June 4, 1784, quoted in Taylor, *Divided Ground*, 142.
10. *PA*, 2:3:518–22.
11. *Freeman's Journal*, April 3, 1782.
12. *PA*, 2:3:518–22.

13. Samuel Wharton quoted in Silver, *Our Savage Neighbors*, 288.
14. Richter, "Onas, the Long Knife," 208.
15. *Journals of the Continental Congress*, 683.
16. Allan MacLean to Frederick Haldimand, May 18, 1783, quoted in Taylor, *The Divided Ground*, 112.
17. *Journals of the Continental Congress*, 686, emphasis added.
18. Dickinson, "John Dickinson to Congress, April 29, 1783."
19. *PA*, 1:10:54.
20. *EAID*, 19:299–301; Sadosky, *Revolutionary Negotiations*, 128–29.
21. *EAID*, 19:299–301.
22. Ibid.
23. Ibid., 18:305–12.
24. Sadosky, *Revolutionary Negotiations*, 132–34.
25. Articles of Confederation, NA, https://www.ourdocuments.gov/doc.php?flash=false&doc=3&PAge=transCRipt.
26. Sadosky, *Revolutionary Negotiations*, 119–47; *EAID*, 18:313–21.
27. *DCHSNY*, 5:368.
28. Ibid., 5:367–68, emphasis added; Sadosky, *Revolutionary Negotiations*, 133–34.
29. *EAID*, 18:313–21.
30. Evans and Raup, "Journal of Griffith Evans," 211.
31. Pennsylvania commissioner quoted in Richter, "Onas, the Long Knife," 212.
32. *EAID*, 18:325.
33. Ibid., 18:319.
34. Evans and Raup, "Journal of Griffith Evans," 212.
35. Graymont, *The Iroquois in the American Revolution*, 278.
36. John Dease to "Major Fraser," November 26, 1784, Forney, *Henry S. Manley*, 293.
37. *EAID*, 18:319.
38. Richter, "Onas, the Long Knife," 212–13.
39. *PA*, 1:10:740–41.
40. *EAID*, 18:320; *PA*, 2:4:627–28; *CR*, 16:501, 505.
41. Evans and Raup, "Journal of Griffith Evans," 214.
42. *John Hughes v. Henry Dougherty*, October 1792, *Reports of Cases Ruled and Adjudged in the Courts of Pennsylvania*, 1:497.
43. Calloway, *The American Revolution in Indian Country*, 156–57.
44. Frederick Haldimand, "A Census of the Six Nations on the Grand River," 1785, Johnston, *The Valley of the Six Nations*, B19; Shannon, *Iroquois Diplomacy*, 170–209.
45. Way-Way, Grand River, Canada, July 14, 1837, Murray, *A History of Old Tioga Point*, 169–70; Calloway, *The American Revolution in Indian Country*, 139.
46. Way-Way, Grand River, Canada, July 14, 1837, Murray, *A History of Old Tioga Point*, 169–70.
47. Calloway, *The American Revolution in Indian Country*, 282–83.

48. Way-Way, Grand River, Canada, July 14, 1837, Murray, *A History of Old Tioga Point,* 169.
49. Obermeyer, *Delaware Tribe in a Cherokee Nation,* 44; Haldimand, "A Census of the Six Nations on the Grand River," B19.
50. Haldimand, "A Census of the Six Nations on the Grand River," B19.
51. *PA*, 1:6:631–32.
52. Maryland State Council quoted in Ruddiman, *Becoming Men of Some Consequence,* 160; Angus McCoy, Revolutionary War Pension Application, in John C. Dann, *The Revolution Remembered: Eyewitness Accounts of the War for Independence* (Chicago: University of Chicago Press, 1980), 314; Bouton, "A Road Closed."
53. Ramsay, *History of the United States,* 46.
54. *PA*, 2:3:450–452, 521.
55. Holton, *Abigail Adams,* 144–218; *PA*, 1:10:357–58.
56. Evans and Raup, "Journal of Griffith Evans," 211.
57. Smith, *Laws of the Commonwealth of Pennsylvania,* 195–96.
58. *Journal of the General Assembly, 1784,* 316, 319.
59. *PA*, 1:10:357–58.
60. Bouton, *Taming Democracy,* 61–87.
61. Brunhouse, *Counter-Revolution,* 170–71.
62. Ibid.
63. *CR,* 14:272–74.
64. Brunhouse, *Counter-Revolution,* 170–71.
65. Ireland, *Religion, Ethnicity, and Politics,* 160.
66. Brunhouse, *Counter-Revolution,* 170–71.
67. Smith, *Laws of the Commonwealth of Pennsylvania,* 195.
68. Bouton, "A Road Closed."
69. Gallo, "'Fair Play Has Entirely Ceased, and Law Has Taken Its Place,'" 428.
70. *PA*, 3:19:787–93.
71. *Hughes v. Dougherty,* 1791, Smith, *Laws of the Commonwealth of Pennsylvania,* 196.
72. *PA*, 2:3:675–79; Wolf, *Fair Play Settlers,* 83–84.
73. Meginness, *Otzinachson,* 470.
74. Benjamin Walker, RWP, W. 14088; Seneca Nation to the Governor and Council of Pennsylvania, August 12, 1790, Timothy Pickering Papers, vol. 61, no. 2a, Massachusetts Historical Society; Taylor, *The Divided Ground,* 235–37.
75. Meginness, *Otzinachson,* 680–82; *PA*, 1:11:721–22; Taylor, *The Divided Ground,* 235–37.
76. *PA*, 1:11:744–46.
77. *Independent Gazetteer,* September 14, 1782; Meginness, *Otzinachson,* 680–82; *PA*, 1:11:744–46; George Washington to Edmund Randolph, October 3, 1790, Founders Online, NA, https://founders.archives.gov/documents/Washington/05-06-02-0248; Taylor, *The Divided Ground,* 235–37, 245; Timothy Pickering to Washington, December 4, 1790, Founders Online, NA, https://founders.archives.gov/documents/Washington/05-07-02-0014; Benjamin Walker, RWP, W. 14088.

78. Ramsay, *A Dissertation on the Manners of Acquiring the Character and Privileges of a Citizen*, 1. For the struggle to define citizenship during the American Revolution, see Bradburn, *Citizenship Revolution*.
79. Guy Graybill, "Pennsylvania's Main Literary Fraud," *The Express*, July 1, 2023, https://www.lockhaven.com/opinion/letters-to-the-editor/2023/07/pennsylvanias-main-literary-fraud/.
80. "Ambush of Innocents: The Plum Tree Massacre," *Williamsport Sun-Gazette*, May 28, 2016, https://www.sungazette.com/news/top-news/2016/05/ambush-of-innocents-the-plum-tree-massacre/.
81. There is a rich and growing scholarship exploring how memory of the past and memorialization in the United States is a continuation of settler colonialism and its "logic of elimination." See, especially, Smith, *Memory Wars*, 1–42; Smith, "Settler Colonialism and the Revolutionary War"; and Rose, "New World Poetics of Place."

BIBLIOGRAPHY

Manuscripts

American Philosophical Society, Philadelphia

Burd-Shippen Papers
Timothy Horsfield Papers
Shippen Family Papers
Jasper Yeates Papers

British National Archives, Kew, England

American Loyalist Claims
Colonial Office Records

Dauphin County Historical Society, Harrisburg, PA

Elder Collection

Historical Society of Pennsylvania, Philadelphia

Cox-Parrish-Wharton Family Papers
Gratz Collection
Miscellaneous Collection
Northumberland Committee of Safety Minutes
Penn Family Papers
Shippen Family Papers

Massachusetts Historical Society, Boston

Adams Family Papers: An Electronic Archive
Timothy Pickering Papers

National Archives, Washington, DC

Revolutionary War Pension Files

Pennsylvania Historical and Museum Commission, State Archives, Harrisburg

Burd-Shippen Family Papers
Oyer and Terminer Papers, 1768
Records of Pennsylvania's Revolutionary Governments, 1775–1790
Records of the Land Office

Public Archives, Ottawa, Ontario, Canada

Claus Family Papers

Newspapers and Magazines

American Magazine (Philadelphia)
The Express (Lock Haven, PA)
Freeman's Journal (Philadelphia)
Harrisburg Telegraph (Harrisburg, PA)
Independent Gazetteer (Philadelphia)
Independent Ledger (Boston)
Lock Haven Express (Lock Haven, PA)
New York Gazette (New York)
Pennsylvania Evening Post (Philadelphia)
Pennsylvania Gazette (Philadelphia)
Pennsylvania Journal (Philadelphia)
Pennsylvania Packet (Philadelphia)
Rivington's New-York Gazetteer (New York)
United States Magazine (Philadelphia)
Universal Magazine of Knowledge and Pleasure (London)
Williamsport Sun-Gazette (Williamsport, PA)
Der Wöchentliche Pennsylvanische Staatsbote (Philadelphia)

Published Primary Sources

Allen, James. "Diary of James Allen, Esq., of Philadelphia, Counselor-at-Law, 1770–1778." *Pennsylvania Magazine of History and Biography* 9 (1885–86): 2:176–96, 3:278–96, 4:424–41.
American Archives. Edited by Peter Force. Fourth Series, vol. 6. Washington, DC, 1843.
Annals of the American Pulpit. Edited by William B. Sprague. New York, 1858.
Articles of Association in Pennsylvania, for the Defence of American Liberty. Philadelphia, 1775.

The Baptismal Register of Fort Duquesne. Translated and edited by A. A. Lambing. Pittsburgh, 1885.

Blackstone, Sir William. *The Commentaries of Sir William Blackstone, Knight, on the Laws and Constitution of England*. Chicago: American Bar Association, 2009.

Bouquet, Henry. *The Papers of Col. Henry Bouquet*. Edited by Sylvester K. Stevens and Donald H. Kent. Harrisburg: Pennsylvania Historical Commission, 1941.

Burnaby, Andrew. *Travels through the Middle Settlements in North America: In the Years 1759 and 1760. With Observations upon the State of the Colonies*. London, 1775.

Calloway, Colin G. *The World Turned Upside Down*. Boston: Bedford/St. Martin's, 2016.

The Colonial and State Records of North Carolina. Volume 7. Edited by William Laurence Saunders. Raleigh, NC, 1886.

Colonial Records. Edited by Samuel Hazard. 17 vols. Harrisburg, PA, 1851–60.

Correspondence between William Penn and James Logan and Others, 1700–1750. Volume 1. Edited by Edward Armstrong. Philadelphia, 1870.

Croghan, George, and Nicholas B. Wainwright. "George Croghan's Journal, April 3, 1759 to April 30, 1763." *Pennsylvania Magazine of History and Biography* 71, no. 4 (1947): 313–444.

Davies, Samuel. *Religion and Public Spirit: A Valedictory Address to the Senior Class, Delivered in Nassau Hall*. New York, 1761.

———. *A Sermon on Man's Primitive State; and the First Covenant, Delivered before the Reverend Presbytery of New-Castle*. Philadelphia, 1748.

Dickinson, John. "John Dickinson to Congress, April 29, 1783." *Magazine of History with Notes and Queries* 3 (1910): 228–29.

Documents of the American Revolution, 1770–1783. Colonial Office Series. Edited by K. G. Davies. 7 vols. Shannon: Irish University Press, 1972–81.

Documents of the Senate of the State of New York. 35 vols. Albany, NY, 1842–1920.

Documents Relative to the Colonial History of the State of New York. Edited by E. B. O'Callaghan. 15 vols. Albany, NY, 1849–51.

Early American Indian Documents: Treaties and Laws, 1607–1789. 20 vols. Edited by Alden T. Vaughan. Bethesda, MD: University Publications of America, 1979–2003.

Early Western Travels, 1748–1846. Volume 1. Edited by Reuben Gold Thwaites. Cleveland: Arthur H. Clark, 1904.

Evans, Griffith, and Hallock F. Raup. "Notes and Documents: Journal of Griffith Evans, 1784–1785." *Pennsylvania Magazine of History and Biography* 65, no. 2 (1941): 202–33.

Evans, Israel. *A Discourse, Delivered at Easton*. Philadelphia, 1779.

Extracts from the Votes and Proceedings of the Committee of Observation of Lancaster. Lancaster, PA, 1775.

Franklin, Benjamin. *The Papers of Benjamin Franklin*. Edited by Leonard W. Labaree et al. 44 vols. New Haven, CT: Yale University Press, 1959–2023.

Goodlet, John. *A Vindication of the Associate Synod*. Philadelphia, 1767.

Heckewelder, John. *History, Manners, Customs of the Indian Nations Who Once Inhabited Pennsylvania and the Neighbouring States*. Philadelphia, 1876.

Heckewelder, John, and Peter S. Du Ponceau. "Biographical Sketches." *Transactions of the American Philosophical Society* 4 (1834): 351–96.

Historical Collections of the State of Pennsylvania. Edited by Sherman Day. Philadelphia, 1843.

Indian Treaties Printed by Benjamin Franklin, 1736–1762. Edited by Julian P. Boyd. Philadelphia: Historical Society of Pennsylvania, 1938.

Johnson, William. *The Papers of Sir William Johnson*. Edited by James Sullivan. 14 vols. Albany: University of the State of New York, 1921–65.

Johnston, Charles M. *The Valley of the Six Nations: A Collection of Documents on the Indian Lands of the Grand River*. Toronto: University of Toronto Press, 1964.

Journal of the General Assembly, 1784. Philadelphia, 1785.

Journals of the Continental Congress, 1774–1789. Volume 25. Washington, DC: Government Printing Office, 1922.

Journals of the Military Expedition of Major General John Sullivan against the Six Nations of Indians in 1779. Edited by Frederick Cook. Auburn, NY, 1887.

Kenny, James, and John W. Jordan. "Journal of James Kenny, 1761–1763." *Pennsylvania Magazine of History and Biography* 37, no. 2 (1913): 152–201.

Linn, John Blair, ed. *History of Centre and Clinton Counties*. Philadelphia, 1883.

Mackraby, Alexander. "Philadelphia Society before the Revolution: Extracts from Letters of Alexander Mackraby to Sir Philip Francis." *Pennsylvania Magazine of History and Biography* 11 (1887): 3:276–87, 4:491–94.

McCrea, Kenneth D. *Pennsylvania Land Applications*, vol. 2, *New Purchase Applications, 1769–1773*. Harrisburg: Genealogical Society of Pennsylvania, 2003.

Memorials of the Moravian Church. Volume 1. Edited by William C. Reichel. Philadelphia, 1870.

Merrell, James H. *The Lancaster Treaty of 1744 with Related Documents*. Boston: St. Martin's, 2008.

Mittelberger, Gottlieb. *Journey to Pennsylvania in the Year 1750 and Return to Germany in the Year 1754*. Translated and Edited by Carl T. Eben. Philadelphia: John Jos. McVey, 1898.

Montgomery, Joseph. *A Letter, from a Clergyman in Town*. Philadelphia, 1764.

Moraley, William. *The Infortunate: The Voyage and Adventures of William Moraley, Indentured Servant*. Edited by Susan E. Klepp and Billy G. Smith. University Park: Pennsylvania State University Press, 2005.

Navarre, Robert. *Journal of Pontiac's Conspiracy*. Edited by M. Agnes Burton, translated by R. C. Ford. Detroit: Clarence Monroe Burton, 1912.

Papers Relating to the History of the Church in Pennsylvania, 1680–1778. Edited by William Stevens Perry. Privately printed, 1871.

The Parliamentary History of England from the Earliest Period to the Year 1803. Volume 23. Edited by William Cobbett. London, 1814.

The Paxton Papers. Edited by John R. Dunbar. The Hague: Martinus Nijhoff, 1957.

Pennsylvania Archives. Series 1–8. Edited by Samuel Hazard et al. Harrisburg, PA, 1852–1935.

Peters, Richard. "Some Selections from the 'Peters Papers,' in the Library of the Historical Society of Pennsylvania." *Pennsylvania Magazine of History and Biography* 29, no. 4 (1905): 451–66.

Ramsay, David. *A Dissertation on the Manners of Acquiring the Character and Privileges of a Citizen*. Charleston, SC, 1789.

———. *The History of the United States, from Their First Settlement as English Colonies, in 1607, to the Year 1808*. Volume 3. Philadelphia, 1818.

Reed, Joseph. *Life and Correspondence of Joseph Reed*. Edited by William Bradford Reed. 2 vols. Philadelphia, 1847.

The Register of Pennsylvania Devoted to the Preservation of Facts and Documents and Every Other Kind of Useful Information Respective to the State of Pennsylvania. Edited by Samuel Hazard. 12 vols. Philadelphia, 1829–33.

Report of a Treaty with the Western Indians. Edited by Reuben Gold Thwaites. Madison: Wisconsin Historical Society, 1908.

Reports of Cases Ruled and Adjudged in the Courts of Pennsylvania before and since the Revolution. Edited by Alexander J. Dallas. 4 vols. New York, 1882–89.

Rockingham, Marquis. *Memoirs of the Marquis of Rockingham*. Edited by George Thomas, Earl of Albermarle. 2 vols. London, 1851–52.

Sanderson, W. H. "Recollections of His Great Grandfather, Robert Covenhoven, August 29, 1919." *Journal of Lycoming County Historical Society* 5, no. 1 (Spring 1968): 15–18.

Smith, Charles. *Laws of the Commonwealth of Pennsylvania*. Volume 2. Philadelphia, 1810.

Smith, James. *An Account of the Remarkable Occurrences in the Life and Travels of Col. James Smith*. Lexington, KY, 1799.

The Statutes at Large of Pennsylvania from 1682 to 1809. Edited by Robert L. Cable. 18 vols. Harrisburg, PA: Legislative Reference Bureau, 2001.

The Susquehannah Company Papers. Edited by Julian P. Boyd and Robert J. Taylor. 11 vols. Ithaca, NY: Cornell University Press, 1962–71.

Thomson, Charles. *Enquiry into the Causes of the Alienation of the Delaware and Shawanese Indians from the British Interest*. London, 1759.

Washington, George. *The Papers of George Washington Digital Edition*. Charlottesville: University of Virginia Press, Rotunda, 2008.

Washington-Irvine Correspondence: The Official Letters. Edited by C. W. Butterfield. Madison, WI, 1882.

Williams, Elisha. *The Essential Rights and Liberties of Protestants*. Boston, 1744.

Woolman, John. *The Journal and Essays of John Woolman*. Edited by Amelia Mott Gummere. New York: Macmillan, 1922.

Zeisberger, David. "David Zeisberger's History of the Northern American Indians." Edited by Archer Butler Hulbert and William Nathaniel Schwarze. *Ohio Archaeological and Historical Quarterly* 19, no. 1 (1910): 1–189.

Secondary Sources

Anderson, Fred. *Crucible of War: The Seven Years' War and the Fate of Empire in British North America, 1754–1766*. New York: Vintage Books, 2001.

Anderson, Virginia DeJohn. *Creatures of Empire: How Domestic Animals Transformed Early America*. New York: Oxford University Press, 2006.

———. "King Philip's Herds: Indians, Colonists, and the Problem of Livestock in Early New England." *William and Mary Quarterly*, 3rd series, 51, no. 4 (1994): 601–24.

Bell, Whitfield J., Jr. "Samuel Purviance, Jr. (1728?–1788)." In *Patriot-Improvers: Biographical Sketches of Members of the American Philosophical Society*, edited by Charles Greifenstein, 430–40. Philadelphia: American Philosophical Society, 1997.

Blaakman, Michael, A. "Speculation Nation: Land and Mania in the Revolutionary American Republic, 1776–1803." PhD diss., Yale University, 2016.

Bouton, Terry. "A Road Closed: Rural Insurgency in Post-Independence Pennsylvania." *Journal of American History* 87, no. 3 (2000): 855–87.

———. *Taming Democracy: "The People," the Founders, and the Troubled Ending of the American Revolution*. New York: Oxford University Press, 2007.

Bradburn, Douglas. *The Citizenship Revolution: Politics and the Creation of the American Union, 1774–1804*. Charlottesville: University of Virginia Press, 2009.

Broderick, Francis L. "Pulpit, Physics, and Politics: The Curriculum of the College of New Jersey, 1764–1794." *William and Mary Quarterly*, 3rd series, 6, no. 1 (1949): 42–68.

Brooking, Greg. *From Empire to Revolution: Sir James Wright and the Price of Loyalty in Georgia*. Athens: University of Georgia Press, 2024.

Brown, Malcolm B. "'Is It Not Our Land?': An Ethnohistory of the Susquehanna-Ohio Indian Alliance, 1701–1754." PhD diss., Oklahoma State University, 1996.

Brunhouse, Robert L. *The Counter-Revolution in Pennsylvania, 1776–1790*. Harrisburg: Pennsylvania Historical Commission, 1942.

Bullock, Steven C., and Sheila McIntyre. "The Handsome Tokens of a Funeral: Glove-Giving and the Large Funeral in Eighteenth Century New England." *William and Mary Quarterly*, 3rd series, 69, no. 2 (2012): 305–46.

Calloway, Colin G. *The American Revolution in Indian Country: Crisis and Diversity in Native American Communities*. Cambridge: Cambridge University Press, 1995.

———. *The Chiefs Now in This City: Indians and the Urban Frontier in Early America*. New York: Oxford University Press, 2021.

———. *The Indian World of George Washington: The First President, the First Americans, and the Birth of the Nation*. New York: Oxford University Press, 2018.

———. *The Scratch of a Pen: 1763 and the Transformation of North America*. New York: Oxford University Press, 2006.

Campbell, William J. "An Adverse Patron: Land, Trade, and George Croghan." *Pennsylvania History* 76, no. 2 (2009): 117–40.

Campbell, William J. *Speculators in Empire: Iroquoia and the 1768 Treaty of Fort Stanwix*. Norman: University of Oklahoma Press, 2015.

Carter, Susan B., et al. *Historical Statistics of the United States, Earliest Times to the Present: Millennial Edition*. New York: Cambridge University Press, 2006.

Cave, Alfred. "The Delaware Prophet Neolin: A Reappraisal." *Ethnohistory* 46, no. 2 (1999): 265–90.

Cohen, Norman. "William Allen: Chief Justice of Pennsylvania, 1704–1780." PhD diss., University of California, Berkeley, 1966.

Cronon, William. *Changes in the Land: Indians, Colonists, and the Ecology of New England*. New York: Hill and Wang, 2011.

Dowd, Gregory Evans. *A Spirited Resistance: The North American Indian Struggle for Unity, 1745–1815*. Baltimore: Johns Hopkins University Press, 1993.

———. *War under Heaven: Pontiac, the Indian Nations and the British Empire*. Baltimore: Johns Hopkins University Press, 2002.

Edelson, S. Max. *The New Map of Empire: How Britain Imagined America before Independence*. Cambridge, MA: Harvard University Press, 2017.

Fogelman, Aaron Spencer. *Hopeful Journeys: German Immigration, Settlement, and Political Culture in Colonial America, 1717–1775*. Philadelphia: University of Pennsylvania Press, 1996.

Forney, Joyce Manley. *Henry S. Manley (1892–1967): His Life and Writings*. Bloomington, IN: iUniverse, 2010.

Futhey, J. Smith, and Gilbert Cope. *History of Chester County, Pennsylvania, with Genealogical and Biographical Sketches*. Philadelphia, 1881.

Gallo, Marcus. "'Fair Play Has Entirely Ceased, and Law Has Taken Its Place': The Rise and Fall of the Squatter Republic in the West Branch Valley of the Susquehanna River, 1768–1800." *Pennsylvania Magazine of History and Biography* 136, no. 4 (2012): 405–34.

Gerstle, Gary. *Liberty and Coercion: The Paradox of American Government from the Founding to the Present.* Princeton, NJ: Princeton University Press, 2015.

Gordon, Thomas F. *The History of Pennsylvania from Its Discovery by Europeans to the Declaration of Independence in 1776.* Philadelphia, 1829.

Gould, Eliga H. *The Persistence of Empire: British Political Culture in the Age of the American Revolution.* Chapel Hill: University of North Carolina Press, 2000.

Graymont, Barbara. *The Iroquois in the American Revolution.* Syracuse, NY: Syracuse University Press, 1972.

Greene, Jack P. *The Constitutional Origins of the American Revolution.* Cambridge: Cambridge University Press, 2011.

Greer, Allan. *Property and Dispossession: Natives, Empires and Land in Early Modern North America.* Cambridge: Cambridge University Press, 2018.

Griffin, Patrick. *American Leviathan: Empire, Nation, and Revolutionary Frontier.* New York: Hill and Wang, 2007.

———. *The People with No Name: Ireland's Ulster Scots, America's Scots Irish, and the Creation of a British Atlantic World, 1689–1764.* Princeton, NJ: Princeton University Press, 2001.

———. *The Townshend Moment: The Making of Empire and Revolution in the Eighteenth Century.* New Haven, CT: Yale University Press, 2017.

Grimes, Richard S. "The Emergence and Decline of the Delaware Indian Nation in Western Pennsylvania and the Ohio Country, 1730–1795." PhD diss., West Virginia University, 2005.

Grumet, Robert S. *The Munsee Indians: A History.* Norman: University of Oklahoma Press, 2009.

Hämäläinen, Pekka. *Indigenous Continent. The Epic Contest for North America.* New York: Liveright, 2022.

Handlin, Oscar, and Mary Handlin. *Commonwealth: A Study of the Role of Government in the American Economy—Massachusetts, 1774–1861.* Cambridge, MA: Belknap Press of Harvard University Press, 1947.

Harper, Steven C. "Delawares and Pennsylvanians after the Walking Purchase." In *Friends and Enemies in Penn's Woods: Indians, Colonists, and the Racial Construction of Pennsylvania,* edited by William A. Pencak and Daniel K. Richter, 167–79. University Park: Pennsylvania State University Press, 2004.

———. "Making History: Documenting the 1737 Walking Purchase." *Pennsylvania History* 77, no. 2 (2010): 217–33.

Hartz, Louis. *The Liberal Tradition in America: An Interpretation of American Political Thought since the Revolution.* New York: Harcourt, 1955.

Hinderaker, Eric. "Declaring Independence: The Ohio Indians and the Seven Years' War." In *Cultures in Conflict: The Seven Years' War in North America,* edited by Warren R. Hofstra, 105–25. New York: Rowman and Littlefield, 2007.

———. *Elusive Empires: Constructing Colonialism in the Ohio Valley, 1673–1800.* Cambridge: Cambridge University Press, 1997.

Hirsch, Alison Duncan. "The Celebrated Madame Montour: 'Interpretress' across Early American Frontiers." *Explorations in Early American Culture* 3 (2000): 81–112.

Holton, Woody. *Abigail Adams: A Life*. New York: Atria, 2010.
———. *Forced Founders: Indians, Debtors, Slaves, and the Making of the American Revolution in Virginia*. Chapel Hill: University of North Carolina Press, 1999.
Horle, Craig W., et al., eds. *Lawmaking and Legislators in Pennsylvania: A Biographical Dictionary*. 3 vols. Harrisburg: Commonwealth of Pennsylvania House of Representatives, 2005.
Humphrey, Thomas J. "Crowd and Court: Rough Music and Popular Justice in Colonial New York." In *Riot and Revelry in Early America*, edited by William Pencak, Matthew Dennis, and Simon P. Newman, 107–24. University Park: Pennsylvania State University Press, 2002.
Hunter, William A. *Forts on the Pennsylvania Frontier, 1753–1758*. Harrisburg: Pennsylvania Historical and Museum Commission, 1960.
———. "The Upper Susquehanna in the French and Indian War." *The Settler: A Quarterly Magazine of History and Biography* 3 (1955–56): 148–64.
Huston, Charles. *An Essay on the History and Nature of Original Titles to Land in the Province and State of Pennsylvania*. Philadelphia, 1849.
Hutson, James. *Pennsylvania Politics, 1746–1770: The Movement for Royal Government and Its Consequences*. Princeton, NJ: Princeton University Press, 1972.
Ireland, Owen S. *Religion, Ethnicity, and Politics: Ratifying the Constitution in Pennsylvania*. University Park: Pennsylvania State University Press, 1995.
Irvin, Benjamin H. *Clothed in Robes of Sovereignty: The Continental Congress and the People Out of Doors*. Oxford: Oxford University Press, 2011.
Jennings, Francis. *The Ambiguous Iroquois Empire: The Covenant Chain Confederation of Indian Tribes with English Colonies from Its Beginnings to the Lancaster Treaty of 1744*. New York: Norton, 1984.
———. *Empire of Fortune: Crowns, Colonies, and Tribes in the Seven Years War in America*. New York: Norton, 1988.
Jensen, Merrill. "The American People and the American Revolution." *Journal of American History* 157, no. 1 (1970): 5–35.
———. *The Founding of a Nation: A History of the American Revolution, 1763–1776*. Indianapolis, IN: Hackett, 1968.
Jordan, Kurt A. "Incorporation and Colonization: Postcolumbian Iroquois Satellite Communities and Processes of Indigenous Autonomy." *American Anthropologist* 115, no. 1 (2013): 29–43.
Kars, Marjoleine. *Breaking Loose Together: The Regulator Rebellion in Pre-Revolutionary North Carolina*. Chapel Hill: University of North Carolina Press, 2002.
Keith, Charles P. *The Provincial Councilors of Pennsylvania Who Held Office between 1733 and 1776*. Philadelphia, 1883.
Kenny, Kevin. *Peaceable Kingdom Lost: The Paxton Boys and the Destruction of William Penn's Holy Experiment*. New York: Oxford University Press, 2009.
Knouff, Gregory T. *The Soldiers' Revolution: Pennsylvanians in Arms and the Forging of Early American Identity*. University Park: Pennsylvania State University Press, 2004.
Koehler, Rhiannon. "Hostile Nations: Quantifying the Destruction of the Sullivan-Clinton Genocide of 1779." *American Indian Quarterly* 42, no. 4 (2018): 427–53.
Landsman, Ned C. "Religion, Expansion, and Migration: The Cultural Background to Scottish and Irish Settlement in the Lehigh Valley." In *Backcountry Crucibles: The Lehigh Valley*

from Settlement to Steel, edited by Jean R. Soderlund and Catherine S. Parzynski, 104–18. Bethlehem, PA: Lehigh University Press, 2008.

Lemon, James. *The Best Poor Man's Country: A Geographical Study of Early Southeastern Pennsylvania*. New York: Norton, 1972.

Linn, John Blair. "Indian Land and Its Fair-Play Settlers, 1773–1785." *Pennsylvania Magazine of History and Biography* 7, no. 4 (1883): 420–25.

Mancall, Peter C. *Valley of Opportunity: Economic Culture along the Upper Susquehanna, 1700–1800*. Ithaca, NY: Cornell University Press, 1991.

Marietta, Jack D. "The Distribution of Wealth in Eighteenth-Century America: Nine Chester County Tax Lists, 1693–1799." *Pennsylvania History* 62, no. 4 (1995): 532–45.

Marietta, Jack D., and G. S. Rowe. *Troubled Experiment: Crime and Justice in Pennsylvania, 1682–1800*. Philadelphia: University of Pennsylvania Press, 2006.

Marshall, Peter. "Colonial Protest and Imperial Retrenchment: Indian Policy, 1764–1768." *Journal of American Studies* 5, no. 1 (1971): 1–17.

———. "Empire and Opportunity in Britain, 1763–75; The Prothero Lecture." *Transactions of the Royal Historical Society* 56 (1995): 111–28.

Maxey, David W. "The Honorable Proprietaries v. Samuel Wallis: 'A Matter of Great Consequence' in the Province of Pennsylvania." *Pennsylvania History* 70, no. 4 (2003): 361–95.

McConnell, Michael N. *A Country Between: The Upper Ohio Valley and Its Peoples, 1724–1774*. Lincoln: University of Nebraska Press, 1992.

McConville, Brendan. "The Rise of Rough Music: Reflections on an Ancient New Custom in Eighteenth-Century New Jersey." In *Riot and Revelry in Early America*, edited by William Pencak, Matthew Dennis, and Simon P. Newman, 87–106. University Park: Pennsylvania State University Press, 2002.

———. *These Daring Disturbers of the Public Peace: The Struggle for Property and Power in Early New Jersey*. Philadelphia: University of Pennsylvania Press, 2003.

McCusker, John J., and Russell R. Menard. *The Economy of British America, 1607–1789*. Chapel Hill: University of North Carolina Press, 1985.

Meginness, John F. *History of Lycoming County, Pennsylvania*. Chicago, 1892.

———. *Otzinachson; or, A History of the West Branch Valley of the Susquehanna*. Philadelphia, 1857.

Meier, Kathryn Shively. "'Devoted to Hardships, Danger, and Devastation': The Landscape of Indian White Violence in Wyoming Valley, Pennsylvania, 1753–1800." In *Blood in the Hills: A History of Violence in Appalachia*, edited by Bruce E. Stewart, 53–79. Lexington: University of Kentucky Press, 2012.

Merrell, James H. "'I Desire All That I Have Said . . . May Be Taken Down Aright': Revisiting Teedyuscung's 1756 Treaty Council Speeches." *William and Mary Quarterly*, 3rd series, 63, no. 4 (2006): 777–826.

———. *Into the American Woods: Negotiators on the Pennsylvania Frontier*. New York: Norton, 1999.

———. "Shamokin, 'the Very Seat of the Prince of Darkness': Unsettling the Early American Frontier." In *Contact Points: American Frontiers from the Mohawk Valley to the Mississippi, 1750–1830*, edited by Andrew R. L. Cayton and Fredrika J. Teute, 16–59. Chapel Hill: University of North Carolina Press, 1998.

Merritt, Jane T. *At the Crossroads: Indians and Empires on a Mid-Atlantic Frontier, 1700–1763*. Chapel Hill: University of North Carolina Press, 2003.

Mickley, Joseph. *Brief Account of Murders by the Indians, and the Cause Thereof in Northampton County, Pennsylvania*. Philadelphia, 1875.

Middleton, Richard. *Pontiac's War: Its Causes, Course and Consequences*. New York: Routledge, 2007.

Minderhout, David J. *Native Americans in the Susquehanna River Valley, Past and Present*. Lanham, MD: Bucknell University Press, 2013.

Mintz, Max M. *Seeds of Empire: The American Revolutionary Conquest of the Iroquois*. New York: New York University Press, 1999.

Moyer, Paul B. *Wild Yankees: The Struggle for Independence along Pennsylvania's Revolutionary Frontier*. Ithaca, NY: Cornell University Press, 2007.

Munger, Donna Bingham. *Pennsylvania Land Records: A History and Guide for Research*. Wilmington, DE: Scholarly Resources, 1991.

Murphy, Brian Philips. *Building the Empire State: Political Economy in the Early Republic*. Philadelphia: University of Pennsylvania Press, 2015.

Murray, Louise Welles. *A History of Old Tioga Point and Early Athens, Pennsylvania*. Wilkes-Barre, PA: Raeder Press, 1908.

Nash, Gary. "Poverty and Politics in Early American History." In *Down and Out in Early America*, edited by Billy G. Smith, 1–28. University Park: Pennsylvania State University Press, 2004.

———. *Quakers and Politics: Pennsylvania 1681–1726*. Boston: University of New England Press, 1993.

———. "Up from the Bottom in Franklin's Philadelphia." *Past and Present* 77 (1977): 57–83.

Nelson, Brett A. "The Greening of the West Branch." In *Pennsylvania's Pine Creek Valley and Pioneer Families*, edited by Spencer L. Kraybill, 5–100. Baltimore: Gateway Press, 1991.

Newman, Paul Douglas. "The 'Four Nations of Indians upon the Susquehanna': Mid-Atlantic Murder, Diplomacy, and Political Identity, 1717–1723." *Pennsylvania History* 88, no. 3 (2021): 287–318.

Novak, William J., and Steven Pincus. "Revolutionary State Formation: The Origins of the Strong American State." In *State Formations: Global Histories and Cultures of Statehood*, edited by John L. Brooke, Julia C. Strauss, and Greg Anderson, 138–55. Cambridge: Cambridge University Press, 2018.

Obermeyer, Brice. *Delaware Tribe in a Cherokee Nation*. Lincoln: University of Nebraska Press, 2009.

Owens, Robert M. *Red Dreams, White Nightmares: Pan-Indian Alliances in the Anglo-American Mind, 1763–1815*. Norman: University of Oklahoma Press, 2015.

Parkinson, Robert G. *The Common Cause: Creating Race and Nation in the American Revolution*. Chapel Hill: University of North Carolina Press, 2016.

———. *Thirteen Clocks: How Race United the Colonies and Made the Declaration of Independence*. Chapel Hill: University of North Carolina Press, 2021.

Parkman, Francis. *The Conspiracy of Pontiac and the Indian War after the Conquest of Canada*. 2 vols. 1903; reprint Lincoln: University of Nebraska Press, 1994.

Pearl, Christopher R. *Conceived in Crisis: The Revolutionary Creation of an American State*. Charlottesville: University of Virginia Press, 2020.

———. "'Our God, and Our Guns': Religion and Politics on the Revolutionary Frontier." *Pennsylvania History* 85, no. 1 (2018): 58–89.

———. "Pulpits of Revolution: Presbyterian Political Thought in the Era of the American Revolution." *Journal of Presbyterian History* 95, no. 1 (2017): 4–17.

———. "Such a Spirit of Innovation: The American Revolution and the Creation of States." In *From Independence to the U.S. Constitution: Reconsidering the Critical Period of American History*, edited by Douglas Bradburn and Christopher R. Pearl, 152–92. Charlottesville: University of Virginia Press, 2022.

Preston, David L. *The Texture of Contact: European and Indian Settler Communities on the Frontiers of Iroquoia, 1667–1783*. Lincoln: University of Nebraska Press, 2009.

Richter, Daniel K. *Facing East from Indian Country: A Native History of Early America*. Cambridge, MA: Harvard University Press, 2003.

———. "His Own, Their Own: Settler Colonialism, Native Peoples, and Imperial Balances of Power in Eastern North America, 1660–1715." in *The World of Colonial America: An Atlantic Handbook*, edited by Ignacio Gallup-Diaz, 209–34. New York: Routledge, 2017.

———. "Native Americans, the Plan of 1764, and a British Empire That Never Was." In *Cultures and Identities in Colonial British America*, edited by Robert Olwell and Alan Tully, 269–92. Baltimore: Johns Hopkins University Press, 2006.

———. "Onas, the Long Knife: Pennsylvanians and Indians after Independence." In *Trade, Land, Power: The Struggle for Eastern North America*, edited by Daniel K. Richter, 202–26. Philadelphia: University of Pennsylvania Press, 2013.

———. *Ordeal of the Longhouse: The Peoples of the Iroquois League in the Era of European Colonization*. Chapel Hill: University of North Carolina Press, 1992.

———. *Trade, Land, Power: The Struggle for Eastern North America*. Philadelphia: University of Pennsylvania Press, 2013.

———. "War and Culture: The Iroquois Experience." *William and Mary Quarterly*, 3rd series, 40, no. 4 (1983): 528–59.

Ries, Linda. "'The Rage of Opposing Government': The Stump Affair of 1768." *Cumberland County History* 1, no. 1 (1984): 21–45.

Rose, Deborah Bird. "New World Poetics of Place along the Oregon Trail and in the National Museum of Australia." In *Rethinking Settler Colonialism: History and Memory in Australia, Canada, Aotearoa New Zealand and South Africa*, edited by Annie E. Coombes, 228–44. Manchester, UK: Manchester University Press, 2006.

Rowe, G. S. "The Frederick Stump Affair, 1768, and Its Challenge to Legal Historians of Early Pennsylvania." *Pennsylvania History* 49, no. 4 (1982): 259–88.

Ruddiman, John A. *Becoming Men of Some Consequence: Youth and Military Service in the Revolutionary War*. Charlottesville: University of Virginia Press, 2014.

Russell, Hellen H. "The Big Runaway of 1778." *Now and Then* 16, no. 7 (1970): 357–63.

Ryerson, Richard Alan. *The Revolution Is Now Begun: The Radical Committees of Philadelphia, 1765–1776*. Philadelphia: University of Pennsylvania Press, 1978.

Sadosky, Leonard J. *Revolutionary Negotiations: Indians, Empires, and Diplomats in the Founding of America*. Charlottesville: University of Virginia Press, 2009.

Schutt, Amy C. *Peoples of the River Valleys: The Odyssey of the Delaware*. Philadelphia: University of Pennsylvania Press, 2007.

Schwartz, Sally. *"Mixed Multitude": The Struggle for Toleration in Colonial Pennsylvania*. New York: New York University Press, 1987.

Shannon, Timothy J. *Indians and Colonists at the Crossroads of Empire: The Albany Congress of 1754*. Ithaca, NY: Cornell University Press, 2009.

———. *Iroquois Diplomacy on the Early American Frontier*. New York: Viking, 2008.

Shirai, Yoko. "The Indian Trade in Colonial Pennsylvania, 1730–1768: Traders and Land Speculation." PhD diss., University of Pennsylvania, 1985.

Silver, Peter. *Our Savage Neighbors: How Indian War Transformed Early America*. New York: Norton, 2008.

Simler, Lucy. "The Landless Worker: An Index of Economic and Social Change in Chester County, Pennsylvania, 1750–1820." *Pennsylvania Magazine of History and Biography* 114, no. 2 (1990): 163–99.

———. "Tenancy in Colonial Pennsylvania: The Case of Chester County." *William and Mary Quarterly*, 3rd series, 43, no. 4 (1986): 542–69.

Sipe, C. Hale. *The Indian Wars of Pennsylvania*. Harrisburg, PA: Telegraph Press, 1929.

Smith, Abbott Emerson. *Colonists in Bondage: White Servitude and Convict Labor in America, 1607–1776*. Chapel Hill: University of North Carolina Press, 1947.

Smith, A. Lynn. *Memory Wars: Settlers and Natives Remember Washington's Sullivan Expedition of 1779*. Lincoln: University of Nebraska Press, 2023.

Smith, Andrea Lynn. "Settler Colonialism and the Revolutionary War: New York's 1929 'Pageant of Decision.'" *Public Historian* 41, no. 4 (2019): 7–35.

Smith, Billy G. "Best Poor Man's Country?" In *Down and Out in Early America*, edited by Billy G. Smith, xi–xix. University Park: Pennsylvania State University Press, 2004.

Snyder, Charles Fisher. "The Militia of Northumberland County during the Revolution." *Northumberland County Historical Society* 18 (1948): 48–85.

Spero, Patrick. *Frontier Country: The Politics of War in Early Pennsylvania*. Philadelphia: University of Pennsylvania Press, 2016.

———. *Frontier Rebels: The Fight for Independence in the American West, 1765–1776*. New York: Norton, 2018.

Starna, William A. "The Diplomatic Career of Canasatego." In *Friends and Enemies in Penn's Woods: Indians, Colonists, and the Racial Construction of Pennsylvania*, edited by William A. Pencak and Daniel K. Richter, 144–66. University Park: Pennsylvania State University Press, 2004.

———. "Retrospecting the Origins of the League of Iroquois." *Proceedings of the American Philosophical Society* 152, no. 3 (2008): 279–321.

Taylor, Alan. *American Revolutions: A Continental History, 1750–1804*. New York: Norton, 2016.

———. *The Divided Ground: Indians, Settlers, and the Northern Borderland of the American Revolution*. New York: Knopf, 2006.

Trask, Roger R. "Pennsylvania and the Albany Congress, 1754." *Pennsylvania History* 27, no. 3 (1960): 273–90.

Vest, Jay Hansford. "An Odyssey among the Iroquois: A History of Tutelo Relations in New York." *American Indian Quarterly* 29, nos. 1–2 (2005): 124–55.

Waddell, Louis M. "Thomas and Richard Penn Return Albany Purchase Land to the Six Nations: The Power of Attorney of November 7, 1757." *Pennsylvania History* 72, no. 2 (2005): 229–40.

Wallace, Anthony F. C. *King of the Delawares: Teedyuscung, 1700–1763*. Syracuse, NY: Syracuse University Press, 1990.

Wallace, Paul A. *Conrad Weiser, 1696–1760: Friend of Colonist and Mohawk*. Philadelphia: University of Pennsylvania Press, 1945.

———. "Conrad Weiser and the Delawares." *Pennsylvania History* 4, no. 3 (1937): 139–52.
———. *Indians in Pennsylvania*. Harrisburg: Pennsylvania Historical and Museum Commission, 1961.
Webb, Stephen Saunders. "The Peaceable Kingdom: Quaker Pennsylvania in the Stuart Empire." In *The World of William Penn,* edited by Richard S. Dunn and Mary Maples Dunn, 173–94. Philadelphia: University of Pennsylvania Press, 1986.
Weslager, C. A. "Delaware Indian Name Giving and Modern Practice." In *A Delaware Indian Symposium,* edited by Herbert C. Kraft, 135–45. Harrisburg: Pennsylvania Historical and Museum Commission, 1974.
———. *The Delaware Indians: A History*. New Brunswick, NJ: Rutgers University Press, 1972.
White, Richard. "'Although I Am Dead, I Am Not Entirely Dead. I Have Left a Second of Myself': Constructing Self and Persons on the Middle Ground of Early America." In *Through a Glass Darkly: Reflections on Personal Identity in Early America,* edited by Ronald Hoffman, Mechal Sobel, and Fredrika J. Teute, 404–18. Chapel Hill: University of North Carolina Press, 1997.
———. *The Middle Ground: Indians, Empires, and Republics in Great Lakes Region, 1650–1815*. Cambridge: Cambridge University Press, 1991.
Wolf, George D. *Fair Play Settlers of the West Branch Valley, 1769–1784: A Study of Frontier Ethnography*. Harrisburg: Pennsylvania Historical and Museum Commission, 1969.
Wolfe, Patrick. "Settler Colonialism and the Elimination of the Native." *Journal of Genocide Research* 8, no. 4 (2006): 387–409.
———. *Settler Colonialism and the Transformation of Anthropology: The Politics and Poetics of an Ethnographic Event*. London: Cassell, 1999.

INDEX

Italicized page numbers refer to illustrations.

Adams, Abigail, 266
Adams, John, 1, 223, 224
Adams, Samuel, 170
Albany Congress (1754), 61–65, 81, 97
Alison, Francis, 179
Allen, Andrew, 179
Allen, Anne, 24
Allen, George, 108
Allen, John, 148, 179
Allen, William: basic facts about, 23–24, 25, 149; on ferocity of Seven Years' War, 75; and Fort Stanwix conference (1768), 148; land acquisitions and loyalty to Penn family of, 24–25; and land sold at Albany Congress, 64, 65; and Lehigh River Valley land, 52, 53, 57; on Massachusetts Circular Letter, 170
American Magazine, 31–33
Amherst, Jefferey, 85–86, 91, 99, 128–29
Antes, Henry, 219, 222, 233
Armstrong, John, 109, 238–39
Aroas, 70
Arthur, Robert, 201
Articles of Confederation, 256
Asquash, Jacob, 204, 205
Aubrey, Laetitia Penn, 24

Bailey, Francis, 250
Bald Eagle, 13, 218, 236
Barrington, Lord, 131, 132
Baynton, John, 135, 138
Beaver Wars, 13
Belt of Wampum (Kaghswaghtaniunt), 86–87
Beyerly, Jacob, 65
"Black Boys," 135
Board of Trade: boundary separating Native Americans and colonists, 140, 144, 164; and Grand Ohio Company, 172; and Johnson, 128, 130, 131, 132; and proclamation line of George III, 128, 130, 131, 132; responsibilities of, 128
Bouquet, Henry, 105–6
Boyd, John, 198–99
Braddock, Edward, 67, 71
Bradford, Andrew, 31–33
Brant, Joseph: basic facts about, 226; at Fort Stanwix conference (1784), 257–58; move to Canada of, 262; post–Revolutionary War supporters of, 260; and Revolutionary War, 227, 248
Brant, Molly, 226. *See also* Konwatsitsiaienni

{325}

Britain: and 1768 Fort Stanwix treaty and sovereignty of Haudenosaunee, 165; Coercive Acts, 206, 208; colonial resistance to, 170, 206–13, 214–15, 302n76; King George's War, 20; land ceded by, in 1783 Treaty of Paris, 253–55; mid-1760s rebellions in Empire, 135; Native Americans at war with, 103; peace with Native American nations, 84; and post–Revolutionary War disunity among states, 256; Quartering Act, 169; Quebec Act, 206, 208; relationship with Delaware, 66; relationship with Haudenosaunee, 20–21, 259; Stamp Act, 139; taxation in colonies, 139, 140. *See also* Revolutionary War; Seven Years' War
Brodhead, Charles, 69–70, 73
Brodhead, Daniel, 245
Bryan, George, 239
Burd, James: basic facts about, 23; on behavior of Native Americans at Fort Augusta, 93; and Connecticut settlers, 102; meeting with Susquehanna Nations chiefs at Fort Augusta, 91–92; and "New Purchase" land, 180; and Susquehanna Nations' peace with colonial government, 102–3, 104–5
Burgoyne, John, 222, 223
Butler, John, 231, 232
Butler, Richard, 258
Butler, Zebulon, 184–85, 231, 237, 242

Campbell, William, 222
Canada, 262, 264
Canassatego: assassination of, 60; basic facts about, 41; and colonial government's recognition of Haudenosaunee sovereignty, 41–42; on Delaware as tributary nation of Haudenosaunee, 56; land sale to proprietors by, 42, 43, 46–47, 50, 61, 81; and "Walking Purchase," 56

Canyase, 59
Captain Amos, 84
Captain Bull: attack on Connecticut settlers near Wyoming, 113, 115, 117, 118–19; basic facts about, 109–10, 150; capture of, 113; and Connecticut settlers, 101, 102; at Easton conferences, 110, 111; peace between Native Americans and Britain, 84; and peace with colonial government, 103; and Pontiac's War, 109, 111–12
Captain Harris, 51, 53
Captain John, 51
Captain Peter, 57, 110
Captain Pipe, 227, 228
Carlisle, Earl of, 232
Carson, James, 205
Cayuga: and boundary between Native Americans and colonists, 164; guardians of routes to Onondaga, 13; post–Revolutionary War, 261–62; and Revolutionary War, 225, 226, 228, 231; and settlements beyond 1768 Fort Stanwix boundary line, 188–90
Chambers, James, 199
Champion, Bill, 152
Cherokee: and boundary between Native Americans and colonists, 133, 164; Nanticoke belief, aided colonial expansion, 127; and Seven Years' War, 76
Chickasaw, 70
Chillaway, Job, 102, 221
Chippewa, 228
Circular Letter (Massachusetts), 170
Clapham, William, map of march, *14*
Clark, Francis, 188, 203–4
Clinton, George, 255, 256, 257, 261
Clinton, James, 243–45
Coercive Acts (1774), 206, 208
Colden, Cadwallader, 120

colonists: ability of, to register land claims, 175–76; and boundary separating Native Americans from, 115–17, 118, 121–23, 125–27, 130–31, 132–35, 137–38, 140, 141–42, 143, 144–47, 148, 159–68, 162, 166, 167, 168; and destruction during Pontiac's War, 115; diversity of, 10; government control over actions against Native Americans, 187–88; and hunting by Native Americans, 154; land as priority of, 7–8; Neolin's message and removal of, 123; removal of Native Americans as goal of American Revolution, 8–9, 280n16; rural nature of, 8; and settlements beyond 1768 Fort Stanwix treaty boundary line, 180–82, 183–86; taxation by British of, 139, 140. *See also* squatters/squatting
community: and Fair Play republic governance, 211, 272; and hunting, 90; as integral part of settling land, 198–200; patriarchy and values of, 204–5
Connecticut: and boundary between Native Americans and colonists, 142; and competition among colonies, 67; Congress and claims of, in Northern Susquehanna River Valley, 257; and Fort Stanwix conference (1768), 162–63; Haudenosaunee and claim by, 186–87; land desired by, 61, 62; and "New Purchase" land, 183–85; royal charter for, 96; settlers from, after 1768 Fort Stanwix treaty, 173; —, in Northern Susquehanna River Valley, 97–100, 101–2, 110, 113–14, 115, 117; —, and proclamation line of George III, 131
Conoquieson, 188
Conoy: delegation to colonial government (1749), 19, 20; dispersal of, from Northern Susquehanna River Valley before Revolutionary War, 218; displaced to Northern Susquehanna River Valley, 12,

36; and Fair Play republic, 205; and land sold at Albany Congress, 63; in Maryland, 151; relationship with Delaware, 55; and Revolutionary War, 246; and settlements beyond 1768 Fort Stanwix treaty boundary line, 188–89; and squatters, 38; as tributary of Haudenosaunee, 15, 36; warrior population of, after Pontiac's War, 150
Continental Congress, 206–13
Cook, John, 153
Cooke, William, 190
Cornplanter, 231, 260, 261
Cornwallis, Lord, 246
Coshaughaways, 102
Couc, Isabelle or Elizabeth, 44–45. *See also* Madam Montour; Ostonwackin
"Covenant Chain," 35–36
Covenhoven, Mercy, 233
Covenhoven, Robert, 220, 233–34, 237, 242
Cox, John, 182
Croghan, George: basic facts about, 103–4, 125; and boundary between Native Americans and colonists, 125–26, 135, 137–38, 164; census of Native Americans in Northern Susquehanna River Valley by, 150; on government's inability to control colonists, 187–88; and Grand Ohio Company, 172; and "New Purchase" land, 179; preparations for Fort Stanwix conference (1768), 154–55; refusal to discuss land ceded by France, 103–4

Declaration of Independence, 1, 7, 251
Deganawidah, 21
Delaware: delegation to colonial government (1749), 20; dispersal of, from Northern Susquehanna River Valley before Revolutionary War, 217, 218; displaced to Northern Susquehanna

Delaware (*continued*)
  River Valley, 12–13, 25, 36, 66; and Fair Play republic, 205; and Fort Stanwix conference and treaty (1768), 142–43, 163–66; land granted to proprietors in 1749 treaty, 16; and land sale by Canassatego to proprietors, 50; and land sold at Albany Congress, 63; land speculators' acquisition of land of, 24; leadership, 51; and Lehigh Valley land, 52, 53–54; Morris's declaration of war on, 75–76; in New Jersey, 151; as Ohio Nation, 48; problems resulting from squatters, 38; relationship with British, 66; relationship with Haudenosaunee, 54, 56; and Revolutionary War, 227, 228, 245, 246, 247; and settlements beyond 1768 Fort Stanwix boundary line, 188–89; and Seven Years' War, 69, 70; as tributary of Haudenosaunee, 15, 36, 56; warrior population of, after Pontiac's War, 150
Denny, William, 84–85
Der Wöchentliche Pennsylvanische Staatsbote, 223, 224
Deserontyon, 260, 262
DeWitt, Abraham, 199
Dickinson, John, 154, 269–70
Dodge, Jonathan, 111–12
Dougherty, Henry, 199, 202
Doyle, Samuel, 272, 274
Drinker, Henry, 182
Duane, James, 255
Dunmore, Lord, 185
Dunn family, 197–98, 220
Dyer, Eliphalet, 100

Easton conferences (1756–1758), 77, 78–81, 82–83, 110, 111, 151
Elder, John, 113, 120–21

elite white men: and colonial rights, 173; competition for land immediately after Seven Years' War, 125; Continental Congress and displays of monarchical culture by, 209; and Fort Stanwix conference (1768), 148–49, 178, 179–80, 182; as oligarchy, 212; squatters' declaration of independence and power of, 7. *See also* land speculators; proprietors
equality, defining, 6, 7
Esopus, 12, 15
Evans, Griffith, 266–67
Evans, Israel, 244–45
Evans, Lewis, 166, *166*

Fair Play republic, 211, 272; claims to land in, 203, 214; and Continental Congress's resistance efforts, 209–13; establishment of, 193; fear of Native Americans, 204, 205; foundational fiction of, 276; governance of, 193, 200–204, 211, 272; independence as understood in, 8, 9–10, 251, 252, 264–65; independence declared by, 2–5, *4–5*, 7, 213–15; integration into Pennsylvania of, 16, 271–72; land ownership in, 200–201, 202, 203; as part of 1768 purchase, 268; and Pennsylvania state constitution, 214; post–Revolutionary War fear of land speculators, 251–52; post–Revolutionary War settlement of land conflicts in, 272; punishment in, 203–4; recognition of land claims by 1790s Pennsylvania government, 270–71; and Revolutionary War, conquest/eradication of Native Americans, 250–51; —, evacuation of, 233–34, 250; —, forts constructed by, 221, 228, 229–30, 233, 238; —, mobilization, 219–21, 222, 242–45; —, Native American attacks, 221–22, 229–30; rights granted to veterans of

Revolutionary War, 16–17; sovereignty of, 200; and Susquehanna Nations, 203–4, 205
Ferguson, Thomas, 198, 199
Fish Carrier, 231
Fithian, Philip Vickers, 192, 194–95, 215–16
Fort Augusta, *87, 89;* and boundary between Native Americans and colonists, 134; construction of, 86–88; Fair Play refugees at, 250; Haudenosaunee demanding evacuation of soldiers from, 94–95; Native American populations in area of, 90–91; Native Americans' misgivings about, 91–92; and Pontiac's War, 111; and proclamation line of George III, 136; and Revolutionary War, 222, 233–36; squatters around, 131; and Susquehanna Nations, 93–94, 104, 105, 154; as trade hub, 88–90, 91–93, 95
Fort Stanwix conference and treaty (1768): attendees, 141, 155–56; boundary line between Native Americans and colonists drawn at, 159–68, *162, 166, 167, 168;* complaints of Native Americans prior to, 154–55; foreign interference in, 143; Fort Pitt meeting prior to, 154–55; and Haudenosaunee, 157–58, 159–60, 165, 186; and Hillsborough, 144; Johnson at, 158; land gained by Thomas Penn, 171–72, 173–74; land speculators at, 148–49; Native Americans' threatened boycott of, 142–43; opening ceremonies, 156–58; preparations for, 141–42, 143, 154–55; settlements after, 171–75, 176–82, *178,* 183–86, 188–91, 192, 197, 298n48
Fort Stanwix conference and treaty (1784), 255–62, 266–68
France: cession of Native land by, 103–4; and control of Ohio Valley, 47; and Fort Stanwix conference (1768), 143, 155; Haudenosaunee as bulwark for British against, 20–21; imperial designs in North America of, 21, 61, 62; and post–Revolutionary War disunity among states, 256; as protector of Haudenosaunee tributary nations, 40. *See also* Seven Years' War
Francis, Turbutt, 137, 145, 148, 173–74, 177–78, 179
Franklin, Benjamin, 61–63, 125, 143, 172
Franklin, William, 147, 156, 158, 172
Freeman's Journal, 250
French and Indian War. *See* Seven Years' War
Friendly Association, 79, 92, 93
fur trade, 34–35, 91

Gage, Thomas: evacuation of British forts by, 136–37; and Johnson, 131; and peace with Native Americans, 129; and retribution against Mingo and northern Seneca, 129, 130
Galloway, Joseph: and boundary separating Native Americans from colonists, 116–17, 126, 145, 147; and Continental Congress, 206–7, 208; and Massachusetts Circular Letter, 172; and "New Purchase" land, 182
George III, 127–28, 143. *See also* Royal Proclamation of 1763
Germain, Lord George, 223
Germany, immigrants from, 27, 28
Gideon, 57. *See also* Honest John; Tattenhick; Teedyuscung
Girty, Simon, 45
Gnaddenhutten massacre, 247
Goodlet, John, 196
Grand Council of Chiefs at Onondaga: Fire That Never Dies, 13; and Hamilton's removal of squatters, 44; and land sold at Albany Congress, 63; limits to power of, 59–60; and Ohio Nations, 49; and Seven Years' War, 72

Grand Ohio Company, 125, 172–73
Great Island: abandonment of, 221; British attack on, during Pontiac's War, 109, 111; location of, 13; and proclamation line of George III, 136; Susquehanna move from, 101
"Great Treaty" (1736), 55–56, 62, 81
Great Tree, 243
Grenville, George, 138–39
Griffy, Jonas, 153

Haldimand, Frederick, 247–48, 264
"Half-Kings," 49
Hamilton, James: attempt to purchase land west of Susquehanna River, 39–40, 42; basic facts about, 25; and conferences with Haudenosaunee (1749), 21–22, 38–39, 40–43, 47; and conflicting interests of Haudenosaunee and their tributaries, 38–39; and Connecticut settlers, 102, 110; and Fort Augusta, 94, 95–96; and "New Purchase" land, 176; and Pontiac's War, 106; and squatters, 25, 39, 44; and Teedyuscung, 98, 99
Hamilton, John, 216, 229
Hamilton, Robert, 216
Hancock, John, 1
Hartley, Thomas, 235–37, 238, 239–43, 262
Haudenosaunee: and boundary separating Native Americans and colonists, 132–35, 141–42, 144, 145, 147, 160, 161, 163; as bulwark for British against French, 20–21; claim to Lehigh Valley, 56; claim to Northern Susquehanna River Valley, 13; conflicting interests with tributary nations, 38–39; and Congress, 258; and Connecticut's claim, 186–87; and Connecticut settlers in Northern Susquehanna River Valley, 98–99, 100; control of road to Philadelphia by, 34; and Delaware, 54, 56; delegations to colonial government (1749), 19, 38–39, 40–43, 47; at Easton conferences, 77, 78; at end of Revolutionary War, 249–50; evacuation of soldiers from Fort Augusta demanded by, 94–95; and Fair Play republic, 205; and Fort Stanwix conference and treaty (1768), 157–58, 159–60, 165, 186; and Fort Stanwix conference and treaty (1784), 256–62, 267–68; granting of council fires, 99, 100; and Johnson, 129–30, 131; and King George's War, 20, 21; and land ceded by Britain in 1783 Treaty of Paris, 253–54; Logan's courting of, 55; membership in, 35; Nanticoke belief, aided colonial expansion, 127; need to maintain peaceful relationship with Pennsylvania, 40; and John Penn, 187; post–Revolutionary War treatment of, 255; power of, 12, 43; —, and displacement of tributary nations, 59; —, and Gage's approach to peace, 129; —, and proclamation line of George III, 128; —, and removal of squatters, 20, 21; —, and sale of land, 39–40, 43; —, and Seven Years' War, 93; —, post–Revolutionary War, 259–60; and repopulation of Northern Susquehanna River Valley, 151–52; and Revolutionary War, 218–19, 225–32, 236, 243–44, 245–46, 247; sale of land to Thomas Penn at Albany Congress, 61, 62–65, 97; and settlements beyond 1768 Fort Stanwix boundary line, 188–90; sovereignty of, Canassatego and colonial government's recognition of, 41–42; —, colonial government recognition of, 39, 55; —, as dependents of New York state, 256; —, expansion of, 35–36; —, and Fort Stanwix conference (1784), 259; —, and Fort Stanwix treaty (1768), 165; —, and "Great Treaty," 81; —, post–Revolutionary

War, 255, 256–57, 258–59; —, and Susquehanna Nations' perpetual land ownership, 81; and Susquehanna Nations, 74–75, 94; and Teedyuscung, 58; treatment of Teedyuscung by, 94

Haudenosaunee tributary nations: and Canassatego's sale of land east of Susquehanna River, 42; conflicting interests with Haudenosaunee, 38–39; and dealing with British, 26; France as protector of, 40; Indigenous Christians as, 119; and land sold at Albany Congress, 63; nations, 15, 36, 93; Ohio Nations entreaties to, 47–48; power of Haudenosaunee and displacement of, 59; status of Delaware as, 56; and Susquehanna Nations' perpetual ownership of land, 81; treatment of, 36. *See also* Grand Council of Chiefs at Onondaga; Susquehanna Nations; *and specific nations*

Hendrick, 63, 81
Henry, Patrick, 125, 171
Henry, Thomas, 203
Hiawatha, 21
Hill, Aaron, 259, 260, 268
Hill, Henry, 220, 222, 237, 240–41
Hills, Wills, 143. *See also* Hillsborough, Lord
Hillsborough, Lord: and boundary separating Native Americans and colonists, 144, 164, 165, 171–72; and Grand Ohio Company, 172; and Massachusetts Circular Letter, 170; resignation of, 173; responsibilities of, 143
"Hillsborough paint," 171
Holland, Nathaniel, 93
Honest John: basic facts about, 51, 57, 58; and Nutimus, 52; relocation of, from Lehigh Valley, 57; and "Walking Purchase," 54, 56. *See also* Gideon; Tattenhick; Teedyuscung

Horsfield, Timothy, 111, 284n22
Hughes, James, 201
Hughes, John, 147, 202
Hunter, Robert, 44
Hunter, Samuel, 220–22, 230, 233, 234, 239
hunting: and boundary separating Native Americans and colonists, 161; and colonists, 154; as community effort, 90; fur trade, 34–35; and Juniata River settlements, 19–20; and land cultivation, 33–34; seasonal grounds for, 33; and squatters, 37–38
Huron, 217
Hurst & Company, 185

Illinois-Wabash Company, 125
independence: Fair Play republic declaration of, 2–5, 4, 5, 7, 213–15; Fair Play republic's understanding of, 8, 9–10, 251, 252, 264–65; and frontiers as stated in Declaration of Independence, 251; Haudenosaunee assertion of, at Fort Stanwix conference (1784), 259; of Haudenosaunee tributary nations, 36–37; and Native Americans fighting on British side, 228; and Paine, 212; and Pennsylvania colonial government, 212, 213–14; Philadelphia as synonymous with, 1–2; squatters support for, as essential for legal land ownership, 237–38
Independence Day (July 4), 1
Indiana Company, 125, 126
Indigenous Christians: and Bull's raids, 118–19; displaced to Northern Susquehanna River Valley, 12, 15; as Haudenosaunee tributary nation, 119; and Paxton Boys, 119–20; John Penn and protection of, 119–20; and Revolutionary War, 246–47
Ironcutter, John, 152, 153, 154, 187

Irvine, James, 92, 106, 111, 248
Irwin, Alexander, 197, 199–200

Jackson, Anna, 213, 229–30, 234
Jackson, John, 199
Jacob, Johann, 109–10. *See also* Captain Bull
James, Abel, 182
Jefferson, Thomas, 125, 171
Jersey Shore, Pennsylvania declaration of independence, 2–5, *4*, *5*, *7*
Johnson, Guy, 144, 225
Johnson, Sir William: and Board of Trade reorganization, 128, 130, 131, 132; and boundary separating Native Americans and colonists, 132–35, 137–38, 140, 141–42, 159–60, 161–63, *162*, 164–65; census of populations of Native Americans in Northern Susquehanna River Valley, 90; and Connecticut settlers in Northern Susquehanna River Valley, 99–100; death of, 225; and death of Teedyuscung, 101; and Fort Stanwix conference (1768), boundary drawn, 159–65; —, opening ceremonies, 156–58; —, and peace with Native Americans, 129; —, and Thomas Penn, 147; —, preparations by, 141–42, 143; —, and proclamation line of George III, 128, 131; —, relationship with Haudenosaunee, 129–30, 131; on government's inability to control colonists, 187; and Grand Ohio Company, 172; health of, 141; and Hillsborough, 143–44; on importance of British forts, 136–37; on independence of Susquehanna Nations, 74; land given to, by Mohawk, 134, 147; on Native American alliance with French, 70–71; on Native Americans' view of selves as independent, 9
Juniata River settlements, 19–20, 27, 44, 46, 60, 71, 131

Kaghswaghtaniunt, 86–87
Kanaghragait, 153
Kanak't, 150
Kanigut, 150
Kemplen, Thomas, 201
Kiashuta, 105
Killbuck, John, Jr., 227
Kincaid, John, 195, 199, 204
Kinderuntie, 96
King, Thomas, 94–95, 98–99, 123
King, William, 199
King Beaver, 98
King George's War, 20, 21
kinship terms, use of, 54–55, 56, 75, 80, 132–33
Konwatsitsiaienni, 129–30, 226

Lackawacka, 13
land: as ancient possession of Native Americans, 9; boundary separating Native Americans and colonists, 115–17, 118, 121–23, 125–27, 130–31, 132–35, 137–38, 140, 141–42, 143, 144–47, 148, 159–68, *162*, *166*, *167*, *168*; categories of, 30; ceded by Britain in Treaty of Paris (1783), 253–55; community as integral part of settling, 200; competition for, after Seven Years' War, 124–25; and declarations of independence, 213, 214; Delaware, granted to proprietors in 1749 treaty, 16; desired by France and other colonies, 61, 62; as driving force of immigration, 27, 28; French cession of Native, 103; Haudenosaunee power and sale of, 39–40, 43; measuring, 53; Native American use of, and Eurocentric understanding of use, 30, 31, 32–34; Ohio Nations and sales of, to colonial government, 49; and overhunting, 35; ownership, American independence as essential for squatters' claims, 237–38; —, as decided by settling, 97; —,

defining, 30–32; —, in Fair Play republic, 200–201, 202, 203; —, and positions in colonial government, 202; as payment to Revolutionary War Pennsylvania soldiers, 16–17, 253–54, 265; Thomas Penn and, "reserved" for Susquehanna Nations, 81–82; Penn family's dispensing of, 23; Thomas Penn purchase of, at Albany Congress, 61, 62–65, 81, 97; Thomas Penn's need for, 22–23; and Pennsylvania state constitution, 214, 251; and Pennsylvania state government politics in 1790s, 268, 270; as priority of colonists, 7–8; proclamation line of George III, 127–28, 130–32; purchases from Native Americans in Pennsylvania, 48; and Quebec Act, 206, 208; and Revolutionary War as war of conquest, 245–48; royal patents for, 31; sale by Canassatego to proprietors, 42, 43, 46–47, 50, 61, 81; sale by Pennsylvania after Revolutionary War, 267; sales by unauthorized Native Americans, 52; settlements after 1768 Fort Stanwix treaty, 171–75, 176–82, 178, 183–86, 188–91, 192, 197, 298n48; squatters as deserving, 8; squatters' claim to, 7, 65, 203, 214; squatters' view of uncultivated, 29–30, 32; strains in access to, 26–27; subject to taxation, 30; Susquehanna Nations' perpetual ownership of, 81–83; transferred in 1763 Treaty of Paris, 103–4; West Branch of Susquehanna River as last bastion of Native, in Susquehanna River Valley, 9–10. *See also* Fort Stanwix conference and treaty (1768); West Branch of Susquehanna River

"land jobbing," 22, 251, 266. *See also* land speculators

land speculators: and boundary separating Native Americans and colonists, 125–27, 138, 144–45, 147; and colonial government's system of land registration, 175–76; in Fair Play republic after Revolutionary War, 251–52; formation of Grand Ohio Company by, 172; and Fort Stanwix conference and treaty (1768), 148–49, 172; and land sold at Albany Congress, 64; and "New Purchase," 192; Ohio Company, 125, 126, 171–72; and Penn family, 22–23, 56; and Physick, 174; and price of land, 38; proclamation line of George III, 130, 131; proprietors and success of, 22–25; purchases from unauthorized Native Americans by, 52; and recognition of Fair Play republic land claims, 4, 271; relationships with proprietors, 24; sentiment against, 32; and settlements after 1768 Fort Stanwix treaty, 174–75, 177–80, 181–82, 183, 184, 186, 192, 197; "Suffering Traders," 125, 135, 138, 156, 172; as winners of Revolutionary War, 265–66. *See also specific individuals*

Last Night, 150

Lee, Arthur, 258

Lehigh River Valley: Haudenosaunee claim to, 56; Native Americans relocated to, 51, 52, 57; proprietors' claim to, 53–54; and speculators, 52, 53–54; squatters in, 57

Lenni Lenape. *See* Delaware

liberty, defining, 6, 7

"located land," 30

Logan, James: courting of Haudenosaunee by, 55; Haudenosaunee treaty of alliance with colonial government recognizing, 55; on importance of Haudenosaunee to British, 21; and Lehigh River Valley land, 52, 53–54; on Nutimus, 54; on squatters' view of uncultivated land, 29

Long, Cookson "Cookey," 219, 220, 222, 229

Long, George, 219

Luckey, William, 198–99
Lukens, John, 176, 177, 254
Lycoming Creek, land beyond. *See* West Branch of Susquehanna River
Lydius, John, 63, 82

Maclay, William, 234
Madam Montour, 44–45
Mahhaffey, Thomas, 199
Maryland: and competition among colonies, 67; Nanticoke and Conoy in, 151; royal charter for, 97; southern border dispute with Pennsylvania, 185
Massachusetts, 170, 172, 206
Master of Life, 122–23
McClure brothers, 198
McCrea, Jane, 223–24
McElhatton, William, 199
McElvaine, John, 199
McKee, Alexander, 153, 166
McKee, Thomas, 102, 153
McLlhatton, William, 203
McMeen, William, 198
Mekawawlechon, 101, 103
minerals, 61, 146, 147
Mingo: Gage and retribution against, 129, 130; and northern Seneca, 75; and Revolutionary War, 228, 246; and Susquehanna Nations, 75
Mississippi Company, 125
Mittelberger, Gottlieb, 28
Mohawk: at Albany Congress, 62; and boundary separating Native Americans and colonists, 144; and British, 21; Konwatsitsiaienni's status in, 129; land given to Johnson by, 134, 147; move to Canada of, 262; and New York, 62, 63; relationship with colonial government, 62; and Revolutionary War, 225, 226, 228; and settlements beyond 1768 Fort Stanwix boundary line, 188

Mohican: and 1768 Fort Stanwix treaty boundary line, 165–66; delegation to colonial government (1749), 20; dispersal of, from Northern Susquehanna River Valley before Revolutionary War, 218; displaced to Northern Susquehanna River Valley, 12, 36; and land sale by Canassatego to proprietors, 50; and land sold at Albany Congress, 63; and Revolutionary War, 236; settlements beyond 1768 Fort Stanwix treaty boundary line, 188–89; as tributary of Haudenosaunee, 15, 36; warrior population of, after Pontiac's War, 150
Montour, Andrew, 44, 105
Montour family, 44–45, 264
Morgan, George, 135, 138, 228, 245
Morris, Robert Hunter: on British actions against Native Americans in Northern Susquehanna River Valley, 72; on defeat of Braddock, 71; and Fort Augusta, 87–88; and Native American requests for supplies, 69; on Susquehanna Nations during Seven Years' War, 73; and war on Delaware, 75–76
multiethnic Indigenous communities: and Captain Bull, 109; and family of Honest John, 51; and Fort Augusta, 86, 92; multiple displacements of, during and after Revolutionary War of, 263–64; in Northern Susquehanna River, 12–13, 15, 44, 58; Queen Esther's Town, 218, 241; and settlers from Connecticut, 113–14; and Seven Years' War, 68; and Teedyuscung, 77
Munsee: and 1768 Fort Stanwix treaty boundary line, 166; dispersal of, from Northern Susquehanna River Valley before Revolutionary War, 218; displaced to Northern Susquehanna River Valley, 36; and land sale by Canassatego to proprietors, 50; and Revolutionary War,

236, 246; and Seven Years' War, 70; as tributary of Haudenosaunee, 36; warrior population of, after Pontiac's War, 150. *See also* Delaware

names and naming: of colonial governors by Native Americans, 158; and kinship, 158; of Native Americans, 57–58

Nanticoke: belief Haudenosaunee and Cherokee aided colonial expansion, 127; delegation to colonial government (1749), 19, 20; dispersed from Northern Susquehanna River Valley before Revolutionary War, 218; displaced to Northern Susquehanna River Valley, 12, 36; and Fair Play republic, 205; and land sale by Canassatego to proprietors, 50; and land sold at Albany Congress, 63; in Maryland, 151; problems resulting from squatters, 38; relationship with Delaware, 54–55; and Revolutionary War, 246, 262–63; settlements after 1768 Fort Stanwix treaty, 188–89, 262; and Seven Years' War, 69; as tributary of Haudenosaunee, 36; warrior population of, after Pontiac's War, 150

Nanticoke, Jemmy, 150

Native Americans: attendees at Fort Stanwix conference (1768), 155–56; and boundary separating Native Americans and colonists, 115–17, 118, 121–23, 132–35, 137–38, 140, 141–42, 143, 144–47, 148, 159–68, *162, 166, 167, 168;* complaints of, prior to Fort Stanwix conference (1768), 154–55; displaced, to Northern Susquehanna River Valley, 12–13, 25, 36; effects of trade goods on, 34; erasure of, from popular history/memory, 276–77; fear of, in Fair Play republic, 6, 204, 205; French cession of land of, 103; Gage's approach to peace with, 129; government control over actions of colonists against, 187–88; kinship networks of, 117, 129–30, 153, 158, 225; land of, as ancient possession, 9; land purchases from, in Pennsylvania, 48; names of, 57–58; Neolin's religious message, 122–23; in Northern Susquehanna River Valley during Revolutionary War, 229–48; population diversity among, 117–19; post–Revolutionary War portrayal and treatment of, 250, 255; post–Revolutionary War sovereignty of, 256–57, 258–59; poverty among, 38; problems resulting from squatters, 37–38; and proclamation line of George III, 128; Quakers as perceived cause of colonial government's failure to act against, 115, 119; racialized violence against, 122, 152–53; relocated to Lehigh River Valley, 51, 52; and Revolutionary War, as aggressors, 253, 254; —, alliances with British, 223; —, Haudenosaunee and Susquehanna Nations at end of, 249–50; —, Haudenosaunee during, 218–19; —, as Indian War, 214–15, 216, 221–22, 223–25, 227–48; —, initial neutrality of, 218–19; —, as portrayed by Philadelphia committee, 215; —, as portrayed by press and publicists, 214, 223–24, 232, 242, 302n76; —, Susquehanna Nations during, 218–19, 221–22, 228, 231, 243–44, 246, 262–63; —, as war to conquer/eradicate, 8–9, 244–48, 250–51, 280n16; sale of land by unauthorized, 52; Seven Years' War alliances, 67–68; trade and land, 34; treaties with, as tacit ownership of land by, 32; unpurchased land of, 31, 32; use of land by and Eurocentric understanding of use, 30, 31, 32–34; on West Branch of Susquehanna River, 9–10, 44, 194–96, 198–200, 272–75. *See also specific Native nations*

natural law, uncultivated land as against, 29–30, 32
Neguttewesta, 102
Neolin, 122–23, *124*, 128
Nescopeck, 13
Newalike, 136, 152–53, 188–89, 217, 227
New Jersey, 151, 156
"New Purchase": boundary line declared by Thomas Penn, 186; and Connecticut, 183–85; and land speculators, 176, 179, 180, 182, 192; and Pennsylvania colonial government, 173, 174–75, 185, 187–88, 190–91; squatters attempts to obtain land in, 197, 198, 199, 200; and Tilghman, 174, 176–77, 178–79, 180, 181–82; and Virginia, 185
New York: Haudenosaunee as dependents of state, 256; Haudenosaunee land obtained by, 261–62; and Indigenous Christians, 120; legislature and Quartering Act, 169–70; and Mohawk, 62, 63; royal charter for, 97
Northern Susquehanna River Valley: boundaries of area, 11; and boundary between Native Americans and colonists, 133–34, 141–42, 143, 144–47, 148, 159–68, *162*, *166*, *167*, *168*; condition of Native Americans in, after Pontiac's War, 150; Congress and claims of Connecticut in, 257; Delaware in, 66; dispersal of Native Americans in, before Revolutionary War, 217; erasure of Native Americans from history of, 276–77; as gateway connecting Native nations, 228–29; and Haudenosaunee, 13, 151–52, 261; land gained by Thomas Penn in 1768 Fort Stanwix treaty, 171–72, 173–74; location of "Tiadaghta" creek, 166, 166–68, 167, 168, 186; multiethnic Indigenous towns in, 12–13, 15, 44, 58; Native Americans displaced to, 12–13, 25, 36; Ohio Nations' seasonal residences in, 15; populations of Native Americans in, 90–91; and proclamation line, 137; racialized violence against Native Americans in, 152–53; relations between British and Native Americans in, 71–72; and Revolutionary War, 11, 229–48; routes through, 13, 228; settlers from Connecticut in, 97–100, 101–2, 110, 113, 145; Shawnee in, 66; John Shikellamy and settlement in, 60; squatting immediately after Seven Years' War, 124; strategic importance of, 13; Susquehanna Nations' perpetual ownership of land in, 81–83; Teedyuscung as leader of displaced Native Americans in, 59; toll of American Revolution in, 11. *See also* Fair Play republic; Susquehanna Nations
Nutimus: as characterized by Logan, 54; and Connecticut settlers, 102; death of, 150; and Honest John/Teedyuscung, 52; importance of, 52; and Lehigh Valley "deed," 53; and peace with colonial government, 101–2, 107; relocation of, from Lehigh Valley, 57; and "Walking Purchase," 56

Ohio Company, 125, 126, 171–72
Ohio Nations: and boundary separating Native Americans and colonists, 132–35, 163–64; as "Brethren of the Six Nations," 49; entreaties to Haudenosaunee tributary nations, 47–48; and Fair Play republic, 205; and French and Indian War, 65–66; "Half-Kings" in, 49; increase in power of, 48–49; and land sales to colonial government, 49; peace with British, 84; and Revolutionary War, 221–22, 228, 230; seasonal residences in Northern Susquehanna River Valley of, 15; and settlements beyond 1768 Fort

Stanwix treaty boundary line, 188; and Seven Years' War, 76
Ohio River Valley, 21, 47, 245–46
Old Belt, 86
Oneida: at Albany Congress, 63; and boundary separating Native Americans and colonists, 144–45, 161; at Fort Stanwix conference (1768), 156; guardians of routes to Onondaga, 13; and Johnson's proposed boundary line, 159, 160; post–Revolutionary War, 261–62; and Revolutionary War, 225, 227, 228
Oneida Carry, 141
Onondaga: guardians of routes to, 13; importance of, 13; post–Revolutionary War, 261–62; and Revolutionary War, 225, 226, 228
Orby, John, 102
Osternados (Seneca George), 151–52
Ostonwackin, 13. *See also* Madam Montour
Ottawa, 228

Paine, Thomas, 212, 249
Parr, James, 199
patriarchy and community values, 204–5
Patterson, Captain, 168
Paul, William, 201
Paxinosa, 74, 76, 150
Paxtang Rangers, 113, 120–21, 231. *See also* Paxton Boys
Paxton Boys, 117, 119–21, 183, 196, 231
Peale, Charles Willson, 249
Penn, John: at Albany Congress, 62; basic facts about, 24, 25–26; and Haudenosaunee and squatters, 187; Haudenosaunee treaty of alliance with colonial government, 55; and land speculators, 23; promises by, to end racialized violence against Native Americans in Northern Susquehanna River Valley, 152, 153; protection of Indigenous Christians by, 119–20; and settlements beyond 1768 Fort Stanwix treaty boundary line, 189–90; and Joseph Shippen, 147–48
Penn, Richard, 23, 24, 25–26
Penn, Thomas: basic facts about, 22, 25; and boundary between Native Americans and colonists, 134, 142, 145–47, 161–62, 163; and Fort Stanwix conference (1768), 148–49; Haudenosaunee treaty of alliance with colonial government recognizing, 55; and Johnson, 147; and land gained in 1768 Fort Stanwix treaty, 172, 173–75, 176–82, *178*, 183–86, 187–91, 192; land purchased by, at Albany Congress, 61, 62–65, 81; and land speculators, 23; and lands "reserved" for Susquehanna Nations, 81–82; and Native Americans, 25–26; need for land, 22–23; "New Purchase" boundary line declared by, 186; settlements in Northern Susquehanna River Valley, 145, 146–47; supporters of, 22–23
Penn, William, 23, 25, *26*, 53
Penn's Treaty with the Indians (West), 25, 26
Pennsylvania (colony): charter of, 96–97, 212; and competition among colonies, 67; and Continental Congress, 206–7; and death of Teedyuscung, 110; and declarations of independence in, 212, 213–14; encouragement of squatters by, 46; enforcement of proclamation line, 136–37; Haudenosaunee delegations (1749), 19, 38–39, 40; land ownership of officials, 202; land sales to, and Ohio Nations, 49; legal system, 204–5; and Massachusetts Circular Letter, 170; and Mohawk, 62; and "New Purchase" land, 174–75, 185, 187–88, 190–91; Nutimus and peace with, 101–2; and Paxton Boys, 120; and Pontiac's War, 106; as proprietary oligarchy,

Pennsylvania (colony) (*continued*) 212, 213, 215; Quakers as perceived cause of failure of, to act against Native Americans, 115, 119; and racially motivated violence, 122; representation at 1768 Fort Stanwix conference of, 156; rural nature of, 8, 29; and Seven Years' War, 69; southern border dispute with Maryland, 185; and sovereignty of Haudenosaunee, 39, 55, 81; Susquehanna Nations peace with, 102–3, 104–5, 107; and Susquehanna Nations' perpetual ownership of land in Northern Susquehanna River Valley, 82. *See also* Fair Play republic

Pennsylvania (state): conditions of Revolutionary War veterans in, 265–66; and Congress and claims of Connecticut in Northern Susquehanna River Valley, 257; constitution of, 7, 214, 251, 269, 270; Continental Congress's committees in, 210; and Fort Stanwix Treaty (1784), 256, 257, 260–61; land as payment to Revolutionary War soldiers from, 253–54, 265; land purchases from Native Americans in, 48; mobility of population of, 29; modern boundaries of, 16; population diversity of, 116–18; poverty in, 26, 27, 28–29, 38; recognition of Fair Play republic land claims in, 270–71; sale of land by, after Revolutionary War, 267; securities speculation in, 266, 268–70; state government politics in 1780s, 268–70; Supreme Executive Council (SEC), 229, 235, 238, 239, 242, 243; system of land registration and speculators, 175–76. *See also* Fair Play republic

Pennsylvania Evening Post, 223, 224, 232
Pennsylvania Gazette, 112–14, 223
Pennsylvania Journal, 223, 224
Pennsylvania Packet, 223

"people of the Longhouse." *See* Haudenosaunee

Peters, Richard: at Albany Congress, 62; description of Indigenous people by, 46; on Haudenosaunee demands regarding squatters' cabins, 45; and land sold at Albany Congress, 64, 65; removal of squatters by, 45–46; on second 1749 Haudenosaunee delegation, 41; and Shippen Sr., 181–82; and squatters around Juniata, 27; and Teedyuscung's complaint about proprietors, 73

Pettit, Charles, 270, 271

Philadelphia: British capture of, 222–23; celebration of end of Revolutionary War, 249; Continental Congress committee, 212–15; population of, 8; as synonymous with liberty and independence, 1–2; as trade center, 34

Physick, Edmund, 174–76, 177, 180, 181, 182

Pitt, William, 131

Pocopoco, 15, 51, 52

Pontiac's War, 103, 106–9, 110–13, 115, 123, 128, 131, 150

poverty, as fact of life in Pennsylvania, 26, 27, 28–29, 38

proprietors: and Board of Trade boundary separating Native Americans and colonists, 144; claim to Lehigh River Valley, 53–54; and Fair Play republic, 205; as land owners through royal authority, 31; land sale by Canassatego to, 42, 43, 46–47, 50, 61, 81; as part of oligarchic Pennsylvania colonial government, 212, 213, 215; and Pennsylvania charter, 212; sentiment against, 32; and settlements beyond 1768 Fort Stanwix treaty boundary line, 178, 179; and success of land speculators, 22–25. *See also specific individuals*

Pumpshire, John, 80–81
Purviance, Samuel, 179

Quakers: Friendly Association, 79, 92, 93; as perceived cause of government failure to act against Native Americans, 115, 119
Quartering Act, 169
Quebec Act, 206, 208

Ramsay, David, 265–66
Read, Peter, 187
religion: Native American and Neolin, 122–23; and Paxton boys, 121; Presbyterian frontier ministers, 120–21; Presbyterianism, 195–96; uncultivated land as against Christianity, 29–30, 32
Renatus, 118–19
Revolutionary War: abandonment of Great Island during, 221; and Britain, advances of, 222–23; —, early resistance to, 170, 206–13, 214–15, 302n76; —, Native American alliances with, 223; —, as portrayed in press, 223, 224; Carlisle peace terms, 232; as civil war, 10; debt from, 252–63; establishment of committees as commitment to, 208–12; Fair Play republic mobilization during, 219–21, 222; financing, 238; independence urged by Philadelphia Continental Congress committee, 212–14; land as payment to Pennsylvania soldiers, 16–17, 253–54, 265; land speculators as winners of, 265–66; meaning of, 8, 9–10, 251, 252, 264–65; and Native and Native Americans, as aggressors, 253, 254; —, Haudenosaunee and Susquehanna Nations at end of, 249–50; —, Haudenosaunee during, 218–19; —, as Indian War, 214–15, 216, 221–22, 223–25, 227–48; —, initial neutrality of, 218–19; —, as portrayed by press during, 223–24, 232, 242; —, Susquehanna Nations during, 218–19, 221–22, 228, 231, 243–44, 246, 262–63; —, as war to conquer/eradicate, 8–9, 244–48, 250–51, 280n16; Philadelphia celebration of end of, 249; popular vision of, 1–2, 5; and speculation in government securities, 269; squatters' role in memories of, 216; surrender of Cornwallis, 246; toll of, in Northern Susquehanna River Valley, 11; treaty ending, 253–55, 259
Richardson, James, 199
Robinson, Thomas, 180–81
Rockingham, Lord, 131
routes: guardians of, to Onondaga, 13; through Northern Susquehanna River Valley, 13, 228; to Philadelphia, 34
royal authority and land ownership, 31, 32
Royal Proclamation of 1763, 130–31, 132–35, 138, 140

Saiuchtowano, 44
"Sam," the Conoy, 102
Saponi: displaced to Northern Susquehanna River Valley, 12; problems resulting from squatters, 38; as tributary of Haudenosaunee, 15; warrior population of, after Pontiac's War, 150; as Yesay, 35–36
Sattelihu. *See* Montour, Andrew
Sayenqueraghta, 228, 231, 232, 248, 260
scalp hunting, 75–76
Scarouady, 69, 74, 86–87
Scull, Edward, 50–51
Scull, William, 166–67, *167*
Senaxse, 63, 64. *See also* West Branch of Susquehanna River
Seneca: and boundary between Native Americans and colonists, 164; at Easton conferences, 77, 78; and Fort Stanwix conference (1768), 155; at Fort Stanwix conference (1784), 261;

340   INDEX

Seneca (*continued*)
    French and, 21; guardians of routes to Onondaga, 13; Mingo and northern, 75; post-Revolutionary War, 262; and Revolutionary War, 221, 225, 226, 228, 231, 248; and Seven Years' War, 77–78; on West Branch of Susquehanna River after Revolutionary War, 272–75
Seneca George (Osternados), 151–52
"settler colonialism," 275–77, 280n16, 309n81
Seven Years' War: British-Native American relations in Northern Susquehanna River Valley, 71–72; ferocity of, 75; immediate aftermath of, 124–25; Native American alliances during, 67–69, 71–72, 76–78; Ohio Nations during, 65–66; and power of Haudenosaunee over Susquehanna Nations, 93; Susquehanna Nations during, 68–74; taxation to pay for, 69; trade during, 70, 76; treaty ending, 103–4; as world war, 76
Shamokin, 13, 65, 86. *See also* Fort Augusta
Shamokin Daniel, 103
Shawana Ben, 153, 188–89, 217
Shawnee: and boundary between Native Americans and colonists, 133, 142, 163–64; and Delaware, 54–55; dispersal of, from Northern Susquehanna River Valley before Revolutionary War, 218; displaced to Northern Susquehanna River Valley, 12, 36; and Fair Play republic, 205; and Fort Stanwix conference and treaty (1768), 142–43, 166; and land sale by Canassatego to proprietors, 50; and land sold at Albany Congress, 63; in Northern Susquehanna River Valley, 66; as Ohio Nation, 48; problems resulting from squatters, 38; and Revolutionary War, 227, 228, 246, 247; and settlements beyond 1768 Fort Stanwix treaty boundary line, 188–89; and Seven Years' War, 70, 75; as tributary of Haudenosaunee, 36
Shelburne, Lord, 131, 132, 247
Shikellamy: death of, 60; and Haudenosaunee tribute nations, 36; and Logan, 55; treaty of alliance with colonial government, 55; and "Walking Purchase," 56
Shikellamy, John, 60
Shingas ("the Terrible"), 65, 70
Shippen, Edward, Jr., 182
Shippen, Edward, Sr., 23, 91, 181–82
Shippen, Joseph, 88–90, 147–48, 179–80
Silver Heels, 70
Silverthorn, Rachel, 233
Six Nations. *See* Haudenosaunee
slavery, 214
Smith, William, 177, 180
Sock, Will, 119
sovereignty: and Articles of Confederation, 256; Canassatego and colonial government's recognition of Haudenosaunee, 41–42; colonial, 169–70, 171; effect of trade on, 35; of Fair Play republic, 200; of Haudenosaunee, Canassatego and colonial government's recognition of, 41–42; —, colonial government recognition of, 39, 55; —, as dependents of New York state, 256; —, expansion of, 35–36; —, and Fort Stanwix conference (1784), 259; —, and Fort Stanwix treaty (1768), 165; —, and "Great Treaty," 81; —, and Susquehanna Nations' perpetual land ownership, 81; and Native Americans neutrality during Revolutionary War, 219; post–Revolutionary War, 255, 256–57, 258–59; post–Revolutionary War Native American, 256–57, 258–59; Susquehanna Nations pursuit of, 15
Spain and Fort Stanwix conference (1768), 143, 155

squatters/squatting: attempts to obtain "New Purchase" land by, 197, 198, 199, 200, 232; and Board of Trade boundary line separating Native Americans and colonists, 144; claims to land, 7, 65, 203, 214; colonial government encouragement of, 46; competition for land immediately after Seven Years' War, 124; demographics, 26, 27; as deserving land, 8; effects on life of Native Americans of, 37–38; and Fort Augusta, 88; and Fort Stanwix conference and treaty (1784), 266–67; Haudenosaunee demands regarding, 45; and Haudenosaunee tributary nations' independence, 36–37; independence as essential for legal land ownership, 237–38; Juniata River settlements, 19–20, 46, 60, 71, 131; and land sold at Albany Congress, 64–65; and land speculators, 38; in Lehigh Valley, 57; minerals on land of, 61; monikers given to, 29; as only option for better life, 29; and peace agreement after Pontiac's War, 131; and John Penn's relationship with Haudenosaunee, 187; poverty of, 27; preemption rights of, 270, 271; problems posed by, for Hamilton, 25; and proclamation line of George III, 131, 137–38; purpose of American Revolution to, 8; removal of, 20, 21, 39, 44–46; removal of Native Americans as goal of American Revolution, 8–9, 280n16; role in remembrances of Revolution, 216; settlements beyond 1768 Fort Stanwix treaty boundary line by, 184, 186, 187–91, 197, 298n48; view of uncultivated land, 29–30, 32. *See also* Fair Play republic; West Branch of Susquehanna River

Stamp Act (1765), 139
Stewart, Lazarus, 183, 184–85, 231–32
Stuart, John, 128, 164
Stump, Frederick, 137, 152–53, 154, 187, 188
"Suffering Traders," 125, 135, 138, 156, 172
Sullivan, John, 243–45, 263
Susquehannah Company: and boundary between Native Americans and colonists, 134, 142, 145, 163; and Connecticut charter, 134; and settlements, 98, 99–100; settlements beyond 1768 Fort Stanwix treaty boundary line by, 183
Susquehanna Nations: and boundary separating Native Americans and colonists, 132–35, 160, 165–66; confederation forming, 72, 77; and Connecticut settlers, 98–99, 102; dispersal of, from Northern Susquehanna River Valley before Revolutionary War, 217; at end of Revolutionary War, 249–50; and Fair Play republic, 203–4, 205; and Fort Augusta, 87–88, 91, 104, 105, 154; improved relations with Haudenosaunee, 94; independence of, 74–75, 77, 93–94, 111, 113, 149; leadership, 73, 74; move from Great Island, 101; multiple displacements of, during and after Revolutionary War of, 262–64; nations comprising, 12–13; peace negotiations by, 78–81; peace with colonial government, 102–3, 104–5, 107; Thomas Penn and lands "reserved" for, 81–82; and perpetual ownership of land in Northern Susquehanna River Valley, 81–83; and Pontiac's War, 107–9, 111, 149–50; and proclamation line of George III, 136; and Revolutionary War, 218–19, 221–22, 228, 231, 243–44, 262–63; rumors about, preparing for war, 105–6; settlements beyond 1768 Fort Stanwix treaty boundary line, 188–89, 190–91; and Seven Years' War, 68–74, 76–77, 93; sovereignty pursued by, 15; strength of, 74–75; as tributaries of Haudenosaunee, 15. *See also specific nations*

Susquehanna River Valley, 39–40, 42, 43. *See also* West Branch of Susquehanna River
Susquehannock, 13

Tahaiadoris, 105
Tamaqua, 98
Tatteneskund. *See* Gideon; Honest John; Tattenhick; Teedyuscung
Tattenhick, 50–51, 284n22. *See also* Gideon; Honest John; Teedyuscung
taxation: colonial legislatures' opposition to, 169; land subject to, 30; to pay for Seven Years' War, 69; and Pennsylvania state government politics in 1790s, 268–69
Tea Act (1773), 206
Teedyuscung: basic facts about, 73, 78, 79, 99; and Brodhead, 69; complaint about proprietors, 72; and Connecticut settlers, 97–99; conversion to Christianity, 57; and council fire granted by Haudenosaunee, 99, 100; death of, 85, 100–101, 110, 112; on decision to ally with French, 73–74; displacement of, 38; at Easton conferences, 78–81; and "Foundation of our Uneasiness," 42; Haudenosaunee characterized by, 58; Haudenosaunee treatment of, 94; as "King," 74, 77, 78–79; on land speculators, 38; as leader of displaced Native Americans in Northern Susquehanna River Valley, 59; named "the War Trumpet," 73; as peacemaker, 84–85; request for supplies during Seven Years' War, 69, 76; as rival of John Shikellamy, 60; spelling of, 284n22; and Susquehanna Nations' independence, 77; and Susquehanna Nations' perpetual land ownership, 80–81, 82; and Tamaqua, 98; as "The Healer," 84; in Wyoming, 58–59. *See also* Gideon; Honest John; Tattenhick
Telenimut, 102

Tenhoghskweaghta, 225
Tepascowan, 101, 102
Thayendanegea, 226. *See also* Brant, Joseph
The Belt, 60
Thomas T. Taber Museum, 3
Thomson, Charles, 72
"Tiadaghta" (or "Tiadaghton") creek, *166*, 166–68, *167, 168*, 186
Tiadaghton Elm, 3, *4, 5,* 213, 271, 276
Tilghman, James: and Fort Stanwix conference (1768), 148; and "New Purchase" land, 174, 176–77, 178–79, 180, 181–82; and Wallis, 183
Tittamy, Joseph, 80–81
Tohaswuchdioony, 60
Townshend, Charles, 139, 140, 206
trade: Amherst and Native American, 86; British control of best routes, 68; complaints about prices and white encroachment of hunting territory, 154; Continental Congress embargo, 208; by Croghan, 135; and disunity among states, 256; effects of manufactured goods on Native Americans, 34; Fort Augusta as hub of, 88–90, 91–93, 95; illegal, 91; and Indigenous use of land, 34; Philadelphia as center of, 34; and Pontiac's War, 111; prices of manufactured goods and value of skins and furs, 91; and Seven Years' War, 70, 76; and sovereignty of Native polities, 35
Treaty of Fort Macintosh (1785), 262
Treaty of Fort Stanwix (1768). *See* Fort Stanwix conference and treaty (1768)
Treaty of Fort Stanwix (1784). *See* Fort Stanwix conference and treaty (1784)
Treaty of Paris (1763), 103–4
Treaty of Paris (1783), 253–55, 259
Tuscarora: detention of hunting party, 154; and Fair Play republic, 205; and Pontiac's

War, 150; post–Revolutionary War, 261, 262; and Revolutionary War, 225, 227, 228

Tutelo: delegation to colonial government (1749), 19, 20; dispersal of, from Northern Susquehanna River Valley before Revolutionary War, 218; displaced to Northern Susquehanna River Valley, 12; and Fair Play republic, 205; and land sale by Canassatego to proprietors, 50; problems resulting from squatters, 38; as tributary of Haudenosaunee, 15; as Yesay, 35–36

Unalachtigo. See Delaware
Unami. See Delaware
"unlocated land," 30

Virginia: and competition among colonies, 67; and Fort Stanwix conference and treaty (1768), 156, 162, 171–72; land desired by, 61, 62; and "New Purchase" claim, 185; and Ohio Company, 125, 126, 171–72; royal charter for, 97

Walker, Benjamin, 197, 199, 220, 222, 273–75
Walker, Henry, 220, 273–75
Walker, John, 180–81, 197, 220, 273, 274
Walker, Joseph, 220, 273–75
"Walking Purchase" (1737), 12–13, 53–54, 55–56, 73
Wallis, Samuel, 182–83
Walpole, Richard, 172
Walpole, Thomas, 172
Walpole Company, 125, 126
wampum: given to Newalike, 152; given to Teedyuscung, 78–79, 98; importance of, 157; Susquehanna Nations' refusal of, from Haudenosaunee, 74
Washington, George: as land speculator, 125, 171; and Native Americans, 117, 239, 243, 244, 274; as president of United States, 274; and Revolutionary War, 220, 223, 239, 243

Way-Way, 262–63

Weiser, Conrad: on Haudenosaunee treatment of tributary nations, 36; and land sold at Albany Congress, 64, 65; and Osternados, 151; and Susquehanna Nations' perpetual land ownership, 80–81; and "Tiadaghta" (or "Tiadaghton") creek, 167

Welagameka, 51, 52
Wendat/Wyandot (Huron), 217
Wenschpochkechun, 13
West, Benjamin, 25, 26

West Branch of Susquehanna River: as interdependent community of small farm families, 198–200; as last bastion of Native land in Susquehanna River Valley, 9–10; Native Americans in, after Revolutionary War, 272–75; population of, 194–96; removal of squatters on, 44–46; residents of, described, 197–98, 199. See also Fair Play republic

Wetterholt, Nicholaus, 107–8, 111, 112
Wharton, Samuel, 135, 138, 172
Wharton, Thomas, 147, 172, 220
White, Robert, 98
White Eyes, 217–18, 227, 228
Whitefield, George, 24
White Mingo, 153
Williamson, David, 246
Williamsport Sun-Gazette, 276
Woapalanne, 218, 236
Wolcott, Oliver, 258
Woodbridge, Timothy, 100
Woods, George, 198
Wyalusing, 13, 165–66
Wyoming: Captain Bull's attack on, 113–14, 115, 117, 118–19; and Connecticut settlers, 98–99, 100, 101–2, 173–74; location, 13;

Wyoming (*continued*)
  minerals near, 146, 147; and Thomas Penn, 82; and Revolutionary War, 231, 232, 233; and Seven Years' War, 71; and Teedyuscung, 58–59, 98

Yesay, 35–36. *See also* Saponi; Tutelo
Young Captain Harris, 57, 110

Zacharias, 107–8, 110, 112

The Revolutionary Age

Dishonored Americans: The Political Death of Loyalists in Revolutionary America
TIMOTHY COMPEAU

The American Liberty Pole: Popular Politics and the Struggle for Democracy in the Early Republic
SHIRA LURIE

European Friends of the American Revolution
ANDREW J. O'SHAUGHNESSY, JOHN A. RAGOSTA, AND
MARIE-JEANNE ROSSIGNOL, EDITORS

The Tory's Wife: A Woman and Her Family in Revolutionary America
CYNTHIA A. KIERNER

Writing Early America: From Empire to Revolution
TREVOR BURNARD

Spain and the American Revolution: New Approaches and Perspectives
GABRIEL PAQUETTE AND GONZALO M. QUINTERO SARAVIA, EDITORS

The American Revolution and the Habsburg Monarchy
JONATHAN SINGERTON

Navigating Neutrality: Early American Governance in the Turbulent Atlantic
SANDRA MOATS

Ireland and America: Empire, Revolution, and Sovereignty
PATRICK GRIFFIN AND FRANCIS D. COGLIANO, EDITORS

Milton Keynes UK
Ingram Content Group UK Ltd.
UKHW030923131024
449633UK00005B/23

9 780813 951980